CAMBRIDGE TEXTS IN
HISTORY OF PHILOSO]

——

JOHANN GEORG HAMANN
Writings on Philosophy and Language

CAMBRIDGE TEXTS IN THE
HISTORY OF PHILOSOPHY

Series editors
KARL AMERIKS
Professor of Philosophy, University of Notre Dame
DESMOND M. CLARKE
Professor of Philosophy, University College Cork

The main objective of Cambridge Texts in the History of Philosophy is to expand the range, variety and quality of texts in the history of philosophy which are available in English. The series includes texts by familiar names (such as Descartes and Kant) and also by less well-known authors. Wherever possible, texts are published in complete and unabridged form, and translations are specially commissioned for the series. Each volume contains a critical introduction together with a guide to further reading and any necessary glossaries and textual apparatus. The volumes are designed for student use at undergraduate and postgraduate level and will be of interest not only to students of philosophy, but also to a wider audience of readers in the history of science, the history of theology and the history of ideas.

For a list of titles published in the series, please see end of book.

JOHANN GEORG HAMANN

Writings on Philosophy and Language

TRANSLATED AND EDITED BY
KENNETH HAYNES
Brown University

CAMBRIDGE
UNIVERSITY PRESS

CAMBRIDGE UNIVERSITY PRESS
Cambridge, New York, Melbourne, Madrid, Cape Town, Singapore, São Paulo

Cambridge University Press
The Edinburgh Building, Cambridge CB2 8RU, UK

Published in the United States of America by Cambridge University Press, New York

www.cambridge.org
Information on this title: www.cambridge.org/9780521817417

© Cambridge University Press 2007

First published 2007

Printed in the United Kingdom at the University Press, Cambridge

A catalogue record for this publication is available from the British Library

ISBN 978-0-521-81741-7 hardback
ISBN 978-0-521-52067-6 paperback

Contents

Contents

Introduction

Johann Georg Hamann (1730–88) is prominent in the history of German literature, being known above all for an idiosyncratic and sometimes bizarre style that was intransigently at odds with the aesthetics of his time and which fascinated and sometimes influenced writers of the nineteenth century. He is one of the most innovative figures within Lutheran theology and arguably "the most profound Christian thinker of the eighteenth century";[1] his insistence on the historical truth of the Bible led him to a radical rethinking of the nature of both history and truth. Finally, he is a philosopher who wrote penetrating criticisms of Herder, Jacobi, Kant, and Mendelssohn; who gave philosophical attention to language in a way that, at times, seems strikingly modern; but whose own philosophical positions and arguments remain elusive.

Hamann was a minor civil servant for most of his adult life, working in Königsberg as part of the widely hated tax administration of Frederick the Great. He never attained any sort of significant professional success; friends had to intervene to prevent the sale of his library and to fund the education of his children. On the other hand, he had the freedom of his failure inasmuch as he was not obliged to meet the expectations of any particular audience. He exercised his freedom in several respects: to develop a rebarbative and enigmatic style, to reject basic assumptions of his contemporaries, and to range freely across disciplines.

Hamann, however, was not merely moving across disciplines but finding his deepest themes reiterated in a variety of material: ancient and

---

[1] Hendrik Kraemer, as quoted by James C. O'Flaherty, "Some Major Emphases of Hamann's Theology," *Harvard Theological Review* 51:1 (January 1958), 39.

contemporary; sacred and secular; historical, political, economic, theological, literary, and journalistic; and in a wide range of languages. Some of his most profound writing was composed at the intersection of philology, theology, and philosophy. Often he has been considered from only one of those perspectives, which is not only inadequate but also ironic insofar as his own emphasis was on unity. The powerful criticism which Hamann made in opposition to his age was at once stylistic, theological, and philosophical.

Hamann and literary style

Hamann formed his style after experiencing a religious crisis. In 1757, while working for a firm run by the family of a friend, he went on a business trip to England, where he was not successful, either professionally or personally. After some months he began to despair of the life he was leading; this led to a religious crisis in which he recovered and radicalized the Christian faith of his childhood. When he returned to Königsberg, his friends Kant and Johann Christoph Berens sought to redirect him toward his previous, more secular and Enlightened, orientation, suggesting that he translate articles from the *Encyclopédie*. After an initial effort, Hamann gave up and began his own writing career in earnest. The style he cultivated was the opposite of that of the *Encyclopédie*, obscure rather than perspicuous, personal and even private rather than disembodied and anonymous, erudite and sometimes obscene rather than polite and complaisant. The style was a reproach to the language used by Enlightenment writers; it was a critique of their language by means of his language.

For example, the first dedication of *Socratic Memorabilia* (1759) is addressed to the "public," but it is far from ingratiating itself with a potential audience; rather, it presents the public as a phantom and an idol, a fraud perpetuated by the cultured elite and no different from the fraud attempted by the prophets of Baal or the priests of Bel. Throughout his career, Hamann had an extraordinary sensitivity to the keywords of his age – like "public" – which he found evasive, obsequious, and self-contradictory. The word "public" seems to imply the existence of such an entity, but who is the public, and how do the many voices of people become the single voice of the public? After parodying a flattering appeal to this putative public,[2] which concludes with a scatological classical allusion, Hamann adds a second dedication to two friends. From this book onwards, his style makes use of parody, local referents, biblical quotations, obscenity, and wide-ranging allusions. The style is not polite; Hamann writes that it is not made for taste.

Hamann's parody is motivated by a desire to refuse claims implicit in other ways of writing. He is never happier than when using it to show, or imply, that a reasonable position set out in a reasonable style is actually a fanatical and mystical one – where all three adjectives, "reasonable," "fanatical," and "mystical," were strongly charged keywords of the time. In the dedication to *Socratic Memorabilia*, faith in a public is equated to faith in Baal. When Hamann began, in the last part of his life, to write about philosophical texts directly, he applied an analogous skepticism to philosophical terms. The term "metaphysics," for example, is a linguistic accident that has infected the whole study.[3] A preposition which should indicate, empirically and spatially, the standard position within his corpus of one book of Aristotle's relative to his *Physics* has come to mean, abstractly and transcendentally, that something goes "beyond" physics and is sometimes alleged to secure the valid meaning of the merely physical. For Hamann this "beyond," like the "public," has become an object of superstitious veneration disguised as reasonableness.

Kant, for example, in the *Critique of Pure Reason*, refers to a "transcendental object," which he glosses as "a something = x, of which we know, and with the present constitution of our understanding can know, nothing whatsoever." In his *Metacritique on the Purism of Reason* (1784), Hamann responds to Kant's claim by presenting this equation as every bit as mystical and superstitious as the scholastic philosophy condemned by the *philosophe* Helvétius (see p. 210 below):

---

[2] More sophisticated discussions of public discourse had to wait twenty years; see the essays by Klein, Bahrdt, Moser, and Fichte on the public use of reason collected in James Schmidt, ed., *What is Enlightenment?: Eighteenth-Century Answers and Twentieth-Century Questions* (Berkeley, CA, 1996), as well as the more famous essays by Kant (on which see especially Onora O'Neill, "The Public Use of Reason," *Constructions of Reason* (Cambridge, 1999), 28–50). Parodies of dedications to the public continued into the nineteenth century; cf. the dedication to E. T. A. Hoffmann's *Life and Opinions of the Tomcat Murr* (1819).

[3] "The hereditary defect and leprosy of ambiguity adheres to the very name 'metaphysics' . . . the birthmark of its name spreads from its brow to the bowels of the whole science" (p. 209).

Through this learned troublemaking it works the honest decency of language into such a meaningless, rutting, unstable, indefinite something $= \mathrm{x}$ that nothing is left but a windy sough, a magic shadow play, at most, as the wise Helvétius says, the talisman and rosary of a transcendental superstitious belief in *entia rationis*, their empty sacks and slogans.

Removed from their context and the system in which they make sense, Kant's words invite the scorn which Enlightenment figures had directed against their opponents. Hamann seeks to undercut the ground by which reason and faith are contrasted, so that neither receives a special status. Kant's arguments are not answered by Hamann (and may not have been understood by him). Parody does not make arguments or respect them; it proceeds by exaggeration, ironic juxtaposition, and misapplication. This serves Hamann's purpose since he is not interested in rebutting a philosophical stance with philosophical arguments, but rather in using mockery to deny a philosophical problem its status as a problem, to be freed from its grip.

From the early *Socratic Memorabilia* to the late *Metacritique*, a consistent target of Hamann's parodies is the contrast between reason on the one hand and mysticism, superstition, faith, and prejudice on the other. Another is the contrast between the abstract purity of philosophy and the embodied history of lived experience. In the *Metacritique*, Hamann objects to the threefold purism, as he sees it, of Kant's vain effort to make reason free from history, experience, and language. In the following example, he mocks first the mysticism and then the sexual sterility of the analysis of pure reason (see pp. 214–15 below):

I would open the eyes of the reader that he might perhaps see – hosts of intuitions ascend to the firmament of pure understanding and hosts of concepts descend to the depths of the most perceptible sensibility, on a ladder which no sleeper dreams – and the dance of the Mahanaim or two hosts of reason – the secret and vexing chronicle of their courtship and ravishing – and the whole theogony of all the giant and heroic forms of the Shulamite and muse, in the mythology of light and darkness – to the play in forms of an old Baubo with herself – *inaudita specie solaminis*, as Saint Arnobius says – and of a new immaculate virgin, who may not however be a Mother of God for which Saint Anselm took her – .

The old woman Baubo, according to Arnobius, was able to cheer Demeter after a long period of mourning by exposing herself and causing the goddess to laugh, an "unusual form of consolation," which Hamann compares to Kant's philosophy. He then contrasts it with the Virgin Mary, whom Protestants do not believe was immaculately conceived; why should reason be more greatly privileged? Hamann delights in associating Kant with Jewish mysticism and Catholic sexuality. To complain that the mockery is unfair to Kant is to miss Hamann's point: it is not that particular philosophical arguments need to be refuted but that the motivation behind them (a desire for mathematical certainty, Hamann alleges in Kant's case) stands in need of scrutiny and exposure.

In the *Metacritique* as in all his parodies, Hamann cultivates a deliberate impurity. If philosophy desires to become independent of history and tradition, he writes with continual references to historical tradition; if it is concerned with truths that are independent of experience, he inserts the body and all its functions; if philosophy is to be reasonable, abstract, and transparent, his style will be obscure, weighted with concrete details, strange; in his prose the fact of language, especially in its non-representational aspects, is centrally obtruded.

Parody is parasitic, dependent on other people's words to make its points, and so Hamann's essays quote or allude to other texts with great frequency. In addition to these textual references, however, his essays also introduce many personal and local ones. The *Socratic Memorabilia*, for example, is prefaced by two dedications: the first parodies contemporary appeals to the "public" while the second is addressed to two specific friends, Kant and Berens. The motive for introducing contingent facts of his personal biography has been called "metaschematism" (a word Hamann derived from 1 Corinthians 4:6). James C. O'Flaherty discusses it in this way:[4]

> For Hamann to metaschematize meant to substitute a set of objective relationships for an analogous set of personal or existential relationships or the reverse, in order to determine, through the insight born of faith, their common meaning . . . Thus Hamann's literary method requires *direct* personal involvement and *indirect* communication . . . In the *Memorabilia* Hamann is in effect saying: my relationship to Berens and Kant as typical representatives of the

[4] James C. O'Flaherty, *Hamann's Socratic Memorabilia* (Baltimore, MD, 1967).

present rationalistic age is essentially the same as that of Socrates to the Sophists of fifth-century Athens. Therefore, I will translate our personal relations into the objective historical relations of Socrates in order to bring my adversaries to a full awareness of their true situation.

Metaschematism is an extension of typology, the practice of reading the Bible in such a way that people and events of the New Testament are foreshadowed or figured by those of the Old. For Hamann, typology did not come to an end with the early Christian Church and is not limited to biblical sources; the present continues to be made legible by reference to the past, and only in this way. Past, present, and future are in this sense bound together and mutually illuminated by prophecy (a theme of *Aesthetica in Nuce* and the second *Cloverleaf,* more fully developed in the conclusion of the first version of *Disrobing and Transfiguration*).

Hamann's writings have a peculiar texture, being made up of sustained and parodic allusions to the particular texts he is investigating, biblical quotations, references to ancient history and literature, as well as items of recent history and personal biography. The style belongs in part to the "tradition of learned wit,"[5] exuberant demonstrations of learning that had characterized prose of the early modern period. By Hamann's time, however, literary aesthetics abandoned the copia of such writing in favor of a transparent and perspicuous style. Literature that valued clarity and impersonal demonstration was not interested in the views of past authorities, and it disdained personal idiosyncrasy. Hamann's response to an aesthetic which made irrelevant the learning of the past, the authority of Scripture, and present biography was to write in a style in which these had continual – although indirect – relevance.

He has often been found obscure. He himself, metaschematically identifying his style with Socrates', described it as a group of islands lacking "the bridges and ferries of method necessary for their close association" (p. 8). The obscurity of the writing is not generally resolved only by providing further information, a necessary but not a sufficient step; to read Hamann means to consider the many possible ways by which this information is related to his text, whether by parody, irony, analogy, typology, or other means.

---

[5] Cf. D. W. Jefferson, "The Tradition of Learned Wit," *Essays in Criticism* 1:3 (1951), 225–48.

Hamann and theology

Hamann's style has theological and philosophical implications, just as his theology has stylistic and philosophical ones, and his philosophy stylistic and theological ones. Theology is grammar, according to Hamann, who took the equation from Luther.[6] Two Lutheran emphases in particular are strongly marked in his writing. The first is a theme found in all his writings, kenosis, the self-renunciation, self-emptying of God. This is the paradox in Christianity whereby power manifests itself in powerlessness, as omnipotence in the helplessness of an infant or divinity tortured and killed as a criminal. The biblical support comes mainly from the Sermon on the Mount and other parables ("so the last shall be first, and the first last") and the kenotic hymn, so-called, of Philippians 2, one of Hamann's base-texts. It is one of the main currents of interpretation of Christ's crucifixion and marks especially the Lutheran (and Augustinian) tradition.

Hamann's own style is kenotic insofar as it cultivates despised forms, makes rude references, and places unreasonable demands on readers; at a period when good taste was very highly praised, to write in bad taste could be kenotic. Hamann takes as the preeminent example of a kenotic style that of the New Testament. In the first of the *Cloverleaf of Hellenistic Letters*, he defends the Greek of the New Testament for the same reasons it was a scandal to literary men of his time: its impurity, as in the traces of Aramaic audible in its idiom; its lack of ornament and rhetoric; its lowliness and even degenerate condition relative to Attic standards. In the *New Apology of the Letter h*, Hamann argues even about orthography in these terms, which give him grounds to defend a useless, redundant, and traditional element of spelling.

Moreover, for Hamann kenosis is a principle of critique quite generally. His was a unique voice insisting that Frederick the Great was a tyrant and that the philosophical activity of the Berlin Enlightenment was a way of justifying Frederick's despotism. The contrast between "Fritz in the purple cradle" (Frederick the Great) and "Fritz *in praesepio*" (Fritz, an average German, in a cradle) organizes his essays (see p. 102). *To the Solomon of*

---

[6] See *Miscellaneous Notes on Word Order in the French Language*, p. 22, below; the quotation from Luther is mediated through an eighteenth-century Lutheran theologian. In a letter to Friedrich Heinrich Jacobi (*Briefe*, vol. VII, p. 169), Hamann asks, "Do you now understand my language-principle of reason and that with Luther I turn all philosophy into a grammar?" (Fritz Mauthner gives this passage as an epigraph to the first section of his *Beiträge zu einer Kritik der Sprache*, 1906).

Prussia is an uncompromising indictment, and an occasionally scurrilous one, of Frederick the Great and the culture which supported and was supported by him. The title "Golgotha and Sheblimini!" (Hamann's rebuttal to Moses Mendelssohn's *Jerusalem*) sets up the same contrast: "Golgotha" is Calvary, where Christ was crucified, and "Sheblimini!," Hebrew for "Sit thou at my right hand" (see Psalms 110:1 and Hebrews 1:13), is taken as the command by which Christ was exalted. Hamann believes that Mendelssohn's arguments for religious toleration and natural law were complicit with the machinery of Frederick's absolutist state – and not just Mendelssohn's arguments, but those of the Berlin Enlighteners generally, all of whom Hamann suspected of seeking to give a blank check to secular power.

Throughout his career language was Hamann's great theme. On August 6, 1784, he wrote to Johann Gottfried Herder, "If I were only as eloquent as Demosthenes, I would need to do no more than repeat one phrase three times: reason is language, Λόγος; on this marrowbone I gnaw and will gnaw myself to death over it" (*Briefe*, vol. v, p. 177). Hamann's understanding of language was always theological. In his earlier writings, he was concerned to emphasize the many and diverse phenomena involving language, denying primacy to its function of communicating propositions. He emphasized language, including the language of nature,[7] as the means of God's revelation to humankind. In his later writing, he began to understand language in sacramental terms that were closely informed by the Lutheran doctrine sometimes known as "consubstantiation" (though the term is contested). Unlike members of the Catholic and Calvinist confessions, Luther had insisted that both the body and blood of Christ *and* the bread and wine of the elements were present in the Eucharist, not only one or the other.[8] For Hamann, this became a means of distinguishing

---

[7] "Further underlying the subordination of philosophy to poetry is Hamann's basic conviction . . . that from the beginnings of humanity 'every phenomenon of nature was a word,' a conviction canceling any philosophical pretensions to being able to distinguish between sign (spirit) and signified (nature)," Daniel O. Dahlstrom, "The Aesthetic Holism of Hamann, Herder, and Schiller," in Karl Ameriks, ed., *The Cambridge Companion to German Idealism* (Cambridge, 2000), 81.

[8] Although there were many gradations among the three positions, Catholics maintained the doctrine of transubstantiation (the substance of the Eucharist was wholly converted to the blood and body of Christ, though the appearance of bread and wine remained), Lutherans subscribed to what is commonly called "consubstantiation," and Calvinists, at least of the Zwinglian variety, took the Eucharist to be symbolic and memorial. Despite attempts at rapprochement between Lutherans and Calvinists, Luther's insistence on this position created a rupture between the confessions that was never bridged.

kinds of writing. Letter and spirit must both be present, body and symbol must co-inhere, if an utterance is to be authoritative (that is, a *Machtwort*, which transforms elements into a sacrament).

Hamann is often seen as a proponent of holism,[9] and this is an adequate description so long as it is seen in the appropriate context. At least since Augustine, Christianity has insisted on the value of the letter (in contrast to the allegorizing of the Greeks) and on the value of the spirit (in contrast to the legalism of the Jews). A peculiar richness resulted from the presence of two distinct systems of truth obligation, and Hamann sought to preserve this, insisting on the unity of letter and spirit against what he took to be the impoverishing discourse of Enlightenment philosophy. Furthermore, holism is present above all in the incarnation of Christ, who unites human and divine attributes. Hamann, like Luther, invokes the doctrine of the *communicatio idiomatum*, whereby the attributes of each of the two natures are shared by the other in Christ. Hamann extends the principle, seeing in language the interrelation of human and divine generally.[10]

Hamann's holism, then, has a primary theological orientation which lies behind his rejection of the opposition between, and even the dualism of, faith and reason, idealism and realism, objectivity and subjectivity, body and spirit. By the 1780s, Hamann formulates this rejection of opposites in another way, in "the one important exception to Hamann's general refusal to appeal to a metaphysical principle,"[11] the *coincidentia oppositorum*, the union of opposites (as they are experienced by us) in God. Hamann believes that human knowledge is piecemeal, contradictory, and not resolvable by philosophical analysis.

Holism motivates his attacks on Mendelssohn's and Kant's philosophies. To Mendelssohn's argument that actions and convictions must be treated independently, Hamann replies that "actions without convictions and convictions without actions are a cleaving of complete and living duties into two dead halves" (p. 179), resulting in the dead body of the state and a scarecrow-ghost of a church. Of Kant's distinction of the

---

[9] In *Poetry and Truth* (1811–22), Goethe influentially characterized Hamann's writings: "The principle underlying all of Hamann's utterances is this: 'Everything a human being sets out to accomplish, whether produced by word or deed or otherwise, must arise from the sum of his combined powers; anything isolated is an abomination.'" In Goethe's account, however, Hamann is interested only in the unity of self, and the theological, political, and social dimensions of unity are overlooked.

[10] Fully discussed in Friedemann Fritsch, *Communicatio Idiomatum: Zur Bedeutung einer christologischen Bestimmung für das Denken Johann Georg Hamanns* (Berlin, 1999).

[11] James C. O'Flaherty, *Johann Georg Hamann* (Boston, MA, 1979), 91.

sensibility and the understanding, Hamann asks, "To what end is such a violent, unjustified, willful divorce of that which nature has joined together! Will not both branches wither and be dried up through a dichotomy and rupture of their common root?" (p. 212).

Hamann and philosophy

Hamann's own philosophy has sometimes been called fideist or irrationalist. In particular, older scholarship often represented him as a member of a German Counter-Enlightenment, along with Herder, Jacobi, and sometimes Justus Möser, figures supposed to be united in rejecting the claims of reason and the methods of science.[12] However, as historians have become skeptical about the utility of the phrase "The Enlightenment," the claims of "The Counter-Enlightenment" to a coherent program have come to seem even more exiguous.[13] Hamann is perhaps the figure most uncompromisingly at odds with the Enlightenment, but even he has been described as radicalizing, rather than rejecting, the Enlightenment.[14] Moreover, Hamann could be as absolute in his criticism of Herder or Jacobi as he was in dissenting from Kant or Mendelssohn, as demonstrated by his three essays translated below on Herder's treatise on the origin of language (*The Last Will and Testament of the Knight of the Rose-Cross*, *Philological Ideas and Doubts*, and *To the Solomon of Prussia*).

The fundamental divide between Hamann and Jacobi makes clear how inadequate it is to regard Hamann as a philosopher of irrationalism or an advocate of faith opposed to reason. In *David Hume on Faith, or Idealism or Realism: A Dialogue* (1787), Jacobi defended himself against the charge of irrationalism by invoking Hume to insist on the necessary primacy of faith (or belief, as the same word in German, *Glaube*, can mean either). In a letter to Jacobi written from April 27 to May 3,

---

[12] Lewis White Beck, *Early German Philosophy* (Cambridge, MA, 1969), 361–92; Isaiah Berlin, "The Counter-Enlightenment," in Philip P. Wiener, ed., *Dictionary of the History of Ideas* (New York, 1973), vol. II, pp. 100–12.

[13] "Central elements usually identified with the counter-Enlightenment were in fact fundamental to the Enlightenment itself," writes Jonathan B. Knudsen, *Justus Möser and the German Enlightenment* (Cambridge, 1996), 148. See also J. G. A. Pocock, "Enlightenment and Counter-Enlightenment, Revolution and Counter-Revolution: A Eurosceptical Enquiry," *History of Political Thought* 20:1 (Spring 1999), 125–39 and the essays in Joseph Mali and Robert Wokler, eds., *Isaiah Berlin's Counter-Enlightenment* (Philadelphia, PA, 2003). I have drawn on an unpublished paper of James Schmidt, "The Idea of Counter-Enlightenment: A Critique of Isaiah Berlin."

[14] See Oswald Bayer, *Zeitgenosse im Widerspruch: Johann Georg Hamann als radikaler Aufklärer* (Munich, 1988).

1787,[15] Hamann is relentless in attacking what he takes to be Jacobi's errors – reducing being to a property or an object rather than understanding it as the general relation in which we are enmeshed prior to cognitive acts; taking faith as a self-evident part of human experience but then attempting to defend it by arguments from Spinoza and Hume; distinguishing faith from reason and realism from idealism although those distinctions have no basis in experience. The irrationalist or fideist philosopher attempts to close the gulf (or, as Lessing called it, the "ugly broad ditch") that has opened up between faith and reason, while the rationalist or skeptic philosopher is intent on preserving the distance between them, but both recognize the gulf. For Hamann, on the other hand, "it is pure idealism to separate faith and sensation from thought";[16] no special faculty for faith should be imputed, which could then be found in opposition to the faculty of reason. Jacobi, from Hamann's perspective, has been betrayed by his initial jargon into investing metaphysical wraiths with real substance. It makes no sense to isolate certain features from reality, combine them into a larger abstraction, and then attempt to infer reality from that abstraction. Jacobi's faith then becomes a desperate way out of "the impossible situation of having to retrieve existence in general out of thought in general"[17] instead of a routine and ordinary part of daily existence.

Occasionally Western thinkers have launched linguistic critiques of philosophy (as done by Valla, Lichtenberg, Maimon, Mauthner, and Wittgenstein),[18] and it is possible to see Hamann as such a figure. Yet he rarely engages with the details and implications of a specific vocabulary and is not interested to offer improvements or think through the consequences of an alternative vocabulary. For the most part Hamann prefers to offer a metacritique instead, that is, he seeks to isolate what he considers to

[15] Hamann, *Briefe*, vol. VII, pp. 161–81. [16] Ibid., p. 174.
[17] George di Giovanni, introduction to Friedrich Heinrich Jacobi, *The Main Philosophical Writings and the Novel Allwill* (Montreal, 1994), 115. In addition to di Giovanni's valuable discussion of this letter (see especially pp. 103–5 and 115–16 of his introduction), see Renate Knoll, "Hamanns Kritik an Jacobi mit Jacobis Briefen vom 1., 6. und 30. 4. 1787 und Hamanns Briefen vom 17., 22. und 27. 4. 1787," in Bernhard Gajek, ed., *Johann Georg Hamann, Acta des Internationalen Hamann-Colloquiums in Lüneburg 1976* (Frankfurt, 1979), 214–76.
[18] See Lorenzo Valla's attack on Aristotle in the *Dialecticae disputationes*, discussed for example by Brian P. Copenhaver and Charles B. Schmitt, *Renaissance Philosophy* (Oxford, 1992), 218–19; the aphorisms by Lichtenberg on language treated by J. P. Stern, *Lichtenberg: A Doctrine of Scattered Occasions* (Bloomington, IN, 1959), 156–68; Solomon Maimon, "The Philosophical Language-Confusion," in Jere Paul Surber, ed. and tr., *Metacritique: The Linguistic Assault on German Idealism* (Amherst, NY, 2001), 71–84; and Fritz Mauthner, *Beiträge zu einer Kritik der Sprache*, discussed for example by Gershon Weiler, *Mauthner's Critique of Language* (Cambridge, 1970).

be the *proton pseudos*, the initial and fundamental error, of a philosopher. He does so by using exaggeration and grotesque parody to render foolish what he takes to be the initial impulse behind a philosophical problem. In the case of Kant, for example, Hamann believes that what motivates the *Critique of Pure Reason* is no more than prejudice in favor of mathematics and a predilection for purity. Mathematics may yield certainty, but to favor it relegates human reason to a position inferior to the "infallible and unerring instinct of insects" (p. 211). Why should philosophy be concerned with certainty?

This linguistic assault on philosophy is carried out in Hamann's distinctive style of parody. Hamann believes that philosophy deals with unreal problems created by the misapplication of language ("language is the centerpoint of reason's misunderstanding with itself," p. 211); his object, therefore, is not to refute a philosophical position but to expose and make ridiculous its pretensions. In this sense, his "metacritique" may have more in common with Aristophanes' mockery of Socrates than with philosophical texts. It is possible, of course, to imagine fuller rebuttals of Kant and Mendelssohn and others along the lines which Hamann has sketched, by tracing more precisely and systematically the philosophical implications of what he saw as the impurities of human existence – that we speak a language we did not invent, inherit a history we did not make, and live in a body we did not create – and such rebuttals would soon be offered, and these would, in their turn, be subject to further refutations and restatements. However, Hamann always refrained from doing so.

Should Hamann then be considered a philosopher at all? He scarcely develops his suggestive remarks about reason, language, sociability, and history, and nowhere does he demonstrate a talent for consecutive logical thought. However, rather than take him as a confused precursor of philosophical themes and arguments to come, it does more justice to him to respect his antagonism to philosophical abstraction and argumentation. Jacobi, who introduced the term "nihilism" into the European languages, found skepticism[19] philosophically threatening and attempted to rebut it. Hamann had no such anxiety; skepticism did not present worrisome

---

[19] On eighteenth-century skepticism and its perception, see the essays in Richard H. Popkin, Ezequiel De Olaso, and Giorgio Tonelli, eds., *Scepticism in the Enlightenment* (Dordrecht, 1997). See also John Christian Laursen, "Swiss Anti-skeptics in Berlin," in Martin Fontius and Helmut Holzhey, eds., *Schweizer im Berlin des 18. Jahrhunderts* (Berlin, 1996), 261–81, and the essay by Richard H. Popkin on skepticism in Knud Haakonssen, ed., *The Cambridge History of Eighteenth-Century Philosophy* (Cambridge, 2006), 426–50.

arguments that needed to be rebutted. Hamann, after all, was not tempted to find first principles on which to ground knowledge with certainty, nor did faith and reason collide in his understanding. Since he did not see himself as confronted by philosophical difficulties, he was not tempted to find a way out of them, for example by making covert appeals to unavowed philosophies, as in giving to common sense an epistemological status it cannot easily bear, or in appealing to the authority of everyday experience that is taken to be incipiently or inherently philosophical, or in making a leap of faith. It is often difficult, especially when confronted with matters of great import, to refrain from making or implying philosophical statements, and Hamann is an unexcelled guide to this therapy.

The essays

This selection, emphasizing the essays on language, is made up of twelve of Hamann's writings, ten complete, and two in part, spanning more than twenty-five years of his life. His two most sustained philosophical essays (the *Metacritique on the Purism of Reason*, a response to Kant, and *Golgotha and Sheblimini!*, a response to Mendelssohn) have been included entire.

The twelve pieces fall broadly into three periods. The early period is represented by the two dedications to *Socratic Memorabilia* (1759) and several essays from his 1762 collection *Crusades of a Philologist* (the *Aesthetica in Nuce*, his most famous and influential work, and three essays tackling more narrowly linguistic topics which nonetheless provide him with an opportunity to begin his assault on fundamental assumptions of his contemporaries about the nature of language). A second period begins a decade later with the three essays he wrote in response to Herder's prize-winning essay on the origin of language (1772). In them, as also in an essay opposing a spelling reform, *New Apology of the Letter h* (1773), Hamann deepens his reflections on language, his central theme, and ties them more aggressively to politics; because of his mocking opposition to Frederick the Great, some of the essays could not be published. A final period can be dated from his intensive re-reading of Luther in 1780 and includes three works, his most profound: the *Metacritique* (1784), *Golgotha and Sheblimini!* (1784), and *Disrobing and Transfiguration* (1786). The last work exists in two versions; the conclusion of the first version has been translated here.

The first extract in this selection comes from Hamann's *Socratic Memorabilia* of 1759, the work which inaugurated his career. In it he recovered Socrates' traditional role as defender of foolishness against the world's wisdom (Erasmus had aligned Socrates with Christ), pitting this image against one which many Enlightenment writers favored, Socrates as a supreme rationalist.[20] The two dedications to this work are translated, the first addressing and guying the "public" and the second metaschematically equating Hamann's friends Kant and Berens with the sophists of Socrates' Athens. Among the themes being developed in this work Hamann treats language, implicitly in his claim "to have written about Socrates in a Socratic way" (p. 7) and explicitly in his comparison of coins and words as things that have their value relationally rather than intrinsically (see, for example, *Werke*, vol. II, pp. 71–2). Hamann continues to ponder the relational nature of language in most of his subsequent writings.

In the years immediately after *Socratic Memorabilia*, he writes a number of short pieces on literary and philological topics, collecting them and adding a few more in *Crusades of the Philologist*, where the title refers "to the zigzag sallies of the Teutonic Knights past the megaliths scattered throughout the Baltic area in order that they might avoid participating in an actual crusade."[21] The collection consisted of thirteen essays, four of which are translated here. The first of these, *Essay on an Academic Question*, was provoked by the topic which the Berlin Academy set for the prize essay of 1759, on the mutual influence of language and opinions (the contest was won by Johann David Michaelis, a philologist of Oriental languages who was to become Hamann's particular *bête noire*). Hamann objects to the evasiveness of the Academy's question, which he believes was set out in fashionable and vague terms in order to promote the influence of the French language and French opinion (the public language of the Academy, like that of Frederick the Great, was French). The next essay, *Miscellaneous Notes on Word Order in the French Language*, begins with an allusion to Friedrich Carl von Moser's *Master and Servant* (1759), a work of political theory much influenced by the French writers of the time. The bulk of the essay is devoted to a discussion of the relation between money and language and between word order and thought; the latter question was

---

[20] For the full range of the Socrates reception in the eighteenth century, see Benno Böhn, *Sokrates im achtzehnten Jahrhundert* (Neumünster, 1966 [1929]).

[21] O'Flaherty, *Johann Georg Hamann*, 63–4; cf. Josef Nadler, *Johann Georg Hamann 1730–1788: Der Zeuge des Corpus Mysticum* (Salzburg, 1949), 126.

part of a wide contemporary debate originating in France on the "natural order of thought." Both essays are significant for their exploration of the political dimension of language, and in particular for introducing and scrutinizing the theoretical grounding of what would become linguistic nationalism.

The three letters that make up *Cloverleaf of Hellenistic Letters* are concerned, respectively, with the language of the New Testament, the value of Greek literature, and the language of the Hebrew Bible. The first letter revisits an old debate on the quality of the Greek of the New Testament, which in comparison with Attic Greek seems barbarous and debased. Hamann defends it for the same reasons others had condemned it; its lowliness is evidence of divine purpose. Moreover, its Greek bears traces of the languages of the Jews and the Romans, and its hybrid and impure state is superior to mere purity. The second letter considers the poets, philosophers, and historians of ancient Greece, finding that it is only through a kind of prophecy that they may be understood and enable the present to be understood, that is, only through understanding the connection of past, present, and future. The third letter responds to Michaelis' *Opinion on the Means Used to Understand the Defunct Hebrew Language* (1757). Without venturing to contradict the book's precise claims about Hebrew and Arabic, Hamann attacks its philology more broadly, denying its claim to read truthfully or in good faith. Hamann shares Nietzsche's intense ambivalence toward philology as at once truth-denying and truth-giving.

The *Aesthetica in Nuce*, the last of the four works translated from the 1762 *Crusades*, continues to attack Michaelis, opposing to his rationalist criticism of the Bible a new aesthetics, elements of which would be found congenial by Romantic writers: poetry has a priority over prose, emotions and images lose their primordial force when they are subject to abstraction, the "oriental" style of the Bible is superior to the etiolated good taste of the French, mimesis has as its proper object the divine creative process and not mere created things, and so on. These propositions, as propositions, had been anticipated by other writers;[22] Hamann's originality lies elsewhere,

---

[22] The poetic superiority of ancient languages over modern, derivative ones was emphasized by Jean-Baptiste Dubos in 1719 and became a commonplace; Homer's primitive style had been praised by Thomas Blackwell and others on the grounds of its passionate superiority to later rules governing taste; the belief that the earliest stages of a language are the most vivid and come closest to bridging speech and action is found in several authors of the eighteenth century.

in the weird originality of his style and in the status he gives to poetry and art as the primary mode of human and Christian existence.

In 1771, Johann Georg Herder won the prize offered by the Berlin Academy for the best answer to the question of the origin of language. The topic had been discussed since antiquity, and for much of the eighteenth century it was debated with a particular intensity.[23] Herder's answer was resolutely naturalist, which elicited several ripostes from Hamann, including the three that are translated here: *The Last Will and Testament of the Knight of the Rose-Cross, Philological Ideas and Doubts,* and *To the Solomon of Prussia.* Hamann, despite his friendship with Herder, thought that the debate was foolish and its terms (natural vs supernatural) hopelessly compromised. For him, the proponent of the supernatural version of the origin of language (viz., Süßmilch) hides under a blanket and shouts "Here's God!," while the naturalist Herder walks onto the stage and says, "Look, I am a man!" (*Werke*, vol. III, p. 17). *The Knight of the Rose-Cross* opens by rejecting this picture of the world in which natural and supernatural are divided and opposed to each other; it ends by uniting them, in a retelling of the biblical creation story in which Adam's discovery of language was "as natural, as close and easy, as a child's game" (p. 109). *Philological Ideas and Doubts* proceeds by parody and pays close attention to Herder's own words and arguments. (The "ideas" of the title translates *Einfälle* and could also be rendered "raids" or "incursions.") Hamann seizes on the weaknesses of Herder's account of the origin of language – the capacious role played by the ill-defined faculty of "reflection," the asocial and ahistorical anthropology which invokes "freedom" and "reason" as constant human qualities and which claims that language could be invented by a man in isolation – and makes them appear ridiculous. *To the Solomon of Prussia,* written in French, does not continue the polemic with Herder; instead, it addresses Frederick directly, calling on him to emulate Solomon, expel the French, recognize Herder's genius, and renew Prussia. Hamann's rage is carefully controlled and subordinated throughout this parodic address, which stood no chance of being published.

Hamann's and Herder's philosophies of language have been repeatedly examined in modern scholarship, but unfortunately no consensus about

---

[23] Allan Megill's unpublished Ph.D. thesis, "The Enlightenment Debate on the Origin of Language and its Historical Background" (Columbia University, 1975), is a valuable and comprehensive survey. See also Hans Aarsleff, "Philosophy of Language," in Haakonssen, ed., *The Cambridge History of Eighteenth-Century Philosophy,* 451–95.

them has emerged.[24] Their differences have been described in diverse, and sometimes invidious, ways. Moreover, while some historians emphasize their continuity with previous thinkers, especially French, others largely assimilate them to the German Romantics of a subsequent generation. Finally, neither Hamann nor Herder is particularly consistent. The task of clarifying the "linguistic turn" in German philosophy at the end of the eighteenth and the beginning of the nineteenth century is obdurate.

The *New Apology of the Letter h* was written in response to an orthographic reform proposed in an appendix of Christian Tobias Damm's *Observations on Religion* (1773). Damm, in common with a number of eighteenth-century writers, worried over the irrational spelling of German words, in which letters (especially the letter *h*) do not always correspond to sounds. Hamann reacts strenuously to the proposed rationalized spelling, attacking Damm's confused arguments but also defending the letter on religious grounds (as Jakob Boehme had previously interpreted the letter); Hamann then adds a statement spoken in the voice of *h* itself, one of his most effective instances of a favored rhetorical device, prosopopoeia. The essay has been well described by Jonathan Sheehan:[25]

> Like other grammarians of the eighteenth century, Hamann viewed the *h* as a visual representation of the bodily expulsion of breath. Unlike these grammarians, however, Hamann cherished a language that did not exist for the clear expression of thoughts, and a writing exceeding its function as a mirror of speech. Rather, writing was to preserve the speech of God or, even more precisely, the breath of God . . . The *h*, furthermore, not only represented the breath but was itself the very sign of superabundance and overflow in human language that hearkened to God's hidden hand . . . [F]or Hamann, the excess of God's creation "still displays itself in nature," and thus still was present in language and testified to this original act of creation . . . Rather than just reversing the terms of the reformers, then, Hamann's theology of the *h* displaces the terms by asking the principal question at stake: what is language for?

---

[24] Ian Hacking has a witty account of some recent polemics in "How, Why, When, and Where Did Language Go Public?," in *Historical Ontology* (Cambridge, MA, 2002), 121–39.

[25] Jonathan Sheehan, "Enlightenment Details: Theology, Natural History, and the Letter h," *Representations* 61 (Winter 1998), 38–9.

Golgotha and Sheblimini! (1784) is Hamann's response to Mendelssohn's *Jerusalem*, published the year before. Mendelssohn's plea for religious toleration is divided into two parts: in the first half he argues,
from within the framework of social contract theory, that matters of conscience cannot be regulated either by church or by state; in the second
he represents Jewish doctrine as the natural religion of eternal truths and
interprets Jewish ceremonial law as a particularly vivid way of motivating
right action in accordance with those truths. The careful distinctions of
Mendelssohn's argument – between actions and convictions, eternal and
historical truths, church and state – are rejected by Hamann, who sees in
them "the serpent's deception of language" (p. 172), a "cleaving" of a complete whole "into two dead halves" (p. 179). In contrast to Mendelssohn,
he insists on the temporal truths of history, unique and unrepeated, which
become truths only by the authority of the tradition which has preserved
them.

The *Metacritique on the Purism of Reason*, Hamann's response to Kant's
Critique of Pure Reason and *Prolegomena to Any Future Metaphysics*, was
written in 1784. Herder and Jacobi read it in manuscript; it was published
posthumously in 1800. He objects to Kant's division of knowledge into
sensibility and understanding, and more generally of his dualism of phe-
nomenal and the noumenal, on the grounds that such a division cannot
be overcome to correspond with the unity of experience. The dualism is
arbitrarily made and then arbitrarily overcome. Moreover, it breaks the
bond connecting reason and language, taking reason to be a priori whereas
it is always found in language and history and can be represented as prior
to them only by an ungrounded abstraction.[26]

Disrobing and Transfiguration: A Flying Letter to Nobody, the Well Known
(1786) is both a defense of his writing and a continuation of the disagree-
ment with Mendelssohn, who died early in the year at the height of the
"pantheism controversy" between Jacobi and himself.[27] It exists in two
versions; in both, Hamann first recalls his *Socratic Memorabilia* and then
defends *Golgotha and Sheblimini!* against a hostile review, indicating that
he no longer needs to temper his remarks out of consideration for his

---

[26] Frederick C. Beiser, *The Fate of Reason: German Philosophy from Kant to Fichte* (Cambridge, MA,
1987), 40–3.
[27] Best represented in English by Gérard Vallée, *The Spinoza Conversations between Lessing and Jacobi*
(Lanham, MD, 1988), which contains excerpts from Mendelssohn and Jacobi; the most famous
contribution to the debate is Kant's essay "What is Orientation in Thinking?"

friendship with Mendelssohn. The conclusions to the two versions differ more substantially, though both are critical of Mendelssohn's *Jerusalem* and his *Morning Hours* (1785). The conclusion of the less polemical first version has been translated here.

Hamann's striking and provocative sentences have always attracted attention, even when readers were stymied by the essays in which they appeared. Nor is it improper that individual statements by Hamann, read aphoristically, have aroused excitement; his style encourages and occasionally demands it. On the other hand, not all readings need to take this form, and my translation and commentary is intended to encourage further readings by removing some of the extrinsic obstacles to the essays. Aquiring the relevant information, however, is only the first step in understanding why Hamann writes what he writes, how he moves from one thought to another, what motivates particular references and allusions. That task is for readers.

Chronology

1730 Johann Georg Hamann is born on August 27 in Königsberg, the capital of East Prussia, to parents of modest circumstances and Pietist orientation.

1740 Frederick II becomes King of Prussia, attacks Silesia, and begins the War of the Austrian Succession (1740–8).

1746 After being tutored at home and attending a few schools (including the Kneiphof Gymnasium), Hamann enrolls at the University of Königsberg to study theology, later switching to law.

1749 For over a year, Hamann collaborates with friends to produce *Daphne*, a weekly literary journal for women.

1752 Failing to take a degree, Hamann leaves the university and becomes a tutor to the sons of minor nobility in Livonia and Courland. He regularly visits his friend from the university, Johann Christoph Berens, in Riga.

1756 Undertakes a somewhat obscure mission to London as an agent of the Berens family's firm. En route to London, he visits Berlin (meeting Mendelssohn and other figures of the Berlin Enlightenment) and other cities in Germany and the Netherlands. Frederick II invades Saxony, and the Seven Years War begins.

1757 Arriving in London, he fails to deliver a message to the Russian Embassy. He spends the next months accumulating debt and, according to his subsequent account, lives a life of dissipation.

1758 Alone in London, Hamann undergoes a spiritual crisis and recovers his Christian faith in a radicalized form. He reads the

Bible in its entirety and in *Biblical Reflections* writes a commentary on its personal meaning for him. He returns to Riga in July, staying with the Berenses; he fell in love with but was refused permission to marry his friend's sister.

1759 Hamann returns to Königsberg, living in his father's house. *Socratic Memorabilia* is published.

1762 *Crusades of the Philologist* appears; it includes the essays *Essay on an Academic Question*, *Miscellaneous Notes on Word Order in the French Language*, *Cloverleaf of Hellenistic Letters*, and *Aesthetica in Nuce*, most of which were published previously.

1763 With the peasant woman Anna Regina Schumacher, who was caring for his father, Hamann begins a devoted and intimate relationship though they never marry. They have four children (the oldest in 1769 and the youngest in 1778). He works briefly for the municipality of Königsberg and then for the Department of War and Crown Lands for Prussia.

1764 Hamann resigns in order to care for his ailing father (who dies in 1766); he tutors and becomes the friend of Johann Gottfried Herder. From the summer and over the next years he travels and seeks employment outside of Prussia.

1766 To increase the efficiency of tax revenue, Frederick II creates a new financial ministry, the General Excise Administration, as a tax farming agency; it is run by a consortium of Frenchmen.

1767 Returning to Königsberg, Hamann finds a job as clerk and translator for the General Excise Administration.

1772 Herder's *Essay on the Origin of Language* is published; Hamann writes in response *The Last Will and Testament of the Knight of the Rose-Cross*, *Philological Ideas and Doubts*, and *To the Solomon of Prussia* (the latter two were not published). First partition of Poland.

1773 *New Apology of the Letter h.*

1774 Hamann responds to Herder's *Oldest Document of the Human Race* with *On the Most Recent Interpretation of the Oldest Document of the Human Race*.

1775 Hamann writes on mystery and religion in *Hierophantic Letters* and on marriage and sexuality in *Essay of a Sibyl on Marriage*.

1777 Hamann is promoted to Superintendent of the Customs Warehouse.

1780 Hamann translates Hume's *Dialogues concerning Natural Religion.*

1781 Hamann reads Kant's *Critique of Pure Reason* in proofs and writes, but does not publish, a review.

1782 Hamann's income is reduced after a reform of the perquisites of his job. He enters into correspondence with Friedrich Heinrich Jacobi.

1783 Mendelssohn's *Jerusalem, or on Religious Power and Judaism.*

1784 *Metacritique on the Purism of Reason* is written but not published; *Golgotha and Sheblimini!* is published.

1786 *Disrobing and Transfiguration.*

1787 Hamann is discharged by his employers after petitioning for a leave. He visits Münster at the invitation of Princess Gallitzin and also visits Jacobi and others.

1788 Hamann dies in Münster.

Further reading

Standard editions and commentaries

Josef Nadler's edition of Hamann's writings (*Sämtliche Werke*, 6 vols., Vienna, 1949–57) and Walther Ziesemer and Arthur Henkel's edition of Hamann's letters (*Briefwechsel*, 7 vols., Wiesbaden/Frankfurt am Main, 1955–79) are the standard editions. Vol. VI of Nadler's *Werke* includes an index which also serves as a glossary and commentary. Of the five volumes that were published in the series *Hamanns Hauptschriften erklärt* (Gütersloh, 1956–63), three are relevant to essays included here: vol. II, on the *Sokratische Denkwürdigkeiten* (ed. Fritz Blanke, 1959); vol. IV, covering Hamann's essays on the origin of language (ed. Elfriede Büchsel, 1963), and vol. VII, on *Golgatha und Scheblimini!* (ed. Lothar Schreiner, 1956). The commentary by Sven-Aage Jørgensen on the *Sokratische Denkwürdigkeiten* and the *Aesthetica in Nuce* is valuable (Stuttgart, 1968), as is the commentary on *Aesthetica in Nuce* by Hans-Martin Lumpp in *Philologia Crucis* (Tübingen, 1970). Three further editions give essential commentary on essays included in this selection: Karlheinz Löhrer's *Kleeblatt hellenistischer Briefe* (Frankfurt am Main, 1994); Oswald Bayer's edition, commentary, and discussion of the *Metakritik über den Purismus der Vernunft* which appears in his *Vernunft ist Sprache* (Stuttgart, 2002); and Reiner Wild's *"Metacriticus Bonae Spei": Johann Georg Hamanns "Fliegender Brief"* (Frankfurt am Main, 1975).

Translations

Hamann seems to have made a single appearance in English in the nineteenth century; most of his early (pre-conversion) essay on the French political economist Plumard de Dangeul was published in Frederic H. Hedge, ed., *Prose Writers of Germany* (Philadelphia, 1848). A wide selection from both the writings and the letters of Hamann, mainly in the form of extracts, was translated by Ronald Gregor Smith in *J. G. Hamann: A Study in Christian Existentialism* (New York, 1960). A translation with a full commentary on the *Socratic Memorabilia* was made by James C. O'Flaherty in Hamann's *Socratic Memorabilia: A Translation and Commentary* (Baltimore, MD, 1967). Stephen N. Dunning appends an unannotated translation of *Golgotha and Sheblimini!* to *The Tongues of Men: Hegel and Hamann on Religious Language and History* (Missoula, MT, 1979). Joyce P. Crick's translation and annotation of *Aesthetica in Nuce* was first published in H. B. Nisbet, ed., *German Aesthetic and Literary Criticism* (Cambridge, 1985). Gwen Griffith Dickson translated, with explication as well as annotation, *Socratic Memorabilia, Aesthetica in Nuce, The Last Will and Testament of the Knight of the Rose-Cross, Philological Ideas and Doubts, Essay of a Sibyl on Marriage, Metacritique on the Purism of Reason*, and a few others in *Johann Georg Hamann's Relational Metacriticism* (Berlin, 1995). James Schmidt edited *What is Enlightenment?: Eighteenth-Century Answers and Twentieth Century Questions* (Berkeley, CA, 1996), in which an earlier version of my translation of the *Metacritique on the Purism of Reason* appears; it also includes an annotated translation of Hamann's letter of 1784 to Christian Jacob Kraus in which Hamann responds to Kant's essay "What is Enlightenment?" Arnulf Zweig's translation of Kant's *Correspondence* (Cambridge, 1999) includes five letters from Hamann. Jere Paul Surber translates the *Metacritique* and discusses its genesis in *Metacritique: The Linguistic Assault on German Idealism* (Amherst, NY, 2001).

Angelo Pupi translated several of Hamann's works into Italian (*Scritti cristiani*, 1975; *Scritti sul linguaggio: 1760–1773*, 1977); French translations have been made by Pierre Klossowski, Henry Corbin, and Romain Deygout (see the latter's *Aesthetica in nuce, Métacritique du purisme de la raison pure, et autres textes*, 2001).

Secondary literature in English

James C. O'Flaherty's introductory survey of Hamann's life and writings (*Johann Georg Hamann*, Boston, MA, 1979) remains a good starting point from which to learn about Hamann. Two other works of his may be consulted: *Unity and Language: A Study in the Philosophy of Hamann* (Chapel Hill, NC, 1952) and *The Quarrel of Reason with Itself: Essays on Hamann, Michaelis, Lessing, Nietzsche* (Columbia, SC, 1988). Isaiah Berlin's introductory study *The Magus of the North: J. G. Hamann and the Origins of Modern Irrationalism* (London, 1993, but written in 1965) is a valuable introduction which illustrates Berlin's gift for finding suggestive quotations.

For further background to Hamann in relation to his contemporaries, four works may be recommended: Robert T. Clark, Jr., *Herder: His Life and Thoughts* (Berkeley, CA, 1955); Alexander Altmann, *Moses Mendelssohn: A Biographical Study* (London, 1973); the long introduction by George di Giovanni to his translation of Friedrich Heinrich Jacobi, *The Main Philosophical Writings and the Novel Allwill* (Montreal, 1994); and Manfred Kuehn, *Kant: A Biography* (Cambridge, 2001).

Lewis White Beck in *Early German Philosophy: Kant and His Predecessors* (Cambridge, MA, 1969), and Frederick C. Beiser in *The Fate of Reason: German Philosophy from Kant to Fichte* (Cambridge, MA, 1987) discuss Hamann in the context of intellectual history. E. A. Blackall devotes a chapter of *The Emergence of German as a Literary Language* (Cambridge, 1959) to Hamann's style. Other monographs include W. M. Alexander, *Johann Georg Hamann: Philosophy and Faith* (The Hague, 1966) and Terence J. German, *Hamann on Language and Religion* (Oxford, 1981).

On Hamann and Socrates, see Denis Thouard, "Hamann and the History of Philosophy," in C. R. Ligota and J.-L. Quantin, eds., *History of Scholarship* (Oxford, 2006), 413–36. For Hamann's essays on the origin of language, important studies in English include Allan Megill's unpublished Ph.D. thesis, "The Enlightenment Debate on the Origin of Language and its Historical Background" (Columbia University, 1975) and James H. Stam, *Inquiries into the Origin of Language* (New York, 1976). For Hamann's essay opposing orthographic reform, see Jonathan Sheehan, "Enlightenment Details: Theology, Natural History, and the Letter h," *Representations* 61 (Winter 1998), 29–56. Sheehan's full-length study, *The Enlightenment Bible: Translation, Scholarship, Culture* (Princeton, NJ, 2005) examines, among other topics, the contested relation between German philology and theology, and is an excellent, wide-ranging survey of the period. On Hamann's *Miscellaneous Notes*, see Gérard Genette, *Mimologics* (Lincoln, NE, 1995), 143–78, in regard to eighteenth-century debates about word order and the order of thought. For Hamann's response to Mendelssohn's *Jerusalem*, see Stephen H. Dunning, *The Tongues of Men: Hegel and Hamann on Religious Language and History* (Missoula, MT, 1979).

Secondary literature in German and other languages

A large bibliography of secondary literature on Hamann ("Bibliographie der Hamann-Literatur") is currently maintained at http:// members.aol.com/agrudolph/bib.html.

The International Hamann-Kolloquium meets approximately every four years and publishes the proceedings of its meetings; the full range of Hamann's writings, life, and context come in for examination. Joseph Kohnen has edited several books about the culture of Königsberg; several essays in them are devoted to Hamann (*Königsberg*, 1994; *Königsberg-Studien*, 1998; *Königsberger Beiträge*, 2002).

Important studies devoted specifically to Hamann and language include Bernhard Gajek, *Sprache beim jungen Hamann* (Berne, 1967); Georg Baudler, *"Im Worte Sehen": Das Sprachdenken Johann Georg Hamanns* (Bonn, 1970); Helmut Weiss, *Johann Georg Hamanns Ansichten zur Sprache: Versuch einer Rekonstruktion aus dem Frühwerk* (Münster, 1990); and Helmut Weiss, "Johann Georg Hamann," in Herbert E. Brekle et al., eds., *Bio-bibliographisches Handbuch zur Sprachwissenschaft des 18. Jahrhunderts*, vol. IV (1996), pp. 39–55. An older work of scholarship on Hamann and the Enlightenment, Rudolf Unger's *Hamann und die Aufklärung* (Halle an der Saale, 1925), should be read in conjunction with Oswald Bayer's *Zeitgenosse im Widerspruch: Johann Georg Hamann als radikaler Aufklärer* (Munich, 1988).

Hegel's long review in 1828 of Hamann's collected works can be found in *Werke in zwanzig Bänden*, vol. XI, pp. 275–353.

Angelo Pupi published a large biography in Italian of Hamann (7 vols., Milan, 1988–2004); it includes much translation of Hamann into Italian.

Note on the text, translation, and annotation

For the *Metacritique on the Purism of Reason*, I have translated the text printed in Oswald Bayer, *Vernunft ist Sprache* (2002); for the excerpt from *Disrobing and Transfiguration*, I have followed that of Reiner Wild, *"Metacriticus Bonae Spei": Johann Georg Hamanns "Fliegender Brief"* (1975). Otherwise, the texts translated here are those printed by Josef Nadler in his edition of Johann Georg Hamann, *Sämtliche Werke* (1949, 6 vols.). Nadler reproduces Hamann's typographical errors and introduces a few of his own; these have not been indicated in the translation. In a few other instances, I have departed from Nadler's texts; as a rule these have been indicated in the annotation.

All Hamann's writings after his rediscovery of his Christian faith are densely allusive to the Bible. I have generally replaced allusions to the Luther Bible (or, in the case of *To the Solomon of Prussia*, the French Bible of Olivetan) with allusions to the King James Bible. On some occasions, it has not been possible to reproduce the allusion because of an important difference in wording; fuller explanations of such cases generally follow in the notes. Many of Hamann's essays react to the precise wording of another piece of writing. In the case of the *Metacritique on the Purism of Reason*, a response to Kant's *Critique of Pure Reason*, and of *Golgotha and Sheblimini!*, a response to Mendelssohn's *Jerusalem*, I have followed the English translations by Norman Kemp Smith and Allan Arkush, respectively.

In general, I have avoided the temptation to simplify Hamann's words. This has meant sometimes translating an obscure word in German by an obscure word in English (plus a note); not always resolving ambiguities

(Hamann tended to be careless about the referents of pronouns); and occasionally reproducing idiosyncratic features of punctuation (especially the dash). In addition, it has meant preserving the multilingual aspect of Hamann's writing. Hamann believed that speaking a language, like having a body, was a fundamental aspect of human finitude. To present his writings in a seamless web of a single language would have betrayed both his practice and his convictions. Quotations in foreign languages are presented in keeping with modern conventions (Greek and French words are given diacritical marks, Latin is spelled with "u" as a vowel and "v" as a consonant); these passages are translated in the notes. In one respect, I have simplified Hamann's text: I do not reproduce his extensive italics. Often these indicate that a word or phrase is a quotation or a proper name, and this information is provided by the annotation.

I have deliberately modeled my translation of *Aesthetica in Nuce* on that by Joyce P. Crick, which appears in *Classic and Romantic German Aesthetics*, ed. J. M. Bernstein (Cambridge Texts in the History of Philosophy, 2003).

Full annotation, though desirable, would run to great length and is not possible here. Only one example exists in English: James C. O'Flaherty's *Hamann's Socratic Memorabilia* (1967), which devotes more than 200 pages to a 25-page essay by Hamann. Several fully annotated editions of Hamann's work exist in German (see Further Reading); the most recent is Oswald Bayer's *Vernunft ist Sprache* (2002), an explication of an eight-page essay which runs to more than 500 pages. The notes offered in this volume have had to be highly disciplined; for the most part, they serve only to help make an immediate sense of the words. Contextual and interpretative remarks are rare; cross-references to Hamann's other writings have been made only in exceptional cases (*Briefe* indicates the seven-volume edition of letters prepared by Ziesemer and Henkel, and *Werke* the six-volume edition of writings prepared by Nadler); and references to secondary literature are generally avoided.

In translating and annotating Hamann, I have benefited from the help given by colleagues and friends who have reduced the number of errors in my work: Nicolas de Warren, Adam Gitner, David Konstan, Matthew Spencer, and Zachary Sng. I am especially indebted and grateful to James Schmidt. I gratefully acknowledge the support of the Howard Foundation. I wish also to thank Cambridge University

Press and Karl Ameriks, the general editor of the series Cambridge Texts in the History of Philosophy. An earlier version of my translation "Metacritique on the Purism of Reason" was published in James Schmidt, ed., *What is Enlightenment? Eighteenth-Century Answers and Twentieth-Century Questions* © 1996, The Regents of the University of California.

Writings on philosophy and language

Socratic

Memorabilia

Collected
for the
Boredom[1] of the
Public by a
Lover of
Boredom

With
a Double Dedication
to Nobody and to Two

O curas hominum! o quantum est in rebus inane!
Quis leget haec? – – – Min' tu istud ais?
                    Nemo hercule – –Nemo? –
Vel DVO vel NEMO – – –

Persius[2]

Amsterdam, 1759[3]

---

[1] That is, as a specific against boredom, "for whiling away the time."

[2] Persius, *Satire* 1.1–3: "O the cares of mankind! the emptiness in things!" "Who will read these things?" "Are you talking to me? No one, by Hercules." "No one?" "Either TWO or NO ONE." (Hamann's capitals).

[3] The book was published in Königsberg; the fictitious place of publication seems to have been added at the whim of the publisher (permission for publication had been obtained from the government, and so there was no need to suppress the genuine location).

To the Public,
or
Nobody, the Well-Known

– ὅδ' ΟΥΤΙΣ, ποῦ 'στιν; – –

Euripides, Κύκλωψ[4]

You bear a name and need no proof of your existence, you find faith and do no miracles[5] to earn it, you get honor and have neither concept nor feeling thereof. We know that there is no idol in the world.[6] Neither are you human, yet you must be a human image which superstition has made a god. You lack nor eyes nor ears, which nonetheless do not see, do not hear;[7] and the artificial eye you form, the artificial ear you plant,[8] is like your own, blind and deaf. You must know everything, and you learn nothing;[a] [9] you must judge everything, and you understand nothing, ever learning,

---

[a] Proverbs 9:13 ["A foolish woman is clamorous: she is simple, and knoweth nothing."]

[4] Euripides, *Cyclops* 675: "this No one, where is he?"

[5] John 3:2: "Rabbi, we know that thou art a teacher come from God: for no man can do these miracles that thou doest, except God be with him." Luther and Hamann have *Zeichen* ("signs") for "miracles."

[6] Cf. 1 Corinthians 8:4: "we know that an idol is nothing in the world."

[7] Cf. Psalms 115:5–6, Jeremiah 5:21, Matthew 13:13.

[8] Psalm 94:9: "He that planted the ear, shall he not hear? he that formed the eye, shall he not see?"

[9] Proverbs 9:13 does not seem relevant; cf. Proverbs 14:7: "Go from the presence of a foolish man, when thou perceivest not in him the lips of knowledge." For "perceivest not . . . the lips of knowledge" Luther and Hamann have *lernst nichts* ("learn nothing").

4

and never able to come to the knowledge of the truth;[b] you are talking, or you are pursuing, you are on a journey, or peradventure you sleep,[10] while your priests lift up their voice, and you should answer them and their mockery with fire.[11] Offerings are offered you every day, which others consume at your expense, in order that, on the grounds of your hearty meals, your existence seem probable.[12] For all your fastidiousness, you nonetheless welcome all, if only they do not appear before you empty.[13] I throw myself, like the philosopher, at the hearing feet of a tyrant.[14] My gift is in nothing but the lumps by which a god, like you, once burst in sunder.[15] So let them be given to a pair of your worshipers, whom I wish to purge with these pills from devotion to your vanity.[16]

Because you wear the features of human ignorance and curiosity on your face, I will confess to you the identity of the two on whom I intend to perform, through your hands, this pious fraud. The first[17] works on the philosopher's stone like a friend of mankind who views it as a means to promote industry, bourgeois virtues, and the welfare of the commonwealth. I wrote for him in the mystical language of a sophist, because wisdom will always be the most hidden secret of political economy, even if alchemy succeeds in its goal to make all men rich, who by means of the fertile maxims of the Marquis de Mirabeau[18] must soon (!) populate

---

[b] 2 Timothy 3:7 ["Ever learning, and never able to come to the knowledge of the truth"]

[10] 1 Kings 18:27: "either he is talking, or he is pursuing, or he is in a journey, or peradventure he sleepeth." More literally, Hamann (following Luther) writes, "you are musing, have work to do, are afield, or perhaps asleep."

[11] In 1 Kings 18, Elijah challenged the prophets of Baal to a contest. They and he each prepared a sacrifice, one to Baal and one to God, and each prayed for fire to consume the sacrifice.

[12] In Bel and the Dragon 1:3–22, Daniel exposes the fraud whereby the priests of Bel had convinced the king that Bel was a living god because he consumed so much food and wine every day.

[13] Exodus 23:15: "none shall appear before me empty."

[14] The philosopher Aristippus threw himself at the feet of the tyrant Dionysius. He defended himself by saying, "It is not I who am to blame, but Dionysius who has ears in his feet" (Diogenes Laertius, *Lives of Eminent Philosophers* 2.8.79, tr. Hicks, Loeb Classical Library).

[15] Bel and the Dragon 1:27: "Then Daniel took pitch, and fat, and hair, and did seethe them together, and made lumps thereof: this he put in the dragon's mouth, and so the dragon burst in sunder: and Daniel said, Lo, these are the gods ye worship."

[16] The phrase "devotion to vanity" appears in a cantata by Bach, BWV 204; the libretto was adapted from poems by Christian Friedrich Hunold.

[17] Johann Christoph Berens (1729–92), merchant in Riga, friend (and patron) of Hamann, and friend of Kant.

[18] Victor de Riqueti, marquis de Mirabeau (1715–89), physiocrat and disciple of Quesnay, author of *L'Ami des hommes, ou, traité de la population* (1756–8; "The friend of mankind, or, treatise on population").

France. According to today's plan of the world, the art of making gold remains, justly, the highest project and highest good of our statesmen.

The other[19] would like to be as universal a philosopher and as good a Warden of the Mint as Newton was.[20] No aspect of critical analysis is more certain than that which has been devised for gold and silver. Therefore, the confusion in Germany's coinage cannot be as large as the confusion which has stolen into the textbooks that are quite ordinarily found among us. We are lacking accurate conversion tables to determine how much of the prescribed intrinsic value[21] an idea must have if it is to pass as a truth, etc.[c]

Since these lumps must not be chewed, but swallowed, like those the Cosmic family in Florence adopted on their coat of arms,[22] they are not made for their taste. As far as their effects are concerned, it was because of a feeling similar to what they produce that Vespasian first learned to recognize the good fortune of your name and is said to have cried out on a stool that was not his throne: VTI PVTO, DEVS FIO![23]

---

[c]

> ὦ Ζεῦ, τί δὴ χρυσοῦ μὲν ὃς κίβδηλος ᾖ,
> τεκμήρι' ἀνθρώποισιν ὤπασας σαφῆ·
> ἀνδρῶν δ' ὅτῳ χρὴ τὸν κακὸν διειδέναι
> οὐδεὶς χαρακτὴρ ἐμπέφυκε σώματι·
> Euripides, *Medea*

[Euripides, *Medea* 516–19. "O Zeus, why, when you gave to men sure signs of gold that is counterfeit, is there no mark on the human body by which one could identify base men" (tr. Kovacs, Loeb Classical Library)].

[19] Immanuel Kant.

[20] Isaac Newton became Master of the Mint in 1699, retaining the office until his death in 1727.

[21] In German, "an Korn und Schrot." *Korn* is the amount of precious metal in a coin (that is, its intrinsic value), and *Schrot* is the gross weight of a coin. Hamann plays on the expression "von echtem Schrot und Korn," as in a man "of sterling qualities."

[22] The emblem of the Medici family (the political dynasty was founded by Cosimo) consisted of a number of red balls on a gold shield; these were variously interpreted, including as medicinal pills, an allusion to the family name, "doctors."

[23] "I think I'm becoming a god." Hamann's source is the Latin translation of Bacon's essay "On Death," which conflates Vespasian's words (from Suetonius, *Lives of the Caesars* 8.23) with the manner of his death (an attack of diarrhea, 8.24).

To the Two

The public in Greece read the memorabilia of Aristotle on the natural history of animals, and Alexander understood them.[25] Where an ordinary reader may see nothing but mold, the feeling of friendship will perhaps reveal to you, gentlemen, a microscopic forest in these pages.

I have written about Socrates in a Socratic way. Analogy[d] was the soul of his reasoning, and he gave it irony for a body. Let ignorance and confidence be as characteristic of me as they may; they must nonetheless be regarded here as aesthetic imitations.

In the works of Xenophon a superstitious devotion predominates, and in Plato's works, an enthusiast's devotion; a vein of similar feelings runs

---

[d] "Analogy, man's surest guide below," Edward Young, *Night Thoughts* 6. [Edward Young (1683–1765) wrote his most famous work, the long poem *The Complaint, or, Night-Thoughts on Life, Death, and Immortality* in 1742–6; Hamann quotes from l. 734 of Night 6.]

[24] Sophocles, *Electra* 450: "They are small things but nonetheless that which I have."

[25] In chap. 7 of book 1 of the *Advancement of Learning* (1605), Francis Bacon writes that when Alexander the Great read Aristotle's books on nature, he wrote a letter to the philosopher "wherein he expostulateth with him for publishing the secrets or mysteries of philosophy." Hamann's source was Bacon's *De augmentis scientiarum* (1623); see p. 157 of vol. II of Bacon's *Works* (1857–74), ed. Spedding, Ellis, and Heath. Bacon's source was Plutarch's life of Alexander (7.4).

therefore through all parts of this mimetic labor. The easiest thing here would have been for me to be more like the heathens in their frankness; I have had, however, to make the effort of lending my religion the veil which a patriotic St. John[26] and a platonic Shaftesbury[27] wove for their respective unbelief and misbelief.

Socrates, gentlemen, was no mean critic. In the works of Heraclitus he distinguished what he did not understand from what he did understand in them, and he made a very equitable and modest inference from the comprehensible to the incomprehensible.[28] On this occasion Socrates talked of readers who could swim.[e] A confluence of ideas and feelings in that living elegy of the philosopher perhaps turned his sentences into a group of small islands which lack the bridges and ferries of method necessary for their close association.

As you are both my friends, your biased praise and your biased blame will be equally welcome to me. I am, etc.

---

[e] "Atque hic tam docilis ad cetera, natare nesciit." Suetonius, *Caligula.* ["And yet as varied as were his accomplishments, the man could not swim." Suetonius, *Lives of the Caesars*, 4.54, tr. Rolfe, Loeb Classical Library].

[26] Henry St. John, Viscount Bolingbroke (1678–1751), politician and author, published (privately) *The Idea of a Patriot King* and *A Letter on the Spirit of Patriotism* in 1739. In *Letters on the Study and Use of History* (privately printed, 1738), Bolingbroke treated with skepticism the Jewish history of the Old Testament and in particular the chronology of Scripture.

[27] Anthony Ashley Cooper, third earl of Shaftesbury (1671–1713), wrote his most famous work, *Characteristicks of Men, Manners, Opinions, Times*, in 1711. Shaftesbury was skeptical of many aspects of traditional Christianity, and in particular he ridiculed religious enthusiasts; at the same time, he defended a Platonic notion of enthusiasm.

[28] Diogenes Laertius, *Lives of Eminent Philosophers* 2.22: "Euripides gave [Socrates] the treatise of Heraclitus and asked his opinion upon it, and that reply was, 'The part I understand is excellent, and so too is, I dare say, the part I do not understand; but it needs a Delian diver to get to the bottom of it'" (tr. Hicks, Loeb Classical Library). The story is also told in François Charpentier, *La Vie de Socrate* (1650); one of Hamann's chief sources for the *Socratic Memorabilia* was the German translation of Charpentier published in 1720.

Essay on an Academic Question[1]

by
Aristobulus[2]

Horatius
− − nos proelia virginum
sectis in iuvenes unguibus acrium
cantamus vacui, sive quid urimur,
non praeter solitum leves.[3]

---

[1] In 1759, the Berlin Academy set as the topic for its essay contest of that year the question of the mutual influence of language and opinions. Johann David Michaelis won the competition, and his essay was published in 1760.

[2] In the preface to *Crusades of a Philologist* (1762), Hamann identifies "Aristobulus" as the figure from 2 Maccabees 1:10, the "schoolmaster" of King Ptolemeus; see *Werke*, vol. II, p. 115.

[3] Horace, Ode 1.6.17–20: ". . . we sing the contests of maidens, who with sharp nails are fierce against the youths, either fancy-free or, if we are at all fired by love, cheerfully as usual."

FORTVNAMPRIAMICANTABOTNOBILEBELLVM
Scriptor cyclicus olim⁵

⁴ "Proverb."
⁵ Horace, *Ars poetica* 136–7: "[nor will you begin as] the writer of epic cycles in times past: 'I shall sing the fortune of Priam and noble war' [fortunam Priami cantabo [e]t nobile bellum]."

The title of this short essay is so problematic that I cannot think any of my readers capable of guessing what it means. I will therefore declare myself that I wish to put on paper some thoughts about the topic that had been issued by the Berlin Academy for the year 1759. This celebrated society thought it worthwhile to communicate to the world the prize essay together with six of its competitors under the following title: *Dissertation qui a remporté le prix proposé par l'Academie royale des sciences et belles lettres de Prusse, sur l'influence réciproque du langage sur les opinions, et des opinions sur le langage; avec les pieces qui ont concouru, à Berlin, MDCCLX, 4.*[6]

In my view it would be easier to survey the answer to the question of the mutual influence of opinions and language if this topic had been clarified prior to proceeding on to its solution.[a] However,

---

[a] περὶ παντός, ὦ παῖ, μία ἀρχὴ τοῖς μέλλουσι καλῶς βουλεύσεσθαι, εἰδέναι δεῖ περὶ οὗ ἂν ᾖ ἡ βουλή, ἢ ἅπαντος ἁμαρτάνειν ἀνάγκη. τοὺς δὲ πολλοὺς λέληθεν ὅτι οὐκ ἴσασι τὴν οὐσίαν ἑκάστου. ὡς οὖν εἰδότες οὐ διομολογοῦνται ἐν ἀρχῇ τῆς σκέψεως, προελθόντες δὲ τὸ εἰκὸς ἀποδιδόασιν· οὔτε γὰρ ἑαυτοῖς οὔτε ἀλλήλοις ὁμολογοῦσιν. ἐγὼ οὖν καὶ σὺ μὴ πάθωμεν ὃ ἄλλοις ἐπιτιμῶμεν . . . ὁμολογίᾳ θέμενοι ὅρον, εἰς τοῦτο ἀποβλέποντες καὶ ἀναφέροντες τὴν σκέψιν ποιώμεθα. Socrates in Plato's *Phaedrus*. ["There is only one way, dear boy, for those to begin to take counsel wisely about anything. One must know what the counsel is about, or it is sure to be utterly futile, but most people are ignorant of the fact that they do not know the nature of things. So, supposing that they do know it, they come to no agreement in the beginning of their enquiry, and as they go on they reach the natural result – they agree neither with themselves nor

[6] "Dissertation which won the prize set by the Royal Academy of Sciences and Literature of Prussia, on the reciprocal influence of language on opinions, and of opinions on language; with essays which also competed, in Berlin, 1760, quarto." Michaelis' essay was published in German in this collection; it was translated into French in 1762 and from French into English in 1769 (reprinted in 1771 and 1973).

scholars[b] do not consider such dry thoroughness to be necessary in order to understand each other, or perhaps they have themselves written most richly and cheaply on indeterminate propositions; therefore, common readers might be done a service to see this lack, if not made good, yet at least pointed out in the present pages.

The meaning of the word "opinions" is ambiguous, because they can be now regarded as truth and now opposed to it,[c] and what "language" refers to is very varied. That there exists a relationship and a connection between our soul's faculty of knowledge and our body's faculty of ostension is a rather familiar perception, but little has yet been attempted about the nature and limits of that relationship and connection. There must be similarities among all human languages based on the uniformity of our nature and similarities that are necessary within small spheres of society.

With the word "influence" a hypothesis is presupposed which appears to conform with neither the taste of a Leibnizian nor that of an Academist. The former would perhaps have said "harmony," and a doubter is far too cautious to infer the existence of some effect of things on each other merely on the basis of their relationship, since far too often a single language is

with each other. Now you and I must not fall into the error which we condemn in others . . . let us first agree on a definition of love, its nature and its power" (tr. Fowler, Loeb Classical Library). Plato, *Phaedrus* 237b–d.]

[b] ΔΟΞΟΣΟΦΟΙ γεγονότες ἀντὶ σοφῶν. Socrates in Plato's *Phaedrus*. ["They are not wise but only APPEAR WISE" (tr. Fowler, Loeb Classical Library). Plato, *Phaedrus* 275b. Hamann capitalizes the word that contains the Greek δόξα in the context in which it means "opinion," in order to attack Michaelis, whose treatise praised the Greeks for their glory, another meaning of the word (see pp. 10–12 of the English translation of Michaelis' essay). In addition, it emphasizes the uncertainty of the Academy's question which focused on "opinions."]

[c] ΔΟΞΑΣΤΙΚΗΝ . . . περὶ πάντων ἐπιστήμην ὁ σοφιστὴς ἡμῖν ἀλλ᾽ οὐκ ἀλήθειαν ἔχων ἀναπέφανται. The Stranger from Elis in Plato's *Sophist*.

Δύο γάρ, ἐπιστήμη τε καὶ ΔΟΞΑ, ὧν τὸ μὲν ἐπίστασθαι ποιεῖ, τὸ δὲ ἀγνοεῖν· ἡ μὲν οὖν ἐπιστήμη ποιέει τὸ ἐπίστασθαι, ἡ ΔΟΞΑ τὸ ἀγνοεῖν· τὰ δὲ ἱερὰ ἐόντα πρήγματα ἱειροῖσιν ἀνθρώποισι δείκνυται· βεβλήλοισι δὲ οὐ θέμις, πρὶν ἢ τελεσθῶσιν ὀργίοισιν ἐπιστήμης. With these words the Νόμος of Ἱπποκράτης concludes. [The first quotation is said by the Eleatic stranger in Plato, *Sophist* 233c, "The sophist has been shown to possess a sort of knowledge about everything BASED ON OPINION, and not true knowledge" (Hamann's capitals).

The second quotation comes from the short work *Law* ("Νόμος") attributed to the most famous doctor of antiquity, Hippocrates of Cos, who lived in the fifth century BC. He has not been confidently identified as the author of any of the writings attributed to him. "For there are two things, knowledge and opinion; the former makes people know well and the latter makes them ignorant. Knowledge then makes knowledge, and OPINION makes ignorance. But the things which are holy are revealed to holy men. It is not lawful for the profane to learn them until they are initiated in the mysteries of science."]

found for contradictory opinions and vice versa. Actually, I will be happy to tolerate this expression because I do indeed think that an author could have an effect on the majority of voices through a tacit influence on the opinions and language of a scholarly guild even though this investigation touches on casuistry and the algebra of luck. Now I will attempt no more than to parse the manifold sense which the losing academic topic can possess into some arbitrary propositions which are the easiest for me to survey and assess, somewhat as the Macedonian youth untied the Gordian knot and gained the fulfillment of the oracle.[7]

First of all: the natural mode of thinking has an influence on language. Universal history as well as the story of individual peoples, societies, sects, and men and women, a comparison of several languages and of a single language in different associations with time, place, and objects, yield here an ocean of observations which a learned philosopher could reduce to simple principles and general classes. If our conceptions are oriented around the point of view of the soul, and if this point of view in turn is determined, in the opinion of many people, by the condition of the body, then something similar may be applied to the body of an entire people. The lineaments of a people's language will therefore correspond with the orientation of its mode of thinking, which is revealed through the nature, form, laws, and customs of its speech as well as through its external culture and through a spectacle of public actions. The Ionian dialect has been compared with their traditional dress; and the legal punctiliousness which rendered the Jewish people so blind at the time of the divine visitation is obvious in their language. From this orientation of the mode of thinking arises the comparative wealth in some areas of the language and the poverty that runs parallel to it in other areas, there arise all phenomena deriving from such disparity, now reckoned perfection, now imperfection, as well as the willfulness perceived in idiotisms[8] and all that is understood in the term "genius of a language." This natural temperament must not be confounded either with grammar or with eloquence, no more than the resemblance of a painting is confounded with

---

[7] Alexander the Great, from Macedonia, "untied" the Gordian knot by cutting it and subsequently fulfilled the prophecy that whoever untied the knot would conquer Asia.

[8] "Idiotism" has a range of linguistic meanings, including the language peculiar to a group, the idiomatic character of a language, and a personal peculiarity of expression. "Willfulness" translates *Eigensinn*.

the regularity of the design or of the blend of colors or of the light and shadow, of any sort, but rather it is independent of both. Readers who are well informed at least about a good newspaper page or library will easily recall the names of two scholars who possess excellent ideas and merits, the elder in the grammar and study of the German language and the younger in the grammar and study of oriental languages.[9] However, as regards the genius of language they have adopted and wish to erect publicly many prejudices of philosophical myopia and philological touting as the guiding principles of their judgment. The honorary title of language-master and polyhistor[10] is not necessary for whoever will have the fortune of meeting with the genius of their profession. Here also Hesiod's self-praise about seafaring is true:

> δείξω δή τοι μέτρα πολυφλοίσβοιο θαλάσσης,
> οὔτέ τι ναυτιλίης σεσοφισμένος οὔτε τι νηῶν – – –
> ἀλλὰ καὶ ὡς ἐρέω Ζηνὸς νόον αἰγιόχοιο·
> Μοῦσαι γάρ μ' ἐδίδαξαν ἀθέσφατον ὕμνον ἀείδειν.[11]

Since our mode of thinking is based on sensory impressions and the sensations connected with them, the presumption is that the instruments of feeling agree with the coil springs of human speech. Nature makes a certain color or cut of the eye characteristic of a people, and just as easily it may impart to tongues and lips modifications unnoticed by us. Thomas Willis (*Cerebri anatome nervorumque descriptio et usus*, chap. xxii)[12] found in the branching of the fifth pair of nerves the reason why flirtatious glances and kisses serve as a universal dictionary for this eloquent passion.

---

9 The younger scholar is presumably Michaelis, as an expert in oriental languages; the older scholar is Johann Christoph Gottsched (1700–66), the literary critic who introduced French classicism into Germany. Hamann indicates Gottsched's identity by referring to a "library": Gottsched edited the *Neuer Büchersaal der schönen Wissenschaften und freyen Künste* ("New Library of Fine Sciences and Free Arts").

10 A language-master (*Sprachmeister*) gave instruction in languages; a polyhistor was a scholar with encyclopedic tendencies (see, for example, Anthony Grafton, "The World of the Polyhistors," in *Bring Out Your Dead: The Past as Revelation* (Cambridge, MA, 2001), pp. 166–80).

11 Hesiod, *Works and Days* 648–9 and 661–2: "I will show you the measures of the resounding sea, being altogether unskilled in seafaring and in ships . . . but even so I will tell the thought of aegis-bearing Zeus; for the Muses have taught me to sing unlimited song."

12 Thomas Willis (1621–75), English physician. In 1664, he published *Cerebri anatome: cui accessit nervorum descriptio et usus* ("The Anatomy of the Brain, to which has been added a description and use of the nerves"). See pp. 142–3 of the English translation by Samuel Pordage (1681, repr. in facsimile 1965).

Dealings with the deaf and the mute shed much light on the nature of the oldest languages. The mere breath of a sound is sufficient to make the artificial distinctions. The voices of animals seem to us more restricted for their social intercourse than they may actually be, because our senses are infinitely more blunt. With the ease of speaking[d] and the habit of listening, distraction grows on both sides as well as the need for new aids. Rhythm and accentuation represented the newer dialectic;[13] an ear that keeps good time and a throat rich in tones once transmitted hermeneutical and homiletic principles which were the equal of ours in thoroughness and convincingness. From here it is seen how the condition of attention and the objects of attention can expand and restrict the language of a people and give it this or that tincture.

Second: fashionable truths, prejudices of appearance and esteem, which circulate among a people more or less make up the artificial and accidental mode of its thinking and have a particular influence on its language. The appearance of mathematical method and the esteem of French and English writers have produced among us large and contradictory changes. It has been a real piece of luck for our language that the craving for translation and for logical demonstration have kept each other going; the latter would have become a rosary of enumerated neologisms, and the former would have been made into a net that captures and takes good and foul fish of every class. Whoever wants to carry out an investigation into the influence of opinions on the language of people must not overlook this twofold distinction. The first class of opinions constitutes the immovable mode of thinking of a people and the second the movable. The former can very reasonably be considered the most ancient, and the latter as the most recent. The story of the hat in Gellert's fable[14] may serve as a parable, or the medical doctrine of how our body is constantly transformed in a brief

---

[d] Samuel Werenfels, "Dissertatio de loquela" in *Opuscula theologica, philosophica et philologica*, pp. 760, 761. [Samuel Werenfels (1657–1740), Reformed theologian in Basel. Hamann refers to his "Dissertatio de loquela" ("Essay on speech"), which appeared in his *Opuscula theologica, philosophica et philologica* (1739, first published 1718; "Brief theological, philosophical, and philological works").]

[13] That is, mode of thinking.

[14] Christian Fürchtegott Gellert (1715–69) wrote a number of fables and stories in verse. "Die Geschichte von dem Hute" ("The story of the hat") appeared in the first book of *Fabeln und Erzählungen* (1746; "Fables and stories") and told the story of a hat that passes through several heirs.

cycle of years and yet remains the same, through the entire economy of natural life, from conception to decay.[e]

Is it the Abbot Pluche in his *Mécanique des langues*[15] or Herr Diderot in his pastoral letter on the deaf and dumb written for the useful instruction of those who already know how to ask and answer questions,[16] who blamed scholastic philosophy for having introduced a rigid hierarchy in French syntax? I leave this conjecture here for what it is worth; but what influence have opinions not had on grammars of defunct and living languages? Most of the methods to understand the former and propagate the latter are either the tangled paths of transformation according to the paternal way or those of this and that fashionable truth which a scholar (παραλογιζόμενος ἐν πιθανολογίᾳ)[f] knows how to make plausible to his audience.

Third: the domain of language stretches from the letters of the alphabet to the masterpieces of poetry and of the subtlest philosophy, of taste and criticism; and its character falls partly on word choice and partly on the

---

[e] ἡ θνητὴ φύσις ζητεῖ κατὰ τὸ δυνατὸν ἀεί τε εἶναι καὶ ἀθάνατος, δύναται δὲ ταύτῃ μόνον, τῇ γενέσει, ὅτι ἀεὶ καταλείπει ἕτερον νέον ἀντὶ τοῦ παλαιοῦ· ἐπεὶ καὶ[. . .]ἓν ἕκαστον τῶν ζῴων ζῆν καλεῖται[. . .]ἀλλὰ νέος ἀεὶ γιγνόμενος, τὰ δὲ ἀπολλύς, καὶ κατὰ τὰς τρίχας καὶ σάρκα καὶ ὀστᾶ καὶ αἷμα καὶ ξύμπαν τὸ σῶμα, καὶ μὴ ὅτι κατὰ τὸ σῶμα, ἀλλὰ καὶ κατὰ τὴν ψυχὴν· οἱ τρόποι, τὰ ἤθη, δόξαι, ἐπιθυμίαι, ἡδοναί, λῦπαι, φόβοι, τούτων ἕκαστα οὐδέποτε τὰ αὐτὰ πάρεστιν ἑκάστῳ· ἀλλὰ τὰ μὲν γίγνεται, τὰ δὲ ἀπόλλυται· πολὺ δὲ τούτων ἀτοπώτερον ἔστιν, ὅτι καὶ αἱ ἐπιστῆμαι μὴ ὅτι αἱ μὲν γίγνονται, αἱ δὲ ἀπόλλυνται ἡμῖν, καὶ οὐδέποτε οἱ αὐτοί ἐσμεν οὐδὲ κατὰ τὰς ἐπιστήμας, ἀλλὰ καὶ μία ἑκάστη τῶν ἐπιστημῶν ταὐτὸν πάσχει. Diotima in Plato's *Symposium*. [Plato, *Symposium* 207d–208a, "The mortal nature ever seeks, as best it can, to be important, but it can succeed in only one way, that is by generation, since it can always leave behind a new creature in place of the old. Since each living thing is called living, he is continually becoming a new person, and there are things also which he loses, as appears by his hair, his flesh, his bones, and his blood and body altogether, and not only in his body but in his soul: manners, habits, opinions, desires, pleasures, pains, or fears, none abide the same in his particular self; some things grow in him, while others perish. And here is something much stranger: with regard to the possessions of knowledge, not merely do some of them grow and others perish in us, so that neither in what we know are we ever the same persons, but a like fate attends each single sort of knowledge" (tr. Fowler, Loeb Classical Library, adapted).]

[f] Colossians 2:4. ["Beguiling with enticing words," adapted from Colossians 2:4: "lest any man should beguile you with enticing words."]

[15] Noël-Antoine Pluche (1688–1761), priest, professor of rhetoric, and natural historian, wrote as "l'Abbé Pluche" and published *La Mécanique des langues, et l'art de les enseigner* ("The mechanism of languages and the art of teaching them") in 1751.

[16] Denis Diderot (1713–1784), French philosopher, wrote the *Lettre sur les sourds et muets, à l'usage de ceux qui entendent et qui parlent* ("Letter on the deaf and mute for the use of those who hear and speak") in 1751. The first few pages of the essay are concerned with the inversion of normal word order in French. Diderot writes that "it is perhaps due to the peripatetic philosophy [i.e., the Aristotelianism of the scholastics] . . . that in our language we almost no longer have what we call inversions in the classical languages."

cultivation of expressions. Since the concept of that which is understood by "language" is of such diverse meaning, it would be best to determine it according to its purpose as the means to communicate our thoughts and to understand the thoughts of others. The relation of language to this double purpose would then be the main doctrine from which the phenomena of the reciprocal influence of opinions and language could be both explained and asserted in advance.

Since I know that the readers of the *Wöchentliche Frag- und Anzeichnungsnachrichten*[17] cannot care very deeply about the evolution of this concept, and since from the voices of your judgment I may not expect anything, either for my name or for my income, I am relieved of the effort to solve the Academy's question with this key itself. A philosopher who finds it more convenient to write a dozen treatises about a scholastic proposition than to read the half dozen already printed will be as content with the clue to the relationship (to which he is now referred) as that old philosopher was at the sight of a geometrical figure because he would no longer see an unknown land as an uncultivated desert.[18]

We are not lacking in observations by which the relation of language to its variable usage can be determined rather precisely. Insight into this relation and the art of applying it belongs to the spirit of the law[19] and the secrets of governing.[g] It is just this relation which makes classical writers. The trouble caused by confounding languages and the blind faith in certain signs and formulas are at times coups d'état which have more to

---

[g] πειρῶνταί τινες συνάγειν ὡς ὈΝΟΜΑΚΡΙΤΟΥ μὲν γενομένου πρώτου δεινοῦ περὶ νομοθεσίαν, γυμνασθῆναι δ᾽ αὐτὸν ἐν Κρήτῃ Λοκρὸν ὄντα καὶ ἐπιδημοῦντα, κατὰ τέχνην μαντικήν· τούτου δὲ γενέσθαι Θάλητα ἑταῖρον· Θάλητος δ᾽ ἀκροατὴν Λυκοῦργον καὶ Ζάλευκον· Ζαλεύκου δὲ Χαρώνδαν – Aristotle, *Politics* chapter 12 of Book 2. [Aristotle, *Politics* 1274a (chapter 12 refers to an older division of the book and is equivalent to chapter 9 in some more recent texts): "Some try also to establish connections, on the grounds that ONOMACRITUS was the first expert in lawmaking, a Locrian who trained in Crete, during a visit there in pursuit of his art of soothsaying; and that Thales was his comrade; and that Lycurgus and Zaleucus were pupils of Thales; and Charondas of Zaleucus" (tr. Saunders, adapted). Hamann capitalizes the name "Onomacritus," literally "judge of names." In the next sentence, Aristotle repudiates these putative connections. Onomacritus was a sixth-century priest of Attica who (according to Herodotus) forced oracles. Hamann connects the invention of language (Onomacritus as judge of names) and the invention of law (the legend of Onomacritus as the first lawgiver).]

[17] Hamann's essay was first published in the *Wöchentliche Königsbergische Frag- und Anzeigungsnachrichten* ("Weekly Königsberg Enquirer and Advertiser") in 1760.
[18] Perhaps a reference to Descartes, who in *A Discourse on Method* compares his geometrical method of philosophy with the methods used by surveyors to lay out regular plans for cities.
[19] Montesquieu's *De l'esprit des lois* ("The spirit of the laws") was published in 1748.

them in the kingdom of truth than the most powerful, freshly exhumed word-radical or the unending genealogy of a concept; coups d'état which would never enter the head of a scholarly blatherer[20] and an eloquent journeyman, not even in his most propitious dreams.

I want to conclude with a pair of examples in which language seems to have an influence on opinions and opinions on language. Whoever writes in a foreign language must like a lover accommodate his mode of thinking to it.[h] – – Whoever writes in his native language has the authority of a husband in his own house,[i] if he is in command of it. A head that thinks at its own expense will always trespass on language; but an author in the pay of a society approves the words that have been prescribed to him like a mercenary poet composing verses to set rhymes (bouts-rimés)[21] which lead him to the tracks of those thoughts and opinions which are the most suitable. For marketable writers of this sort, the community most often has the weakness of an appointed schoolmaster toward children who can rattle off the lesson even if they happened to understand no more of it than Herr Merian[22] understands of the new native language of the republic of letters. I read the succinct and charming extract made by this distinguished member of the prize-winning essay with all the more pleasure because through it I am able to take the opportunity to think back to the honor of being associated with him, and I avail myself of the occasion to acclaim with the most due respect the memory of his friendship.

---

[h] Every language demands a mode of thinking and a taste that are proper to it: that is the reason Ennius boasted with a three-fold heart, almost like Montaigne with his soul of three floors. Q. Ennius tria corda habere sese dicebat, quod loqui Graece & Osce & Latine sciret. Aulus Gellius, *Noctes Atticae*, Bk. xvii, chap. 17. [Aulus Gellius, *Attic Nights* 17.17: "Q[uintus] Ennius used to say that he had three hearts because he spoke Greek and Oscan and Latin." Hamann may be referring to Montaigne's tower library and what he called the arrière-boutique of his soul (in the essay "De la solitude"). Here as elsewhere, he spells "Montaigne" as "Montagne."]

[i] – – soloecismum liceat fecisse marito. Juvenal, *Satire* 6, line 456. ["let a husband be allowed to make a grammatical slip."]

[20] "Kannengießer," here translated as "blatherer," entered into German as a term for an "ignoramus who spews political advice" as a result of the German translation (1743) of Ludvig Holberg's comedy *Den Politiske Kandestøber* ("Der politische Kannengießer," "The political tinker").

[21] Bouts-rimés are "a List of Words that rhyme to one another, drawn up by another Hand, and given to a Poet, who was to make a Poem to the Rhymes in the same Order that they were placed upon the List" (*Oxford English Dictionary*, quoting Addison).

[22] Johann Bernhard Merian (1723–1807), Swiss member of the Berlin Academy, prepared the French summary of Michaelis' essay which appeared in the *Dissertation*.

Ἡ ἈΓΑΠΗ οὐδέποτε πίπτει· εἴτε δε ΠΡΟΦΗΤΕΙΑΙ, καταργηθήσον-
ται. εἴτε ΓΛΩΣΣΑΙ, παύσονται· εἴτε ΓΝΩΣΙΣ, καταργηθήσεται. ἘΚ
ΜΕΡΟΥΣ δὲ γινώσκομεν καὶ ἘΚ ΜΕΡΟΥΣ προφητείομεν — —[23]

---

[23] 1 Corinthians 13:8–9: "CHARITY never faileth: but whether there be PROPHECIES, they shall
fail; whether there be TONGUES, they shall cease; whether there be KNOWLEDGE, it shall vanish
away. For we know IN PART, and we prophesy IN PART" (Hamann's capitalization).

Miscellaneous Notes

on Word Order in the French Language

Thrown Together,
with Patriotic Freedom,
by a
Highly Learned German-Frenchman[1]

LECTORI MALEVOLO S.[2]

Adulescens! quoniam sermones habes non publici saporis, et quod
rarississimum est, amas bonam mentem, non fraudabo te arte secreta.

T. PETRONIUS ARBITER.[3]

---

[1] The title makes an allusion to Friedrich Carl von Moser's treatise of 1759, *Der Herr und der Diener geschildert mit patriotischer Freiheit* ("Master and servant, portrayed with patriotic freedom"; by "servant" is meant "civil servant" or "minister"). Moser (1723–98) was the first minister of the landgraviate of Hessen-Darmstadt, and his treatise on governmental administration adopted French ideas of the Enlightenment (see, e.g., p. 5: "In general it is an almost universal error of the small and middling German courts: They do not think and act systematically"). The title describes Moser as "Highly Learned"; the German word is *Hochwohlgelehrten*, similar to *Hochwohlgebornen*, a term of address used by the lower classes to a superior. In 1763, Moser will call Hamann "the Magus of the North."

[2] "Hello, malicious reader."

[3] *Satiricon* 3.1–2: "Young man, because your discourse is of unusual quality and, what is very rare, you love understanding, I will not disguise from you the secret of our art."

Num furis? an prudens ludis me obscura canendo?

Horace, Book II, Satire 5[4]

21

The investigation of money and language is as profound and abstract as their use is universal. They stand in a closer relationship[a] than one might suspect. The theory of one explains the theory of the other; they therefore appear to be derived from common ground. The wealth of all human knowledge rests on the exchange of words;[b] and it was a theologian of penetrating wit[5] who pronounced theology, – the oldest sister of the higher sciences, – to be a grammar of the language of Holy Writ. On the other hand, all the goods of civil or social life take money as their universal standard, which even Solomon,[c] according to some translations, is said to have recognized.

There is then no reason to be surprised that in the operations of state in ancient times eloquence carried just as much weight as finances in the discretion and fortune of our own time.[d] In the present century Julius

---

[a] See Leibniz, "Unvorgreiffliche Gedancken, betreffend die Ausübung und Verbesserung der Teutschen Sprache" in *Collectanea etymologica*. [Hamann cites Leibniz's essay of 1697, "Modest thoughts concerning the use and improvement of the German language" added to the end of the first part of the posthumous collection *Collectanea etymologica* (1717; "Etymological miscellany"). In §5 of Leibniz's essay (p. 257 of *Collectanea etymologica*) Leibniz draws a parallel between money and language.]

[b] "Speech, thought's canal! speech, thought's criterion too!" Young. [Edward Young, *The Complaint, or Night Thoughts* (1742–5), Night 2, line 469.]

[c] רהכסף יענה את הכל:, Ecclesiastes 10:19 – – ἓν δή τι δεῖ εἶναι, τοῦτο δ᾽ ἐξ ὑποθέσεως· διὸ νόμισμα καλεῖται· τοῦτο γὰρ πάντα ποιεῖ σύμμετρα· μετρεῖται γὰρ πάντα νομίσματι, Aristotle, *Nico-machean Ethics*, Book V, chapter 8. In the first book of the *Politics*, he takes money to be στοιχεῖον καὶ πέρας τῆς ἀλλαγῆς. [Ecclesiastes 10:19: "but money answereth all things."

Aristotle, *Nicomachean Ethics* 1133b: "There must therefore be some one standard, and this accepted by agreement, which is why it is called *nomisma*, customary currency; for such a standard makes all things commensurable, since all things can be measured by money (tr. Rackham, Loeb Classical Library, adapted). *Nomisma* is derived from the Greek *nomos*, "law" or "convention."

Aristotle, *Politics* 1257b: for money is "unit of trade and the limit of it."]

[d] ἀμοιβῇ γὰρ ἔοικε νομίσματος ἡ τοῦ λόγου χρεία – Plutarch, *De Pythiae oraculis metricis*. Plutarch again in the life of Phocion: ὡς ἡ τοῦ νομίσματος ἀξία πλείστην ἐν ὄγκῳ βραχυτάτῳ δύναμιν ἔχει, οὕτω λόγου δεινότης [ἐδόκει] πολλὰ σημαίνειν ἀπ᾽ ὀλίγων. [Plutarch, "The Oracles at Delphi No Longer Given in Verse," chap. 24 (*Moralia* 406b): "For the use of language is like the exchange of money." (Hamann gives a Latin title of Plutarch's essay, which may be translated as "On the metrical oracles of the Pythia.")

Plutarch, *Parallel Lives*, "Phocion," chap. 5: "As the value of money has greater power in smaller bulk, so the forceful words [seemed] to indicate a great deal from very little."]

[5] Martin Luther. In the preface (§14) to Johann Albrecht Bengel's *Gnomon Novi Testamenti* (1742; "Index of the New Testament"), Hamann found a quotation attributed to Luther: "nil aliud esse Theologiam, nisi Grammaticam in Spiritus Sancti verbis occupatam" ("that theology is nothing else but grammar engaged with the words of the Holy Spirit"). See *Briefe*, vol. II, p. 10 (February 19, 1760). I have not found the exact wording in Luther, but see the *Weimar Ausgabe* vol. XXXIX, part 1, p. 69 and vol. XXXIX, part 2, pp. 14–15 and 303–4.

Caesar[e] may well have found it as useful to be an extraordinary master of the mint as it was praiseworthy in his time to be a fine grammarian. His books *De analogia*[6] have gone missing and presumably were not as rich in content as the history of his heroic deeds, as every critical reader can easily believe.

We should not be any more startled at the fact that a Varro holds the title of most learned Roman[f] through his works on agriculture and etymology, seeing that an astronomical travel report on the Milky Way, the apologia for a metaphysical slogan, and the recommendation of new *concinnitates et ingeniosae ineptiae* (as Bacon expressed himself somewhere)[7] in physics and ethics often give wings, at least waxwings, to the name of our most recent writers.

The indifference of most businessmen, particularly successful ones, does a good deed for the community, which with clearer ideas in the absence of patriotic virtues would risk something far greater than the harm it may now suffer through the embezzlement of their fig leaves. Law,[8] the famous stockbroker, had studied money as a philosopher and a statesman; he knew trade better than the game of chance which he obliged by becoming an errant knight. His heart, however, was not the equal of his intellect; this broke the neck of his plans and made his memory hateful. I limit his rehabilitation to his surviving writings.

Also, the ignorance of scholars in the depths[g] of language lends a hand to abuses without end, but perhaps it will forestall yet greater abuses which

---

[e] See de la Pause in his French translation of Suetonius' *Lives*, pp. xxxiv–xxxv. [Suetonius' *Lives of the Caesars* was translated by "Henri Ophellot De La Pause" – the name is an anagram of "le philosophe de la nature" and the pseudonym of Delisle de Sales (1741–1816) – in 1770. On pp. xxxiv–xxxvi of his introduction to the work, the translator insists that the ancient Romans made rational grammar the basis of their knowledge and refers to Julius Caesar's treatise on analogy.]

[f] "Doctissimus togatorum," Cicero, *Quaestiones academicae*. ["Most learned of the Roman citizens." Hamann appears to combine two Ciceronian sources: a fragment from Book III of the *Academica* in which Varro is called "sine ulla dubitatione doctissimo" ("without doubt most learned") and a passage from *De oratore* (3.11) in which Q. Valerius Soranus is called "litteratissimum togatorum omnium" ("most learned of all Roman citizens").]

[g] L'établissement des langues n'a pas été fait par des raisonnements et des discussions académiques mais par l'assemblage bizarre en apparence d'une infinité de hazards [co]mpliqués; et cependant il y règne au fond une espèce de Métaphysique fort subtile, qui a tout conduit – Un des plus pénibles

[6] Julius Caesar's work on style and grammar in two books, *De analogia*, has not survived but is attested by Suetonius and other ancient sources.

[7] "Ingenious charms and clever absurdities"; the quotation has not been traced.

[8] John Law (1671–1729), Scottish adventurer who became a French citizen and then finance minister in France; he was forced into exile when his financial system collapsed.

would be the more harmful to the human race the less that the sciences fulfill their promise to improve the human spirit in the present day. This reproach shames the literary artists and the philologists the most, as they can be seen as the banquiers[9] of the republic of letters. *Pace Vestra liceat dixisse, primi omnium – –* Petronius.[10]

In the comparison drawn between Latin and French on the occasion of a disputed question, an investigation was also launched into the theory of inversions of word order.[11] It is known how much liberty exists in the Roman language to alter the order of words and that in schools it is customary to destroy this beauty of ancient writers by "construing" them, as it is called; by this methodical nonsense the ears of youth are deprived of practice in the melody that belongs to a Latin period, and also the emphasis of the sense is generally lost, which through the placement of the words should awaken and maintain in stages the attention of the reader or listener.[h]

---

soins – est de développer – cette Métaphysique, qui se cache et ne [peut être] apperçue que par des yeux assez perçans. L'esprit d'ordre, de clarté, de précision necessaire dans ces recherches délicates est celui qui sera la clef des plus hautes sciences, pourvu qu'on l'y applique de la manière qui leur convient. Fontenelle, vol. III, p. 382 etc. [Bernard Le Bovier de Fontenelle (1657–1757), French polymath. Hamann cites the *Œuvres de Fontenelle* (1742): "Languages were not established by academic reasonings and discussions but a combination, bizarre in appearance, of an infinite number of complicated accidents; nonetheless there reigns at bottom a very subtle metaphysics, which has led everything . . . One of the most tedious concerns . . . is that of developing . . . this metaphysics, which is hidden and perceived only by eyes that are sufficiently penetrating. The spirit of order, clarity, the necessary precision in delicate researches is what will be the key to the highest sciences, provided that it is applied in the appropriate manner." See pp. 512–13 of vol. V of *œuvres complètes* (1989–2001), ed. Niderst.]

[h] *Œuvres du comte Algarotti*, vol. VII, p. 304. [Count Francesco Algarotti (1712–64), writer of the Italian Enlightenment, a friend of Voltaire's and Frederick II's; on the page cited (from a letter of 1752) he understands inverted word order as a mark of linguistic barbarism.]

[9] French for "bankers."

[10] Petronius, *Satiricon* 2.2, "Pace vestra liceat dixisse, primi omnem eloquentiam perdidistis," "Permit me with your leave to say that you were the first to lose all eloquence." (Hamann's adaptation may be translated, "Permit me with your leave to say that the first of all . . .").

[11] In France, a wide-ranging and sometimes heated debate was conducted in the eighteenth century on the relative advantages of Latin and French word order. The debate had been started by Laboureur's *Avantages de la langue françoise sur la langue latine* (1669, "Advantages of French over Latin"), in which the author maintained that French word order reproduced the natural order of thought (Cicero, therefore, thought in French before speaking in Latin). Subsequently, Lamy and Condillac denied that thought had a natural order, while Diderot, d'Alembert, Du Bellay, and Beauzée favored the word order of French as closest to the order of thought. Diderot's *Lettre sur les sourds et muets* (1751, "Letter on the deaf and dumb") begins with a discussion of the origin and scope of hyperbaton (that is, the inversion of normal word order) before turning to a more general discussion of natural word order.

The German language is by its nature more capable than others of these inversions; and its boldness contributes to the high esteem of our poetical style. I will offer a simple example. With no loss of pureness or clarity we can say:

> Er hat mir das Buch gegeben.
> Mir hat er das Buch gegeben.
> Das Buch hat er mir gegeben.
> Gegeben hat er mir das Buch.[12]

The first sentence is the most direct, or perhaps emphasis can be placed on the man who gave. In the second, the main idea rests on the word *mir* ("me"); in the third, *Buch* ("book") is pointed to; in the last, the action of the verb. It is evident, then, that this inversion is not simply arbitrary or random, but rather is subject to the judgment of the intellect and the sense of hearing.

The reason why the syntax of some languages permits this alteration of word order to a greater or lesser degree depends largely on the nature of their grammatical etymology. The more characteristic the etymology,[13] the more inversions occur in the word order. The greater the diversity and sensuousness with which the etymology of grammar indicates changes in the movable parts of speech (namely nouns and verbs), the less rigidly bound its syntactic order can be. The etymology of French grammar, however, has features that are neither so numerous nor so recognizable, and therefore the use of inversions in its word order is forbidden of itself.

French is entirely lacking in case endings and consequently declensions.[i] To indicate the dependence of nouns, the French prepositions *de* and *à* are most often used, like the English *of* and *to*, which might be compared with + and − (the signs of the two main operations in arithmetic).

---

[i] Φρύγες σμικρόν τι παρακλίνοντες. Socrates in Plato's *Cratylus*. [Plato, *Cratylus* 410a: "The Phrygians altering it slightly." In context, "Well, this word πῦρ ['fire'] is probably foreign; for it is difficult to connect it with the Greek language, and besides, the Phrygians have the same word, only altering it slightly" (tr. Fowler, Loeb Classical Library, adapted).]

[12] The four sentences, all meaning "He gave me the book," are re-arranged so that different parts of the sentence come first and so receive an emphatic stress.

[13] "Characteristic" in the sense of the original "character" (ideogram, hieroglyph) of words.

A noun, if it is governed immediately (that is, without a preposition) by the verb, must therefore assume its position behind the verb if I am to be aware of its dependence:

> Le jeune Hébreu tua le géant.
> Le géant tua le jeune Hébreu.

"Mêmes articles: mêmes mots: & deux sens contradictoires,"[14] wrote the author from whom I salvaged this example.[j] German in contrast tolerates an alteration of word order without reversing the sense.

> Der hebräische Jüngling erlegte den Riesen.

or:

> Den Riesen erlegte der hebräische Jüngling.[15]

The endings of the German articles and nouns are sufficient to distinguish the field of the verbum, and the position of the words does not remove this distinction.

As the Latin form of declension has been insinuated into French grammar through a misapplication, so too the theory of articles fell into confusion through a superficial observation. For the sake of brevity,[k] I refer to the *Grammaire* of Restaut,[16] which I may not take pains either to summarize or to amplify.

Attempts have been made to attribute the origin of the article to the Saracens, with how much justification I do not know. Should

---

[j] *La Mécanique des langues, et l'art de les enseigner.* By Pluche, published in Paris in 1751; in the first book. [Noël-Antoine Pluche (1688–1761), priest, professor of rhetoric, and natural historian, wrote as "l'Abbé Pluche" and published *La Mécanique des langues, et l'art de les enseigner* ("The mechanism of languages and the art of teaching them") in 1751.]

[k] "– – qua nihil apud aures vacuas atque eruditas potest esse perfectius." Quintilian, Book x. [Quintilian at *Institutes* 10.1.32 refers to Sallust's brevity, "than which nothing can be more perfect for erudite and leisured ears."]

[14] "The young Hebrew killed the giant. The giant killed the young Hebrew. The same articles, the same words, and two contradictory senses."

[15] Both sentences mean "The Hebrew youth brought down the giant."

[16] Pierre Restaut (1696–1764) wrote *Principes généraux et raisonnés de la grammaire françoise* ("General and rational principles of French grammar") in 1730; it went through several editions in his lifetime.

chimes and the tinkling of rhymes not also have been introduced into poetry?[l] [m]

In a treatise by Bishop Pontoppidan about Danish,[17] I remember having read that this language has the peculiar characteristic of adding the article after the nouns.[n] A rather similar contrast is made by the *emphasis aramaea*[18] in the oriental languages.

[l] "Rhythmi cum alliteratione avidissimae sunt aures Arabum," Albert Schultens in *Florilegium sententiarum Arabicarum*, which was added to Thomas Erpenius' *Rudimenta linguae Arabicae*, p. 160. In the preface Schultens writes of this anthology: "Florilegium Sententiarum excerptum ex MS Codice Bibliothecae publicae, in quibus linguae arabicae Genius egregie relucet, nativumque illum cernere licet caracterem qui per rhythmos & alliterationes mera vibrat acumina. – – Elnawabig vel Ennawawig, inscribitur istud Florilegium venustissimum, quod vocabulum designat scaturientes partim poetas, partim versus vel rhythmos nobiliore quadam vena sese commendantes. – – Dignum est totum illud opusculum commentario Zamachsjarii, Philogorum arabum facile principis, illustratum, quod diem lucemque adspiciat." [Albert Schultens (1686–1750), Dutch Orientalist with expertise in Arabic and Hebrew philology, republished in 1733 Thomas Erpenius' Arabic grammar *Rudimenta linguae Arabicae* (1613; "The rudiments of the Arabic language"). He added to it a discussion of the linguistic relation between Hebrew and Arabic (*Clavis dialectorum*, "Key to the dialects") as well as a Latin translation from an anthology of Arabic proverbs, *Nawabigh al-kalim*, which had been assembled by Zamakhshari (1075–1144), a Persian-born Arabic philologist and theologian.

The Latin passages may be translated as follows:
"The ears of the Arabs are most eager for rhythm with alliteration."
"The anthology of proverbs has been excerpted from a manuscript codex of a public library; in it the genius of the Arabic language shines forth admirably and it is possible to discern the native character which brandishes its pure points through rhythm and alliteration . . . This very lovely anthology is entitled Elnawabig or Ennawawig; the name signifies in some cases gushing poets or in others verses or rhythms which recommend themselves by a certain rather noble vein . . . The whole short work, with a commentary by Zamakhshari (easily the greatest of Arab philologists) should see the light of day."]

[m] This notion is already accepted as historical truth by many scholars. Just recently I read in Giannone's history of Naples (Book 4, chap. 10) that the Sicilians are said to be the first to have adopted rhymes from the Arabs, and afterwards the rest of the Italians. Tommasso Campanella knew a Slavic song by heart in which it was stated that the Arabs brought rhyme to Spain. The editor. [Pietro Giannone (1676–1748) wrote *Istoria civile del Regno di Napoli* ("Civil history of the Kingdom of Naples") in 1723. Tommasso Campanella (1568–1639) was an Italian philosopher and utopian writer. In the English translation of Giannone (1729), the relevant passage is found on pp. 220–1: "And some have said, that it was the Arabians who first taught the Sicilians and afterwards the other Italians, as also the Spaniards; and Thomas Campanella, in order to confirm that, brings a Sclavonian song for a Testimony, wherein the same is affirm'd, and which he was wont to repeat by Heart."]

[n] 'Les Basques désignent le même sens par une particule enclitique qu'ils mettent à la fin des noms'. Beauzée in the *Grammaire générale*, vol. 1, p. 313. ["The Basques indicate the same meaning [as the French do by placing the article before the word] by an enclitic particle which they put at the end of nouns." Nicolas Beauzée (1717–89) published his *Grammaire générale* ("General grammar") in 1767.]

[17] Perhaps Erik Eriksen Pontoppidan (1616–78) in *Grammatica Danica* (1668); or the more famous Erik Pontoppidan (1698–1764) in one of his numerous works on the history, antiquities, and language of Denmark. Both were bishops.

[18] "Aramaic emphasis." Cf. possibly Matthew 26:73 and Mark 14:70, where Peter denies Christ although his accent inculpates him.

The correct use of articles is primarily logical[o] and serves to limit the meaning of a word or to give it a particular bearing.

However, the actual nature of the determination by the articles *le* and *la* and the varieties of this determination have not yet been explained with sufficient clarity.[p] The fault, in my opinion, lies mainly in the defective explanation of the correct concept of noun and adjective (*nomen substantivum* and *nomen adiectivum*), which would earn a high place among ontological problems. All *nomina propria* are simply adjectives,[q] and therefore they do not require articles; if articles are added, they become *nomina appellativa*,[19] in the same way that *adiectiva* become *substantiva* in French. On this basis are founded the main rules of the gender of words in Latin and other languages. This ambiguity in the

---

[o] Articulus numeralis (*a*, *an*) notat vocis generalis particulari cuiusdam (sive speciei, sive individuo saltem vago) applicationem – – Articulus demonstrativus (*the*) notat particularium unius pluriumve (quibus actu applicatur vox generalis) determinationem [. . .] Neuter horum articulorum praefigitur vel voci generali generaliter significanti (utpote cuius significatio particularibus actu non applicatur) vel nomini proprio (quod ex se satis innuit & individuum & quidem determinatum) vel etiam ubi aliud aliquod adiectivum adest, quod hos articulos virtualiter contineat (redundarent enim). John Wallis, Geometriae Professor Savilianus, *Grammatica linguae Anglicanae*, Oxford 1653, chap. 3. [John Wallis (1616–1703) was the Savilian professor of geometry at Oxford; published *Grammatica linguae Anglicanae* ("Grammar of the English language") in 1653, a work which went through many editions. Chapter 3 is concerned with articles; from it Hamann condenses several paragraphs on pages 71–2 (or pp. 79–80 of the fifth edition, the one most commonly reprinted now): "The numerical article (*a*, *an*) indicates the application of a general word to some particular word (either to a species or at least to an indefinite individual) . . . The demonstrative article (*the*) indicates the delimiting of one or more particulars (to which a general word is actually applied)[. . .]Neither of these articles is placed before a general word with a general meaning (as its meaning is not actually applied to particulars), or before a proper name (which sufficiently signals on its own that it is individual and delimited), or where some other adjective is present which virtually contains these articles (for they would be redundant)."]

[p] *Grammaire générale et raisonnée . . . Ouvrage de l'invention du Grand Arnaud, et de la composition de Dom Cl. Lancelot*, edition by J. J. Meynier at Erlang, 1746, p. 49. [Antoine Arnauld (1612–94) collaborated with Claude Lancelot (1616–95) to produce the *Grammaire générale et raisonnée* ("General and rational grammar") in 1660, more commonly known as the "Port-Royal grammar." See the English translation of 1753, pp. 49–50: "the use of the articles is to determine the signification of the common nouns; but it is a difficult matter to point out precisely, what this determination consists in, because the practice is not alike in all languages, that have articles."]

[q] Leibniz, as is well known, made an axiom out of this: "Omnia nomina propria aliquando fuisse appellativa." [On the first page of the *Brevis designatio meditationum de originibus gentium, ductis potissimum ex indicio linguarum* ("Brief outline of thoughts on the origins of peoples, deduced primarily from the evidence of language"), Leibniz writes that he "holds it for an axiom, that all nouns which we call proper had once been common nouns." The essay was printed in the *Miscellanea Berolinensia* (Berlin, 1710), 1–16.]

[19] "Nomen proprium" is a proper name; "nomen appellativum" is a common noun.

grammatical quality of nouns has not been removed by the *Réflexions philosophiques sur l'origine des langues et la signification des mots* of a Maupertuis[20] – –

> (Quis desiderio sit pudor aut modus
> Tam cari capitis – – ?)[21]

Readers who see not only what one is writing about but also what one intends to be understood[r] can easily and happily continue these notes without further guidance about the etymological signature of verbs, which in French strike the eye more than the ear. Suitable for children, into whose mouth you have to thrust ready morsels of porridge, are writers who are pedagogues more thorough than an annotator may be. Connoisseurs and admirers who themselves know how to make notes are not lacking in others' talent to use theirs and the adroitness to solve the ellipses of a treatise without a Lambert Bos.[s]

In general the serviceability of personal pronouns in French is a convenient symbol of verbs which rarely differ in their endings from nouns and modifiers, and the otherwise unavoidable misunderstanding of persons (as would be the case in German) is thereby totally averted.

In French the symbol of negation *ne* and the adverbial pronouns *y* and *en* are placed in front of the verbs; arguably they must have selected this position themselves for the sake of their own security, since their monad-bodies are of infinite importance to the meaning of a sentence. The ordering of all these tiny parts of speech (including some other pronouns)

---

[r] "In omnibus eius operibus intelligitur plus semper quam pingitur," Pliny says of Timanthes' brush, in *Natural History*, Book 35, chap. 36. [Pliny, *Natural History* 35.74: "In all his works more is always implied than is painted"; Hamann alters the quotation slightly.]

[s] A Dutch scholar, whose glossary on elliptical constructions in Greek is well known in schools. [Lambert Bos (1670–1707), professor of Greek at Franeker, first published the *Ellipses Graecae* in 1702 (translated as "Greek Ellipses" in 1830).]

[20] Pierre-Louis Moreau de Maupertuis (1698–1759), French mathematician and astronomer, member of the Berlin Academy (and president from 1745 to 1753), published his *Réflexions philosophiques sur l'origine des langues et la signification des mots* ("Philosophical reflections on the origin of language and the meaning of words") in 1747.

[21] Horace, Ode 1.24.1–2: "What shame or regret can there be for our desire for one so dear . . .," on the death of his friend Quintilius.

seems to be arranged in accordance with the fluidity of expression and some accidents of merging them.

> Ordinis haec virtus erit et Venus (aut ego fallor)
> ut iam nunc dicat, iam nunc debentia dici
> pleraque differat et praesens in tempus omittat;
> hoc amet, hoc spernat promissi carminis auctor.
>
> HORATIUS ad PISONES[22]

I now shake off the dust of the workshop from my pen, which, for a change, is to risk a sally into the more open field of observation and taste, now that I have reminded those who accuse French of monotony in its word order that a regular monotony in Latin is inevitable because of its audible endings and their more frequent meeting.

Rousseau, the philosopher of Geneva, tried in a letter on French music to deny to France, on the basis of the qualities of its language, all its claims to merit in music.[23] His game is won, whether the church music of our colonists[24] is taken as a model for comparison, or the enthusiastic voice of foreign eunuchs is made the umpire of harmony. However, the defects with which languages are burdened always stem from the incompetence of an author or a composer in the choice of material or the way of treating it.

> Suam quique culpam auctores ad negotia transferunt.[t]
>
> – – Cui lecta potenter erit res,
> nec facundia deseret hunc, nec lucidus ordo.[u]

To see that the French language is itself disposed toward epic poetry, look at some vaudevilles rather than the *Henriade*.[25] The inference from

---

[t] Sallust in *The Jugurthine War* 1. ["Those who are themselves at fault each blame their faults on circumstance." Modern texts have "quisque" for "quique."]

[u] Horace, *Epistle to the Pisones*. [Horace, *Art of Poetry* 40–1: "Neither eloquence will forsake him, nor lucid order, by whom a subject is selected effectively."]

[22] Horace, *Ars poetica* (also known as the "Epistle to the Pisones") 42–5: "This will be the strength and the charm of order (if I am not mistaken), that he say what needs to be said at the moment, that he postpone and omit much in the present time; let the author of the promised poem love this, spurn that."

[23] Jean-Jacques Rousseau wrote his polemic *Lettre sur la musique française* ("Letter on French music") in 1753.

[24] Huguenot immigrants to Prussia.

[25] A vaudeville is a popular song, often topical or satiric; Voltaire published his epic poem *La Henriade* in 1728.

a street ballad to the future reality of a heroic poem will not seem strange
to anyone since the discovery by a master hand of the origin of a more
important work, that is an epic in France derived from a trivial vaudeville.
"Les Bourbons," a credible historian of their house confesses,[v] "sont gens
fort appliqués aux batagelles − − peut être moi-même aussi bien que les
autres − −"[26]

The purity of a language dispossesses it of its wealth; a correctness that
is all too rigid takes away its strength and manhood. − − In a city as big

---

[v] See *Master and Servant, Depicted with Patriotic Freedom*, p. 147. To make good the title of my
Miscellaneous Notes, I avail myself of this chance quotation in order to vent my highly educated
patriotism on the portrayal of master and servant. − − This rhapsody is partly spun from French
silk, which is why they have been so conscientious to reimburse France at a usurious rate for
the use of the material. Another proof of German honesty, which is nonetheless injurious to the
growth of shrewdness. Since the lustrous skin has attracted much attention, a summary analysis
of the inner structure should be inserted here. "The author appears to be a stranger in the cabinet,
yet better known in lecture halls and the chancellery. − − The true art of government, too active
and cunning to linger over *pia desideria*, must also not be confused with commercial advantages
and ceremonial laws. − − His knowledge of books and the world is unreliable, *fundusque mendax*,
and what Horace said about relations with matrons may be applied to him:
> − − unde laboris
> Plus haurire mali est, quam [ex] re decerpere fructus.

A magazine of good taste cannot take the place of the documents of erudition. The unsteady eye
of the curious observer (without the fixed gaze of an examiner) becomes, particularly on trips and
above all at court, fatigues without satisfying, diverts more than instructs, becomes accustomed
to admiration but not to judgment, which must be more correct and precise in censure than in
praise. − − The matter is indigestible, which makes the style unhealthy, which tastes more of gall
and vinegar than of salt and spice." A pedagogue of small princes (who nonetheless have large
servants, it is said, and in fact would need them the most; see Part xi of the *Briefe der Neueste
Litteratur Betreffend*, the postscript to the 180th letter, p. 37) will know to accept this *licentia poetica*
of a scholiast with the same moderation that is advisable for advanced age and the fruits thereof, as
the preface prophesies. The heart of Herr von Moser is in any case too noble to prefer the kisses
of a washerman to the well-intentioned blows of an admirer. ["Pia desideria" ("pious desires") is
not uncommon as a title for works of devotional literature; the major work of the Pietist Phillipp
Jacob Spener (1635–1705) carried this title.

"Fundusque mendax," "the deceitful farm" (i.e., the farm that bears less than the expected
crop), is a phrase from Horace, Ode 3.1.30.

The quotation beginning "unde laboris" comes from Horace, Satire 1.2.78–9: "from which
more trouble is to be derived than fruits from success gathered." Horace is referring to the
amorous pursuit of matrons.

Briefe die neueste Literatur betreffend ("Letters concerning the most recent literature") was a
review edited by Lessing, Mendelssohn, Nicolai, and others. On the page indicated, Hamann's
footnote on Moser has been reproduced.

In the preface to *Master and Servant*, Moser justifies publishing his work at age thirty-five
rather than waiting till age fifty.]

[26] "The Bourbons are very diligent at bagatelles, myself perhaps as much as the others." The
quotation, as Hamann notes, appears on p. 147 of Friedrich Carl von Moser's *Der Herr und
der Diener geschildert mit patriotischer Freiheit* ("Master and servant, portrayed with patriotic
freedom"). Moser cites as his source *Mémoires de Mademoiselle de Montpensier*, vol. I. p. 179.

as Paris, forty learned men are procured each year, at no expense, who infallibly know what is pure and polite in their mother tongue and what is necessary for the monopoly of this junkshop.[27] – Once in centuries, however, it happens that a gift of Pallas,[28] – a human image, – falls from heaven, with full authority to manage the public treasury of a language with wisdom, – like a Sully; or to increase it with shrewdness, – like a Colbert.[29]

[27] The French Academy, founded in 1635, consists of forty members; Hamann alludes to its responsibility to prepare a dictionary which reflects the best usage of words.

[28] The "human image" of Sully and Colbert is contrasted with the image of Pallas Athena, the Palladium, which fell from heaven and protected Troy so long as the city preserved it.

[29] The Duke of Sully (1560–1641) was a minister to Henri IV, and Jean-Baptiste Colbert (1619–83) was the controller general of finance under Louis XIV.

Cloverleaf
of Hellenistic[1] Letters

Paul to the Romans 15:15
τολμηρότερον δὲ ἔγραψα[2] – –

---

[1] In the eighteenth century, "Hellenistic" had a specific reference to the language of the Greek New Testament, which many regarded as either a specific dialect or as a debased form of Greek, with impure mixtures from other languages.

[2] "Nevertheless . . . I have written the more boldly."

Lucretius, Lib. VI

Tv mihi supremae praescripta ad candida calcis
Currenti spatium praemonstra, callida musa,
Calliope, requies hominum divumque voluptas!3

---

3 Lucretius, *De rerum natura* 6.93–4: "Show me the course, Calliope, ingenious muse, as I hasten to the white line that marks the goal, Calliope, respite for men and delight for gods!"

First letter

-- 1759

Most noble Sir,[4]

For the kind communication of your manuscript, you have my bounden gratitude, most noble Sir. I was encouraged by it to read the *Observationes sacrae*[5] once again, since I believe myself capable of making greater use of it now than when I first skimmed it in Courland.[6]

A slight indisposition today prevents me from continuing in my Homer; and your polemical treatise led me to all sorts of ideas which I intend to capture with my pen, to keep the time until bed from being so long – – With good reason you emphasize to the reader the correctness of the word *Observationes* in the title of the book; however, I see no reason why such *observationes* are called *sacrae* and not *profanae, criticae*, etc., since they are no more than a picnic[7] contributed by profane writers;

---

[4] The German "H. H." (= "Hochedelgeborener Herr") is a more precise title than "Most noble Sir." For example, Goethe's father, as Imperial Councillor, was entitled to it, and it was also applied honorifically to professors (see the *Deutsches Rechtswörterbuch*). Hamann's addressee, if real, is not known with certainty; for a discussion, see Karlheinz Löhrer, ed., *Kleeblatt hellenistischer Briefe* (Frankfurt am Main, 2004), 17–23.

[5] Georg David Kypke (1723–79), *Observationes sacrae in Novi Foederis libros ex auctoribus potissimum graecis et antiquitatibus* ("Sacred Observations on the books of the New Testament mainly from Greek authors and antiquities," 2 vols., 1755). Kypke was the professor of Oriental languages at the University of Königsberg, translator of Locke's *Of the Conduct of Human Understanding*, and inspector of the Königsberg synagogue. *Observationes sacrae* rebutted the charge that the New Testament was badly written in a debased version of the Greek language, partly by finding parallels in classical Greek authors and partly by identifying and defending the Hebraisms in it.

[6] In 1756; see the letter from the end of February 1756 (*Briefe*, vol. I, p. 156).

[7] Picnics, in the eighteenth century, were fashionable gatherings to which each participant brought some of the provisions.

35

a question therefore from Haggai 2:12. If one bear holy flesh in the skirt of his garment, and with his skirt do touch bread, or pottage, or wine, or oil, or any meat, shall it be holy? And the priests answered and said, No![8]

The dispute over the language and style of the New Testament is not wholly unknown to me; so I doubt that a study of its language alone would suffice to resolve contradictions among opinions. One must know not only what good Greek is, as the reviewer says,[9] but also what language in general is; not only what is the elegance of a classical author but also what style in general is. On both topics, few philosophical insights are available. The lack of general principles, however, is mostly responsible for the scholastic quarrels. Here is really the place for a higher philosophy on the basis of which a very praiseworthy blot is imputed to the author of the *Observationes sacrae*. Since, however, it is not given to me to say much about it κατ' ἐξοχήν, I will therefore make my observations κατ' ἄνθρωπον.[10]

It is very easy for me to believe that the books of the new covenant were written Ἑβραϊστί, Ἑλληνιστί, Ῥωμαϊστί like the title of the cross (John 19:20).[11] If it is true that they were drafted in Jewish lands under the dominion of the Romans by people who were not *literati* of their *saeculum*,[12] then the character of their literary style is the most authentic proof for the author, place, and time of these books. In the reverse case, the critic would have infinitely more reason to be incredulous toward their reliability.

Since these books were not written for Greeks (1 Corinthians 1:22–3)[13] and scholars who are prejudiced for and against the purity of their

---

[8] Hamann gives Luther's translation. Luther's marginal note glosses, "The sacred does not sanctify the profane, but the profane pollutes the sacred."

[9] The review of Kypke's work in the *Göttingische Anzeigen von gelehrten Sachen* ("Göttingen notices on scholarly matters," vol. 1, pp. 690–3) of June 23, 1755 may be relevant; Johann David Michaelis (1717–91), theologian and Orientalist and favorite target of Hamann, became editor of the journal in 1753.

[10] κατ' ἐξοχήν, *par excellence*; κατ' ἄνθρωπον, like a man.

[11] John 19:19–20: "And Pilate wrote a title, and put it on the cross. And the writing was JESUS OF NAZARETH THE KING OF THE JEWS. This title then read many of the Jews: for the place where Jesus was crucified was nigh to the city: and it was written in Hebrew, and Greek, and Latin." The Greek words mean "in Hebrew, in Greek, in Latin."

[12] "Educated men of their century."

[13] "For the Jews require a sign, and the Greeks seek after wisdom: But we preach Christ crucified, unto the Jews a stumbling block, and unto the Greeks foolishness."

language, and no Greeks by birth but as the chiliarch Claudius Lysias in regard to their art-critical citizenship,[14] may confess in this language that they have won such citizenship with much head-splitting (ἐγὼ πολλοῦ κεφαλαίου τὴν πολιτείαν ταύτην ἐκτησάμην, Acts 22:28),[15] while Paul, in regard to them, could refer to his children's shoes worn out long ago;[16] since furthermore no language can be surveyed from books alone and the language of an author is as a dead language compared to the language of social life; these indications, therefore, are sufficient to show that more heat than light is at the root of all these investigations.

Matthew, the publican,[17] and Xenophon[18] – – Who seeks in a Joachim Lange[19] the style of a von Mosheim,[20] and yet there are chancellors who notwithstanding their dignity are permitted to write like pedagogues, and accept no exception to their style contrary to their rules.[21]

Every mode of thought that becomes a little fashionable, every imperceptible gradation of feeling colors the expression of our concepts. The Christian way (which in every age is called heresy)[22] accordingly also

---

[14] Hamann, echoing Luther's translation of Acts 22:28, writes "Bürgerrecht" ("citizenship"), whereas the King James version has "freedom."

[15] Claudius Lysias was the chief captain (chiliarch) in charge of the Roman troops in Jerusalem, who arrested and then protected Paul (see Acts 21–3). He has a Greek name (Lysias) and spoke with Paul in Greek; he was probably Greek by birth. He tells Paul at Acts 22:28, "With a great sum obtained I this freedom." The Greek word for "sum" is derived from the word "head," on which Hamann puns with his "head-splitting."

[16] Probably a reference to 1 Corinthians 13:11–12, where Paul writes that he spoke as a child when he was a child but put away childish things when he became a man. "Outworn children's shoes" is a literal translation of a common German idiom referring to what one has outgrown.

[17] Matthew 10:3.

[18] In his preface, Kypke refers several times to Xenophon in illustrating the language of the New Testament, as in his commentary on Matthew 8:3.

[19] Joachim Lange (1670–1744), professor of theology in Halle; a pietist and a pedagogical writer.

[20] Johann Lorenz von Mosheim (1694–1755), chancellor of Göttingen University, theologian, known for his eloquence in preaching.

[21] Michaelis is possibly intended here. He is a chancellor in a loose sense, as Secretary of the Royal Society of Sciences and editor of the *Göttingische Anzeigen*. He stands accused of contradicting his own rules because in praising Mosheim he admits to having imitated another writer. On the fifth page of the unpaginated preface to the bound 1755 volume of the *Anzeigen*, he wrote that the obituary of Mosheim in the issue of December 8 was composed with the help of another pen (that of the scholar Johannes Matthias Gesner) whose style he imitated. In his 1758 preface to Lowth's *De sacra poesi Hebraeorum*, Michaelis opposes imitation.

[22] Acts 24:14: "But this I confess unto thee, that after the way which they call heresy, so worship I the God of my fathers."

had to receive a new tongue²³ and a holy style to distinguish it. Go into whichever congregation of Christians you will; the language in the holy place²⁴ will betray their fatherland and genealogy, that they are heathen branches grafted παρὰ φύσιν onto a Jewish stem.²⁵ The more edifying the speaker, the heavier his Galilean shibboleth²⁶ falls on our ears. The more fire, the more of that Canarian²⁷ heresy, which the Ismaelites²⁸ (our Church's children of the flesh)²⁹ mock, (as it is written, χλευάζοντες ἔλεγον ὅτι γλεύκους μεμεστωμένοι εἰσί);³⁰ the more of that dew of youth, in the womb of which³¹ the Sun of righteousness arose unto us with healing in his wings³² – – In short, what is oriental in our pulpit style leads us back to the cradle of our race and our religion, so that we should not take exception to the aesthetic taste of some Christian spokesmen, *si aures* (to speak with a hispanic-fine Latinist[a] of our time) *perpetuis tautologiis, Orienti iucundis, Europae invisis laedant, prudentioribus stomachaturis, dormituris reliquis.*³³

---

[a] Michaelis. Seigneur de Balzac's *Socrate chrestien*, Discours VI ("De la langue de l'Eglise et du Latin de la Messe") et Discours VII ("Des quelques Paraphrases nouvelles"). [Johann David Michaelis (1717–91), theologian and Orientalist, is called a "hispanic-fine Latinist" perhaps in an allusion to the Spanish-born Roman teacher and writer on rhetoric Quintilian. Jean-Louis Guez de Balzac (1594–1654) published *Socrate chrétien* ("Christian Socrates") in 1652. In chapter 6 ("On the language of the Church and the Latin of the Mass"), he defends Church Latin, and in chapter 7 ("On some new paraphrases"), he attacks some excessively ornate paraphrases of the Psalms. Hamann read Balzac's work in 1763 (see *Briefe*, vol. II, p. 205).]

²³ Acts 2:4: "And they were all filled with the Holy Ghost, and began to speak with other tongues, as the Spirit gave them utterance."

²⁴ Acts 21:28: "and further brought Greeks also into the temple, and hath polluted this holy place."

²⁵ Romans 11:24: "For if thou wert cut out of the olive tree which is wild by nature, and wert graffed contrary to nature (παρὰ φύσιν) into a good olive tree."

²⁶ Cf. Matthew 26:73.

²⁷ The Canary Islands as the source of "sweet wine"; see n. 30 below.

²⁸ Descendants of Ishmael (Genesis 16:11–12, 21:9–13); sometimes used to refer to Arabs or to Muslims generally.

²⁹ Romans 9:8: "They which are the children of the flesh, these are not the children of God."

³⁰ Acts 2:13: "Others mocking said, These men are full of new wine." Luther and Hamann have "sweet wine."

³¹ Psalm 110:3: "Thy people shall be willing in the day of thy power, in the beauties of holiness from the womb of the morning: thou hast the dew of thy youth."

³² Malachi 4:2: "But unto you that fear my name shall the Sun of righteousness arise with healing in his wings."

³³ "If they should injure the ears with their unending tautologies, dear to the Orient, hated by Europe, irritating to experts, soporific to everyone else." Hamann adapts some of Michaelis' words from his preface to an edition of Robert Lowth's *De sacra poesi Hebraeorum* (Göttingen, 1758). The exact quotation is given in the second letter of the *Cloverleaf*, below.

It is part of the unity of the divine revelation that the Spirit of God, through the man's pen[34] belonging to the holy men whom it has led,[35] humbled itself and made itself of no majesty, just as the Son of God did through the form of a servant,[36] and as the whole creation is a work of the highest humility. Simply to admire in nature God only wise[37] is perhaps an offense similar to the affront which is shown to a decent, reasonable man whose worth the crowd estimates according to his cloak.

So if the divine style of writing chooses even what is silly – superficial – ignoble, to put to shame the strength and ingenuity of all profane writers, then there is certainly a need for the illuminated, inspired, jealous eyes of a friend, a confidant, a lover, to recognize in such a disguise the rays of heavenly splendor. *Dei dialectus, soloecismus*, says a well-known exegete.[38] – Here also it is true: *Vox populi, vox Dei*.[39] The emperor says *schismam*,[40] and the gods of the earth are little concerned to be masters of language. – What is sublime about Caesar's style is its carelessness.

We have this treasure of divine documents, to say with Paul, ἐν ὀστρακίνοις σκεύεσιν, ἵνα ἡ ὑπερβολὴ τῆς δυνάμεως ᾖ τοῦ Θεοῦ καὶ

---

34 Isaiah 8:1: "Take thee a great roll, and write in it with a man's pen."

35 Romans 8:14: "For as many as are led by the Spirit of God, they are the sons of God."

36 Philippians 2:7–8: "But made himself of no reputation, and took upon him the form of a servant, and was made in the likeness of men: And being found in fashion as a man, he humbled himself, and became obedient unto death, even the death of the cross."

37 Romans 16:27: "To God only wise, be glory through Jesus Christ."

38 "The dialect of God is ungrammatical," said by John Lightfoot (1602–75), English biblical scholar, who was quoted by Johann Albrecht Bengel, Hamann's source, in his commentary on the New Testament, *Gnomon Novi Testamenti* (1742). In the section on Revelation 11:15, the opinion of the Church Father Dionysius of Alexandria that the book was written in bad Greek is rebutted with the quotation by Lightfoot: "Johannes enim θεοδίδακτος passim in sua Apocalypsi veteris Testamenti stylum assumebat: hic autem, qui Hebraeae linguae erat ignarus, id omne, quod DEI DIALECTUS erat, SOLOECISMO imputabat, et quod intelligere nequibat, barbarum esse credebat" (an edition of Bengel from 1850 is quoted here). "For John, being taught of God, adopted the style of the Old Testament throughout Revelation: but this man [i.e., Dionysius of Alexandria] who was ignorant of Hebrew accounted all that was the DIALECT OF GOD for a SOLECISM, and believed that what he was unable to understand was a barbarism." Lightfoot's words appear (without the capitalized words and phrases) in his brief essay on the authorship of Revelation included in the *Opera posthuma*, p. 149, which is included in the *Opera omnia* of 1699 with the same pagination.

39 "The voice of the people is the voice of God."

40 Refers to an anecdote which exists in several variant forms (including one told by Luther). The version from Julius Wilhelm Zincgref, *Teutsche Apophthegmata* (1644) seems to fit the context: At the Council of Constance, Emperor Sigismund made a solecism in saying that "We do not want a schism"; he declined the word "schism" incorrectly, saying "schismam" rather than "schisma." When his error was pointed out, he answered that as emperor he was higher than grammarians.

μὴ ἐξ ἡμῶν[b] [41] and the *stylus curiae*[42] of the kingdom of heaven remains, to be sure, especially in comparison with Asianic[43] courts, the meekest and lowliest.[44] The outward appearance of letters is more like the colt whereon man never sat,[45] the foal of an ass,[46] than like those proud stallions which broke the neck of Phaethon; – *nec nomina novit equorum.*[47]

The style of newspapers and letters, according to all rhetoricians, belongs to the *genus humile dicendi,*[48] and little that is analogous has survived in the Greek language. Nevertheless, this is the taste by which to judge the style of the New Testament books, and in this respect they are in a way original.

Acts and Revelation are historical writings in the proper sense. Of the style in which future incidents must be stated we have nothing isoperimetrical[49] but perhaps fragments of Delphic and Sibylline oracles.

Since words and usages are signs, their history and philosophy is very similar and mutually dependent. The question: whether the heathen judaize in their religious practices, or whether the Jews consecrated to

---

[b] Socrates, in Plato's *Ion*, expresses himself similarly about the foolishness of poets: – – ὁ θεὸς ἐξαιρούμενος τούτων τὸν νοῦν τούτοις χρῆται ὑπηρέταις καὶ τοῖς χρησμῳδοῖς καὶ τοῖς μάντεσι τοῖς θείοις, ἵνα ἡμεῖς οἱ ἀκούοντες εἰδῶμεν ὅτι οὐχ οὗτοί εἰσιν οἱ ταῦτα λέγοντες οὕτω πολλοῦ ἄξια, οἷς νοῦς μὴ πάρεστιν, ἀλλ' ὁ θεὸς αὐτός ἐστιν ὁ λέγων, διὰ τούτων δὲ φθέγγεται πρὸς ἡμᾶς – – [Plato's *Ion* 534c–d: "And for this reason God takes away the mind of these men and uses them as his ministers, just as he does soothsayers and godly seers, in order that we who hear them may know that it is not they who utter these words of great price, when they are out of their wits, but that it is God himself who speaks and addresses us through them" (tr. W. R. Lamb, Loeb Classical Library).]

[41] 2 Corinthians 4:7: "in earthen vessels, that the excellency of the power may be of God, and not of us."

[42] "the pen/style/dagger of the court."

[43] *Oxford English Dictionary*: "pertaining to or characterized by the florid and inflated literary style characteristic of the Asiatic Greeks in the three centuries preceding the Christian era." Cicero, too, was criticized for an Asianic style.

[44] Matthew 11:29: "for I am meek and lowly in heart."

[45] Mark 11:2 and Luke 19:30.   [46] Matthew 21:5.

[47] In Book II of the *Metamorphoses*, Ovid tells the story of Phaethon, the son of Helios, the sun-god. Phaethon drove his father's chariot of the sun with disastrous results. Hamann quotes the line "nor does he know the names of the horses" (2.192), indicating Phaethon's helplessness with the chariot.

[48] "The genre of speaking humbly." In the classical theory of rhetoric, the lowest of the three styles, and the one most often seen as suited to Christian writers.

[49] "Having a perimeter of the same length"; Joseph-Louis Lagrange had recently formulated a method of dealing with isoperimetrical problems, a major advance in mathematics (he established the calculus of variations).

their God the theft of superstitious customs?[50] This question is to be ana-
lyzed according to similar principles with the racial registers of the idioms
which languages have in common amongst themselves. Photius[c] extends
the warfare of Paul (to bring into captivity everything to the obedience of
Christ)[51] unto the heathen flowers of speech and catch-phrases.

French in our time is as widespread as Greek was formerly. How
could it be supposed otherwise possible but that it has to degenerate
in London and Berlin just as much as Greek in Jewish lands, especially
in Galilee, would have been spoken with a broken accent? The purpose,
place, time of an author all qualify his expression. Court, school, the
business of everyday life, closed guilds, gangs, and sects have their own
dictionaries.

The migrations of the living languages give us light enough on the
qualities which dead languages share with them and on the variable schema
of all languages in general. For a while I have found the word "salamalec"[52]
in the more recent works of wit, as in France, but until I unexpectedly

[c] – – ὁ πολλὰ πολλάκις σοφῶς αἰχμαλωτίσας Παῦλος εἰς τὴν ὑπακοὴν τοῦ Χριστοῦ, οὐδὲν δὲ
ἧττον καὶ τῶν ἔξω φωνῶν οὐχ ὅση κομψὴ καὶ γλῶττα καὶ εὔηχος, ἀλλ᾽ ὅση γνησία σημᾶ-
ναι καὶ παραστῆσαι τὸ προκείμενον. Photius in his answers to Amphilochius, which Johann
Christoph Wolf appends to the last part of his *Curae philologicae et criticae* on the New Testament,
p. 743. [Photius, the ninth-century Patriarch of Constantinople, is a major figure in the history of
the Christian church and in classical scholarship. The passage comes from his theological work
Amphilochia, Question 133 (it also appears as Epistle 256, addressed to Photius' brother Tarasios;
see the Teubner edition of Photius' *Epistulae et Amphilochia*, vol. II, pp. 197–8). The question
is headed "What does the Apostle call offscouring?" (for "offscouring" see 1 Corinthians 4:13).
The Greek means, "Paul, who many times speared many things wisely for obedience to Christ,
did so no less with whatever in the outer language was not boastfulness and speech and sonorous
but was authentic so as to signify and present the subject." Hamann's source for the quotation
was the New Testament commentary by Johann Christoph Wolf (1683–1739), *Curae philologicae
et criticae*, vol. IV (1735; "Philological and critical concerns"), p. 743.]

50 The indebtedness of Judaism to Egyptian religious practices was much discussed in the eighteenth
century; see Jan Assmann, *Moses the Egyptian* (Cambridge, MA, 1997), 91–143. For the Christian
indebtedness to heathen practices, see Georg Christoph Hamberger, *Rituum quos Romana ecclesia
a maioribus suis gentilibus in sua sacra transtulit enarratio* (1751; "Account of the rituals which the
Roman church transferred into their sacred rites from their pagan ancestors"). Hamann returns
to the question subsequently in the *Hierophantische Briefe* (1775; "Hierophantic letters") directed
against Johann August Starck, *De tralatitiis ex gentilismo in religionem Christianam* (1774; "On
transfers from paganism into the Christian religion").
51 2 Corinthians 10:3–5: "we do not war after the flesh: (For the weapons of our warfare are not
carnal but mighty through God to the pulling down of strong holds;) Casting down imaginations,
and every high thing that exalteth itself against the knowledge of God, and bringing into captivity
every thought to the obedience of Christ."
52 "Salamalec" is the French form of the Eastern salutation.

came across it in the travel writings of the Chevalier d'Arvieux[53] I did not understand that "salamalec" means an oriental bow or throwing oneself at another's feet – –

I am now reading Prince Dimitrie Cantemir's history of the Ottoman Empire[54] for a change, and I found yesterday some news of Misri Effendi, Sheik of Prusa, in the reigns of Ahmed II and Mustapha II. My fresh memory and pleasure at these passages moves me to conclude with this extraordinary man, who is said to have been a brilliant poet and a clandestine Christian. The mufti did not dare to pass judgment on his verses and is said to have declared, "The interpretation and meaning of them is known to none but God and Misri" – – The mufti also ordered his poetry to be collected in a volume, in order to examine it. He read it, committed it to the flames, and passed this fatwa: "Whoever speaks and believes as Misri Effendi, ought to be burnt, except Misri Effendi alone: for no fatwa can be passed upon those that are possessed of Enthusiasm."[d]

How do you, most noble sir, like the mufti? Does he not put many popes and critics to shame? – – Whatever you wish with this frightful scrawl, only no fatwa on

Your,

etc. etc.

[d] "Ce n'est pas la peine d'être inspiré pour être commun," says another mufti in his *Remarques sur les Pensées de Pascal*. [The other mufti is Voltaire, "It's not worth the trouble of being inspired to be commonplace." The sentence comes from No. VIII of the "Additions aux Remarques sur les Pensées de M. Pascal" (see the *Lettres philosophiques*, ed. Gustave Lanson, 1937, vol. II, p. 242).]

[53] Laurent d'Arvieux, *Mémoires du chevalier d'Arvieux*, ed. Jean Baptiste Labat, 6 vols. (1735), vol. I, p. 85.

[54] Dimitrie Cantemir (1673–1723), Voivode of Moldavia, member of the Berlin Academy, wrote a history of the Ottoman empire in Latin. The manuscript was first published in an English translation by N. Tindal, *The History of the Growth and Decay of the Othman Empire* (1734–5); a French translation was made from the English in 1743, and a German one in 1745. See the English edition, pp. 387–8, for the passage which Hamann quotes. Ahmed II was the sultan of the Ottoman Empire from 1691 to 1695 and Mustafa II from 1695 to 1703.

Second letter

March 1, 1760

Most noble Sir,

I am not sorry to have followed the hint of Quintilian concerning Euripides.[55] The edition is altogether good for me; it helps me read less haltingly and facilitates my mental translation.[56] Since I am enquiring only into the spirit of the ancients, and since I care more about the genius than the grammar of the Greek language, the schoolmaster's face with which Gesner and Ernesti[57] spoil translations[e] for their audience does not concern me. I shall be very satisfied if I understand my Greek roughly in the way

---

[e] Batteux describes these as a kind of "Dictionnaire continu, toujours ouvert (devant ceux, qui entendent le texte en partie; mais qui ont besoin de quelque secours par l'entendre mieux) et présentant le mot dont on a besoin." The mistakes of most translations are firmly printed by most dictionaries. Or as Pope whispers to the philologist:

> Nor suffers Horace more in wrong Translations
> By Wits, than Cricticks in as wrong Quotations.
> *Essay on Criticism.*

[Charles Batteux (1713–80), abbé, teacher of rhetoric and professor of Greek and Latin at the Collège de France. The quotation is adapted from several sentences on pp. viii–ix of the preface to his translation of Horace (first published in 1750). Batteux calls translations "a kind of running dictionary, always open (for those who understand the text in part but need some assistance to understand it better) and giving the word one needs." The quotation from the poet Alexander Pope (1688–1744) comes from *An Essay on Criticism*, ll. 663–4.]

55 Quintilian, *Institutio oratoria* 10.1.67, finds that, although it is disputed whether Sophocles or Euripides is the greater poet, Euripides at any rate is much more useful for those who are pleading in court.

56 On Hamann's intensive reading in Greek from 1759 to 1763, see Löhrer, *Kleeblatt*, p. 15. The "edition" of Euripides may be a Greek–Latin one.

57 Johann Matthias Gesner (1691–1761), of Göttingen University, and Johann August Ernesti (1707–81), of Leipzig University, were classical philologists.

the bearer of this letter understands his mother tongue – – as food for the body and its needs – – more through the *influxus physicus* of those who look after me than through the *harmonia praestabilita*[58] of learned Aristarchuses.[59]

As you, most noble sir, are the greatest promoter of my Greek *studium*, and as I set my hopes on yet more assistance for my small *otia*[60] from your favorable disposition, so today I shall make a pastime for myself out of duty and give you an accounting of my labors. I communicate to you something from a draft, with which I can be reminded and corrected by no one better. My time is short – and my strengths are suited more for leisure than for business. Since in any case I must handle my predilections as Alexander handled his untamed Bucephalus,[61] I cannot study carelessly and hastily enough a language as obsolete as Greek has become, in part, even among scholars. I must make use of all advantages which playfully and at the same time profitably create my day's work – – nothing but to cut the diagonals – – to act from opposed or composed *principia* and make the shortest line into the track of my goal.

You know, most noble Sir, that I have made a start with Homer, Pindar, and the poets of Greece. Concerning the others still remaining, I do not intend to set myself definite boundaries, but to leave their precise determination to time and opportunity.

Whereupon I think I will pass on to the philosophers,[62] from among whom I will expose to my attention not more than three: Hippocrates, Aristotle, and Plato. Their writings represent for us the circle of the sciences, where hypotheses – systems – and observations are the first and last thing. In my opinion Plato and Aristotle deserve to be read in comparison as paradigms of eclectic and encyclical philosophy.[63] Here is

---

[58] The *influxus physicus* (physical influx) and the *harmonia praestabilita* (pre-established harmony) were competing theories of causation. The theories were especially prominent in debates about the mind–body problem to which Descartes gave a new urgency. Leibniz is the most famous adherent of the latter theory. Hamann associates the discredited theory of direct physical contact between body and soul with learning languages naturally, and the new theory of pre-established harmony with the abstract study of language.

[59] Aristarchus, an important Hellenistic philologist, produced critical editions of major Greek writers, most prominently of Homer.

[60] "Otium" means leisure; in the plural "otia" may signify the products of one's leisure.

[61] Alexander's favorite horse, which he tamed as a boy when his father's attendants were unable to do so; the story is told in Plutarch's life of Alexander, chapter 6.

[62] Including natural philosophers (for example, the medical writings of Hippocrates).

[63] Plato is called eclectic because of his perceived dependence on Egyptian and Pythagorean sources (as the next paragraph specifies). Aristotle is called encyclical because of his encyclopedic range

Scylla and Charybdis, and one must fare past them as happily as Ulysses was taught. – – Leibniz, it is said, was not systematic and Wolff[64] not eclectic enough. Examining for oneself, however, only too often reverses the judgments of appearance – – Aristotle is an exemplary draftsman, Plato a colorist.

> Neighbor to the sun, a mercurial Leibniz thinks
> Seven thoughts at once – – –

is written in the dream of the sickbed.[65] Wolff's *Opera* overflows from pure exergasias[66] and tautologies, flows over and over, more than our litanies, *auresque perpetuis repetitionibus, Orienti iucundis, Europae invisis laedunt, prudentioribus stomachaturis, dormituris reliquis,*[67] as the learned editor of Lowth remarks,[68] every bit as profoundly as astutely, in the preface to the first part of the lectures on the sacred poetry of the Hebrews. – – Aristotle and Plato also deserve, each for himself, to be studied, since I expect to find in the writing of the former the ruins of Greek wisdom, and in Plato's on the other hand the loot of Egyptian and Pythagorean wisdom,[69] and more therefore in both sources than in Laertius and Plutarch.[70]

After the philosophers, it is the turn of the historians. Sagacity and the *vis divinandi* [71] are almost as necessary for reading the past as for the future. Just as in school the New Testament is begun with the Gospel of John, so the historians are regarded as the easiest writers. But can the past be understood when not even the present is understood? – – And who will form correct ideas of the present without knowing the future?

("encyclical" means "encyclopedic" in the pedagogical sense of a complete general education), or perhaps because of his importance to Catholic theology.

[64] Christian Wolff (1679–1754), chancellor of the University of Halle, extended the philosophical rationalism of Leibniz and wrote voluminously on a wide range of scholarly topics.

[65] A citation from Johann Heinrich Öst, *Der Traum: Des Siechbetts Zweiter Gesang* (1752, "The Dream: Canto II of The Sickbed"), a sequel to his poem *Das Siechbett* (1750, "The Sickbed"). The opening of the second canto begins with a vision of the universe. Leibniz is mercurial through being associated with the planet Mercury of the vision, nearest neighbor to the sun.

[66] A rhetorical term for repeating one point with much amplification and variety of sentences.

[67] "And they injure the ears with their unending repetitions, dear to the Orient, hated by Europe, irritating to experts, soporific to everyone else"; see n. 33 above.

[68] Michaelis; see n. 33 above.

[69] Plato's dialogues *Timaeus* and *Critias*, in particular, have been associated with esoteric traditions of Egyptian wisdom. Pythagoras, a philosopher from the sixth century BC, had some influence on Plato's views of mathematics, the soul, and other topics.

[70] Diogenes Laertius, probably of the first half of the third century AD, wrote lives of the philosophers. Plutarch (died c. 120 AD) discussed many philosophical topics in his moral essays.

[71] "Divinatory faculty."

The future determines the present, and the present determines the past, as the purpose determines the nature and use of the means – – we are nevertheless already accustomed here to a ὕστερον πρότερον[72] in our way of thinking: through our actions we reverse all moments, like images in the eye, without even noticing anything of it. – – In order to understand the present, poetry helps us in a synthetic, and philosophy in an analytic, way. Apropos of history, I am struck by a learned man who reads every day a page of the *Etymologicum magnum*[73] and retains three or four words from it, in order to be the best historian in his neighborhood; yet the less one has learned oneself, the more apt one is to teach others. – –

I would rather view anatomy as a key to γνῶθι σεαυτόν[74] than seek the art of living and ruling in our historic skeletons, as they tried to tell me in my youth. The field of history seemed to me like that open valley that was full of bones – – and, lo, they were very dry.[75] No one but a prophet can prophesy of these bones that sinews and flesh will be brought up upon them and skin will cover them. – – Nor is any breath in them – – until the prophet prophesies unto the wind and says the word of the Lord to the wind[76] – – – – Are you not, most noble Sir, of the opinion that I may rejoice at the steps which I will be able to make in the Greek historians, and that the poets and philosophers will serve as the transport? – –

The man to whom history (by virtue of its name)[77] yields science, and philosophy knowledge, and poetry taste not only becomes eloquent himself but almost the equal of the ancient orators. They used occasions

---

[72] In Aristotle, the logical fallacy of establishing "the antecedent [*proteron*] by means of its consequents [*hysteron*]; for demonstration proceeds from what is more certain and is prior" (*Prior Analytics* 2.16).

[73] A large etymological dictionary of Greek words, compiled mainly in the twelfth and thirteenth centuries, and based on earlier works. Nadler believes that the "learned man" is Hamann himself, some of whose word-lists have survived, and that the dictionary referred to was Johann Georg Wachter's *Glossarium Germanicum* (1737).

[74] "Know thyself."

[75] Ezekiel 37:1–2: "The hand of the Lord . . . set me down in the midst of the valley which was full of bones, And caused me to pass by them round about: and, behold, there were very many in the open valley; and, lo, they were very dry." The pun is more exact in German, which has "Feld" ("field") rather than valley.

[76] Ezekiel 37:4–9: "Again he said unto me, Prophesy upon these bones, and say unto them, O ye dry bones, hear the word of the Lord. Thus saith the Lord God unto these bones; Behold, I will cause breath to enter into you, and ye shall live: And I will lay sinews upon you, and will bring up flesh upon you, and cover you with skin, and put breath in you, and ye shall live . . . And when I beheld, lo, the sinews and the flesh came up upon them, and the skin covered them above: but there was no breath in them. Then said he unto me, Prophesy unto the wind, prophesy, son of man, and say to the wind, Thus saith the Lord God."

[77] "History" is derived from a word meaning "learning by inquiry."

as the basis and made a chain of keys which became decisions and passions in their audience.[78]

From orators were made talkers; from historical experts, polyhistors;[79] from philosophers, sophists; from poets, wits. For me it is here that the high school of Greece would begin, in all four faculties; my study might then become nothing but unfettered enthusiasm – from clever Athenaeus to Longinus' cock-crow περὶ ὕψους[80] – –

You see, most noble Sir, my long course! – Perhaps you will shout to me from a minor poet,[f] whose Angler-language you have read,

> Go, with elastic arm impell the bowl
> Erring victorious to its envy'd goal!

Yet this entire plan is like the colorful Iris,[g][81] a child of sun and mist, from one to the other end of the horizon under which I write – a delight for my eyes, to possess which I will not need my feet – perhaps of the same duration as the kikayon, that son of a night, whose shadow did Jonah so much good[82] – – –

---

[f] *The Anglers: Eight Dialogues in Verse.*
Rura mihi et rigui placeant in vallibus amnes
Flumina amem silvasque inglorius – –
London, 1758. The author is said to be a clergyman, Mr. Scott.

[Thomas Scott (1705–75), was a poet and independent minister. On the title page of his poem *The Anglers* (1758) appeared two lines from Virgil's *Georgics* (2. 485–6): "May fields and flowing streams in valleys please me, and may I, inglorious, love rivers and fields."]

[g] Hail, many-coloured messenger, that ne'er
Dost disobey the wife of Jupiter!
Who with thy saffron wings upon my flowers
Diffusest honey-drops, refreshing showers:
And with each end of thy blue bow do'st crown
My bosky acres, and my unshrubb'd down,
Rich scarf to my proud earth – –
Ceres in Shakespeare's *Tempest*
[Act IV, Scene 1].

[78] Classical rhetoric was concerned with fitting a speech to its occasion; it also prescribed distinct parts of a speech in a distinct order, for maximum effectiveness in persuading the audience.

[79] Erudite and encyclopedic compilers of scholarly subjects, characteristic especially of the seventeenth century.

[80] Athenaeus, fl. c. 200 AD, wrote the *Deipnosophistai*, which quotes many hundreds of Greek authors; "Longinus" is the traditional author of *On the Sublime* (περὶ ὕψους).

[81] Iris is the rainbow, or the Greek messenger-goddess of the rainbow.

[82] A "kikayon" is the Hebrew word translated as "gourd" in Jonah 4 in the King James Bible. In that chapter, God prepared a gourd for Jonah, "that it might be a shadow over his head, to deliver him from his grief" (v. 6). But the next day God prepared a worm to smite the gourd, and it withered.

One large question would make my diligence go astray, a question that matters to me as much as the dogma of the best world matters to a jack-of-all-trades (M.A.),[83] or natural or international law matters to a Maltese *neutrius generis*.[84] – This question has a close connection with the principle of all fine arts.[85] Without understanding it, the replies Yes! and No! are proved most easily. That is, some maintain that antiquity makes fools wise, while others may confirm the contrary, that nature makes people more clever than the ancients can. Which of them should be read and which imitated? Where is an explanation of the two that opens our understanding? Perhaps the ancients have the same relation to nature as the scholiasts to their author? Whoever studies the ancients without knowing nature is reading the notes without the text; and whoever reads over a small fragment in the large quarto edition of Petronius makes himself at least a Doctor, perhaps without knowing a hair better what kind of creature an *arbiter elegantiarum*[86] was at the house of a Roman Caesar. – For him who has no skin over his eyes, Homer has no cover. For him who has not yet seen the bright day, neither Didymus nor Eustathius[87] will work that miracle. We either lack the principles to read the ancients, or we succeed with them as our old countryman taught the congregation to sing: "The spirit does not wish to leave the flesh, demanded most of all by the law (of imitation)."[88] – – Rage dispels all my thoughts, most noble Sir, when I bring to mind how a gift of God as noble as the sciences is laid waste, torn apart – by the free spirits in

---

[83] Leibniz. "Tausendkünstler," literally "thousand-artist," has been rendered as "jack-of-all-trades." In German, there are puns on "thousand." First, in the preface to his poem *Der Traum: Des Siechbetts Zweiter Gesang* (see n. 65 above), Öst writes of Leibniz that "One head never thinks the thoughts of a thousand heads" (p. 5). Second, Leibniz's Master's Degree, the "M. A.," may be read as with the "M." for *mille* ("thousand") rather than *magister* ("master"). In treating the problem of evil, Leibniz argued that this world was the best of all possible worlds.

[84] Christian Wolff, who wrote treatises on natural law (*Jus naturae*, 1740) and international law (*Jus gentium*, 1749). He is called a Maltese "of the neuter gender" perhaps because like the Knights of Malta he is neither entirely clerical nor entirely secular.

[85] Namely, mimesis, imitation.

[86] "An authority on etiquette"; Tacitus called Petronius the *elegantiae arbiter* at the court of Nero.

[87] Didymus, Alexandrian scholar of the first century BC, provided commentaries and textual information much used by the scholiasts; Eustathius, Byzantine scholar of the twelfth century AD, compiled commentaries drawing on old scholia and other works. Both are known especially for their work on Homer.

[88] From a Lutheran hymn by Paul Speratus ("Es ist das Heil uns kommen her," "Salvation unto us has come"). Hamann adds the parenthesis "(of imitation)" to his source, to specify which law is meant.

coffee bars, trampled[h] by lazy monks in academic fairs,[89] – and how it is possible that young people can fall in love with the old fairy, erudition, with no teeth and no hair, or with false ones. διάπειρά τοι βροτῶν ἔλεγχος.[90]

I thus return to my Euripides, from whom I expect many benefits; more pleasure, however, from Sophocles, whose *Ajax*[91] I know from afar. Because the character of Ulysses in that play is outlined in accordance with the design of Father Homer, and because he also plays his role in the *Hecuba* of Euripides, a comparison of how this main figure of mythology was treated by both poets provides me with a fair light on their mode of thought. Euripides seems to have condescended to the taste of the parterre and, in the formation of his characters and their manners, to have flattered the reigning prejudice of the great crowd; so too his emotions lapse too often into declamation. Presumably all these merits form the basis of Quintilian's favorable opinion, who recommends him especially to those in public occupations and who have dealings with the people.[92] As a professor of eloquence,[93] he had even more reasons to praise the reading of this poet. On the other hand, Ajax alone teaches me that Sophocles has understood the nature of men, poetry, and the dramatic art philosophically.

As Cervantes with his *Don Quixote* sought to spoil the romance for Spaniards, so it is thought that Homer in his *Odyssey* sought to open up for his compatriots a new route to fame and to oppose cleverness to merit in bodily advantage. This purpose seems known to Sophocles at least and to have been held before his eyes. The character which he gives Ulysses is venerable, holy, secret; hence he is hated by the Greek rabble, and it is strange that with Euripides a clever man may be slandered as a deceiver and fanatic. – – However, I fear from my dithyrambic letter what vafer Flaccus[94] says:

---

[h] Matthew 7:6. ["Give not that which is holy unto the dogs, neither cast ye your pearls before swine, lest they trample them under their feet, and turn again and rend you."]

[89] In German, "Messe" may refer either to Mass or to book-fairs ("Buchmessen"); the pun is lost in English.

[90] Pindar, *Olympian* 4.18, "Trial is the proof of men."

[91] See *Briefe*, vol. II, p. 5 (January 2, 1760). [92] Quintilian, *Institutio oratoria* 10.1.67; see n. 55.

[93] Quintilian was the first rhetorician to receive a state salary.

[94] "Sly Flaccus," that is, Horace; so called by Persius, *Satires* 1.116.

– – – occiditque legendo.[95]

From a surfeit of print, I avenge myself on white paper, without considering whether the reader of this has as much free time to waste as the below undersigned. I commend myself, most noble Sir, to your kind forbearance as etc. etc.

[95] "And kills by reading," Horace, *Ars poetica* 475.

Third letter

February 25, 1760

Most noble Sir,

To you, most noble sir, I return the *Opinion on the Means Used to Understand the Defunct Hebrew Language* with the liveliest gratitude.[96] This small octavo volume is perhaps thicker than Schulten's quartos on the Hebrew language could be.[97]

I once took the liberty with you of dropping an opinion concerning the writings of Herr Michaelis. At present his strengths and weaknesses shine forth excellently. As he mentions from time to time the *déshabillé* of his reading hours, the author knows how to give himself an advantageous *air* in this condition;[98] the episodes too of his future authorship are very apt to maintain his audience's devotion and faith.[99]

---

[96] Johann David Michaelis, *Beurtheilung der Mittel, welche man anwendet, die ausgestorbene hebräische Sprache zu verstehen* (Göttingen, 1757).

[97] Hamann used the second edition of Albert Schultens' *Origines Hebraeae, sive Hebraeae linguae antiquissima natura et indoles, ex Arabiae penetralibus* (1761; "Hebrew Origins, or the Ancient Nature and Genius of the Hebrew Language, from the Depths of Arabia"), to which was added a short work, *De defectibus hodiernis linguae Hebraeae* ("On the Defects of the Hebrew Language Today"), and also *Vindiciae originum Hebraeorum et opusculi de defectibus hodiernis linguae Hebraeae* ("Defense of Hebrew Origins and of the Short Work on the Defects of the Hebrew Language Today"). The volume is in the format of a quarto.

[98] In the *Beurtheilung*, Michaelis refers several times to his classes in which he gives oral instruction in the Hebrew Bible, and Hamann represents him as doing so informally (deshabillé).

[99] That is, faithful and patient devotion to Michaelis. See, for example, pp. 120–1 of the *Beurtheilung*, "Here is not the place to clarify my remark with examples . . . I ask that whoever would like more of this be patient until I can give my critical class on Habakkuk in print, as a trial of this kind of work."

Germany has few writers who have accomplished so much and who are in the position to accomplish even more, whose works one accepts thankfully, and whose promises and their fulfillment one must await with longing – as with Herr Michaelis. His extensive and intensive insights are something rare; the gift of conveying them goes along with this. Gracefulness and thoroughness! – which I would call popular and plausible in order to distinguish them from the philosophical, because they conform more to the canon of fashion[100] or the great world of readers who render decisions[101] than to the true inner nature of the subject matter – –

For all the merits of this author I find a πρῶτον ψεῦδος[102] in the earliest and the most recent writings of his that I have yet received to read, and which suddenly struck me in his opinion concerning improper uses in learning the Hebrew language[103] more forcefully than ever. It is so closely connected with his whole way of thinking that it is as impossible for me to point it out with my finger as it would be for one to be able to say to the portion of Jezreel: that is Jezebel![i] – – The Platonic[j] idea of my neighbor

---

[i] 2 Kings 9:37, Revelation 2:20–3. [2 Kings 9:37: "And the carcase of Jezebel shall be as dung upon the face of the field in the portion of Jezreel; so that they shall not say, This is Jezebel." The verses from Revelation describe the false prophetess Jezebel.]

[j] Ἦ που τὸν τῆς ὑφαντικῆς γε λόγον αὐτῆς ταύτης ἕνεκα θηρεύειν οὐδεὶς ἂν ἐθελήσειε νοῦν ἔχων, ἀλλ᾽ οἶμαι, τοὺς πλείστους λέληθεν, ὅτι τοῖς μὲν τῶν ὄντων ῥᾳδίως καταμαθεῖν αἰσθηταί τινες ὁμοιότητες πεφύκασιν, ἃς οὐδὲν χαλεπὸν δηλοῦν, ὅταν αὐτῶν τις βουληθῇ τῷ λόγον αἰτοῦντι περί του μὴ μετὰ πραγμάτων ἀλλὰ χωρὶς λόγου ῥᾳδίως ἐνδείξασθαι. τοῖς δ᾽ αὖ μεγίστοις οὖσι καὶ τιμιωτάτοις οὐκ ἔστιν εἴδωλον οὐδὲν πρὸς τοὺς ἀνθρώπους εἰργασμένον ἐναργῶς, οὗ δειχθέντος τὴν τοῦ πυνθανομένου ψυχὴν ὁ βουλόμενος ἀποπληρῶσαι, πρὸς τῶν αἰσθήσεών τινα προσαρμόττων ἱκανῶς πληρώσει· διὸ δεῖ μελετᾶν λόγον ἑκάστου δυνατὸν εἶναι δοῦναι καὶ δέξασθαι· τὰ γὰρ ἀσώματα, κάλλιστα ὄντα καὶ μέγιστα, λόγῳ μόνον ἄλλῳ δὲ οὐδενὶ σαφῶς δείκνυται· τούτων δὲ ἕνεκα πάντ᾽ ἐστὶ τὰ νῦν λεγόμενα· ῥᾷων δ᾽ ἐν τοῖς ἐλάττοσιν ἡ μελέτη παντὸς πέρι μᾶλλον ἢ περὶ τὰ μείζω. The stranger from Elis in Plato's *Statesman*. [Plato, *Statesman* 285d–286b: "Still less would any rational man seek to analyze the

[100] Michaelis refers to the "fashionable meanings," sometimes false, that have become attached to Hebrew words (*Beurtheilung*, p. 322).

[101] Ibid., p. 365 (the last sentence of the book): "I believe I am certain that this is the correct way; whether I am correct in so thinking or not, after having given my reasons every reader is the judge."

[102] The "first falsehood," that is, the initial false premise invalidating the later deductions; the term derives from Aristotle's *Prior Analytics* 2.18 (66a).

[103] Much of Michaelis' *Beurtheilung* is concerned with the improper ways of understanding Hebrew (especially regarding the improper use of etymology and dialects). Here Hamann may be referring to Michaelis' opposition to using the Bible as the main text from which to learn Hebrew (p. 353).

(who, as you know, disdains no reheated cabbage[104]) does not seem to me to be incorrect, that the most powerful truths as well as the most powerful lies agree with the monads.[105]

A reader who hates the truth may find much in the *Opinion on the Means Used to Understand the Defunct Hebrew Language* to comfort him, and which could serve him as a whetstone to sharpen the weapons of unrighteousness.[106] A reader who seeks after truth might become a hypochondriac out of dread. Who loves and has the truth can read the author with the greatest application and judgment.

It has been very pleasant for me to discover that the proposal for my summer's work agrees with the direction of so great a master.[107] God give me life to carry it out; so may I perhaps in time be able to succeed at a fundamental understanding of the things themselves.

Regardless of the fact that I understand neither Hebrew nor Arabic, the reprimands of the author are not all just Greek to me, and I trust that you, most noble sir, will have as much patience as that old general, listening to a sophist prattle on about warfare.[108]

Since I have applied my prodigal hours to nothing more than a quick examination of this book, I can give no proof *in forma*[109] that the Arabic

---

notion of weaving for its own sake. But people seem to forget that some things have sensible images, which may be easily shown, when any one desires to exhibit any one of them or explain them to an inquirer, without any trouble or argument; while the greatest and noblest truths have no outward image of themselves visible to man, which he who wishes to satisfy the longing soul of the inquirer can adapt to the eye of sense, and therefore we ought to practise ourselves in the idea of them; for immaterial things, which are the highest and greatest, are shown only in thought and idea, and in no other way, and all that we are saying is said for the sake of them; moreover, there is always less difficulty in fixing the mind on small matters than on great" (tr. Jowett).]

[104] A Greek and Latin proverb, "twice-served cabbage is death," came to mean in later use a poor bit of writing that was repeated ad nauseam. Elsewhere Hamann glosses this passage with the explanation "A philologist must not despise meals" (*Werke*, vol. 11, p. 239).

[105] Hamann connects abstract grammatical analysis with Leibniz's doctrine of pre-established harmony between monads. Michaelis' approach to the Bible cannot distinguish truth from falsehood.

[106] The allusion to 2 Corinthians 6:7 is more exact in German, which has "the weapons [*Waffen*] of righteousness," not as in the English Bible, "the armour of righteousness."

[107] Michaelis (*Beurtheilung*, pp. 215–17) recommends studying Arabic in preparation for learning Hebrew.

[108] The anecdote of the general Hannibal and the sophist Phormio is told by Cicero in *De oratore* 2.75–6.

[109] *In forma* seems to be used as a synonym for *par excellence* or κατ' ἐξοχήν (see n. 10 above), though it may mean no more than a formal proof.

concordance with all the provisos[110] is a means quite as unreliable and misleading as those methods which have deteriorated into improper uses and whose weakness the author has uncovered with such thoroughness that one need only collect his own remarks and direct them appropriately in order to challenge him. – – Thus a teacher always behaves with greatest safety when he does not make his students too wise, and, if need be, a concise program of man's obligation to speak the truth can be elaborated;[111] the exercise of this duty however is not a philological gift.

The art of taking up a fortified position does the greatest honor to the author of this work. Yet what help is the most forbidding fortress if one suffers hunger there and right away makes a pilgrimage in spirit to Rome to assemble manuscripts[112] and right away must stoop to the bare pens with which masterpieces[113] are written, to rail at subscriptions. All of Christianity – but no academy, least of all Kirjath-sepher[114] – can interpret a scholar's inclination towards Arabic as a heresy; but one must not accept the customs of a people whose language one loves, nor cover up small coups d'état with the gold plate of language, nor dupe young people and Maecenases[115] into believing that one can fence as soon as one knows how to parry and thrust and hold the epée and body.

The scraps as the author digresses about the origin of the languages and his division of words into poetic and arbitrary do not strike me as much more definite than the ideas of the hieroglyphic system.[116] The intermediate idea between anointing and measuring, covering and making,[117]

---

[110] Michaelis, who includes many provisos in the arguments of the *Beurtheilung*, insists on the value of Arabic in order to understand Hebrew.

[111] In a footnote on p. 362, Michaelis refers to his "program of the obligation of men to speak the truth."

[112] Michaelis, on p. 238 of the *Beurtheilung*, contrasts the paucity of Syrian literature in Germany with their easy availability in Rome.

[113] Michaelis, p. 184 of the *Beurtheilung*, refers to the desirability of memorizing the masterpieces of a language, as is the custom of Arabs.

[114] Joshua 15:15 and Judges 1:11; literally, "city of books," and Hamann presumably has the Berlin Academy in mind.

[115] Patrons.

[116] In sections 19–21 of the *Beurtheilung*, Michaelis digresses about the origin of language. He opposes a hieroglyphic account (whereby the image of a letter is immediately connected with its meaning), but in order to make his case he first distinguishes between the "natural" and the "arbitrary" meanings of words.

[117] Hamann refers to various attempts in Michaelis' *Beurtheilung* to interpret a Hebrew word by a word in another language with a different meaning. See p. 286, where Michaelis writes "How the same word can mean both measure and anoint at the same time is not to be pursued further here," or p. 165, where "cover" and "make" are traced in different dialects (see also p. 3).

etc., etc., is almost as fanciful as when Gousset hits on something out of context.[118]

A more exact investigation and explanation of dialect would have been all the more necessary as this is the entelechy of the whole text. The art critic however appears as little able to imagine an oriental dialect[k] [119]

---

[k] From the following lines of ore from Schulten's *Origines* the whole thread binding the quires may be inferred: Dialectus est unius linguae variatio externa et accidentalis, quae ad internam eius substantiam non pertingit, sed fundamentum integrum illibatumque conservat – Hae variationes externae, quae in veram Dialectum cadunt, versantur.

   I. circa elementa literarum, sonos ac pronunciandi modos
1. Fons huius variationis temperies aeris, in quo vivitur. Si crassior asperiorque, asperi rudiores adsciscentur soni; sin subtilior delicatiorque, in delicatam quandam mollitiem vel tenuitatem sponte devenietur.
2. ipsorum hominum temperamentum, sese in partem vel politiorem vel impolitiorem exerens.
3. linguae lubrica mobilitas quam proclivissime delabens in literarum vicinarum praesertim, aut unius organi commutationem absque ulla intentione.
4. intentio, cura, industria, qua hoc ipsum iam captatur et tanquam vel dignius vel venustius vel commodius adoptatur.
5. Accentus, quem Regem appellare possum universae pronunciationis, à cuius nutu sic omnia pendent, ut si vel tantillum in eo figendo variaverit consuetudo publica alicuius gentis, diversae et peregrinae mox appareant Linguae, quae iisdem natalibus, iisdem cretae radicibus, germana consanguinitate iunguntur.

  II. circa significationes verborum
1. Gravissimum divortium, quum in propria ac primaria notione alicuius verbi non conspiratur.
2. vocabulum aliquod in una Dialecto frequentatum, in altera plane non occurrens; sive prior aliquid novaverit, sive posterior id emori siverit.
3. differitatem satis grandem formant secundariae et metaphoricae notiones, quae ex primaria aliqua enasci solent. Saepe enim fit, ut in secundariis istis usibus pugna quaedam ac discordia oriatur inter Dialectos sororias. Tristia et aegritudo apud Atticos, quod apud Iones laetitia exultans. (The Low German word *grynen* or *greinen** also has opposite meanings in different provinces and imitates those men of whom a common proverb says that they have laughter and weeping in one bag which after the art of analysis must be sought in the course of tears. – – I may be permitted to insert one detail here. I know someone who is quite an admirer of irony and who is seeking to educate his taste in this figure of rhetoric in a very unusual way, in Golius' Arabic dictionary; he does this because he finds examples of irony nowhere more frequently than in the roots of this language. The etymology of this phenomenon may be derived, if not as scholarship then as devotion, from the original sin of Ishmael.) Aliquando etiam in una Dialecto plures propullulant potestates secundariae, in altera pauciores. Reperio denique quasdam Dialectos sic usibus secundariis indulsisse, ut primariae penitus in oblivionem iverint, quae in alia magno studio conservatae fuerunt et recenti semper memoria viguerunt.

[118] Jacques Gousset (1635–1704), author of *Lexicon linguae Hebraicae* and *Commentarii linguae Ebraicae*, was the target of Michaelis' criticism in sections 9 and 10 for his undisciplined attempts to gloss the meaning of Hebrew words. Gousset opposed on principle the application of comparative philology to Hebrew, a sacred language.

(Footnote 'k' *cont.*)
  III. circa constructionem, loquendi formas totumque orationis ambitum. – – Phrases aliter in hac, aliter in illa Dialecto conceptae conformataeque, in summo consensu radicalis verborum materiae, incredibilem pariunt dissensum quoad universum ambitum orationis formamque ac velut faciem domesticam Dialectorum.

  Omnes linguae habent aliquid singulare, domesticum, privum, praesertim circa Origines, quod in alias linguas non eadem virtute, dignitate, venustate et amplitudine transfundi potest. Hic character prae omnibus aliis ob summam antiquitatem eminet in lingua hebraea eiusque Dialectis, Chaldaica, Syriaca et Arabica. – Omnes linguae sub uno vocabulo unam tantum significationem propriam et primariam possident. Haec primaria, princeps, propria, una in omnibus linguis est rarissimi usus; ex adverso metaphoricae et secundariae regnant.

  Nulla Dialectus sibi sufficit ad Origines sibi suas praestandas; sed omnes mutuam opem lucemque desiderant. Nulla satis docte, solide, profunde tenetur, nisi omnes sub conspectu habeantur. Is conspectus non in Lexicis panditur sed in libris, quos qui non assidue versat, nunquam ad vivum et vegetum harum linguarum sensum perveniet.

  In linguis nil fluxius fallatiusque illa circinatione, quam dexteritas fabri efficit, non Natura ipsa et Origo.

  *Cf. *Œuvres du comte Algarotti*, vol. II, p. 241. The footnote.

  [See n. 119 for a translation, with comments, on this note.]

[119] The long quotation consists of three passages from Albert Schultens, *Origines Hebraeae* (on which see n. 97 above) and one digression.

  The first quotation runs from the beginning until the end of the first paragraph after the Roman numeral III (". . . Dialectorum") and adapts pp. 196–7 of Schultens' work. It may be translated:

  Dialect is the external and accidental variation of a single language which does not affect the substance of the language but preserves its foundation whole and intact. Those external variations which occur with a true dialect involve:

  I. The alphabet, sounds, and manners of pronunciation.
      1. The source of this variation is the climate in which one lives. If it is rather rough and harsh, harsh and rather rude sounds will be adopted; if, on the other hand, it is more rarefied and delicate, the dialect will naturally take on a certain delicate softness or thinness.
      2. The temperament of the men themselves, which reveals itself either on the side of politeness or of rudeness.
      3. The slippery mobility of the tongue, extremely prone to lapse into altering letters that are very close or changing one organ without any intention.
      4. The mental effort, care, and diligence by which a thing is now seized upon and adopted as more appropriate, polished, or convenient.
      5. Accent, which I may call the King of universal pronunciation, from whose assent everything depends to such a degree that if the custom of a people should vary even the smallest amount in its expression, diverse and foreign tongues would soon appear, which are connected by birth, roots, and consanguinity.
  II. The significations of words.
      1. Most serious divergence when there is no agreement regarding a word's proper and fundamental meaning.
      2. A name that is common in one Dialect but does not usually occur in another; whether an innovation was introduced before, or permitted to die off later.
      3. Large differences are formed by secondary and metaphorical meanings, which tend to arise from the primary meaning. Indeed it often happens that in these secondary usages quarrel and discord arises between sister Dialects. Sadness and sickness among the Attic Greeks is exultant happiness among the Ionians. Sometimes one Dialect teems with secondary

without Arabic as an infirm philosopher can imagine a soul without thinking of the situation of his body.

To conclude in keeping with the *Opinion*, the Hebrew language is like
the apocalyptic beast who was, and is not, and yet is.[120] Defunct, according
to the title;[121] – – Wounds, deadly wounds[122] until the epoch – – when
we shall burst anew into song:

(Footnote 119 *cont.*)
> definitions, but another has rather fewer. Lastly I find that some Dialects
> have been so tolerant of secondary usages that the primary meanings
> have been altogether lost in obscurity, while in another dialect they were
> preserved with great care and have always flourished with fresh memory.
> III. Syntax, morphology, and the period of speech.
> > Style, which is conceived and shaped differently among Dialects, even
> > when in agreement about the root matter of words, yields an unimaginable
> > disagreement as far as the general period of speech, and the grammatical
> > form, and the familiar face, so to speak, of Dialects.

Hamann inserts a digression after 11.3, adducing a parallel case of a single word with opposite
meanings in different dialects, which leads him to make another allusion to Michaelis, who used
the word "weep" as an example in his discussion of true and false uses of etymology (p. 19). This
"art of analysis" is incapable of treating tears. The relevant German proverb runs, "Children
have laughter and weeping in the same bag." The Dutch Orientalist Jacob Golius published
a Latin–Arabic dictionary (*Lexicon Arabico–Latinum*) in 1653, and Michaelis was critical of its
limitations (p. 22 of the *Beurtheilung*). The further note which Hamann added to this note refers to
an anecdote recorded by the Italian Enlightenment writer Count Francesco Algarotti (1712–64),
a friend of Voltaire's and Frederick II's, in his "Essai sur la peinture"; it tells the story of a painter
who demonstrates how easy it is to change the representation of a weeping child into that of a
laughing child. The original sin of Ishmael is mockery; see Genesis 21:9 (and recall that "Isaac"
means "he laughs").

The second passage from Schultens consists of two paragraphs from the appended *Vindiciae*
("Defense"), running from "Omnes . . ." to ". . . perveniet," pp. 453–4:
> All languages have something unique, familiar, particular, especially regarding
> Origins, which cannot be transfused into other languages with the same virtue, dig-
> nity, grace, and amplitude. This characteristic above all others is preeminent on
> account of its antiquity in the Hebrew language and its Dialects (Chaldee, Syriac, and
> Arabic). – All languages have only one such proper and primary meaning for each
> name. This one primary, foremost, proper signification in all languages is of the rarest
> usage; on the other hand, metaphorical and secondary meanings dominate.

> No Dialect is sufficient by itself to ascertain its own Origins; rather, they all require
> shared aid and mutual illumination. None is known with sufficient learning, firmness,
> or profundity, unless all the Dialects be held in view. Such a view is not disclosed in
> dictionaries, but in books, and whoever does not study them assiduously, will never
> arrive at a living and lively perception of these languages.

The third passage, the first half of a sentence on p. 232 of Schultens' *Origines Hebraeae*, may be
translated, "In languages nothing is more fluid and more deceptive than that circular path which
the skill of the craftsman creates, not Nature herself and the Original."
[120] Revelation 17:8 ("beast that was, and is not, and yet is") and 11.
[121] "Defunct" refers to Michaelis' title, *Opinion on the Means Used to Understand the Defunct Hebrew
Language.*
[122] Revelation 13:3: "And I saw one of his heads as it were wounded to death; and his deadly wound
was healed."

Aurum de Arabia
Thus et Myrrham de Saba
Tulit in ecclesia
Virtus asinaria[123] –

Whether more can be expected from the most recent methods to awaken the defunct Hebrew language than from the design of that errant knight who sought to gather and reconcile the scattered limbs of the people,[124] time must tell.

If then the doctrine of the Hebrew language were like the woman in the gospel, who took seven brothers for her husband, without having an heir,[125] then of course such an exploit would place in the hands of the Sadducees a new parable against our religion. However, despite all artificial means it could also be true here: You do not understand the scriptures, nor the power of GOD,[126] neither their inspiration nor interpretation, which does not depend on philosophical reasons.

The *Origines* of the Hebrew dialect hence may be as dead as the *uterus* of Sarah:[127] – the most miraculous researchers into language are also, from time to time, the most impotent exegetes; – – the strongest lawgivers are the destroyers of their tables,[128] or they will become one-eyed through the fault of their children.[129]

I found an idea about languages in Pascal, and I am surprised that it has not yet been challenged. He takes all languages to be potentially decipherable (as far as my memory serves), because they are related to each other as one hidden script to another.[130] That a head so practiced in mathematics can commit such an obvious fallacy is easy to understand, so long as we do not turn the weakness of human knowledge into a mere *locus communis* or slip-hole of his sophistries. From his proposition, in case I have

---

[123] "Gold from Arabia and frankincense and myrrh from Sheba were brought within the church by the strength of an ass"; see Isaiah 60:6 and Matthew 2:11 for the gold, frankincense, and myrrh.

[124] Perhaps a reference to Christ; see Matthew 23:37.

[125] Matthew 22:24–7, Mark 12:19–23, Luke 20:28–32. The Sadducees attempt to trick Jesus by asking him a question about the resurrection of a woman who married seven brothers.

[126] Matthew 22:29: "Jesus answered and said unto them, Ye do err, not knowing the scriptures, nor the power of God."

[127] Genesis 18:10–14.

[128] See Exodus 32:19, where Moses destroys the two tables with the ten commandments.

[129] Perhaps a reference to Eli's sons and his blindness in 1 Samuel 2–3.

[130] Probably refers to the remark, "Languages are ciphers where letters are not changed into letters but words into words, so that an unknown language is decipherable," in Pascal's *Pensées* (§45 of section 1 in Brunschvicg's edition).

remembered or understood him correctly, precisely the opposite conclusion follows. – –

P.S. I am reading over what I have written, and it occurs to me that I have extended frankness into impertinence. We are now so timid in thought and demure in speech that we must give offense when we want to speak or hear the truth.

The clarity of certain books is often deceptive and deficient, and exposed to much improper use. Those who know nothing but the mechanism of the sciences have good credit and need not look after readers. A Stahl[1] will always be an obscure author because he knows nature and is always coming upon those places which are as difficult to translate as the original beauties of a thousand-year-old or heterocosmic poet[131] – – –

> Surgamus! solent esse graves cantantibus umbrae;
> Iuniperi gravis umbra. Nocent et frugibus umbrae.
> Ite domum saturae, venit Hesperus, ite capellae![132]

---

[1] See Leibniz's judgments in the collection of his letters ed. by Kortholt (vol. 1, Epistle 128, 193). [Georg Ernst Stahl (1660–1734), chemist and physician, wrote prolifically on scientific topics. In Leibniz's *Epistolae ad diversos* (4 vols., 1734–42), ed. Christian Kortholt, Leibniz occasionally praises Stahl, as in the letters which Hamann cites (see pp. 185–6 and 305 of vol. 1).]

[131] Perhaps a reference to the author of the Koran, praised by Michaelis in his *Beurtheilung*.

[132] Virgil, *Eclogues* 10.75–7 (the final lines of the *Eclogues*, slightly altered): "Let us rise, the shades are too heavy for singers; the shade of the juniper is heavy. Shades harm even the fruits. Well-fed goats, go home; go, the evening star is coming."

Aesthetica in Nuce[1]

A
Rhapsody
in
Cabbalistic
Prose

Book of Judges 5:30[2]

שלל צבעים רקמה
צבע רקמתים לצוארי שלל:

---

[1] "Aesthetics in a nutshell," probably an allusion to a satirical work by Christoph Otto von Schönaich, *Die ganze Ästhetik in einer Nuß* (1754; "Complete aesthetics in a nutshell"). The term "aesthetica" was put into wide circulation with the publication of Alexander Baumgarten's treatise *Aesthetica* (1750); Baumgarten had coined the term in a previous work.

I have deliberately modeled my translation of *Aesthetica in Nuce* on that by Joyce P. Crick, which appears in *Classic and Romantic German Aesthetics*, ed. J. M. Bernstein (Cambridge Texts in the History of Philosophy, 2003).

[2] "A prey of divers colours of needlework, of divers colours of needlework on both sides, meet for the necks of them that take the spoil."

Elihu in the Book of Job 32:19–22[3]

הנה־בטני כיין לא־יפתח
כאבות חדשים יבקע:
אדברה וירוח־לי
אפתח שפתי ואענה:
אל־נא אשא פני־איש
ואל־אדם לא אכנה:
כי לא ידעתי אכנה
כמעט ישאני עשני:

---

[3] "Behold, my belly is as wine which hath no vent; it is ready to burst like new bottles. I will speak, that I may be refreshed: I will open my lips and answer. Let me not, I pray you, accept any man's person, neither let me give flattering titles unto man. For I know not to give flattering titles; in so doing my maker would soon take me away."

HORATIUS

Odi profanum vulgus et arceo.
Favete linguis! carmina non prius
audita, Musarum sacerdos,
virginibus puerisque canto.
Regum timendorum in proprios greges;
reges in ipsos imperium est Iovis,
clari giganteo triumpho,
cuncta supercilio moventis.[4]

Not a lyre! – nor a painter's brush! – a winnowing-fan for my Muse, to purge the threshing-floor of holy literature.[5] – Hail to the Archangel[6] over the relics of Canaan's language[7] – on white asses[a] he is victorious in

---

[a] Book of Judges 5:10. ["Speak, ye that ride on white asses, ye that sit in judgment, and walk by the way."]

[4] Horace, Ode 3.1.1–8: "I hate and spurn the vulgar crowd. Keep sacred silence. I, priest of the Muses, sing to maids and youths songs not heard before. The rule of dread kings is over their subjects; the rule of Jove, famed for his triumph over the giants, who moves all things with his nod, is over the kings themselves."

[5] Matthew 3:12: "Whose fan is in his hand, and he will throughly purge his floor."

[6] The archangel Michael puns on Johann David Michaelis (1717–91), professor at the University of Göttingen, philologist, theologian, and rationalist critic of the Bible.

[7] Reference to Johann David Michaelis, *Beurtheilung der Mittel, welche man anwendet, die ausgestorbene Hebräische Sprache zu verstehen* ("Opinion on the means used to understand the defunct Hebrew language"; Göttingen, 1757).

the contest; – but the wise idiot of Greece[8] borrows Euthyphro's[b] proud stallions for the philological exchange of words.

Poetry is the mother-tongue of the human race, as the garden is older than the ploughed field; painting, than writing; song, than declamation; parables, than logical deduction;[c] barter, than commerce.[9] A deeper sleep was the repose of our most distant ancestors, and their movement was a frenzied dance. Seven days they would sit in the silence of thought or wonder; – – and would open their mouths[10] – to winged sentences.

The senses and passions speak and understand nothing but images. All the wealth of human knowledge and happiness consists in images. The

---

[b] See Plato's *Cratylus*. Hermogenes: καὶ μὲν δή, ὦ Σώκρατες, ἀτεχνῶς γέ μοι δοκεῖς ὥσπερ οἱ ἐνθουσιῶντες ἐξαίφνης χρησμῳδεῖν.

Socrates: καὶ αἰτιῶμαί γε, ὦ Ἑρμόγενες, μάλιστα αὐτὴν ἀπὸ Εὐθύφρονος τοῦ Παντίου προσπεπτωκέναι μοι· ἕωθεν γὰρ πολλὰ αὐτῷ συνῆν καὶ παρεῖχον τὰ ὦτα. κινδυνεύει οὖν ἐνθουσιῶν οὐ μόνον τὰ ὦτά μου ἐμπλῆσαι τῆς δαιμονίας σοφίας, ἀλλὰ καὶ τῆς ψυχῆς ἐπειλῆφθαι. δοκεῖ οὖν μοι χρῆναι οὑτωσὶ ἡμᾶς ποιῆσαι, τὸ μὲν τήμερον εἶναι, χρήσασθαι αὐτῇ – αὔριον δ᾽ ἂν καὶ ὑμῖν συνδοκῇ, ἀποδιοπομπησόμεθά τε αὐτὴν καὶ καθαρούμεθα, ἐξευρόντες ὅστις τὰ τοιαῦτα δεινὸς καθαίρειν, εἴτε τῶν ἱερέων τις εἴτε τῶν σοφιστῶν – – – προβαλέ μοι, ὄφρα ἴδηαι οἷοι ΕΥΘΥΦΡΟΝΟΣ ΙΠΠΟΙ. [Plato, *Cratylus* 396e–397a and 407d. Hermogenes: "Indeed, Socrates, you do seem to me to be uttering oracles, exactly like an inspired prophet (*enthousiôntes*)."

Socrates: "Yes, Hermogenes, and I am convinced that the inspiration came to me from Euthyphro the son of Pantios. For I was with him and listening to him a long time early this morning. So he must have been inspired [*enthousiôn*], and he not only filled my ears but took possession of my soul with his superhuman wisdom. So I think this is our duty: we ought today to make use of this wisdom . . . but tomorrow, if the rest of you agree, we will conjure it away and purify ourselves, when we have found some one, whether priest or sophist, who is skilled in that kind of purifying . . . but ask me, so that you may see what kind EUTHYPHRO'S HORSES are like" (tr. Fowler, Loeb Classical Library, adapted). The final words echo Homer, *Iliad* 5.221–2 and 8.105–6: "so that you may see what Tros' horses are like."]

[c] "– ut hieroglyphica literis: sic parabolae argumentis antiquiores," says Bacon, my Euthyphro. [Francis Bacon, *De augmentis scientiarum* (1623), Book 2, chap. 13; the equivalent passage appears in *The Advancement of Learning* (1605), Book 2, chap. 4: "as hieroglyphics were before letters, so parables were before arguments." For the Latin passage, see p. 224 of vol. II of Bacon's *Works* (1857–74), ed. Spedding, Ellis, and Heath.]

[8] Socrates was the archetype of the wise fool; Hamann, who identifies himself with Socrates, published his *Socratic Memorabilia* in 1759.

[9] Rudolf Unger, in a long footnote on pp. 653–5 of *Hamann und die Aufklärung* (1925), finds antecedents to most of these comparisons in Antoine-Yves Goguet, *De l'origine des loix, des arts et des sciences et leur progrès chez les anciens peuples* (1758; translated in 1761 as *The Origin of Laws, Arts, Sciences, and Their Progress among the Most Ancient Nations*). On barter and commerce, see vol. I, p. 264 of Goguet; on painting and writing, see vol. I, p. 164; on the antiquity of song and poetry, see vol. I, pp. 328–31. Goguet (1716–58) was trained as a lawyer. His interest in ancient history was primarily focused on the social and physical environments of ancient civilizations.

[10] Job 2:13–3:1: "So they sat down with him upon the ground seven days and seven nights, and none spake a word unto him: for they saw that his grief was very great. After this opened Job his mouth."

first outburst of creation, and the first impression of its chronicler; – – the first manifestation and the first enjoyment of nature are united in the words: "Let there be light!"[11] Here begins the perception of the presence of things.[d]

At last GOD crowned the sensory revelation of his majesty with the masterpiece of man. He created man in God's image; – – in the image of God created he him.[12] The will of the Author in this unravels the most convoluted knots of human nature and its destiny. Blind heathens acknowledged the invisibility which man has in common with GOD. The veiled figure of the body, the countenance of the head, and the extremities of the arms are the visible schema[13] in which we move along; yet in truth they are nothing but a finger pointing to the hidden man within us.

Exemplumque DEI quisque est in imagine parva.[e]

The first nourishment was from the plant kingdom; the milk of the ancients, wine; the oldest poetry was called by its learned scholiast (as with the tale of Jotham and Joash)[f] botanical;[g] even man's first apparel was a rhapsody of fig-leaves.[14]

---

[d] πᾶν γὰρ τὸ φανερούμενον, φῶς ἐστιν. Ephesians 5:13. ["For whatsoever doth make manifest is light."]

[e] Manilius, *Astronomica*, Book IV [Line 895: "Each one is an instance of GOD in miniature" (Hamann's capitalization)].

[f] Judges, chap. 9; 2 Chronicles 25:18. [In Judges 9, Jotham tells a parable of trees in search of a king. 2 Chronicles 25:18: "And Joash king of Israel sent to Amaziah king of Judah, saying, The thistle that was in Lebanon sent to the cedar that was in Lebanon, saying, Give thy daughter to my son to wife: and there passed by a wild beast that was in Lebanon, and trode down the thistle."]

[g] – – cum planta sit poesis, quae veluti a terra luxuriante absque certo semine germinaverit, supra ceteras doctrinas excrevit et diffusa est. Bacon, *De augmentis scientiarum*, Book 2, chap. 13. See Herr Councillor John David Michaelis' notes on Robert Lowth, *De sacra poesi Hebraeorum praelectiones academicae Oxonii habitae*, p. 100 (note 18). [Francis Bacon, *De augmentis scientiarum* (1623) book 2, chap. 13 (see p. 226 of vol. II of Bacon's *Works*). The equivalent passage in *The Advancement of Learning* (1605) appears in book 2, chap. 4: "For [poesy] being as a plant that cometh of the lust of the earth, without a formal seed, it hath sprung up and spread abroad more than any other kind."

Michaelis, the "learned scholiast," published an edition of Robert Lowth's *De sacra poesi Hebraeorum praelectiones academicae Oxonii habitae* ("Lectures held at Oxford on the sacred poetry of the Hebrews") in 1758–61. In Note 18 of this work, Michaelis observes that Hebrew poetry took many metaphors from nature, particularly foliage and flowers; he calls such poetry "botanical."]

[11] Genesis 1:3: "And God said, Let there be light: and there was light."
[12] Genesis 1:27: "So God created man in his own image, in the image of God created he him."
[13] Philippians 2:8: "and being found in fashion [ἐν σχήματι] as a man."
[14] Genesis 3:7: "And the eyes of them both were opened, and they knew that they were naked; and they sewed fig leaves together."

But the LORD GOD made coats of skins and put them on – unto our
ancestors,[15] whom the knowledge of good and evil had taught shame. –
If necessity is the inventress of conveniences and arts, then we have good
reason to wonder with Goguet[16] how the fashion of clothing could have
arisen in Eastern lands, and why for that matter in the skins of beasts.
May I venture a conjecture that strikes me as at least ingenious? – – I
set the origin of this costume within the universal persistence of animal
characters,[17] which became known to Adam through his association with
the ancient poet (called Abaddon in the language of Canaan but Apollyon
in the Hellenistic language[18]) – This moved the first man under his borrowed pelt to transmit an intuitive knowledge of past and future events
to posterity – – –

Speak, that I may see you![19] – – This wish was fulfilled by creation,
which is a speech to creatures through creatures; for day unto day utters
speech, and night unto night shows knowledge. Its watchword traverses
every clime to the end of the world, and its voice can be heard in every
dialect.[20] – – The fault may lie where it will (outside or in us): all we have
left in nature for our use are jumbled verses[21] and *disjecti membra poetae*.[22]
To gather these together is the scholar's modest part; to interpret them,

---

[15] Genesis 3:21: "Unto Adam also and to his wife did the LORD God make coats of skins, and clothed them."

[16] Goguet argued in *De l'origine des loix, des arts et des sciences et leur progrès chez les anciens peuples* (1758), vol. I, pp. 114–15, that since clothing was first worn in warm Eastern countries, the original purpose of clothing cannot have been the need for warmth.

[17] Satirical reference to Lessing's rationalist discussion of fables, in which he refers to the "universally known persistence of animal characters." See his essay "Von dem Gebrauch der Tiere in der Fabel" ("On the use of animals in fable") in Lessing's *Werke*, ed. Göpfert, vol. V, p. 398.

[18] Revelation 9:11: "And they had a king over them, which is the angel of the bottomless pit, whose name in the Hebrew tongue is Abaddon, but in the Greek tongue hath his name Apollyon."

[19] An ancient saying, revived by Erasmus (for more information, see Kenneth Haynes, "*Loquere ut te uideam*: Towards the Life of an Apophthegm," *Literary Imagination* 4:2 (Spring 2002), 266–71).

[20] Psalm 19:2–4: "Day unto day uttereth speech, and night unto night sheweth knowledge. There is no speech nor language, where their voice is not heard. Their line is gone out through all the earth, and their words to the end of the world."

[21] In German, "Turbatverse," which were used to teach students to write Latin verse. The words of a single verse would be re-arranged to produce a grammatical but unmetrical line. Students would attempt to turn the jumbled words back into the metrical form which scanned correctly.

[22] Horace, *Satire* 1.4.62: "limbs of the dismembered poet."

the philosopher's; to imitate[h] them – or bolder still – bring them into right order, the poet's.

To speak is to translate – from an angelic language into a human language, that is, to translate thoughts into words, – things into names – images into signs, which can be poetic or curiological,[i] [23] historic or symbolic or hieroglyphic – – and philosophical or characteristic.[j] This kind of translation (that is, speech) resembles more than anything else the wrong side of a tapestry:

h   Rescisso discas componere nomine versum;
                       Lucili vatis sic imitator eris.
                           Ausonius, Epistula V.

[Ausonius, Epistle 15 (in the modern edition by R. P. H. Green), lines 37–8, slightly altered: "May you learn to compose verses with split nouns; thus you will become an imitator of the poet Lucilius."]

i For an explanation, the first section of Wachter's *Naturae et scripturae concordia: commentatio de literis ac numeris primaevis, aliisque rebus memorabilibus, cum ortu literarum coniunctis* (Leipzig and Copenhagen, 1752) can be consulted. [Johann Georg Wachter (1673–1757), philologist and freethinker, distinguishes three stages of writing (curiological, symbolic or hieroglyphic, and characteristic) in the passage of the work cited ("The concord of nature and scripture: A commentary on the first letters and numbers, and on other noteworthy items connected with the origin of writing").]

j The following passage from Petronius is to be understood as this kind of sign. I am obliged to quote it in context, even granting that it may be read as a satire on the philologist himself and his contemporaries: nuper ventosa istaec et enormis loquacitas Athenas ex Asia commigravit, animosque iuvenum ad magna surgentes veluti pestilenti quodam sidere adflavit, simulque corrupta eloquentiae regula stetit et obmutuit. Quis postea ad summam Thucydidis? (He is called the Pindar of historians.) quis Hyperidis (who bared Phryne's bosom to convince the judges of his good cause) ad famam processit? Ac ne carmen quidem sani coloris enituit; sed omnia, quasi eodem cibo pasta, non potuerunt usque ad senectutem canescere. PICTVRA quoque non alium exitum fecit, postquam AEGYPTIORVM AVDACIA tam magnae artis COMPENDIARIAM invenit. This may be compared with the profound prophecy which Socrates put into the mouth of the Egyptian King Thamus about the invention of Thoth, which made Phaedrus exclaim, "ὦ Σώκρατες, ῥᾳδίως σὺ Αἰγυπτίους καὶ ὁποδαποὺς ἂν ἐθέλῃς λόγους ποιεῖς." [Petronius, *Satiricon* 2: "Your flatulent and formless flow of words is a modern immigrant from Asia to Athens. Its breath fell upon the mind of ambitious youth like the influence of a baleful planet, and when the old tradition was broken, eloquence halted and grew dumb. In a word, who after this came to equal the splendor of Thucydides? . . . Or of Hyperides? . . . Even poetry did not glow with the color of health, but the whole of art, nourished on one universal diet, lacked the vigor to reach the grey hairs of old age. The decadence in PAINTING was the same, as soon as EGYPTION CHARLATANS had found a SHORT CUT to this high calling" (tr. Heseltine, Loeb Classical Library; Hamann's capitals). The "philologist" in question is Michaelis.

Hyperides was a Greek orator; an ancient anecdote relates how he bared the breast of the beautiful Phryne to convince a jury of her innocence (Athenaeus 13. 590e–591a).]

Phaedrus' words (from Plato, *Phaedrus* 275b) may be translated "Socrates, you easily make up stories about Egyptians or any country you please."

[23] "Curiological" refers to the stage when objects are represented by pictures and not by symbols.
    "Characteristic" refers to alphabetic writing. With these three phases, Hamann connects poetry, history, and philosophy, respectively.

And shews the Stuff, but not the Workman's skill,

or it can be compared with an eclipse of the sun, which can be looked at in a vessel of water.[k]

Moses' torch illuminates even the intellectual world, which also has its heaven and its earth. Hence Bacon compares the sciences with the waters above and below the vault of our vaporous globe.[24] The former are a sea of glass, like unto crystal mixed with fire;[25] the latter, by contrast, are little clouds from the ocean, no bigger than a man's hand.[26]

The creation of the setting, however, bears the same relation to the creation of man as epic to dramatic poetry. The former takes place by means of the word, the latter by means of action. Heart, be like unto the tranquil sea! – – Hear the counsel: "Let us make men in our image, after our likeness, and let them have dominion!"[27] – – Behold the deed: And the LORD GOD formed man of the dust of the ground[28] – – Compare counsel and deed: worship the mighty speaker with the Psalmist;[l] worship the

---

[k] The one metaphor comes from the Earl of Roscommon's "Essay on Translated Verse" and Howell's *Letters*. Both, if I am not mistaken, borrowed the comparison from Saavedra. The other is borrowed from one of the most excellent weekly journals (*The Adventurer*). Yet there they are used *ad illustrationem* (to adorn the garment); here they are used *ad involucrum* (as a covering for the bare body), as Euthyphro's muse teaches us to distinguish. [Roscommon, "Essay on Translated Verse" (1684), l. 44, on translating Horace into prose.

In the posthumous, fifth edition of James Howell's *Familiar Letters* (1678), he writes that "Some hold Translations not unlike to be, / The wrong-side of a Turky Tapistry" (p. 246); he expands that comparison in prose on p. 422.

"Saavedra" is Miguel Cervantes de Saavedra. In chap. 62 of Part 2 of *Don Quixote*, he compares translation from vernacular languages to viewing Flemish tapestries from the wrong side.

On p. 294 of *The Adventurer*, No. 49 (April 24, 1753), the author writes that to read Aristotle or Greek tragedy in modern French versions "is like beholding the orb of the sun, during an eclipse, in a vessel of water."

Bacon distinguishes between parables that act *ad involucrum* from those that act *ad illustrationem* in *De augmentis scientiarum*, Book 2, chap. 13 (see Bacon's *Works*, vol. II, p. 224). In *The Advancement of Learning*, Book 2, chap. 4, he opposes two kinds of "poesy parabolical": one "that tendeth to demonstrate and illustrate that which is taught or delivered" and another that tends to "retire and obscure it – that is, when the secrets and mysteries of religion, policy, or philosophy, are involved in fables or parables."]

[l] Psalm 33:9. ["For he spake, and it was done; he commanded, and it stood fast."]

[24] Bacon, *The Advancement of Learning*, Book 2, chap. 4: "The knowledge of man is as the waters, some descending from above, and some springing from beneath: the one informed by the light of nature, the other inspired by divine revelation." Cf. *De augmentis scientiarum*, Book 3, chap. 1 (see Bacon's *Works*, vol. II, p. 251).

[25] Revelation 4:6: "And before the throne there was a sea of glass like unto crystal."

[26] I Kings 18:44: "Behold, there ariseth a little cloud out of the sea, like a man's hand."

[27] Genesis 1:26: "And God said, Let us make man in our image, after our likeness: and let them have dominion."

[28] Genesis 2:7: "And the LORD God formed man of the dust of the ground."

supposed gardener[m] with her who bore the news to the disciples; worship the free potter[n] with the Apostle to Hellenistic philosophers and the Talmudic scribes![29]

The hieroglyphic Adam is the history of the entire race in the symbolic wheel: – – the character of Eve is the original of Nature's beauty and of systematic economy, which is not written with methodical sanctity on the plate worn on the forehead,[30] but is wrought beneath the earth and lies hidden – in the bowels, in the very reins of things.[31]

Virtuosos[32] of the present aeon, upon which the LORD GOD caused a deep sleep to fall! You noble few! Make use of this sleep, and build from this Endymion's rib[33] the latest edition of the human soul, which the bard of midnight songs beheld in his morning dream[o] – – but not from close at hand. The next aeon will awake like a giant from a drunken stupor to embrace your muse and rejoice and bear witness to her: This is now bone of my bone and flesh of my flesh![34]

If some modern literary Levite[35] were to take note in passing of this rhapsody, I know in advance that he will bless himself like Saint

---

[m] John 20:15–17. ["Jesus saith unto her, Woman, why weepest thou? whom seekest thou? She, supposing him to be the gardener, saith unto him, Sir, if thou have borne him hence, tell me where thou hast laid him, and I will take him away. Jesus saith unto her, Mary. She turned herself, and saith unto him, Rabboni; which is to say, Master. Jesus saith unto her, Touch me not; for I am not yet ascended to my Father: but go to my brethren, and say unto them, I ascend unto my Father, and your Father; and to my God, and your God."]

[n] Romans 9:21. ["Hath not the potter power over the clay, of the same lump to make one vessel unto honour, and another unto dishonour?"]

[o] See Dr. Young's "Letter to the Author of *Sir Charles Grandison*" on original composition. [Edward Young (1683–1759) prefaced a "Letter to the Author of *Sir Charles Grandison*" (i.e., Samuel Richardson) to his *Conjectures on Original Composition* (1759); in it he defends a notion of progress, asking whether "heaven's latest editions of the human mind may be the most correct" (p. 74).]

[29] Paul, both "a man which am a Jew" (Acts 22:3) and "the apostle of the Gentiles" (Romans 11:13).

[30] The plate worn on the forehead (*Stirnblatt*) appears in Exodus 28:36 and 39:30. Worn by Aaron, it is inscribed with the words, "Holiness to the Lord."

[31] Psalm 139: 13–15: "For thou hast possessed my reins: thou hast covered me in my mother's womb . . . My substance was not hid from thee, when I was made in secret, and curiously wrought in the lowest parts of the earth."

[32] Before it acquired the sense of "connoisseur," "virtuoso" denoted more generally a scholar or scientist.

[33] Genesis 2:21: "And the LORD God caused a deep sleep to fall upon Adam, and he slept: and he took one of his ribs." Hamann combines the story of Eve's creation from Adam's rib with the story of Endymion, the handsome youth whom the moon-goddess loved and who now enjoys an eternal sleep.

[34] Genesis 2:23: "And Adam said, This is now bone of my bones, and flesh of my flesh."

[35] The Levite is contrasted with the good Samaritan in Luke 10:32–3. Hamann is referring to Moses Mendelssohn.

Peter[p] before the great sheet knit at the four corners, wherein he caught sight at a glance and beheld four-footed beasts of the earth, and wild beasts, and creeping things, and fowls of the air[36] – – – "Oh no, you man possessed, you Samaritan"[37] – – (that is how he will scold the philologist in his heart) – "for readers of orthodox tastes, low expressions and unclean vessels are not proper" – – Impossibilissimum est, communia proprie dicere[38] – Behold, that is why an author whose taste is but eight days old, but circumcised,[39] will soil his swaddling clothes with pure white covered gentian[40] – to the honor of human needs! – – The old Phrygian's fabled ugliness was in fact never so dazzling as the aesthetic beauty of Aesop the younger.[41] Today, Horace's typical ode to Aristus[q] is fulfilled, that the poet who sings the praises of sweet-smiling Lalage, whose kiss is still sweeter than her laughter, has made fops out of Sabine, Apuline, and Mauretanian monsters.[42] – True, one can be a man without finding it necessary to become an author. But whoever expects his good friends to think of the writer apart from the man[43] is more inclined to poetic than to philosophical abstractions. Therefore do not venture into the metaphysics of the fine arts without being initiated into the

---

[p] Acts 10:11. ["And saw heaven opened, and a certain vessel descending upon him, as it had been a great sheet knit at the four corners, and let down to the earth."]

[q] Ode 1.22. [See n. 42.]

[36] Acts 10:11–12: "And saw heaven opened, and a certain vessel descending upon him, as it had been a great sheet knit at the four corners, and let down to the earth: Wherein were all manner of fourfooted beasts of the earth, and wild beasts, and creeping things, and fowls of the air." The vision belonged to Peter, who at first resisted God's instruction to eat the "common or unclean" animals (Acts 10:14).

[37] The Jews asked Jesus in John 8:48, "Say we not well that thou art a Samaritan, and hast a devil?"

[38] "It is most impossible to speak of common things in a particular way"; Hamann alludes to Horace, *Ars poetica* 128, substituting "most impossible" for Horace's "difficult." In Hamann's context "common things" refer to vulgar or unclean matters (cf. Acts 10:14).

[39] Genesis 17:12: "And he that is eight days old shall be circumcised among you."

[40] "White gentian" was recorded in Adelung's dictionary as an expression among commoners for the white excrement of dogs.

[41] Aesop, whom tradition records as extremely ugly, is contrasted with Lessing, who published his *Fabeln* ("Fables") in 1759.

[42] The ode, addressed to Aristius (not "Aristus") Fuscus, begins by saying that the man who is pure of heart needs no weapons to defend himself in dangerous territory; as an example, Horace recalls that a monstrous wolf fled from him when he was singing, unarmed, of Lalage; it ends with Horace's declaration, "I shall love sweetly smiling Lalage, sweetly speaking." Hamann gives the monsters geographic designations that recall places mentioned in Horace's ode.

[43] In Letter 7 (January 18, 1759) of Part 1 of *Briefe, die neueste Literatur betreffend* ("Letters concerning the most recent literature"), Lessing wrote, "What does the private life of a writer matter to us?" (p. 35).

orgies[r] and Eleusinian mysteries. But the senses belong to Ceres, and to Bacchus the passions, – the ancient foster-parents of nature the beautiful.

> Bacche! veni dulcisque tuis e cornibus uva
> Pendeat, et spicis tempora cinge Ceres![s]

If this rhapsody should indeed be honored with the judgment of a master of Israel,[44] then let us go meet him in holy prosopopoeia,[t] which is as welcome in the realm of the dead as it is in the realm of the living[45] (– – si NUX modo ponor in illis):[46]

Most Worthy and Learned Rabbi!

"The postilion of the Holy Roman Empire,[47] who bears the device *Relata refero*[48] on the shield of his escutcheon, has made me crave the second half of the homilies[49] *de sacra poesi*.[50] I burn with desire for them – and have waited in vain until this very day, even as the mother of the Hazorite captain looked out of the window for her son's chariot and cried

---

[r] "Orgia nec Pentheum nec Orpheum tolerant." Bacon, *De augmentis scientiarum*, Book 2, chap. 13. ["The orgies of Bacchus cannot endure either Pentheus or Orpheus." Bacon explains: a ruling passion is hostile both to curious inquiry [Pentheus] and to wholesome advice [Orpheus]. See Bacon's *Works*, vol. II, p. 249; the passage is translated in *Works*, vol. VIII, p. 468.]

[s] Tibullus, Elegy 2.1. [Lines 3–4: "Bacchus, come, let the sweet grapes hang from your horns; and wreathe your temples with ears of corn, Ceres."]

[t] "L'art de personnifier ouvre un champ bien moins borné et plus fertile que l'ancienne Mythologie," Fontenelle in *Sur la poésie en général*, vol. VIII. ["The art of personification [prosopopoeia] opens a field that is much less restricted and more fertile than ancient mythology," Bernard Le Bovier de Fontenelle (1657–1757), French polymath, in *Sur la poésie en général* (1751; "On poetry in general"); see Fontenelle's *Œuvres complètes*, ed. Niderst (9 vols.; 1989–2001), vol. V, p. 549. (Hamann refers to an eighteenth-century edition of Fontenelle.) Lowth's thirteenth lecture was devoted to "prosopopoeia, or personification."]

44 John 3:10: "Jesus answered and said unto him, Art thou a master of Israel, and knowest not these things?" Michaelis is meant.

45 One popular form of prosopopoeia in the period was the genre of "dialogues of the dead." It has been suggested that Lowth's distinction between the two kinds of prosopopoeia (attributed either to a fictitious or a real character) gave rise to Hamann's contrast between living and dead.

46 ps-Ovid, *Nux* l. 19: "If as a nut-tree I am counted among them"; "nux" ("nut" or "nut-tree") alludes to the title of Hamann's essay.

47 A reference to the weekly newspaper, Frankfurt's *Kayserliche Reichs-Postzeitungen* ("Imperial kingdom's post-newspaper").

48 "I report what I have been told."

49 In Michaelis' preface to Lowth (p. xxvi), he prefers that the "orationes sacrae" of an "eloquent philosopher" be called "homilies."

50 The newspaper presumably announced the publication of the second half of Michaelis' edition of Robert Lowth's lectures on Hebrew poetry, *De sacra poesi Hebraeorum praelectiones Oxonii habitae* ("Lectures held at Oxford on the sacred poetry of the Hebrews"), which was published in 1758–61.

through the lattice[51] – – Do not think ill of me then if I speak to you like the ghost in *Hamlet*, with beckonings,[52] until I have a more suitable occasion to declare myself in *sermones fideles.*[u] [53] Will you believe without proof that *Orbis pictus*, by the renowned enthusiast, school-master, and philologist

[u] John 3:11. The following passage from Bacon, *De augmentis scientiarum*, Book 9, may help to guard against the crude and ignorant idea of pronouncing the present imitation of cabbalistic style to be good or bad: In interpretandi modo [soluto] duo interveniunt excessus. Alter eiusmodi praesupponit in Scripturis perfectionem, ut etiam omnis Philosophia ex earum fontibus peti debeat, ac si Philosophia alia quaevis res profana esset et ethnica. Haec intemperies in schola Paracelsi praecipue, nec non apud alios invaluit; initia autem eius a Rabbinis et CABBALISTIS defluxerunt. Verum istiusmodi homines non id assequuntur, quod volunt: neque enim honorem, ut putant, Scripturis deferunt, sed easdem potius deprimunt et polluunt. – Quemadmodum enim Theologiam in Philosophia quaerere, perinde est ac si vivos quaeras inter mortuos: ita [e contra] Philosophiam in Theologia quaerere, non aliud est, quam mortuos [quaerere] inter vivos. Alter autem interpretandi modus (quem pro excessu statuimus) videtur primo intuitu sobrius et castus; sed tamen et Scripturas ipsas dedecorat, et plurimo Ecclesiam afficit detrimento. Is est (ut verbo dicamus) quando Scripturae divinitus inspiratae eodem, quo scripta humana, explicantur modo. Meminisse autem oportet, DEO, Scripturarum Auctori, duo illa patere, quae humana ingenia fugiunt: Secreta nimirum cordis et successiones temporis. – – Cum Scripturarum dictamina talia sint, ut et cor scribantur, et omnium saeculorum vicissitudines complectantur; cum aeterna et certa praescientia omnium haeresium, contradictionum et status Ecclesiae varii et mutabilis, tum in communi, tum in electis singulis: interpretandae non sunt solummodo secundum latitudinem et obvium sensum loci: aut respiciendo ad occasionem, ex qua verba erant prolata: aut praecise ex contextu verborum praecedentium et sequentium; aut contemplando scopum dicti principalem: sed sic, ut intelligamus, complecti eas, non solum totaliter, aut collective, sed distributive, etiam in clausulis et vocabulis singulis, innumeros doctrinae rivulos et venas, ad Ecclesiae singulas partes et animas fidelium irrigandas. Egregie enim observatum est, quod Responsa Salvatoris nostri ad quaestiones non paucas, ex iis, quae proponebantur, non videntur ad rem, sed quasi impertinentia. Cuius rei causa duplex est. Altera, quod quum cogitationes eorum, qui interrogabant, non ex verbis, ut nos homines solemus, sed immediate et ex sese cognovisset, ad cogitationes eorum, non ad verba respondet: Altera, quod non ad eos solum locutus est, qui tunc aderant, sed ad nos etiam, qui vivimus et ad omnis aevi ac loci homines, quibus Evangelium fuerit praedicandum. Quod etiam in aliis Scripturae locis obtinet. [See n. 53.]

[51] Judges 5:28: "The mother of Sisera looked out at a window, and cried through the lattice." Sisera was the general of the army under King Jabin of Hazor. The passage is discussed by Lowth as an instance of prosopopoeia in his thirteenth lecture.

[52] *Hamlet*, Act I, Scene 4.

[53] "Sermones fideles" are "faithful sayings"; the phrase in the singular occurs in the Vulgate translation of 1 Timothy 1:15: "This is a faithful saying, and worthy of all acceptation." The Latin translation of Bacon's *Essays* was entitled *Sermones fideles* (1638).

John 3:11: "Verily, verily, I say unto thee, We speak that we do know, and testify that we have seen; and ye receive not our witness."

The long quotation from Bacon's *De augmentis scientiarum* appears on p. 182 of vol. III of Bacon's *Works* (1857–74), ed. Spedding, Ellis, and Heath; it was translated in vol. IX, pp. 353–5 as follows: "in the free way of interpreting Scripture, there occur two excesses. The one presupposes such perfection in Scripture, that all philosophy likewise should be derived from its sources; as if all other philosophy were something profane and heathen. This distemper has principally grown up in the school of Paracelsus and some others; but the beginnings thereof came from the Rabbis and CABALISTS. But these men do not gain their object; and instead of giving honor to the Scriptures as they suppose, they rather embase and pollute them . . . and as to seek theology in philosophy

Amos Comenius,[v] [54] and the *Exercitia* of Muzelius[55] are both books far too learned for children still only pract-is-ing their spell-ing – – and verily, verily, we must become even as little children[56] if we are to receive the spirit of the truth which the world cannot grasp, for it sees it not, and (even if it were to see it) knows it not.[57] – – Blame it on the foolishness of my way of writing, which accords so ill with the original mathematical sin of your earliest writing, and still less with the witty rebirth of your most recent works, if I borrow an example from the spelling-book which doubtless

---

[v] See Kortholt's collection of Leibniz's letters, vol. III, Ep. 29. [Christian Kortholt edited *Leibnitii epistolae ad diversos* ("Letters of Leibniz to various people") in 1734–42. The letter cited is to Magnus Hesenthaler in 1671 (see Leibniz, *Philosophischer Briefwechsel*, ed. Prussian Academy of Sciences, pp. 199–201). Leibniz writes, "Therefore I absolutely agree with Comenius that *Janua linguarum* and a small encyclopedia must be one and the same."]

is to seek the living among the dead, so to seek philosophy in theology is to seek the dead among the living. The other method of interpretation which I set down as an excess, appears at the first glance sober and modest, yet in reality it both dishonors the Scriptures themselves, and is very injurious to the Church. This is, (in a word), when the divinely inspired Scriptures are explained in the same way as human writings. But we ought to remember that there are two things which are known to GOD the author of the Scriptures, but unknown to man; namely, the secrets of the heart, and the successions of time . . . And therefore as the dictates of Scripture are written to the hearts of men, and comprehend the vicissitudes of all ages; with an eternal and certain foreknowledge of all heresies, contradictions and differing and changing estates of the Church, as well in general as of the individual elect, they are not to be interpreted only according to the latitude and obvious sense of the place; or with respect to the occasion whereon the words were uttered; or in precise context with the words before or after; or in contemplation of the principal scope of the passage; but we must consider them to have in themselves, not only totally or collectively, but distributively also in clauses and words, infinite springs and streams of doctrines, to water every part of the Church and the souls of the faithful. For it has been well observed that the answers of our Savior to many of the questions which were propounded to Him do not appear to the point, but as it were impertinent thereto. The reason whereof is twofold; the one, that knowing the thoughts of his questioners not as we men do by their words, but immediately and of himself, he answered their thoughts and not their words; the other, that He did not speak only to the persons then present, but to us also now living, and to men of every age and nation to whom the Gospel was to be preached. And this also holds good in other passages of Scripture" (tr. adapted; Hamann's capitals).

[54] John Amos Comenius (1592–1670) was a Czech educational reformer and devotional writer. Two of his textbooks for instruction in Latin had a large influence in the seventeenth century: *Janua linguarum reserata* (1631; "The gate of languages unlocked") and *Orbis pictus sensualium* (1658; "The visible word in pictures").

[55] Friedrich Muzelius (1684–1753) was an author of school textbooks, including the *Compendium universae Latinitas . . . in exercitia Germanica redactae* (1738; "Compendium of all Latin . . . arranged into German exercises"). On p. 55 of his *Beurtheilung der Mittel* ("Opinion of the means"; see n. 7 above), Michaelis argues against the thesis that no philological help is needed to understand the Bible; this would be the case only if the Bible were Comenius' *Orbis pictus* and Muzelius' *Exercitia*.

[56] Matthew 18:3: "Verily I say unto you, Except ye be converted, and become as little children, ye shall not enter into the kingdom of heaven."

[57] John 14:17: "Even the Spirit of truth; whom the world cannot receive, because it seeth him not, neither knoweth him."

may be older than the Bible. Do the elements of the ABC lose their natural meaning, if in their infinite combinations into arbitrary signs they remind us of ideas which dwell, if not in heaven, then in our brains? – – But if we raise up the whole deserving righteousness of a scribe upon the dead body of the letter, what does the spirit say to that? Shall he be but a groom of the dead chamber to the dead letter, or perhaps a mere esquire to the deadening letter?[58] God forbid! – – According to your copious insight into physical things,[59] you know better than I can remind you that the wind blows where it lists[60] – regardless of whether one hears it blowing; so one looks to the fickle weather-cock to find out where it comes from, or rather, whither it is going – –"

> Ah scelus indignum! solvetur litera dives?
> Frangatur potius legum veneranda potestas.
> Liber et alma Ceres succurrite! – –[w] [61]

---

[w] See the Emperor Octavius Augustus' poetic edict by which Virgil's last will *de abolenda Aeneide* is said to have been nullified. – – One can concede wholeheartedly what Dr. George Benson has to say about the unity of sense, though he has scarcely developed his ideas, rather added them together with little thought, selection, or smoothness. If he had tried to convey some earthly propositions about the unity of reading, his thoroughness would strike us more strongly. – – One cannot leaf through the four volumes of this paraphrastic explanation without a very ambivalent smile, nor miss the frequent passages where Dr. Benson, the beam of popery in his own eye, inveighs against the motes of the Roman Church – passages where he imitates our own theological councillors who loudly applaud every blind and over-hasty idea honoring the creature more than the creator. – – First, one would have to ask Dr. Benson whether unity can exist without multiplicity? – A lover of Homer runs to the same risk of losing his unity of sense by French paraphrasts like de la Motte or a thoughtful dogmatist like Samuel Clarke. – – The literal or grammatical sense, the corporeal or dialectical sense, the Capernaitic or historical sense are all profoundly mystical, and they are determined by minor circumstances of such a fleeting, spiritual, arbitrary nature that without ascending to heaven we cannot find the key of their knowledge. We must not shrink from any journey across the sea or to the regions of such shades as have believed, spoken, suffered for a day, two, for a hundred or a thousand years – mysteries! The universal history of the world can hardly tell us as much about them as the space of the narrowest tombstone, or as can be retained by Echo, that nymph of the laconic memory. – – The man who wants to entrust to us the schemes which intellectual writers in a critical place forge in order to convert their unbelieving brethren must have the keys to heaven and hell. Because Moses placed life in the blood, all the baptized rabbis are afraid of the spirit and life of the prophets, by which the literal understanding, the child of their heart (ἐν παραβολῇ) is sacrificed and the streams of Eastern wisdom turned to blood. – – These stifled thoughts are not for dainty stomachs. – *Abstracta initiis occultis; concreta maturitati conveniunt*, according to Bengel's sun-dial pin – (*plane pollex, non index*). [See n. 61.]

[58] 2 Corinthians 3:6: "for the letter killeth, but the spirit giveth life."

[59] Michaelis emphasizes geography and climate in his biblical exegesis.

[60] John 3:8: "The wind bloweth where it listeth, and thou hearest the sound thereof, but canst not tell whence it cometh, and whither it goeth."

[61] The Latin lines come from the putative "Caesari Augusto tributum" ("What is owed to Caesar Augustus"), a poem numbered 672 in the *Latin Anthology*, in which Augustus overturned Virgil's posthumous instruction that the *Aeneid* be destroyed (*de abolende Aeneide*). The lines quoted

The opinions of philosophers are readings of nature, and the precepts of the theologians are readings of Scripture. The author is the best interpreter of his own words. He may speak through created things – through events – or through blood and fire and vapor of smoke,[x] for these constitute the language of holiness.

---

[x] Acts 2:19. ["And I will shew wonders in heaven above, and signs in the earth beneath; blood, and fire, and vapour of smoke."]

are 4, 20, and 8, respectively: "Oh unworthy crime! Will the rich work be destroyed?"; "Rather, let the august power of the laws be infringed"; "Bacchus and kind Ceres, come to our aid!"

George Benson (1699–1752), Presbyterian minister and theologian, collected his paraphrases on the Pauline epistles in 1752 as *A Paraphrase and Notes on Six of the Epistles of St. Paul*; it was translated into German in 1761 (another of Benson's works was translated by the "theological councillor" Michaelis). The introduction to Benson's volumes is subtitled "An essay concerning on the unity of sense; to show that no text of scripture has more than one sense." On pp. x–xi of the introduction, he discusses a passage of Homer (*Iliad* 4.306–7), in which Eustathius and Anne Dacier found and applauded the multiple meanings. Benson quotes with approval the comment of Samuel Clarke (1675–1729), theologian and classical scholar, on this passage. In his commentary on the *Iliad*, Clarke had sided with Pope and insisted that only one meaning is present in his verses.

Antoine Houdar de la Motte (1672–1731) published a greatly abridged version of Homer's *Iliad* in verse on the basis of Anne Dacier's prose version (as he did not know Greek). In his *Discours sur Homère*, he objected to many aspects of Homer's verse and in particular to repetition of speeches in contradictory contexts which violated the unity of the poem (see his *Œuvres*, vol. II, pp. 47–9, 71–3, 118–19).

The "Capernaitic" sense is historical because when Christ said in Capernaum that he was the bread of life and that any man that should eat of it shall live forever, the Jews objected to the literal meaning of the words (John 6:32–59).

"Key of their knowledge" echoes Luke 11:52.

For shrinking from a "journey across the sea," cf. Deuteronomy 30:13: "Neither is it beyond the sea, that thou shouldest say, Who shall go over the sea for us, and bring it unto us."

The keys of the kingdom of heaven are given to Peter at Matthew 16:19; the keys of hell appear in Revelation 1:18.

"Moses placed life in the blood"; cf. Leviticus 17:11: "For the life of the flesh is in the blood: and I have given it to you upon the altar to make an atonement for your souls: for it is the blood that maketh an atonement for the soul."

ἐν παραβολῇ means "in a figure of speech, in a parable"; it is translated "in a figure" in Hebrews 11:19.

"Turn the streams of Eastern wisdom to blood": rivers are turned to blood in Exodus 7:20 and Revelation 16:4.

Johann Albrecht Bengel (1687–1742) was a textual critic and devotional writer. The sun-dial pin is a gnomon, which is a reference to the title of Bengel's New Testament commentary, *Gnomon Novi Testamenti* (1742; "Index of the New Testament"). The Latin words have not been traced in this work, though they are similar in thought to Bengel's comment on Matthew 1:20. The Latin may be translated, "The abstract suits hidden beginnings; the concrete suits maturity."

"Plane pollex, non index": Cicero, *Letter to Atticus* 13.46 (or 338 in Shackleton Bailey's edition): "a thumb indeed, not an index finger" (Cicero is punning; he is writing to Atticus about an acquaintance named Pollex, "thumb," who does not give him the information he wants; "index" is both "index finger" and "informer."

The book of creation contains examples of general concepts which GOD wished to reveal to creatures through creation. The books of the covenant contain examples of secret articles which GOD wished to reveal to man through man. The unity of the Author is mirrored even in the dialect of his works – in all of them a tone of immeasurable height and depth! A proof of the most splendid majesty and of total self-emptying![62] A miracle of such infinite stillness that makes GOD as nothing, so that in all conscience one would have to deny his existence, or else be a beast.[y] But at the same time a miracle of such infinite power, which fills all in all,[63] that we cannot escape his intense solicitude! –

If what matters is the good taste of the worship consisting in the philosophical spirit and poetic truth,[64] and what matters is the statecraft[z] of the versification, can we present a more credible witness than the immortal Voltaire, who virtually declares religion to be the cornerstone[65] of epic poetry and whose greatest lament is that his religion[aa] is the opposite of mythology?

Bacon represents mythology as a winged boy of Aeolus, the sun at his back, and with clouds for his footstool, and whiling away the time piping on a Grecian flute.[bb]

---

[y] Psalms 73:21–2. ["Thus my heart was grieved, and I was pricked in my reins. So foolish was I, and ignorant: I was as a beast before thee."]

[z] "La seule politique dans un poème doit de faire de bons vers," says Voltaire in his credo on the epic. [In the "Idée de la Henriade"; see p. 310 of vol. II of the Voltaire Foundation's *Complete Works*.]

[aa] What Voltaire understands by religion, grammatici certant et adhuc sub iudice lis est; the philologist has as little to worry about here as his readers. We may regard it as the liberties of the Gallican Church or the sulfuric flowers of purified naturalism; then neither explanation will do harm to the unity of the sense. [Hamann quotes Horace, *Ars poetica* 78, "scholars argue, and the case is still under consideration." By "naturalism" Hamann means natural religion.]

[bb] Fabulae mythologicae videntur esse instar tenuis cuiusdam aurae, quae ex traditionibus nationum magis antiquarum in Graecorum fistulas inciderunt. Bacon, *De augmentis scientiarum*, Book 2, chap. 13. ["Mythological fables seem to be a kind of soft breath from the traditions of more ancient nations, which fell into the pipes of the Greeks." See p. 225 of vol. II of Bacon's *Works* for the Latin, and p. 443 of vol. VIII for the English translation (here slightly modified).]

[62] An allusion to Philippians 2:7: "But made himself of no reputation" [more literally, "emptied himself"].

[63] Ephesians 1:23: "the fulness of him that filleth all in all."

[64] John 4:23: "the true worshippers shall worship the Father in spirit and in truth."

[65] Psalm 118:22: "The stone which the builders refused is become the head stone of the corner."

But Voltaire, high priest in the temple of taste,[66] draws conclusions as compellingly as Caiaphas[cc] and thinks more fruitfully than Herod.[dd] For if our theology is not worth as much as mythology, then it is simply impossible for us to match the poetry of the heathens – let alone excel it, which would be most in keeping with our duty and our vanity.[67] But if our poetry is worthless, our history will look leaner than Pharaoh's kine;[68] but fairy-tales and court gazettes will make good our lack of historians. And it is not worth the trouble of thinking of philosophy; all the more horoscopes! – more than spider-webs in a ruined castle. Every idle fellow who can just about manage dog-Latin or Switzer-German[69] but whose name is stamped by the whole number M or half the number of the academic beast[70] proves such blatant lies that the benches and the clods sitting on them would have to cry "Murder!" if the former only had ears,

---

[cc] "Qu'un homme ait du jugement ou non, il profite également de vos ouvrages: il ne lui faut que de la MEMOIRE," says a writer capable of uttering prophecies to Voltaire's face – – καίτοι οὐκ ἂν πρέποι γε ἐπιλήσμονα εἶναι ῥαψῳδὸν ἄνδρα, Socrates in Plato's *Ion*. [The French quotation is taken from Frederick the Great's letter on March 31, 1738 to Voltaire: "Whether a man has judgment or not, he profits equally from your works; all he needs is memory"; see p. 78 of vol. LXXXIX of the Voltaire Foundation's *Complete Works*.

Plato, *Ion* 539e, "Forgetfulness ill suits a rhapsode."]

[dd] Photius (in his *Amphilochiae quaestiones* 120, which Johann Christoph Wolf has added to his cornucopia of critical and philological whimsies) searches for a prophecy in the words of Herod to the Wise Men of the East ("that I may come and worship him also") and compares them with Caiaphas' pronouncement at John 11:49–52. He notes: Ἴδοις δ' ἂν παραπλησίως τούτοις καὶ ἕτερά τινα, κακούργῳ μὲν γνώμῃ καὶ ὁρμῇ μιαιφόνῳ προενηνεγμένα, πέρας δὲ προφητικὸν εἰληφότα. Photius imagines Herod as a Janus bifrons, who represented the Gentiles by his race and the Jews by his office. – Very many malicious and empty ideas (which masters and servants brag about) would assume an altogether different light for us if we were to remember from time to time to ask ourselves or whether they are speaking on their own or should be understood as prophetic. [Photius, the ninth-century Patriarch of Constantinople, is an important figure in the history of the Christian church and in classical scholarship. The passage quoted comes from his theological work *Amphilochia*, Question 307. The theologian and philologist Johann Christoph Wolf (1683–1739) quoted the passage from Photius in vol. IV of his *Curae philologicae et criticae* (1735). In the modern Teubner edition of the *Amphilochia*, it appears in vol. VI, part 1, p. 106; it may be translated "You may see that other words like these, spoken with a malicious heart and murderous intention, gain a prophetic end."

"Janus bifrons" is "two-faced Janus."]

[66] Cf. Voltaire, *Le Temple du goût* (1733).

[67] Hamann alludes to "Querelle des Anciens et des Modernes" ("Quarrel of the ancients and the moderns"); see for example Peter France, ed., *The New Oxford Companion to Literature in French* (1995), 658–9.

[68] For Pharaoh's lean cows, see Genesis 41.

[69] On Swiss philosophers in Prussia in the eighteenth century, see for example Martin Fontius and Helmut Holzhey, eds., *Schweizer im Berlin des 18. Jahrhunderts* (Berlin, 1996).

[70] "M" stands for the academic master's degree. It also denotes 1,000, half of which is symbolized by "D," which also stands for the academic doctorate.

and if the latter, whom a wretched irony calls auditors, had any practice in hearing with their ears. – –

> "Where is Euthyphro's whip, oh timid jade?
> So that my cart does not get stuck – –"

Mythology here! mythology there![ee] Poetry is an imitation of nature the beautiful – and no doubt the revelations of Nieuwentyt, Newton, and Buffon[71] will be able to replace the lessons of fables in poor taste? – – Obviously they should do so, and they would do so, if they only could. – Why then does it not happen? – Because it is impossible, your poets say.

Nature works through the senses and the passions. But those who maim these instruments, how can they feel? Are crippled sinews fit for movement? – –

Your lying, murderous philosophy has cleared nature out of the way, and why do you demand that we are to imitate her? – So that you can renew the pleasure by becoming murderers of the pupils of nature, too –

Yes, you delicate critics of art!, you go on asking what is truth, and make for the door, because you cannot wait for an answer to this question[72] – Your hands are always washed, whether you are about to eat bread,[73] or whether you have just pronounced a death-sentence[74] – Do you not also ask: what means did you employ to clear nature out of the way? – – – Bacon accuses you of injuring her with your abstractions.[75] If Bacon is a witness to the truth, well then, stone him[76] – and throw lumps of earth or snowballs after his shadow –

[ee] Fontenelle, *Sur la poésie en général*, "Quand on saura employer d'une manière nouvelle les images fabuleuses, il est sûr qu'elles feront un grand effet." [See Fontenelle's *Œuvres complètes*, ed. Niderst (9 vols.; 1989–2001), vol. v, p. 547: "As soon as one knows how to use mythological images in a new way, they will certainly have a great effect."]

[71] Bernard Nieuwentyt (1654–1718), Dutch theologian, physician, and scientist; Georges-Louis Leclerc, comte de Buffon (1707–88), French naturalist.

[72] John 18:38: "Pilate saith unto him, What is truth? And when he had said this, he went out again."

[73] Matthew 15:2: "Why do thy disciples transgress the tradition of the elders? for they wash not their hands when they eat bread."

[74] Matthew 27:24: When Pilate saw that he could prevail nothing, but that rather a tumult was made, he took water, and washed his hands before the multitude, saying, I am innocent of the blood of this just person."

[75] See for example *Novum organon*, Aphorism 51: "to abstract from nature is not as effective as to dissect it" (tr. Rees and Wakely, *The Oxford Francis Bacon*, vol. xi, p. 187). The German word "to abstract" (*abziehen*) can also mean "to flay."

[76] As other witnesses to truth risked or endured stoning; see John 8:59 and Acts 7:59.

If one single truth like the sun prevails, it is day.[77] If you behold, instead of this one truth, as many as the sands of the seashore,[78] – and then behold a little light[ff] which excels in brightness[gg] a whole host of suns, it is a night beloved of poets and thieves. – – The poet[hh] at the beginning of days is the same as the thief[ii] at the end of days – –

All the colors of this most beautiful world grow pale once you extinguish its light, the firstborn of creation.[79] If the belly is your god,[80] then even the hairs on your head are under its guardianship.[81] Every creature will alternately become your sacrifice and your idol. – Subject against its will – but in hope,[82] it groans beneath your yoke or at your vain conduct; it does its best to escape your tyranny, and longs even in the most passionate embrace for that freedom with which the beasts paid Adam homage, when GOD brought them unto man to see what he would call them; for whatsoever man would call them, that was the name thereof.[83]

This analogy of man to the Creator endows all creatures with their substance and their stamp, on which depends fidelity and faith in all

---

[ff]
$$-- \text{et notho} ---$$
$$- \text{lumine} -$$
Catullus, Carmen saeculare ad Dianam
["And with bastard light"; from Catullus, Carmen 34.15–16.]

[gg]
$$-- \text{micat inter omnes}$$
Iulium sidus, velut inter ignes
Luna minores.
Horace, Ode 12, Book I
[Lines 46–8: "The Julian star shines among them all, as the Moon among lesser fires."]

[hh] 2 Corinthians 4:6. ["For God, who commanded the light to shine out of darkness, hath shined in our hearts, to give the light of the knowledge of the glory of God in the face of Jesus Christ."]

[ii] Revelation 16:15. ["Behold, I come as a thief"; cf. 1 Thessalonians 5:2, "For yourselves know perfectly that the day of the Lord so cometh as a thief in the night."]

[77] Genesis 1:16: "And God made two great lights; the greater light to rule the day, and the lesser light to rule the night: he made the stars also."

[78] Jeremiah 33:22: "As the host of heaven cannot be numbered, neither the sand of the sea measured."

[79] Light was firstborn in that it was the first thing God created (Genesis 1:3). But the "firstborn" is also Christ; cf. John 1 and Colossians 1:15: "Who is the image of the invisible God, the firstborn of every creature."

[80] Philippians 3:19: "Whose end is destruction, whose God is their belly, and whose glory is in their shame, who mind earthly things."

[81] Matthew 10:30: "But the very hairs of your head are all numbered."

[82] Romans 8:20: "For the creature was made subject to vanity, not willingly, but by reason of him who hath subjected the same in hope."

[83] Genesis 2:19: "And out of the ground the LORD God formed every beast of the field, and every fowl of the air; and brought them unto Adam to see what he would call them: and whatsoever Adam called every living creature, that was the name thereof."

nature. The more vividly this idea of the image of the invisible GOD[jj] dwells in our heart, the more able we are to see and taste[84] his loving-kindness[85] in creatures, observe it and grasp it with our hands. Every impression of nature in man is not only a memorial but also a warrant of fundamental truth: Who is the LORD. Every reaction of man unto created things is an epistle and seal that we partake of the divine nature,[kk] and that we are his offspring.[ll]

Oh for a muse like a refiner's fire, and like a fuller's soap![mm] – – She will dare to purify the natural use of the senses from the unnatural use of abstractions,[nn] by which our concepts of things are as maimed as the name of the Creator is suppressed and blasphemed. I speak with you, oh Greeks![86] for you deem yourself wiser than the chamberlains with the

---

[jj] – εἰκὼν τοῦ θεοῦ τοῦ ἀοράτου, Colossians 1:15. ["The image of the invisible God."]

[kk] – – θείας κοινωνοὶ φύσεως, 2 Peter 1:4; συμμόρφους τῆς εἰκόνος τοῦ υἱοῦ αὐτοῦ, Romans 8:29. [2 Peter 1:4: "partakers of the divine nature"; Romans 8:29: "conformed to the image of his Son."]

[ll] Acts 17:27, etc. [Acts 17:28: "For we are also his offspring." Cf. Acts 17:29, "we are the offspring of God."]

[mm] Malachi 3:2. ["for he is like a refiner's fire, and like fullers' soap."]

[nn] Bacon, "Aphorismi de interpretatione naturae et regno hominis," 124. Modulos ineptos mundorum et tanquam simiolas, quas in philosophiis (in the theories of the sciences) phantasiae hominum exstruxerunt, omnino dissipandas edicimus. Sciant itaque homines quantum intersit inter humanae mentis Idola et divinae mentis Ideas. Humanae mentis Idola nil aliud sunt quam abstractiones ad placitum: Divinae mentis Ideae sunt vera signacula Creatoris super creaturas, prout in materia per lineas veras et exquisitas imprimuntur et terminantur. Itaque ipsissimae res sunt veritas et utilitas: atque opera ipsa pluris facienda sunt, quatenus sunt veritatis pignora, quam propter vitae commoda (for the sake of the belly). Elsewhere Bacon repeats this reminder that we should use the works of nature not only as *beneficia vitae* but also as *veritatis pignora*. [Hamann adapts a passage from the second part ("Aphorisms concerning the interpretation of nature and the kingdom of man") of *Novum organon*. "I proclaim that the botched and (if you like) apish patterns of worlds which men's fancies have thrown together into philosophical systems should be utterly destroyed. So let men know how great is the gulf between the Idols of the human mind and the Ideas of the divine. The Idols of the human mind are nothing more than abstractions made arbitrarily. The Ideas of the divine are authentic seals that the Creator has stamped upon his creatures according as they are impressed and defined in matter by true and exact lines. Thus truth and utility are the very things themselves: and the very works give much more as warrants of the truth than providers of material benefits" (tr. Rees and Wakely, *The Oxford Francis Bacon*, vol. XI, p. 187; the translation has been adapted to follow Hamann's alterations). "Beneficia vitae" correspond to "the amenities of life" and "veritatis pignora" to "the warrant of truth."]

[84] Psalm 34:8: "O taste and see that the LORD is good."

[85] The word "Leutseligkeit," here translated as "loving-kindness," appears uniquely in the Luther Bible in Titus 3:4: "But after that the kindness and love [*Leutseligkeit*] of God our Saviour toward man appeared."

[86] Perhaps a reference to the art historian Johann Winckelmann (1717–68), who was influential in establishing Greek art as the model to be imitated.

gnostic key;[87] – just try to read the *Iliad* after filtering out, with your abstractions, the two vowels α and ω, and then give me your opinion of the poet's sense and melody![88]

Μῆνιν ·ειδε Θε· Πηληι ·δε· ·χιλῆος

Behold! the large and small Masorah[89] of philosophy has overwhelmed the text of nature, like the Great Flood.[90] Were not all its beauties and riches bound to turn into water? – Yet you perform far greater miracles than the gods ever delighted[oo] to do, with oak-trees[pp] and pillars of salt,[91] with petrified and alchemical metamorphoses and fables to convince the human race – You make nature blind, that she might be your guide! or rather, with your Epicureanism[92] you have put out the light of your own eyes, that you might be taken for prophets who conjure inspiration and expositions out of the empty air. – You would have dominion over nature, and you bind your own hands and feet with your Stoicism, so that in your poetic miscellanies you may sing falsetto on the diamond fetters of fate all the more movingly.

[oo] φιλοπαίγμονες γὰρ καὶ οἱ Θεοί. Socrates in the *Cratylus*. [Plato, *Cratylus* 406c: "For even the gods delight in play."]

[pp] Socrates to Phaedrus: οἱ δέ [γ',] ὦ φίλε, ἐν τῷ τοῦ Διὸς τοῦ Δωδωναίου ἱερῷ δρυὸς λόγους ἔφησαν μαντικοὺς πρώτους γενέσθαι· τοῖς μὲν οὖν τότε ἅτε οὐκ οὖσι σοφοῖς, ὥσπερ ὑμεῖς οἱ νέοι, ἀπέχρη δρυὸς καὶ πέτρας ἀκούειν ὑπ' εὐηθείας, εἰ μόνον ἀληθῆ λέγοιεν. Σοὶ δ' ἴσως διαφέρει τίς ὁ λέγων καὶ ποδαπός, οὐ γὰρ ἐκεῖνο μόνον σκοπεῖς, εἴτε οὕτως εἴτε ἄλλως ἔχει. [Plato, *Phaedrus* 275b–c: "They used to say, my friend, that the words of an oak in the holy place of Dodona were the first prophetic utterances. The people of that time, not being so wise as you young folks, were content in their simplicity to hear an oak or a rock, provided only it spoke the truth; but to you, perhaps, it makes a difference who the speaker is and where he comes from, for you do not consider whether his words are true or not" (tr. Fowler, Loeb Classical Library).]

[87] Presumably a reference to contemporary philosophers around Frederick the Great, including Voltaire. In Acts 8:27, Luther translates as "Kämmerer" (related to "Kammerherr," chamberlain) what the King James Bible translates as "eunuch."

[88] Since Christ is the alpha and the omega (Revelation 1:8, etc.), if Greeks deny him, they would not even be able to read the first line of the *Iliad*, which without those vowels would read as Hamann prints it (approximately, "Sing, · G·ddess, the wr·th ·f Peleus' s·n ·chilles").

[89] "The body of rules, principles, and traditions relating to the text of the Hebrew Scriptures, developed by Jewish scholars in the 6th–9th centuries" (*Oxford English Dictionary*). The small Masorah consists of notes in the margin; the large Masorah, of notes at the head and foot of columns.

[90] See Genesis 7.   [91] Lot's wife is turned into a pillar of salt in Genesis 19.

[92] Epicureanism, traditionally associated with atheism, influenced French skeptical thinkers like Saint-Evremond, Bayle, and Fontenelle.

If the passions are the members of dishonor, do they therefore cease to be instruments of virility?[93] Have you a wiser understanding of the letter of reason than the allegorical chamberlain of the Alexandrian Church had of the letter of the Scriptures when he castrated himself for the sake of the Kingdom of Heaven?[94] The prince of this aeon takes his favorites from among the greatest offenders against themselves; – – his court jesters are the worst enemies of fair nature, who indeed has Corybants and Gauls[95] as her pot-bellied priests,[96] but *esprits forts*[97] as her true worshippers.

A philosopher such as Saul[qq] sets up monastic rules – – passion alone gives hands, feet, and wings to abstractions as well as to hypotheses; – to images and signs it gives spirit, life, and tongue – – Where are swifter syllogisms? Where is the rolling thunder of eloquence begotten, and where is its companion – the monosyllable of lightning?[rr] – –

Why should I paraphrase One Word for you, readers ignorant according to your estate, honor, and office, with an infinite number of words? For you can observe for yourselves the phenomena of passion everywhere in human society; even as everything, however remote, can impulsively strike our hearts in a particular direction; even as each individual feeling extends over the range of all external objects;[ss] even as we know how to

---

[qq] 1 Samuel 14:24. ["For Saul had adjured the people, saying, Cursed be the man that eateth any food until evening, that I may be avenged on mine enemies. So none of the people tasted any food."]

[rr]   Brief as the lightning in the collied night,
          That (in a spleen) unfolds [both] heav'n and earth
          And ere [a] man has power to say, Behold!
          The jaws of darkness do devour it up.
          Shakespeare, *A Midsummer Night's Dream*
                [from Act I, scene 1]

[ss] "C'est l'effet ordinaire de notre ignorance de nous peindre tout semblable à nous et de repandre nos portraits dans toute nature," says Fontenelle in his *Histoire du théâtre français*. "Une grande passion est une espèce d'Ame immortelle à sa manière, et presque indépendante des Organes," Fontenelle in *Eloge de M. du Verney*. [See Fontenelle's *Œuvres complètes*, ed. Niderst (9 vols.; 1989–2001), vol. III, p. 45: "The ordinary effect of our ignorance is to depict us as all alike and to

93 Romans 6:13: "Neither yield ye your members as instruments of unrighteousness unto sin: but yield . . . your members as instruments of righteousness unto God."

94 Origen, a Church Father from Alexandria prone to allegorical exegesis of the Bible, is said to have castrated himself, inspired by a literal reading of Matthew 19:12.

95 Corybants are the mythical attendants of Cybele, the Anatolian mother-goddess; Gauls are Frenchmen, but in connection with Corybants they recall the Galli, the castrated priests of Cybele.

96 Adelung's dictionary records that the term *Bauchpfaffe*, literally "priest of the belly," was applied to ministers more concerned with their own comfort than with their parishioners.

97 An *esprit fort* is "a 'strongminded' person; usually, one who professes superiority to current prejudices, esp. a 'freethinker' in religion" (*Oxford English Dictionary*).

make the most general instances our own by applying them to ourselves personally, and hatch any private circumstances into the public spectacle of heaven and earth. – Each individual truth evolves into the foundation of a design more miraculously than that cow-hide evolved into the domain of a state;[98] and a ground-plan more capacious than the hemisphere is contained by a point of focus. – – In short, the perfection of the designs, the strength of the execution, – the conception and birth of new ideas and new expressions, the labor and rest of the wise man, the consolation and aversion he finds in them, lie buried from our senses in the fruitful womb of the passions.

The philologist's public, his world of readers, seems to resemble that lecture-hall which a single Plato filled.[tt] Antimachus continued confidently, as it is written:

> Non missura cutem nisi plena curoris hirudo.[99]

Just as if our learning were a mere recollection,[100] our attention is constantly directed to the monuments of the ancients, to shape our minds through memory. But why stop at the broken cisterns of the Greeks and forsake the fountain of the most living waters of antiquity?[101] Perhaps we do not really know ourselves what it is in the Greeks and Romans that we admire even to idolatry. This is where that accursed contradiction[uu] in our symbolic textbooks comes from, for to this day they are daintily bound in sheepskin, but within,[102] – verily,

---

extend our portraits over all of nature." The quotation from the eulogy of M. du Verney is found in vol. VII of the *Œuvres complètes*, p. 196: "a great passion is a kind of Soul, immortal in its way and almost independent of the Organs" (Hamann's capitals).]

[tt] Plato enim VNVS instar omnium est. Cicero in *Brutus*. ["For Plato alone is worth all of them." Hamann adapts Cicero's anecdote in *Brutus* LI [191]: When [Antimachus was] reading that long and well-known poem of his before an assembled audience, in the midst of his reading all his listeners left him but Plato; "I shall go on reading," he said, "just the same; for me Plato alone is as good as a hundred thousand" (tr. Hendrickson, Loeb Classical Library).]

[uu] Psalm 59:12. ["For the sin of their mouth and the words of their lips let them even be taken in their pride: and for cursing and lying which they speak."]

[98] Virgil in the *Aeneid* relates that Dido was given only as much land as a cow-hide would enclose; she cut the hide into thin stripes and founded Carthage.

[99] Horace, *Ars poetica* 476: "a leech that will not let go of the skin until it is full of blood."

[100] Cf. Socrates' demonstration in the *Meno* that Meno's slave must be recollecting, not learning, mathematical truths.

[101] Jeremiah 2:13: "For my people have committed two evils; they have forsaken me the fountain of living waters, and hewed them out cisterns, broken cisterns, that can hold no water."

[102] Matthew 7:15: "Beware of false prophets, which come to you in sheep's clothing, but inwardly they are ravening wolves."

within they are full of dead men's bones[103] and full of hypo-critical wickedness.[vv]

Like unto a man beholding his natural face in a glass, but after he beholds himself and goes his way, he straightway forgets what manner of man he was:[104] this is how we treat the ancients. – A painter sits for his self-portrait in a wholly different spirit. – Narcissus (the bulbous plant[105] of *beaux esprits*)[106] loves his image more than his life.[ww] [107]

[vv] See throughout Part 11 of *Briefe, die neueste Literatur betreffend*, a little here, a little there, but mainly p. 131. [On the page which Hamann cites, Friedrich Nicolai anonymously objected to a recent book of poems which included a "Kritische Abhandlung einiger Anmerkungen über das Natürliche in der Dichtkunst und die Natur des Menschen" ("Critical treatment of certain remarks on the natural in poetry and in human nature"). Nicolai wrote that the treatise was like whited sepulchres which indeed appear beautiful outward but are within full of dead men's bones and all uncleanness. Hamann accuses the reviewer of hypocrisy and directs his own biblical allusion against him.]

[ww] Ovid, *Metamorphoses*, Book 3.

[416]   – bibit, visae correptus imagine formae.
Spem sine corpore amat, corpus putat esse, quod umbra est.
Adstupet ipse sibi vultuque inmotus eodem
haeret ut e Pario formatum marmore signum.
Spectat humi positus geminum, sua lumina, sidus
et dignos Baccho, dignos et Apolline crines,
inpubesque genas et eburnea colla, decusque
oris et in niveo mixtum candore ruborem;
cunctaque miratur, quibus est mirabilis ipse.

[438]   – – opaca fusus in herba
spectat inexpleto mendacem lumine formam
perque oculos perit ipse suos; paulumque levatus
ad circumstantes tendens sua bracchia silvas:
'Ecquis, io silvae, crudelius' inquit 'amavit?
(Scitis enim et multis latebra opportuna fuistis) – – –

[446]   Et placet et video; sed quod videoque placetque,
non tamen invenio. Tantus tenet error amantem!
Quoque magis doleam, nec nos mare separat ingens
nec via, nec montes, nec clausis moenia portis.
Exigua prohibemur aqua – – –

[453]   Posse putes tangi. MINIMUM est, quod amantibus obstat.
Quisquis es, huc exi! – –

[457]   Spem mihi nescio quam vultu promittis –

[103] Matthew 23:27: "Woe unto you, scribes and Pharisees, hypocrites! for ye are like unto whited sepulchres, which indeed appear beautiful outward, but are within full of dead men's bones, and of all uncleanness."

[104] James 1:23–4: "For if any be a hearer of the word, and not a doer, he is like unto a man beholding his natural face in a glass: For he beholdeth himself, and goeth his way, and straightway forgetteth what manner of man he was."

[105] The narcissus is a bulbous plant.   [106] A clever wit.

[107] Hamann abridges the story of Narcissus from Ovid, *Metamorphoses* 3.416–510: "He drinks and is smitten by the sight of the beautiful form. He loves an insubstantial hope and thinks that substance

Salvation comes from the Jews.¹⁰⁸ – I had not yet seen them, but I was awaiting sounder concepts in their philosophical writings – to your shame – Christians! – Yet you feel the sting of that worthy name by which

[459]   – – lacrimas quoque saepe notavi
me lacrimante tuas; nutu quoque signa remittis –

[463]   In te ego sum. Sensi, nec me mea fallit imago –

[466]   Quod cupio mecum est: inopem me copia fecit.
O utinam a nostro secedere corpore possem!
Votum in amante novum – –'

[474]   DIXIT et ad faciem rediit male sanus eandem
et lacrimis turbavit aquas, obscuraque moto
reddita forma lacu est; quam cum vidisset abire,

[478]   – clamavit: 'Liceat, quod tangere non est,
adspicere et misero praebere alimenta furori!' –

[502]   Ille caput viridi fessum submisit in herba;
lumina nox clausit domini mirantia formam:
tum quoque se, postquam est inferna sede receptus,
in Stygia spectabat aqua – – –

[508]   Iamque rogum quassasque faces feretrumque parabant,
nusquam corpus erat. Croceum pro corpore florem
inveniunt foliis medium cingentibus albis.

[See n. 107.]

which is only shadow. He looks in speechless wonder at himself and hangs there motionless in the same expression, like a statue carved from Parian marble. Prone on the ground, he gazes at his eyes, twin stars, and his locks, worthy of Bacchus, worthy of Apollo; on his smooth cheeks, his ivory neck, the glorious beauty of his face, the blush mingled with snowy white: all things, in short, he admires for which he himself is admired . . . stretched out on the shaded grass, he gazes on that false image with eyes that cannot look their fill and through his own eyes perishes; raising himself a little, and stretching his arms to the trees, he cries: 'Did anyone, o ye woods, ever love more cruelly than I? (You know, for you have been the favorite haunt of many lovers.) . . . I am charmed, and I see; but what I see and what charms me I cannot find. So great a delusion holds my love! And, to make me grieve the more, no mighty ocean separates us, no mountain ranges, no city walls with close-shut gate. By a thin barrier of water we are kept apart . . . You would think he could be touched. So SMALL a thing it is that separates our loving hearts. Whoever you are, come forth hither! . . . Some ground for hope you offer with your friendly looks . . . and I have often seen tears, when I weep, on your cheeks. My becks you answer with your nod . . . I am in you. I have felt it, I know now my own image . . . What I desire, I have; the very abundance of my riches beggars me. O that I might be parted from my body! A strange prayer for a lover . . .' He SPOKE and, half distraught, turned again to the same image. His tears ruffled the water, and dimly the image came back from the troubled pool. As he saw it thus depart . . . , he cried, 'Still may it be mine to gaze on what I may not touch, and by that gaze to feed my unhappy passion!' . . . He drooped his weary head on the green grass and night sealed the eyes that marveled at their master's beauty. And even when he had been received into the infernal abodes, he kept on gazing on his image in the Stygian pool . . . And now they were preparing the funeral pile, the torches, and the bier; but his body was nowhere to be found. In place of his body they find a flower, its yellow center girt with white petals" (tr. Miller, Loeb Classical Library, adapted; Hamann's capitals).

¹⁰⁸ John 4:22: "for salvation is of the Jews"; Hamann's allusion to the Luther Bible is more exact.

you are called[xx] as little as you feel the honor GOD did himself in taking the derogatory name Son of Man – – – –

Nature and Scripture, then, are the materials of the beautiful, creative, and imitative spirit – – Bacon compares matter with Penelope;[109] – her impudent suitors are the philosophers and scribes. The tale of the beggar who appeared at the court of Ithaca you know, for has not Homer translated it into Greek verse, and Pope into English verse?[110]

But how are we to raise the defunct languages of nature from the dead? – – By making pilgrimages to happy Arabia,[111] by going on crusades to the East, and by restoring their magic art, to steal which, we must employ old women's cunning, for that is the best sort. – Cast your eyes down, you slow bellies,[112] and read what Bacon[yy] thought up about the magic art. – Silken feet in dancing shoes will not bear you on such a burdensome journey, so be ready to be shown a better way through hyperbole[zz] –

[xx] James 2:7. ["Do not they blaspheme that worthy name by the which ye are called?"]

[yy] M AGIA[. . .]in eo potissimum versabatur, ut architecturas et fabricas rerum naturalium et civilium symbolizantes notaret – – Nec similitudines merae sunt (quales hominibus fortasse parum perspicacibus videri possint) sed plane una eademque naturae vestigia aut signacula diversis materiis et subiectis impressa. So Bacon in the third book of *De augmentis scientiarum*, in which he claims to explain the magic art also by means of a "scientia consensuum rerum universalium," and in the light of this, the appearance of the Wise Men at Bethlehem. [Bacon, *De augmentis scientiarum*, Book 3, chap. 1: "But the chief business of the [Persian] magic [so much celebrated] was to note the correspondences between the architectures and fabrics of things natural and things civil . . . Neither are these mere similitudes (as men of narrow observation may perhaps conceive them to be), but plainly the same footsteps of nature treading or printing upon different subjects and matters." The second quotation, "knowledge of the universal consents of things," comes from Book 3, chap. 5 of this work: "For among the Persians magic was taken for a sublime wisdom, and the knowledge of the universal consents of things; and so the three kings who came from the east to worship Christ were called by the name of Magi." The Latin passages are found on pp. 256 and 300 of vol. II of Bacon's *Works*; the English translation, in vol. VIII, pp. 474 and 513.]

[zz] – καὶ ἔτι καθ' ὑπερβολὴν ὁδὸν ὑμῖν δείκνυμι, 1 Corinthians 12:31. ["And yet I shew you unto a more excellent way." In the Greek, the idiom corresponding to "more excellent" (καθ'ὑπερβολήν) suggests "hyperbole."]

[109] In *De augmentis scientiarum*, Book 2, chap. 13 and *De sapientia veterum* ("On the wisdom of the ancients"), chap. 6 ("Pan, or *Nature*"), Bacon discusses the mythological origins of Pan, as springing either from Mercury ("the Word of God") or from Penelope's promiscuous intercourse with all her suitors. See Bacon's *Works*, vol. II, pp. 226–9 (Latin) and vol. VIII, pp. 444–7 (English translation).

[110] Odysseus returned to Ithaca disguised as a beggar and overcame the suitors who had oppressed Penelope. Alexander Pope and his collaborators completed a translation of the *Odyssey* in 1726.

[111] An allusion to the scientific expedition to "Arabia Felix" and elsewhere in Arabic lands under Carsten Niebuhr (1733–1815); it sailed in January 1761. Michaelis provided the main impulse for the expedition.

[112] Titus 1:12: "Cretians are alway liars, evil beasts, slow bellies."

O you who rent the heavens and came down! at whose arrival the mountains flowed down as hot water boils on melting fire, that your name be made known to your adversaries, who nevertheless call themselves by it; and that anointed nations may learn to tremble[113] before the wonders that you do, which are beyond their understanding. – Let new fool's-fire rise in the Orient! – Let the pert curiosity of their magi be roused by new stars, that they bear their treasures in person to our country. Myrrh! frankincense! and their gold! which mean more to us than their magic art![114] – Let kings be gulled by it, let their philosophical muse snort[115] at children and children's lore[116] in vain; but let not Rachel weep in vain![117]

Why should we swallow death from the pots,[118] to make the garnish palatable for the children of the prophets? And how shall we appease the vexed spirit[119] of the Scripture: "Will I eat the flesh of bulls, or drink the blood of goats?"[120] Neither the dogmatic thoroughness of the orthodox Pharisees nor the poetic opulence of the free-thinking Sadducees[121] will renew the mission of the spirit which inspired GOD's holy men (εὐκαίρως ἀκαίρως[122]) to speak and write. – – That bosom disciple[123] of the Only Begotten, which is in the bosom of the Father, has declared it to us:[124]

---

[113] Isaiah 64:1–2: "Oh that thou wouldest rend the heavens, that thou wouldest come down, that the mountains might flow down at thy presence, As when the melting fire burneth, the fire causeth the waters to boil, to make thy name known to thine adversaries, that the nations may tremble at thy presence!"

[114] Matthew 2 relates the story of the Magi.

[115] In German, an allusion to Acts 9:1 is clearer: "And Saul, yet breathing out [*schnaubte*, "snorted"] threatenings and slaughter against the disciples of the Lord."

[116] In contrast to Christ, as at Mark 10:14.

[117] The contempt of Frederick the Great and his court for the childishness of Christianity is compared to Herod's massacre of the innocents. Cf. Matthew 2:18: "In Rama was there a voice heard, lamentation, and weeping, and great mourning, Rachel weeping for her children, and would not be comforted, because they are not."

[118] In 2 Kings 4:38–41, Elisha in a time of dearth orders his servant to prepare food for the sons of the prophets. The servant unknowingly adds a poisonous gourd to the pot. When the men eat, they cry out, "O thou man of God, there is death in the pot" (v. 40). Elisha then adds meal to the pottage, "And there was no harm in the pot" (v. 41).

[119] Isaiah 63:10: "But they rebelled, and vexed his holy Spirit."   [120] Psalm 50:13.

[121] The Pharisees and Sadducees were two of the major Jewish sects at the time of Christ. On some of their differences, see Acts 23. Here, as throughout the essay, Hamann has in mind his own contemporaries.

[122] "In season, out of season," from 2 Timothy 4:2.

[123] John 13:23: "Now there was leaning on Jesus' bosom one of his disciples, whom Jesus loved."

[124] John 1:18: "No man hath seen God at any time, the only begotten Son, which is in the bosom of the Father, he hath declared him."

that the spirit of prophecy lives in the testimony[125] of the ONE NAME, whereby alone we are saved[126] and may inherit the promise of the life that now is and of that which is to come;[127] – the name which no man knows saving he that receives it,[128] the name which is above every name: That at the name of JESUS every knee should bow, of things in heaven, and things in earth, and things under the earth; And that every tongue should confess that JESUS CHRIST is LORD, to the glory of GOD![129] – the Creator, who is blessed for ever, Amen![130]

Thus the testimony of JESUS is the spirit of prophecy,[aaa] and the first sign by which he reveals the majesty in his form of a servant[131] transforms the holy books of the covenant into fine old wine, which deceives the judgment of the governor of the feast[132] and strengthens the weak stomach[133] of the critics. "Lege libros propheticos non intellecto CHRISTO," says the Punic[bbb] [134] Father of the Church, "quid tam insipidum et fatuum

---

[aaa] Revelation 19:10. ["For the testimony of Jesus is the spirit of prophecy.']

[bbb] See pp. 66–7 of the prize-winning answer to the question of the influence of opinions on language and of language, set by the Royal Academy of Sciences in 1759. In this connection *Ars pun-ica, sive Flos linguarum: The art of punning, or, The flower of languages in seventy-nine rules for the farther improvement of conversation and help of memory. By the labour and industry of TOM PUN-SIBI* may also be consulted.

Ex ambiguo dicta vel argutissima putantur, sed non semper in ioco, saepe etiam in gravitate versantur – Ingeniosi enim videtur vim verbi in aliud, atque ceteri accipiant, posse dicere. Cicero, *De oratore*, Book 2.

The second edition of *Ars pun-ica* 1719, octavo. This learned work (alas, I possess a defective copy only) has as its author – Swift, the glory of the priesthood and the shame (*Essay on Criticism*). It begins with logical, physical, and moral definitions. In the logical sense, "Punnata dicuntur id ipsum quod sunt aliorum esse dicuntur aut alio quovis modo ad aliud referentur." According to

[125] Revelation 19:10: "for the testimony of Jesus is the spirit of prophecy."
[126] Acts 4:12: "for there is none other name under heaven given among men, whereby we must be saved."
[127] 1 Timothy 4:8: "godliness is profitable unto all things, having promise of the life that now is, and of that which is to come."
[128] Revelation 2:17: "To him that overcometh will I give to eat of the hidden manna, and will give him a white stone, and in the stone a new name written, which no man knoweth saving he that receiveth it."
[129] Philippians 2:9–11: "Wherefore God also hath highly exalted him, and given him a name which is above every name: That at the name of Jesus every knee should bow, of things in heaven, and things in earth, and things under the earth; And that every tongue should confess that Jesus Christ is Lord, to the glory of God the Father."
[130] Romans 1:25: "who changed the truth of God into a lie, and worshipped and served the creature more than the Creator, who is blessed for ever. Amen."
[131] Philippians 2:7: "But made himself of no reputation, and took upon him the form of a servant."
[132] Christ turned the water into wine at a marriage in Cana (John 2).
[133] 1 Timothy 5:23: "use a little wine for thy stomach's sake."
[134] The Punic Church Father is Augustine. "Punic" (Carthaginian) refers to Augustine's origins in North Africa; with this word Hamann begins an excursus on puns.

(Footnote 'bbb' *cont.*)

the natural science (of the adventurous and capricious Cardano), "Punning is an Art of Harmonious Jingling upon Words, which passing in at the Ears and falling upon the Diaphragma, excites a titillary Motion in those Parts, and this being convey'd by the Animal Spirits into the Muscles of the Face raises the Cockles of the Heart." But according to casuistry, it is "a Virtue, that most effectually promotes the End of Good Fellowship." – – An example of this artful virtue can be found among others of the same ilk in the aforecited answer to the Punic comparison between Mahomet the Prophet and Augustine the Church Father, a comparison which looks plausible to an amphibological lover of poetry (with an imagination half enthusiastic, half scholastic) who is not nearly learned enough to appreciate the figurative language properly, let alone be able to scrutinize religious experience. The good bishop spoke Hebrew without knowing it, just as the bourgeois gentleman spoke prose without knowing it, and just as even today, through learned questions and their answers, a man can reveal without knowing it the barbarism of his age and the treacherous thought of his heart, at the cost of this profound truth: that all have sinned, and come short of the glory that is imputed to them, the lying prophet of Arabia as much as the good African shepherd and also the clever wit (whom I should have mentioned first of all) who thought up that far-fetched comparison between the two believers in providence by putting together such ridiculous parallel passages according to the Punic theory of reason of our modern cabbalists, for whom every fig-leave yields a sufficient reason, and every allusion its own fulfilment. [See n. 134.]

(Footnote 134 *cont.*)

The prize-winning essay was by Michaelis (see Hamann's *Essay on an Academic Question*, above). Michaelis, on pp. 64–5 of the English translation (1769) of his essay, compares Mahomet and Augustine: "They both had a natural bent to poetry . . . Neither of the two had so much learning as to delude themselves from the elusions of figurative style." In particular, Michaelis argues that the doctrine of God's providence was maintained by taking biblical passages in a literal sense when they were meant in a figurative sense. Hamann's excursus on punning is directed here against Michaelis' attack on the figurative language of the Bible and on God's providence; it continues in Hamann's next footnote.

Ars pun-ica, sive Flos linguarum (Hamann gives the full title as it appears on the title page) was identified on the title page of the second edition as the work of Jonathan Swift (both editions appeared in 1719); it is now attributed to Thomas Sheridan (1687–1753).

Cicero, *De oratore* 2.250 [chap. 61]: "Bons-mots prompted by an equivocation are deemed the very wittiest, though not always concerned with jesting, but often with what is important." Cicero, *De oratore* 2.254 [chap. 62]: "for the power to speak the force of a word into a sense quite different from that in which other people understand it seems to indicate a man of talent" (tr. Sutton and Rackham, Loeb Classical Library). This quotation appears on the title page of *Ars pun-ica*.

Alexander Pope in *An Essay on Criticism* (1711) refers to Erasmus, "The Glory of the Priesthood, and the Shame!" (l. 694).

Ars pun-ica begins with "The Logical Definition of Punning" and provides the Latin definition which appears to be a parody of similar Aristotelian and scholastic definitions (cf. Aristotle, *Categories* 6a36). It is followed on p. 2 by a free translation: "PUNS in their very nature and Constitution have a Relation to something else, or if they have not, any other Reason why, will serve as well."

The logical definition is followed by "The Physical Definition of PUNNING, according to Cardan". Girolamo Cardano (1501–75) was an Italian doctor, astrologer, and mathematician. "The Moral Definition of PUNNING" follows next.

An amphibology is a quibble, an ambiguous statement.

"The good bishop spoke Hebrew without realizing it" is a quotation from Michaelis' essay; see p. 65 of the English translation: "Latin indeed was spoken in the cities of Africa, but it was not the Roman Latin, being adulterated with a strong African tinge. If Latin was the body of that language, its soul was formed of the Punic . . . Thus the good bishop spoke Hebrew without knowing it."

88

invenies. Intelliges ibi CHRISTUM, non solum sapit, quod legis, sed etiam inebriat."[135] – "But we must put a stop here to those wicked and high flying spirits, – – The old Adam must first die before he tolerates this and drinks the strong wine. Therefore beware that you do not drink wine while you are still a suckling. There is a limit, a time, and an age for every doctrine."[ccc]

After GOD had grown weary of speaking to us through nature and Scripture, through created things and prophets, through reasonings and figures, through poets and seers, and grown short of breath, he spoke unto us at last in the evening of day through his Son[136] – yesterday and to day![137] – until the promise of his coming, no longer in the form a servant,[138] shall be fulfilled –

> Thou art the King of Glory, O CHRIST,
> Thou art the everlasting SON of the FATHER,
> Thou didst not abhor the Virgin's womb – –[ddd]

[ccc] Our Luther's words (reading Augustine, it is said, spoiled his taste somewhat), taken from his famous preface to the Epistle to the Romans, which I never tire of reading, just as I never tire of his preface to the Psalms. I have introduced this passage by means of an accommodation, as they say, because in it Luther speaks of the abyss of divine providence, and, after his admirable custom, rests assured upon his dictum: "For in the absence of suffering and the cross one cannot deal with predestination without harm and without secret anger against God." [See *Luther's Works* (American Edition) vol. XXXV, p. 378, for both the quotation from Luther in the main text and the one in Hamann's footnote. The "strong wine" is the mystery of predestination. In theology, accommodation is "the adaptation of a text or teaching to altered circumstances" (*Oxford Concise Dictionary of the Christian Church*).]

[ddd] The devout reader will complete the hymn-like cadence of this stanza for himself. My memory abandons me out of sheer wilfulness. – Semper ad eventum – – et quae desperat – relinquit. [The partially quoted stanza in the main text comes from Luther's translation of the "Te Deum." The Latin in the note comes from Horace, *Ars poetica* 148, "always on to the end – and what he despairs of accomplishing – he abandons."]

Monsieur Jourdain, who spoke in prose without knowing it, is the title character from Molière's *Le Bourgeois Gentilhomme*.

Acts 8:22: "Repent therefore of this thy wickedness, and pray God, if perhaps the thought of thine heart may be forgiven thee."

Romans 3:23: "For all have sinned, and come short of the glory of God."

"Sufficient reason" is a Leibnizian doctrine favored by Christian Wolff and other philosophers during the Enlightenment.

[135] Augustine, *In Iohannis Evangelium Tractatus CXXIX* ("129 Tracts on the Gospel of John"), Tract 9 (on John 2:1–11), para. 3: "Read all the prophetic books without perceiving Christ: what will you find so insipid and so silly? Understand Christ there, and what you are reading not only becomes savory, but it also intoxicates" (tr. Rettig, *Tractates on the Gospel of John*, The Fathers of the Church, Catholic University of America).

[136] Hebrews 1:1–2: "God, who at sundry times and in divers manners spake in time past unto the fathers by the prophets, Hath in these last days spoken unto us by his Son."

[137] Hebrews 13:8: "Jesus Christ the same yesterday, and to day."   [138] Philippians 2:7.

We would be bringing a railing accusation[139] if we were to call our clever sophists poor, dumb devils when they compare the law-giver of the Jews to an ass's head and the proverbs of their master-singers to dove's dung;[140] yet them shall the day of the LORD[141] – – a Sabbath darker than the midnight[142] in which indomitable fleets are stubble[143] – – The most complaisant zephyr, herald of the last thunderstorm – as poetical – as the LORD of Hosts could only think and express it, will drown the blasts of even the sturdiest trumpeter: – – Abraham's joy[144] will reach its pinnacle – his cup will run over[145] – The very last tears! more precious beyond measure than all the pearls with which the last Queen of Egypt lived her prodigal life;[146] – these very last tears shed over the last flame of Sodom and the abduction of the last martyr[eee] GOD with his own hand will wipe away[147] from the eye of Abraham, the father of the faithful[148] – –

That day of the LORD, which gives Christians the courage to preach the LORD's death,[149] will reveal the dumbest village-devils among all the angels for whom the fires of hell are prepared.[150] The devils believe and tremble![151] – but your senses, crazed by the subtlety[152] of reason, tremble not – You laugh when Adam the sinner chokes on an apple, and Anacreon

---

[eee] 2 Peter 2:8. ["For that righteous man dwelling among them, in seeing and hearing, vexed his righteous soul from day to day with their unlawful deeds."]

[139] Jude 1:9; 2 Peter 2:11.

[140] 2 Kings 6:25: "and, behold, they besieged it, until an ass's head was sold for fourscore pieces of silver, and the fourth part of a cab of dove's dung for five pieces of silver."

[141] Possibly a reference to Malachi 4:1: "and the day that cometh shall burn them up."

[142] Joel 3:14–15: "for the day of the LORD is near in the valley of decision. The sun and the moon shall be darkened, and the stars shall withdraw their shining"; Amos 5:12, "the day of the LORD is darkness, and not light"; Revelation 6:12: "and the sun became black as sackcloth of hair."

[143] Malachi 4:1: "For, behold, the day cometh, that shall burn as an oven; and all the proud, yea, and all that do wickedly, shall be stubble."

[144] John 8:56: "Your father Abraham rejoiced to see my day."

[145] Psalm 23:5: "my cup runneth over."

[146] According to Pliny (*Natural History* 9.58.119–21), Cleopatra owned the two largest pearls in history. To impress on Antony the luxuriance of a banquet she was hosting, she dissolved one in vinegar and swallowed it.

[147] Isaiah 25:8: "the Lord GOD will wipe away tears from off all faces"; Revelation 7:17: "God shall wipe away all tears from their eyes"; Revelation 21:4, "And God shall wipe away all tears from their eyes."

[148] Romans 4:16: "Abraham; who is the father of us all."

[149] 1 Corinthians 1:23: "But we preach Christ crucified."

[150] Matthew 25:41: "Depart from me, ye cursed, into everlasting fire, prepared for the devil and his angels."

[151] James 2:19: "the devils also believe, and tremble."

[152] 2 Corinthians 11:3: "as the serpent beguiled Eve through his subtilty."

the wise man on the grape-stone![153] – Do you not laugh when the geese fill the Capitol with alarm,[154] – and the ravens feed the patriot[155] whose spirit was Israel's artillery and cavalry?[156] – You congratulate yourself secretly on your blindness when GOD on the cross is numbered among the criminals,[157] – and when some abomination in Geneva or Rome, in the opera or the mosque, becomes apotheosed or colocynthed.[158]

> Pinge duos angues! pueri, sacer est locus; extra
> meiite. discedo – – –
>
> Persius[159]

The birth of a genius will be accompanied, as usual, by the martyr's feast of the holy innocents – I take the liberty of comparing rhyme and meter to innocent children, for our most recent poetry seems to put them in mortal danger.

If rhyme belongs to the same genus as paronomasia[fff] and word-play, then its origins must be almost as old as the nature of language and our sense-impressions. – – He who finds the yoke of rhyme too

---

[fff] See n. 76 by Michaelis in his edition of Lowth's *Praelectiones*, Lecture 15; and Algarotti, vol. III. [In the note to his edition of Lowth (p. 290), Michaelis mentions a work by his father on paronomasia (Christian Benedict Michaelis, *De sacra paronomasia*, 1737); he himself writes that he dislikes such word-play in serious literature.

The works of Francesco Algarotti (1712–64), an Italian philosopher and friend of Frederick the Great, were translated into French and published in seven volumes. His "Essay sur la rime" is found in vol. III; on. pp. 75–6, he writes that rhyme was introduced along with the duel and feudal law as an agreeable contagion; it evolved from leonine verse and infected all the vernacular languages.]

[153] According to Pliny (*Natural History* 7.7.44), Anacreon died by choking on a raisin-stone. The anecdote has been retold by later poets, including Abraham Cowley ("Elegie upon Anacreon: Who was choaked by a Grape-Stone") and Johann Friedrich Lauson ("Das Küßchen," 1754), the latter a friend of Hamann's.

[154] The Capitoline geese warned the Romans that the city was under attack by the Gauls (see for example Livy 5.47).

[155] In the wilderness Elijah was fed by the ravens, 1 Kings 17:4–6.

[156] In 2 Kings 1, Elijah, unarmed, defeats the captains of the king of Samaria.

[157] Mark 15:28: "And he was numbered with the transgressors."

[158] In one interpretation, Hamann is contrasting the Catholic church at Rome and the Calvinist church of Geneva. The elaborate Catholic worship is compared to opera and reaches an apotheosis; the austere Calvinist service is compared to a mosque and is purged by the colocynth, which furnishes a purgative drug (cf. 2 Kings 4, where those who ate the pottage into which the gourd had been mixed called it "death in the pot" and n. 118 above). Additionally, the word "colocynth" recalls Seneca's satire against the deified Claudius, *Apocolocyntosis* ("the gourdification," a pun on apotheosis).

[159] Persius, *Satire* 1.113–14: "Paint two snakes. Children, the place is sacred; piss away from here. I am leaving."

heavy to bear is not thereby justified in denigrating its talent.^{ggg} The bachelor[160] would otherwise have given this frivolous pen as much occasion for a pasquinade as Plato would have had to immortalize Aristophanes' hiccups in the *Symposium*,[161] or Scarron his own hiccups in a sonnet.[162]

The free construction which Klopstock,[163] that great restorer of lyric song, has permitted himself is presumably an archaism, a happy imitation of the mysterious mechanics of sacred poetry among the ancient Hebrews. In it, according to the shrewd observations of the most thorough critics of our time,^{hhh} [164] we apprehend nothing more than "an artful prose broken down into all the small units of the periods, each one of which can be taken as a verse in a particular meter; and the reflections and feelings of the most ancient and sacred poets seem of their own accord" (perhaps just as randomly as the sun motes[165] of Epicurus) "to have arranged themselves into symmetrical lines which are full of harmony, although they have no (prescribed or mandatory) meter."

---

^{ggg} Gently rhyme does steal into the heart, when it is not upon compulsion;
It supports, adorns the harmony, and fixes speech in memory.
Elegien und Briefe (Strasbourg, 1760)

[Ludwig Heinrich von Nicolay (1737–1820) published his *Elegien und Briefe* ("Elegies and letters") in 1760; see p. 81.]

^{hhh} See the editor's fourth note to Lowth's third lecture, p. 49; and see also the fifty-first letter in the third part of *Briefe, die neueste Literatur betreffend*. [The note by Michaelis discusses Lowth's lecture on the free Hebrew meter, which he compares to recitative. Lessing's words (on Klopstock), which Hamann adapts and quotes in the main text, appeared in *Briefe, die neueste Literatur betreffend*, Part 3, letter 51 (August 16, 1759; "Letters concerning the most recent literature"). On p. 103 Lessing wrote, "But what do you say to this kind of verse, if I may even call it verse? For in actuality it is nothing more than an artful prose, broken down into all the small units of the periods, each of which may be taken as verse in a particular meter." On p. 99 he wrote, "They [the expressed sentiments] seem of their own accord to have arranged themselves into symmetrical lines which are full of harmony, although they have no definite meter."]

[160] Elsewhere (*Werke*, vol. II, p. 239) Hamann explains that by "bachelor" he means a verse for which a rhyming line cannot be found.
[161] Plato, *Symposium* 185c–e.
[162] Paul Scarron (1610–60), poet and playwright who specialized in the burlesque style. Shortly before his death, he is said to have wished to write a satire against hiccups; see La Fontaine, "Epigramme sur un mot de Scarron qui était près de mourir."
[163] Friedrich Gottlieb Klopstock (1724–1803), epic and lyric poet, imitated classical meters in German poetry, including what were understood as the "free rhythms" of the Pindaric ode.
[164] The "most thorough critics" are Michaelis and Lessing.
[165] For Democritus and Pythagoras, sun motes are the visible form of the atoms (see Aristotle, *De anima* 1.2, 404a).

Homer's monotonous meter ought to strike us as at least as paradoxical as the unboundenness of our German Pindar.[iii] [166] My amazement at or ignorance of the reason that the Greek poet always used the same meter was tempered when I made a journey through Courland and Lithuania. In certain districts of these regions, you can hear the Lettish or non-German people at work singing just a single cadence of a few notes, which is very much like a poetic meter. If a poet were to emerge among them, it would be quite natural for him to tailor all his lines to this measure established by their voices. It would demand too much time to place this small detail (ineptis gratum fortasse – qui volunt illa calamistris inurere)[167] in the appropriate light, compare it with several other phenomena, trace its causes, and develop fruitful consequences –

> Iam satis terris nivis atque dirae
> grandinis misit Pater et rubente
> dextera sacras iaculatus arces
> terruit urbem,
>
> terruit gentis, grave ne rediret
> saeculum Pyrrhae nova monstra questae,
> omne cum Proteus pecus egit altos
> visere montes. – –

Horace[168]

[iii] Would it not be charming if Herr Klopstock were to specify to his printer or to a Margot la Ravaudeuse (as the philologist's muse) the reasons why he had printed in separate lines his poetic sentiments, which the vulgar think are concerned with *qualitates occultae* and which the language of dalliance calls sentiments par excellence. Despite the gibberish of my dialect, I would quite willingly acknowledge Herr Klopstock's prosaic style to be a model of classical perfection. From having made a trial of a few specimens, I would credit this author with such a profound knowledge of his mother tongue, particularly of its prosody, that his musical versification seems the best suited as the lyric raiment for a singer who seeks to shun the commonplace. – I distinguish the original compositions of our Asaph from his transformations of ancient church hymns, indeed even from his epic, whose story is well-known, and resembles that of Milton, if not entirely, at least in outline. [Louis Charles Fougeret de Monbron (c. 1720–61) published the novel *Margot la Ravaudeuse* ("Margot the mender/darner") in 1750; it was the story of a prostitute. See *Romanciers libertins du XVIIIe siècle*, ed. Lasowski (Paris, 2000), 801–66.

"Qualitates occultae," hidden qualities, a scholastic term; they were opposed by Descartes, Newton, and others.

To Asaph, one of the leaders of David's choir, are attributed Psalms 50 and 73–83. Klopstock is an Asaph because of his religious poetry, which includes his *Geistliche Lieder* ("Spiritual songs") and his epic poem, modeled on Milton, *Der Messias* ("The Messiah").]

[166] Klopstock is the German Pindar. In German the word "unbound" can mean "in prose."
[167] Cicero, *Brutus* 75 [262], slightly adapted: "perhaps gratifying to the inept . . . who want to crimp it with their curling irons."
[168] Horace, *Ode* 1.2.1–8: "Already Jove has sent upon the earth enough snow and fierce hale, and with his red right arm he has struck the sacred citadel and terrified the city; he has terrified the

Apostille[169]

As the oldest reader of this rhapsody in cabbalistic prose, I find myself obliged by the right of primogeniture to bequeath to my younger brethren who will come after me one more example of a merciful judgment, as follows:

Everything in this aesthetic nutshell tastes of vanity! – of vanity![170] – The rhapsodist[jjj] has read, observed, reflected, sought and found agreeable words, quoted faithfully, and like a merchant ship fetched and brought his food from afar.[171] He has added up sentence and sentence as arrows[kkk] are counted on a battle-field; and circumscribed his figures as stakes measure off a tent. Instead of stakes and arrows, he has, with the petit-maîtres[172] and sophomores of his time written * * * * * * * * and – – – – – – – – obelisks and asterisks.[lll]

[jjj] – οἱ ῥαψῳδοί – ἑρμηνέων ἑρμηνεῖς. Socrates in Plato's *Ion*. [Plato, *Ion* 535a: "Rhapsodes – interpreters of interpreters."]

[kkk] Procopius, *De bello Persico* 1.18. [Procopius was a Greek historian of the sixth century AD. His major work is *History of the Wars of Justinian*, of which books 1 and 2 deal with the first Persian war ("de bello Persico"). In 1.18.30–5 of the *History*, Procopius remarks that although the Persians, almost all of them bowmen, shot more rapidly than the Romans, their bows were weak and did not inflict much damage; and that though the Roman bowmen were fewer and much slower, the bows were stiffer and very tightly strung, and so the Romans inflicted a greater number of fatalities.]

[lll] Astericus illuscere facit; obeliscus iugulat et confodit (Jerome in his preface to the Pentateuch; cf. Diogenes Laertius on Plato). A skilful use of these masoretic signs could serve just as well to rejuvenate the writings of Solomon as to interpet two letters of Paul, as one of the most recent commentators has done through the method of §§ and tables. [Jerome's "Preface to the Pentateuch" goes by several names; it is the final section of his "Prefatory Epistles" to the Bible. Hamann adapts a few sentences from the beginning of the section: "an asterisk makes a light shine, the obelisk cuts and pierces." Jerome and his predecessors used the obelisk ("little dagger," represented in ancient times by a straight horizontal stroke) to cut and an asterisk ("little star") to add passages.

Book 3 of Diogenes Laertius' *Lives of Eminent Philosophers* is devoted to Plato. At 3.66, he discusses the various marks used to mark passages; the asterisk indicates agreement with doctrine and the obelus a spurious passage.]

nations that the dread age would return of Pyrrha lamenting new portents, when Proteus drove his whole herd to visit the high mountains."

[169] The official credentials given in a postscript to a document (*Meyers Lexikon*); cf. Niermeyer's *Mediae Latinitatis Lexicon Minus*.

[170] Ecclesiastes 1:2: "Vanity of vanities, saith the preacher; vanity of vanities; all is vanity"; cf. 12:8.

[171] Proverbs 31:14: "she is like the merchants' ships; she bringeth her food from afar."

[172] A petit-maître refers either to a "dandy, fop, coxcomb" or to a "minor master" in the arts; both meanings are derogatory.

Let us now hear the conclusion[173] of his newest aesthetic, which is the oldest:

> Fear GOD, and give glory to him; for the hour of his judgment is come: and worship him that made heaven, and earth, and the sea, and the fountains of waters![174]

---

[173] Ecclesiastes 12:13: "Let us hear the conclusion of the whole matter: Fear God, and keep his commandments: for this is the whole duty of man."
[174] Revelation 14:7.

The Last

Will and Testament

of the

Knight of the Rose-Cross

Concerning the
Divine and Human
Origin of Language[1]

Credidi, propter quod locutus sum.

2 Corinthians 4:13[2]

Hastily translated[3]
from an original cartoon hieroglyphic
by the
hierophant's acolyte[4]

καὶ ἐγὼ ποιήσω Ἱεροφάντην.

Arrian, *Discourses of Epictetus* 3.21[5]

Tempore et loco praelibatis.

Motto of Rabelais[6]

[1] The title-page originally bore the false date of 1770, to imply that the piece had been submitted in the competition over the Berlin Academy's prize-question about the origin of language.

[2] "I believed and therefore have I spoken." In full 2 Corinthians 4:13 reads: "We having the same spirit of faith, according as it is written, I believed, and therefore have I spoken; we also believe, and therefore speak." Cf. Psalm 116:10.

[3] Hamann translated from German into French as a clerk in the General Excise and Customs Administration.

[4] "The title points to the Freemasons, of which Herder became a member in 1766. 'Rose Cross,' or 'Rose Croix,' as the nomenclature is given today, is now and was in Herder's time a degree in the Masonic society . . . The Königsberg lodge, like most others, was presided over by a 'Hierophant,' who quite likely had a *Handlager* [here translated as "acolyte"], or mason's assistant – the German word comes from the stonemason's craft," Robert T. Clark, *Herder: His Life and Thought* (Berkeley, CA, 1953), 160.

[5] "I too will make a hierophant." The motto from Arrian's *Discourses of Epictetus* 3.21.13 was added subsequently by hand. The chapter is an admonition "To those who enter light-heartedly upon the profession of lecturing."

[6] "In the right time and place," from Chapter 42 of *Gargantua*. The identification "motto of Rabelais" was also added subsequently. In the printed version the false date "1770" followed at the bottom of the page; the quotation obliquely indicated the falseness of the date.

Socrates in Plato's *Philebus*

Donum profecto DEORUM ad homines, ut mihi videtur, per Prometheum quendam una cum quodam lucidissimo igne descendit. *Etenim* prisci nobis praestantiores, DIISque propinquiores, haec nobis oracula tradiderunt – –[7]

---

[7] Plato, *Philebus* 16c: "A truly great gift of the gods, as it appears to me, came down to men by some Prometheus together with a most dazzling fire. Indeed the ancients, nobler than we are and nearer to the gods, handed down these oracles to us . . ." Hamann quotes the passage in the Latin translation by Marsilio Ficino, in part because he prefers "oracles" [*oracula*] to "tradition" [φήμην].

Hamann is also aiming at Herder's claim in the *Treatise on the Origin of Language*, Part 1, section 3: "The focal point at which Prometheus' heavenly spark catches fire in the human soul has been determined. With the first characteristic mark language arose." (Herder, *Philosophical Writings*, tr. Forster, p. 97; cf. *On the Origin of Language*, tr. Gode, p. 128).

Favete linguis![8]

If God is supposed[9] to be the origin of all effects in great things and small, or in heaven and in earth,[10] then every numbered hair on our head[11] is as divine as the behemoth, that chief of the ways of God.[12] The spirit of the Mosaic law extends from there to the most disgusting discharge of the human corpse.[13] Consequently, everything is divine, and the question of the origin of evil amounts in the end to word-play and scholastic prattle. Everything divine, however, is also human,[14] because man can neither act nor suffer but by the analogy of his nature,[15] however simple or complex a machine it is said to be. This *communicatio* of divine and human *idiomatum*[16] is a fundamental law and the master-key of all our knowledge and of the whole visible economy.[17]

[8] Horace, Ode 3.1.2: literally, "be propitious with your tongues," but idiomatically, "keep sacred silence."

[9] The prize question had begun "En supposant les hommes abandonnés à leurs facultés naturelles . . . ," "Supposing that men were left to their natural faculties . . ."

[10] "In heaven and in earth" occurs in Psalm 113:6 and Matthew 28:18; "great and small" is also a biblical locution.

[11] Matthew 10:30: "But the very hairs of your head are all numbered"; cf. Luke 12:7.

[12] Job 40:19: "He is the chief of the ways of God."

[13] Cf. Numbers 19:11: "He that toucheth the dead body of any man shall be unclean seven days."

[14] Elsewhere Hamann quotes Hippocrates: "All are divine and all human," from *On The Sacred Disease* (see *Werke*, vol. II, p. 105).

[15] Herder, *Treatise*, Part I, section 3: "the invention of a language out of insipid, empty arbitrary volition is opposed to the whole analogy of his nature" (*Philosophical Writing*, tr. Forster, p. 105; cf. *On the Origin of Language*, tr. Gode, p. 139).

[16] "The interchange of the properties," the theological doctrine that "while the human and Divine natures in Christ were separate, the attributes of the one may be predicated of the other in view of their union in the one person of the Saviour" (*Concise Oxford Dictionary of the Christian Church*); see Luther's "The Word Made Flesh," *Luther's Works* (American Edition), vol. XXXVIII, p. 254. It may also be translated as "communication of idioms."

[17] Or "housekeeping."

99

Because the instruments of language, at least, are a gift of the *alma mater* nature (with whom our *esprits forts*[18] carry on an idolatry more tasteless and malicious than the pagan and papist rabble), and because in accordance with the highest philosophical probability the creator of these artificial instruments desired and was obliged to implant the use of them too, the origin of human language is therefore certainly divine.[a] However, if a higher being or an angel[19] (as in the case of Balaam's ass)[20] is going to take effect through our tongues, any such effect, as with the talking animals in Aesop's fables, must be expressed in analogy with human nature, and in this respect neither the origin of language nor, even less, the progress of language can seem or be anything but human. Thus long ago Protagoras called man the *mensuram omnium rerum*.[b]

Our century is fertile in great souls who revere and claim for themselves the relics of the Epicurean system in the *Œuvres philosophiques de M. de la Mettrie*, in the *Système de la nature*, and in the *Evangile du jour*;[21]

---

[a] – *invenisse* dicuntur necessaria ista vitae, non instituisse; quod antea invenitur, fuit, et quod fuit, non *eius* deputabitur qui invenit, sed eius qui instituit. Erat enim antequam inveniretur. Tertullian, *Apologeticus* 11.7. Tertullian, *De testimonio animae* 5. – DEUS et mentis et vocis et linguae artifex. Lactantius, *De vero cultu*, 6.21. – numquam fuisse homines in terra, qui propter infantiam non loquerentur, intelliget, cui ratio non deest. Lactantius, *De vero cultu*, 6.10. [Hamann refers to four passages from the Church Fathers and quotes three of them. The first comes from Tertullian's *Apology*, chapter 1 (Hamann's Latin deviates slightly from standard editions): "[the gods] are said to have *discovered* those essentials of life, not to have made them. But that which is discovered already existed; and therefore will not be accounted *his* who discovered it, but his who made it. For it existed before it could be discovered."

    The second is not quoted. Tertullian, *On the Testimony of the Soul*, chapter 5, discusses the relation between the knowledge of God that is inborn in the soul and that knowledge which comes from Scripture (the chapter concludes "it does not matter greatly whether the soul's knowledge was shaped by God or by the writings of God").

    The third and fourth passages both come from Book 6 ("Of true worship") of Lactantius, *Divine Institutes*: "God is the contriver of the mind and of the voice and of the tongue" (chapter 21) and "anyone not deprived of sense understands that there were never men on the earth who could not speak [except] on account of infancy" (chapter 10).]

[b] Plato in the *Theaetetus* and the *Cratylus*. ["The measure of all things"; Protagoras' words are quoted in Plato's *Theaetetus* 152a and *Cratylus* 386a.]

[18] An *esprit fort* is "a 'strongminded' person; usually, one who professes superiority to current prejudices, esp. a 'freethinker' in religion" (*Oxford English Dictionary*).

[19] Herder, *Treatise*, Part 1, section 3: "If an angel or heavenly spirit had invented language, how could it be otherwise than that language's whole structure would have to be an offprint of this spirit's manner of thought?" (*Philosophical Writings*, tr. Forster, p. 99; *On the Origin of Language*, tr. Gode, p. 131).

[20] Numbers 22; cf. 2 Peter 2:16: "the dumb ass speaking with man's voice forbad the madness of the prophet."

[21] The "philosophical works" of Julien Offray de la Mettrie (1709–1751) were first published in 1751, and include a posthumously edited "System of Epicurus." The Baron d'Holbach's "system of nature" appeared in 1770. Voltaire edited the "gospel of the day" from 1769 to 1780.

meanwhile, producing the human race from mire or slime still looks to me like a beautifully painted brainless mask. Not a mere potter of plastic forms, but a father of fiery spirits and breathing forces[22] is seen in the whole work.

Someone else may dare to have doubts about the revelations of a Galileo, Kepler, Newton; to me at least the sturdy faith of a Voltaire and Hume in these theories has more than once rendered their evangelical certainty suspect. Also, it hardly makes sense that our wise men of today are so penetrating and dependable in heavenly discoveries but on the other hand so befogged in their domestic affairs. However, just as soon as the spirit of mathematical observation from out of the ethereal spheres will condescend to the horizon of our small moral globe of haze, then the hypothesis of a single human couple[23] and the delusion of a Chinese and Egyptian chronology[24] for the present shape of the earth will appear in a geometric light.[25]

A learned doctor[c] proved not long ago in an oration held at the Anatomy Theater in Pavia that the vertical two-legged gait of man is an inherited and artificial gait. Should the Knight of the Rose-Cross wish to desecrate the diamond writing-pen[26] of his ancestors, just as our leading enthusiasts of Montbard, of Voré, of Ferney en Bourgogne[d] and of — in — desecrate their gaggling goose-quills, then this relic would have become a pragmatic deduction which all the Greek academies of the holy Roman empire would have read to corpses and specters, because I would prove in the jaws of their cannibals and gypsies, leaseholders and swindlers, fouaciers[e] and

---

[c] Moscati. [Pietro Moscati, *Delle corporee differenze essenziali che passano fra la struttura de' bruti, e la umana: discorso accademico letto nel teatro anatomico della Regia Università di Pavia* ("On the essential physical differences that occur between the structure of animals and the human structure: academic oration read in the Anatomy Theater of the Royal University of Pavia"), 1770. It was translated into German the next year.]

[d] Buffon, Helvétius. [Georges-Louis de Leclerc, Comte de Buffon (1707–88), was the most important natural historian of his time; he was born in Montbard, France. Claude-Adrien Helvétius (1715–71), French *philosophe*, retired to his estate in Voré in 1751; his most famous, or infamous, work was *De l'esprit* (1758). Voltaire's moved to Ferney in Burgundy in 1758. The "— in —" presumably refers to an unnamed target.]

[e] Rabelais. [A "fouacier" is a baker of fouaces, flat cakes baked on the hearth. In chapter 25 of Rabelais' *Gargantua*, the fouaciers refuse to sell to those whom they regard as too vulgar.]

[22] Hebrews 1:7: "Who maketh his angels spirits, and his ministers a flame of fire"; cf. Psalms 104:4.

[23] Adam and Eve.

[24] Possibly an allusion to Newton's *The Chronology of Ancient Kingdoms Amended* or similar works.

[25] Geometry in the sense of logical clarity, with perhaps an allusion to the "geometrical method" of Spinoza (*Ethica more geometrico demonstrata*).

[26] Jeremiah 17:1: "The sin of Judah is written with a pen of iron, and with the point of a diamond."

poisoners[27] that even eating and drinking cannot be an innate idea of the human race but rather must simply be an inherited and artificial custom. – Everything, everything debates for this point: the nature of the human stomach, which swallows up into itself skin and hair, stones and veins of ore, like pills, streams of sweat and blood, entire loads of sighs and curses, like distilled liquors;[28] – the element of hunger and thirst, whose avarice or rather attraction makes everything, everything, savory and profitable to the princely palate of our financiers and newfanglers, Cretes and Arabians,[29] even that dung, bearing profit and fruit, which the Jew in the land of the Chaldeans by the river of Chebar[30] scorned in part and in part consumed with care during his prophetic siege[f] against a sovereignly project. The analogy between the cold meals of a Laplander or *indigena*[31] and between the fire-spitting vault of an Apicius or *coquin pendu et parvenu*[32] – between Fritz in the purple cradle[33] and Fritz *in praesepio*,[34] who equally would not have learned to eat either with wooden or with golden spoons had not their wet-nurses or their mothers smeared pap around their gaping little mouths and faithfully awaited the great mystery of digestion. – Come on, do you not know by now, philosophers!, that there

---

[f] Ezekiel 4. [Ezekiel 4:1–2: "Thou also, son of man, take thee a tile, and lay it before thee, and pourtray upon it the city, even Jerusalem: And lay siege against it." Ezekiel 4:12–16: "thou shalt bake it with dung that cometh out of man, in their sight . . . Then said I, Ah Lord God! behold, my soul hath not been polluted: for from my youth up even till now have I not eaten of that which dieth of itself, or is torn in pieces; neither came there abominable flesh into my mouth. Then he said unto me, Lo, I have given thee cow's dung for man's dung, and thou shalt prepare thy bread therewith. Moreover he said unto me, Son of man, behold, I will break the staff of bread in Jerusalem: and they shall eat bread by weight, and with care; and they shall drink water by measure, and with astonishment."]

[27] Hamann's insults are directed primarily against Frederick's officials.
[28] Gwen Griffith Dickson (*Johann Georg Hamann's Relational Metacriticism*, p. 470) points out that here and throughout the paragraph Hamann is parodying Herder's over-emphatic style and his keywords. Cf. near the end of Herder's *Treatise*: "Human invention has everything speaking for it and nothing at all against it: *essence of the human soul* and *element of language*; *analogy of the human species* and *analogy of the advances of language – the great examples of all peoples, times, and parts of the world!*" (*Philosophical Writings*, tr. Forster, p. 163).
[29] Acts 2:11: "Cretes and Arabians, we do hear them speak in our tongues the wonderful works of God."
[30] Ezekiel 1:1: "I was among the captives by the river of Chebar."
[31] Hamann may be referring to himself, a native (*indigena*) of East Prussia; elsewhere, however, he uses the word to indicate Maupertuis, who led an expedition to Lapland in 1736.
[32] Apicius, a rich and decadent gourmet, lived under Augustus and Tiberius, and committed suicide by poisoning himself. The fire-spitting vault is Apicius' kitchen. A *coquin pendu et parvenu* is a rogue that was hanged and had risen in the world.
[33] Purple as the color of emperors, and Fritz as Frederick the Great.
[34] Fritz "in the manger" (Luke 2) makes the kenotic contrast with Frederick the Great.

is no physical connection between cause and effect, means and intent, only a spiritual and ideal one, that is, blind faith, as the greatest earthly chronicler[g] of his country and of the natural church has proclaimed! The happy attempt to hold body and soul together with acorns[35] was thus an invention of our ancestors, who were both imaginative and a quick study, and who were called aborigines or autochthones in a natural pronunciation that was more grunting than bleating.[36] They had the fortune to be born in great forests of oak where they would certainly all have starved under the golden reign of famine had they not swiftly resolved, through the inadvertent tutelage of their subjects and rivals for mast, upon a cynical diet of acorns. – Out of gratitude for this charitable acorn diet, give the swine nutritious husks[37] for these three years, and with which your lost native citizens can keep open table. Meanwhile the gods and colonists guzzle down the gold of the land and leave it behind them. –

Those intimate brothers of the human race, the sophists of Sodom-Samaria, who are edified day and night by the conversations of the Autocrat Mark Antoninus with himself, have certainly read in Chapter 13 of Book six that the *Cheville vivifique*[h] (on which depends the whole preservation and increase of the *âmes moutonnières*)[38] is a *parvi intestini affrictio mucique excretio convulsiva*.[39] But they harness the horses

---

[g] Hume. [David Hume (1711–76) was skeptical about a necessary link between cause and effect, wrote a history of England (and is hence a "chronicler"), and defended natural religion.]

[h] Rabelais. [Rabelais praises the "vivifying peg" in the prologue to the *Third Book*: "I entreat you in the name of . . . the four rumps that begot you and of the vivifying peg that at that time joined them."]

[35] "That acorns (with wild honey) were the food of primitive man, is common knowledge in Antiquity" writes R. A. B. Mynors in his commentary to Virgil, *Georgics* 1.8 (Oxford, 1990). Rousseau in *A Discourse upon the Origin and Foundation of Inequality Among Mankind* laments that he is one of those men "whose passions have forever destroyed their original simplicity, who can no longer live upon grass and acorns, or do without laws and magistrates" (footnote 9). Moscati also refers to acorns as the food of primitive man.

[36] Herder's hypothetical example of the origin of language involved the bleating of a sheep (Part 1, section 3).

[37] Luke 15:16: "And he would fain have filled his belly with the husks that the swine did eat: and no man gave unto him."

[38] "Sheepish souls." Rabelais in *The Fourth Book*, chapter 8, after drowning the sheep that were on the ship, looks round to see whether there remains "any sheepish soul."

[39] Hamann quotes from a Latin translation of Marcus Aurelius Antoninus' description of sex, which consists in a "rubbing of the small member and a convulsive discharge of mucus." The title of his work has been translated as "His Conversation with Himself"; it is more commonly known as *The Meditations* or *Commentaries*.

behind the phaeton[40] – and the wisdom itself of Solomon in the Morning Preacher,[i] like the spikenard of Demetrius (see the large catechism of reason[j] under the heading "Lamia"), smells like a *glans regia*.[41]

Since the Knight of the Rose-Cross knows no Arcadia or El Dorado, where you bless God as you please, his swan-song[42] blesses all the ardent youth and old men, not through his own choice of piety, but from a litany of degrees: "They must be as the grass upon the housetops, which withers afore it grows up, wherewith the mower fills not his hand; nor he that binds sheaves his bosom; and they which go by say,[43] *avez honte pour vos Ancêtres!* "[44]

The imagined or contrived paradise of Sotadic[45] tolerance which Mahomet,[46] *ex utroque Caesar*,[47] just as brazen a *latro*[48] as he is a hypocrite, promises to his proselytes and slaves, is nothing but a dead salt sea

[i] – – que l'on prie Dieu dans mon Royaume comme l'on veut et que l'on y f— comme l'on peut. *Matinées royales, ou Entretiens sur l'art de régner*, 1766. [". . . in my kingdom you pray to God as you please and you f[uck] as you can"; see n. 41.]

[j] Bayle. In the preface to the *Extrait du Dictionnaire historique et critique*, 1765. [See n. 41.]

[40] *Oxford English Dictionary*: "A species of four-wheeled open carriage, of light construction." A reference to Frederick's homosexuality.

[41] Because of its obscene denunciation of Frederick, Hamann's writing is here particularly dense and obscure, and even the handwritten notes he subsequently adds are oblique. The "Morning Preacher" is a cipher for the *Matinées royales*, a satire of uncertain authorship which includes the sentence Hamann quotes in the note.

The remaining allusion is to a story that survives in Athenaeus, *Deipnosophists* (Book 13) but which Hamann found in Pierre Bayle's *Dictionnaire historique et critique*. In a footnote to the article "Lamia," Bayle quotes in Latin the story. King Demetrius desired the flute-girl Lamia and was showing her a variety of perfumes, which she rejected. He called for some spikenard, masturbated, and asked Lamia to smell and tell him how superior it was to the others. She smiled and replied that it smelled the most putrid of all. Demetrius answered that it came from the royal glans [*glans regia*] itself.

The "Extrait" was taken from Bayle's *Dictionary* and published in Berlin, 1765. The preface concludes by insisting that the works of the *philosophes* constitute the "catechism of reason."

[42] That is, his "last will and testament."

[43] Psalms 129 ("A Song of degrees"), verses 6–8: "Let them be as the grass upon the housetops, which withereth afore it groweth up: Wherewith the mower filleth not his hand; nor he that bindeth sheaves his bosom. Neither do they which go by say, The blessing of the LORD be upon you: we bless you in the name of the LORD."

[44] "Be ashamed for your ancestors" (on the grounds they engaged in heterosexual sex?).

[45] "Sotadic" means obscene, from Sotades, Greek poet.   [46] That is, Frederick.

[47] *Ex utroque Caesar*: the ideal of the king as accomplished in both war and the arts (*armis et litteris, arte et marte*). See Ernst H. Kantorowicz, "On Transformations of Apolline Ethics," pp. 265–74 of Konrad Schauenberg, ed., *Charites: Studien zur Altertumswissenschaft* (Bonn, 1957) and Dora and Erwin Panofsky, *Pandora's Box: The Changing Aspects of a Mythical Symbol* (New York, 1956), 40–1; cf. Erwin Robert Curtius, *European Literature and the Latin Middle Ages*, tr. Willard R. Trask (Princeton, 1953), 178–9.

[48] Latin for "thief."

as soon as it means: *mortua est illa pars, qua quondam Achilles eram!*[49] – No thundering chariot, no flame of the air-beating sword,[50] can keep the way to the tree of life more splendidly than the plague of fig-warts[51] on the borders and in the bowels of the state which will shortly be transformed into a Hôtel-Dieu,[52] where the terrible necessity of hardship teaches us to beg. For although Herodes Atticus[53] persecutes the godly foolishness[54] of the Christian faith with the fire of his muse and the sword of his prose, and indeed in an idiom whose syntax St. Diderot[55] considers supremely metaphysical, behold! all laws, orders, and commands not only roar out, more public and more innumerable than the waves and the sand of the foaming sea,[56] the God of grace[57] through whom all that seems to rule really is ruled,[58] but they also snort out the evangelical spirit of usury,[k] which burdens the impoverished and reviled subjects with the nine beatitudes of the preacher on the mount,[59] and Joel's prophecy (2:20–1) is fulfilled once again: "His stink shall come up, and his ill savour shall come up, because he hath done great things. Fear not, O land; be glad and rejoice: for the Lord will do great things." – "Behold! His Contrôleur-Général[60]

---

[k] Γίνεσθε τραπεζῖται δόκιμοι. Johann Albert Fabricius, "De dictis Christi" in *Codex apocryphus Novi Testamenti* (1719) vol. II, p. 330. ["Be a just money-changer," an apocryphal saying of Christ.]

[49] Adapts Petronius, *Satyricon* 129: "Dead is that part in which I was once Achilles."

[50] 1 Corinthians 9:26: "so fight I, not as one that beateth the air" and Genesis 3:24: "and he placed at the east of the garden of Eden Cherubims, and a flaming sword which turned every way, to keep the way of the tree of life."

[51] Syphilitic warts, a variety of condyloma.

[52] Hamann gives the French word for "hospital" because of "Dieu."

[53] Herodes Atticus (101–177) was an important orator and teacher. "Herodes" also invokes the persecuting Herod of the New Testament (the names are identical in German), and "Atticus" refers to the elegant rhetoric and the atheism of the *philosophes*. Hamann is referring to Frederick the Great.

[54] 1 Corinthians 1:25: "Because the foolishness of God is wiser than men; and the weakness of God is stronger than men."

[55] Cf. Diderot's essay "Sur Frédéric II," written in 1760 and published in the *Encyclopédie* in 1765 as a supplement to the article "Prussia." In it, Diderot offers a qualified praise of Frederick's *Œuvres du philosophe de Sans-Souci*; Frederick was wounded by it. See Diderot, *Arts et lettres (1739–1766)*, ed. Jean Varloot (Paris, 1980).

[56] Cf. Hebrews 11:12: "so many as the stars of the sky in multitude, and as the sand which is by the sea shore innumerable."

[57] 1 Peter 5:10: "the God of all grace."

[58] Proverbs 8:15: "By me kings reign, and princes decree justice."

[59] Matthew 5–7, Luke 6.

[60] The Controller-General of Finances in Prussia was the head of the General Excise Administration (or "Regie"), a new ministry Frederick introduced, run by Frenchmen, and responsible for collecting certain taxes.

comes to turn the hearts of the fathers to the native citizens and the unbelievers to the wisdom of the just."[61] –

Therefore if man, according to the universal testimony and example of all peoples, times, and regions,[62] is not in a position to learn by himself and without the sociable influence of his warders and guardians (that is, *iussus*,[1] as it were) how to walk on two legs, nor how to break daily bread without the sweat of his face,[63] nor again, and least of all, to arrive at the masterpiece of the creative brush, how then could the idea come into anyone's head to regard language, *cet art legere, volage, demoniacle* (to speak with Montaigne[m] out of Plato)[n] as an autonomous invention of human art and wisdom? – Our philosophers talk like alchemists about the treasures of productivity, though to judge by their fields and vineyards, you might swear that they do not know how to tell tares from wheat,[64] grapes from thorns, nor figs from thistles[65] – They imitate that charlatan who declared that the *vacuum* of his bag was the great, beautiful, strong spirit who, if it were possible, would seduce the *Élus*[66] themselves. The confusion of language, by which however they seduce and are seduced, is of course a very natural magic of automatic reason, to which it comes at little cost to be transformed into a star of the first magnitude, especially for the pranksters of like blindness.

---

[1] Ovid, *Metamorphoses*, Book 1. [The first book of Ovid's *Metamorphoses* recounts the creation of the world and of man, the degeneration of men after their Golden Age, their destruction at the hands of Jove, and the repopulation of the earth by Deucalion and Pyrrha. "Iussus" ("commanded") perhaps refers to the god who commanded ("iussit") the creation of the world at lines 37, 43, and 55; it also suggests God's commands to Adam in Genesis 2.]

[m] *Essais*, Book 3, chapter 9. [See *Essais*, ed. Thibaudet and Rat (1962), p. 973 ("De la vanité"). "Poetry, says Plato, is an art which is light, winged and inspired by daemons," tr. M. A. Screech, *Essays* (1991), p. 1125 ("On vanity").]

[n] κοῦφον γὰρ χρῆμα ποιητής ἐστιν καὶ πτηνὸν καὶ ἱερόν. Plato, *Ion*. [534b: "a poet is a light and winged and sacred thing."]

[61] Luke 1:17: "And he shall go before him in the spirit and power of Elias, to turn the hearts of the fathers to the children, and the disobedient to the wisdom of the just; to make ready a people prepared for the Lord." Luther has "unbelievers" rather than "disobedient," and so does Hamann. In this instance I have departed from the King James version to render the quotation closer to the German.

[62] Herder, *Treatise*, toward the end: "*the great example of all peoples, times, and parts of the world!*" (*Philosophical Writings*, tr. Forster, p. 163).

[63] Genesis 3:19: "In the sweat of thy face shalt thou eat bread."

[64] Matthew 13:30: "Gather ye together first the tares, and bind them in bundles to burn them: but gather the wheat into my barn."

[65] Matthew 7:16: "Do men gather grapes of thorns, or figs of thistles."

[66] French, "the elect," "the chosen ones."

Without getting myself involved in a fray with ridiculous ideas that do not deserve to be refuted and which cannot be cured by being refuted (for the darkness lies in the eyeball of the *sensus communis* and the trouble lies in the womb of the concept), I shall touch merely on the one bit of nonsense by which these crooked[67] patriarchs of autochthones and aborigines are made into the thrice-blessed inventors of an art whose structure Beauzée (in his *Grammaire générale*)[68] and Harris[69] have written far too much about, but understood far too little of – –

Henceforth, pious brothers, meditate, when and as well as you possibly can, on the birth of the first human couple. – Their nakedness was without shame,[70] their navel[o] a round goblet[71] which never lacks drink, and the voice of a God walking in the cool of the day in the garden was the sincere milk of reason[72] for these little children of creation for the growth of their political destiny: to people the earth and to rule by the word of their mouth[p] – –

---

[o] See Sir Thomas Browne's *Pseudodoxia epidemica*, Book 5, chapter 5. NB: The first humans did not have navels. [Browne argues in Book 5, chapter 5 of this work (1646; sixth edn. 1672) that the representation of Adam and Eve with navels may be an error.]

[p] Qui primus, quod summae sapientiae Pythagorae visum est, omnibus rebus imposuit nomina? Cicero, *Tusculan Disputations*, I.25. – Il ne faut qu'un amant passionné pour inventer l'écriture, mais 30 Leibniz suffiroient à peine pour créer la première langue. *De la philosophie de la nature* (Amsterdam, 1770), vol. III, chap. 2, p. 298. – Philo, *Omnia quae extant opera* (Frankfurt, 1691), pp. 17, 32, 34, 178, 148. [Hamann alters the quotation from Cicero's *Tusculan Disputations* I.25.62 in a minor way: "Who first gave names to things, something which Pythagoras thought required the height of wisdom?"

The second quotation is from a work by Delisle de Sales that was published in Amsterdam in 1770: "It takes only one passionate lover to create writing, but thirty Leibnizes would hardly suffice to create the first language."

The final citation invokes five passages from Philo. In the modern Loeb edition of Philo's works in ten volumes (tr. F. H. Colson and G. H. Whitaker), these correspond to vol. I, pp. 60–5 ("On the Creation" 77–9); vol. I, pp. 110–13 ("On the Creation" 139–42); vol. I, pp. 116–19 ("On the Creation" 147–51); vol. II, pp. 284–9 ("That the Worse is Wont to Attack the Better" 123–30); and vol. II, pp. 170–5 ("The Sacrifices of Abel and Cain" 102–8).]

[67] Hamann has *unschlachtig*, an older equivalent to *ungeschlacht*, "clumsy, coarse, uncouth," but since the word is particularly associated with Luther's translation of Philippians 2:15, "in the midst of a crooked and perverse nation," I have translated it here as "crooked."

[68] Nicolas Beauzée, *Grammaire générale; ou, Exposition raisonnée des éléments nécessaires du langage, pour servir de fondement à l'étude de toutes les langues*, 1767.

[69] James Harris, *Hermes, or A Philosophical Inquiry Concerning Universal Grammar*, 1751; second edn. 1765; third edn. 1771.

[70] Genesis 2:25: "And they were both naked, the man and his wife, and were not ashamed."

[71] Song of Songs 7:2: "Thy navel is like a round goblet."

[72] 1 Peter 2:2: "As newborn babes, desire the sincere milk of the word." Hamann quotes Luther's phrase exactly, but I have departed from the King James version in order to emphasize (as Hamann does) "reason."

Even the inequality of mankind and the social contract are thus consequences of an original institution, for according to the oldest document[73]
a very early event (which is so well suited to the cradle of mankind that
the truth of their narrative bruises the snake's head of skepticism and
makes all the heel-bruises of mockery laughable)[74] long ago gave cause
for woman to submit under the will of the husband[75] – –

Adam was therefore God's,[76] and God himself brought the first-
begotten and the oldest of our race as the feudal tenant and heir of the
world set in order by the word of his mouth. Angels, burning to look
into[77] his heavenly countenance, were the ministers and courtiers of the
first monarch. In the choir of the morning stars all the sons of God shouted
for joy.[78] All tasted and saw,[79] at first hand and red-handed, the goodness
of the master craftsman who rejoiced in the habitable part of his earth and
his delights were for the sons of men[80] – The creature was not yet made
subject, unwillingly, to the vanity and bondage of the corruptible system[81] under which they now yawn, sigh, and are dumb, like the Delphic
tripod[82] and the anti-machiavellian[83] eloquence of Demosthenes with his
silver-quinsy,[84] or at most gasps, rattles, and is stifled finally in the drop-
sied breast of a Tacitus – Every phenomenon of nature was a word, – the
sign, symbol, and pledge of a new, secret, inexpressible but all the more
fervent union, fellowship, and communion of divine energies and ideas.
All that man heard at the beginning, saw with his eyes, looked upon, and

---

[73] Alludes to Herder's work, *The Oldest Document of the Human Race* (1774–6).
[74] Genesis 3:15: "it shall bruise thy head, and thou shalt bruise his heel."
[75] Genesis 3:16: "Unto the woman he said . . . thy desire shall be to thy husband, and he shall rule
over thee." The biblical allusion is closer in German.
[76] Luke 3:38: "Adam, which was the son of God" (in German, "the son" does not appear); 1
Corinthians 3:23: "And ye are Christ's; and Christ is God's."
[77] 1 Peter 1:12: "which things the angels desire to look into."
[78] Job 38:7: "When the morning stars sang together, and all the sons of God shouted for joy?"
[79] Psalm 34:8: "O taste and see that the Lord is good."
[80] Proverbs 8:30–1: "Then I was by him . . . Rejoicing in the habitable part of his earth; and my
delights were with the sons of men." The allusion is closer in German.
[81] Romans 8:20–1: "For the creature was made subject to vanity, not willingly, but by reason of him
who hath subjected the same in hope, Because the creature itself also shall be delivered from the
bondage of corruption into the glorious liberty of the children of God."
[82] On which the priestess of Apollo at Delphi sat and was inspired before delivering oracles.
[83] Frederick the Great published *Anti-Machiavel* anonymously in 1740.
[84] Demosthenes was said to be sufferering from "silver-quinsy" (ἀργυράγχη) when he refrained
from speaking on the grounds that he suffered from quinsy (συνάγχη), but in fact because he
had been bribed. See Plutarch, *Life of Demosthenes*, 25.

his hands handled was a living word;[85] for God was the word.[86] With this word in his mouth and in his heart the origin of language was as natural, as close and easy, as a child's game. For human nature is from the beginning until the end of days as like unto the kingdom of heaven as leaven, with whose smallness every woman can make ferment three measures of meal. –

I would matagrabolize[q] further and wider and deeper if I did not know that much study right now wearies the cheer of the listener as once it wearied the flesh of the spiritual speaker.[87] So I content myself today with having found and named, through a pilgrimage in black ashen sack,[r] the element of language – the A and O[88] – the word.

In conclusion, the Knight of the Rose-Cross invites all the witty and clever fools of the Kingdom of Yvetot[89] and the petrified or animated gawkers *in coemeterio Pisorum*[s] who are not ashamed to be, or to become, German to his hereditary seat, where privileges and livings are not lacking that are lucrative in consecrated ribbons, gloves, wax candles, and sealing-sticks. Meanwhile He Himself, mid-day and midnight, composes a *Roman des œconomies et servitudes*,[t] and broods over the last masterpiece of Roman statecraft, Julian's plan to conquer the Parthians at the border.[90]

---

[q] Matagraboliser, ματαιογραφοβολίζειν. [The word was coined by Rabelais, in *Gargantua* chapter 19. In his note, Hamann invents a Greek word (derived from three Greek roots, μάταιος, "vain, empty"; γράφω, "write"; and βολίζω, "take soundings") that corresponds to Rabelais' neologism.]

[r] *Art royal du Chevalier de Rosecroix à Londres*, 1770. 8. p. 18. [A Masonic text, but since the "Chevalier de Rosecroix" is the French for "Knight of the Rose-Cross," this seems also to be a personal reference to Hamann's repentance during his trip to London in 1758.]

[s] Algarotti. [Frederick raised a monument in Pisa to his friend the philosopher Algarotti, hence "in the cemetery of the Pisans."]

[t] See the original edition of the *Memoirs* of Sully. [The Duc de Sully (1560–1644), a Huguenot, became the head of King Henri IV's financial system. Hamann's French title, "Romance of Economies and Services," adapts the full title of Sully's Memoirs: *Mémoires des sages et royales œconomies d'estat, domestiques, politiques, et militaires de Henry le Grand . . . et des servitudes utiles, obéissances convenables et administrations loyales de Maximilian de Bethune . . .*]

[85] 1 John 1:1: "That which was from the beginning, which we have heard, which we have seen with our eyes, which we have looked upon, and our hands have handled, of the Word of life."

[86] John 1:1: "In the beginning was the Word, and the Word was with God, and the Word was God."

[87] Ecclesiastes 12:12: "and much study is a weariness of the flesh."

[88] Revelation 1:8: "I am Alpha and Omega."

[89] The "King of Yvetot" is "a man of mighty pretensions but small merits" (*Brewer's Dictionary of Phrase and Fable*).

[90] Julian, that is the Roman emperor known as Julian the Apostate, who sought military glory by invading Persia, and died in retreat. Probably a reference to Frederick's partition of Poland in 1772.

The gentlemen *Entrepreneurs à l'enseigne des trois vertus couronnées d'amaranthe*,[91] to whom, in the event of my overhasty *exilium* into a better fatherland, the manuscript of these fragments or the torso of my wasted monument *in agro Pisano Aestiorium*[u] may be of some concern, will be obliged by my dear Junker

Johann. Michel. Joseph. Nazir.[92]

– On his head may the blessings of his father be heaped over and above the blessings of my ancestors, up to the pleasant hill of olden time – may he climb it soon with his eventual[v] sibling!

All assayers to the contrary, who shudder at my dialect larded with French and Latin, I wish that the present acolyte of the hierophant had been a polyglot like Panurge[w] and Quintus Icilius,[93] so that they would not be able to read his translation – *car tel est notre bon plaisir*[94] –

Happy the man who waits two or three, even four years, until the testimony [*Meynung*] of this last will is revealed, whose hidden sense is still sealed!

(L. S.)[95]

Cognovit DOMINVS qui sunt EIVS.
2 Timothy 2:19[96]

---

[u] Caius Herennius Rapidus, *Sermo ad Pisones*. Poem by my blessed teacher Rappolt on *green peas*. [The phrase "in agro Pisano Aestiorum" ("in the Pisan land of the Aestonians") indicates Königsberg. There are three puns: the first contrasts Hamann's wasted monument with the wasteful monument of Algarotti in Pisa. The second echoes the Latin word *pisus*, or pea, the subject of Karl Heinrich Rappolt's poem. The third alludes to the third epistle of the second book of Horace's Epistles, "ad Pisones." Rappolt's pseudonym was Caius Herennius Rapidus, and the title of his book *De Pisis ad Pisones*, published "Pisae Aestiorum" (in Königsberg) in 1740.]

[v] Written on the night of Palm Sunday 1772 a few hours before the birth of my oldest daughter Lisette Reinette. [Elisabeth Regina was born on April 12, 1772.]

[w] Rabelais. [A reference perhaps to Rabelais, *Panurge*, chap. 9, where Panurge and Pantagruel meet, and where Panurge answers him in many languages.]

[91] Sully's *Memoirs* claims to be printed in Amsterdam "chez Alethinosgraphe de Clearetimelee, & Graphexechon de Pistariste, à l'enseigne des trois Vertus couronnées d'Amaranthe."

[92] Johann Michael Hamann was born on September 27, 1769. The name Joseph is added because he received the blessing of Jacob, and Nazir, because that is the pseudonym of Rabelais ("Alcofribas Nasier," an anagram for François Rabelais, is given as the author on the title page of *Gargantua*).

[93] Frederick had given Karl Gottlieb Guichard, a soldier and author whom he liked, the name "Quintus Icilius" (Frederick did this after Guichard had corrected him for misremembering Quintus Caecilius as "Quintus Icilius").

[94] French, "for such is our good pleasure," the formula with which royal edicts conclude.

[95] That is, the "locus sigilli," where the Knight's seal is to be placed.

[96] 2 Timothy 2:19: "The Lord knoweth them that are his."

Philological
Ideas and Doubts
about
an Academic Prize Essay

Psalms 120:4
Sharp arrows of the mighty, with coals of juniper.[1]

– – ἀπομνύω
μὴ τέρμα προβάς, ἄκονθ’ ὥστε χαλκοπάραον ὄρσαι
θοὰν γλῶσσαν.
> Pindar, Nemean Ode 7[2]
> Along with many other passages from this ode,
> each in its place.[3]

Drafted
by the
Magus of the North
In October 1772

Printed at: Here follows the printer of the *Allgemeine
Bibliothek*.[4]

– – neque ego illi detrahere ausim
Haerentem capiti multa cum laude coronam.
Horace, Satire 1.10.48–9.[5]

---

[1] In context, these are related to "a deceitful tongue" (v. 2) and "thou false tongue" (v. 3).

[2] Pindar, Nemean 7.70–2: "I swear that I have not overstepped the mark, launched like a brazen-tipped javelin my swift word."

[3] Pindar's Nemean 7, an ode in praise of a prize-winning athlete, is here applied to Herder's prize-winning essay. Several passages in it are concerned with poetry's awesome power, including its capacity for deception.

[4] Hamann wished to have Friedrich Nicolai, publisher and the editor of the review journal *Allgemeine deutsche Bibliothek* (the "Universal German Library"), publish his work. On Nicolai's rejection of Hamann's work, see Martin Sommerfeld, *Friedrich Nicolai und der Sturm und Drang* (1921), 134–6.

[5] Hamann's Pindaric text differs slightly from modern ones: "Nor would I dare to pull off the wreath clinging to his head with much praise."

(*Göttingische Anzeigen von gelehrten Sachen unter der Aufsicht der Königlichen Gesellschaft der Wissenschaften* No. 78, 1772)

(His style must not be a model for others, but as his own style it agrees with us quite well)[6]

---

[6] A quotation from a review of Herder's essay in the *Göttingen Notices of Scholarly Matters under the Auspices of the Royal Society of Sciences*, No. 78 (June 29, 1772), p. 661.

Aristotle with his customary acumen sought to distinguish voice and language. According to his account,[a] the ᾱ ᾱ ᾱ ᾱ and the παπᾶ παπᾶ παπᾶ παπᾶ παπᾶ παπᾶ παπᾶ of the famous suffering hero,[7] along with that sniffing of the free-loader in *Plutus*, ὔ ὔ ὔ ὔ ὔ ὔ ὔ ὔ,[8] are in the truest understanding sounds of the voice, which is of course the root and

---

[a] ἡ μὲν οὖν ΦΩΝΗ τοῦ ʿΗΔΕΟΣ καὶ ΛΥΠΗΡΟΥ ἐστὶ ΣΗΜΕΙΟΝ, διὸ καὶ τοῖς ἄλλοις ὑπάρχει ζῴοις, μέχρι γὰρ τούτου ἡ φύσις αὐτῶν ἐλήλυθε ὥστε αἰσθάνεσθαι λυπηροῦ καὶ ἡδέος καὶ ταῦτα σημαίνειν ἀλλήλοις. ὁ δὲ ΛΟΓΟΣ ἐπὶ τῷ δηλοῦν ἐστι τὸ ΣΥΜΦΕΡΟΝ καὶ τὸ ΒΛΑΒΕΡΟΝ. ὥστε καὶ τὸ ΔΙΚΑΙΟΝ καὶ τὸ ᾿ΑΔΙΚΟΝ. τοῦτο γὰρ πρὸς τὰ ἄλλα ζῷα τοῖς ἀνθρώποις ἴδιον, τὸ μόνον ᾿ΑΓΑΘΟΥ καὶ ΚΑΚΟΥ καὶ ΔΙΚΑΙΟΥ καὶ ᾿ΑΔΙΚΟΥ καὶ τῶν λοίπων αἴσθησιν ἔχειν. Aristotle, *Politics* 1.1.10 [1253a].

– δεῖ ἔμψυχόν τε εἶναι τὸ τύπτον καὶ μετὰ φαντασίας τινός· ΣΗΜΑΝΤΙΚΟΣ γὰρ δή τις ψόφος ἐστίν ἡ ΦΩΝΗ. Aristotle, *On the Soul* 2.8 [420b]. ["The VOICE, it is true, is a SIGN of PLEASURE and PAIN, and therefore it is also possessed by the other animals for their nature has developed to the point that they perceive pleasure and pain and signify those things to each other. But LANGUAGE is for the purpose of revealing the ADVANTAGEOUS and the HARMFUL. And so the RIGHT and the WRONG. For this in contrast to the other animals is specific to men, the unique perception of GOOD and BAD and RIGHT and WRONG and so on."

"The thing that makes the impact must have a soul and share in imagination, for the VOICE is a SIGNIFYING sound."]

[7] Philoctetes' cries of pain in Sophocles' *Philoctetes*, ll. 731, 739, 745–6, etc. In the first paragraph of Herder's *Essay on the Origin of Language*, he writes: "A suffering animal, no less than the hero Philoctetes, will whine, will moan when pain befalls it" (tr. Gode, p. 87; cf. tr. Forster, p. 65).

[8] Aristophanes, *Plutus*, l. 895. The elaborate sniff follows the line, "I reckon, you villains, that there is much salt fish and roast meat in this house."

stem, the nourishing sap, and the living spirit of language, above all its onomatopoeia.⁹

The concept of stages and kind¹⁰ refers to very arbitrary similarities, and the contrast of these relations has little effect on the knowledge of the things themselves.

Every mechanism posits in advance an organization,ᵇ and every visible life posits both. These three wheels appear everywhere in such large, exceptional amounts that their machinery is as unmistakable in each other as it is, perhaps, indistinguishable.¹¹

Not only does man have life in common with the animals, but he also has similarities both to their organization and to their mechanism, more or less, that is, by stages. The principal difference of man must therefore depend on his way of life.

With respect to sociability, the wise Stagyrite considers man to be neutral.¹² I therefore presume that the true character of our nature consists in the judicial and administrativeᶜ office of a political animal;ᵈ and that consequently man would stand in the same relation to cattle as the prince to the subject.

Now this office [*Würde*] like all honorific positions assumes neither an inner worth [*Würdigkeit*] nor merit in our nature; rather it is, as the latter itself is,¹³ an unmediated gift of grace from the great All-Giver.

ᵇ ʼΟΡΓΑΝΑ δὲ καὶ τὰ τῶν φυτῶν μέρη, ἀλλὰ παντελῶς ἁπλα – – Aristotle, *On the Soul* 2.1 [412b]. ["The parts of plants are also ORGANS, but very simple ones . . ."]

ᶜ πολίτης δ' ἁπλῶς οὐδενὶ τῶν ἄλλων ὁρίζεται μᾶλλον ἢ τῷ μετέχειν ΚΡΙΣΕΩΣ καὶ ἈΡΧΗΣ. Aristotle, *Politics* 3.1.4 [1275a]. ["A citizen is defined simply by nothing other than participation in JUDICIAL FUNCTIONS and MAGISTRACIES."]

ᵈ ΠΟΛΙΤΙΚΑ δ' ἐστὶν ὧν ἕν τι καὶ κοινὸν γίγνεται πάντων τὸ ἔργον. Aristotle, *History of Animals* 1.1 [488a]. ["The political animals are all those that have some one common work."]

⁹ Cf. Herder, *Essay:* "In all aboriginal languages, vestiges of these sounds of nature are still to be heard, though, to be sure, they are not the principal fiber of human speech. They are not the roots as such; they are the sap that enlivens the roots of language" (tr. Gode, p. 91; cf. tr. Forster, p. 68).

¹⁰ Cf. ibid.: "the human species stands above the animals not by stages of more or of less but in kind" (tr. Gode, p. 108; cf. tr. Forster, p. 81).

¹¹ Ezekiel 1:16: "The appearance of the wheels and their work was like unto the color of a beryl: and they four had one likeness: and their appearance and their work was as it were a wheel in the middle of a wheel."

¹² Aristotle, *History of Animals* 1.1 [487b–488a]: "Some [animals] are social, some solitary . . . others show both characteristics . . . Man shows both characteristics." Aristotle is known as the "Stagirite," from the city of Stagira where he was born. In the past, it was also commonly spelled "Stagyrite."

¹³ Merit in the theological sense of "the righteousness and sacrifice of Christ as the ground on which God grants forgiveness to sinners" (*Oxford English Dictionary*).

Every hero or poet, whether he is a type[14] of the Messiah or a prophet of the Antichrist, has periods in life when he has full cause to confess with David: "I am a worm, and no man."[15]

Without the freedom to be evil there is no merit, and without the freedom to be good no responsibility for one's own guilt, and indeed no knowledge of good and evil. Freedom is the maximum and minimum of all our natural powers, as well as both the fundamental drive and the final goal of their entire orientation, evolution, and return.[16]

Hence neither instinct nor the *sensus communis* determines man; neither natural law nor the law of nations determines the prince. Everyone is his own legislator but also the first-born and the neighbor of his subjects.

Without the perfect law of freedom[e] man would not even be capable of imitation, the basis of all education and invention.[17] For man by nature is the greatest pantomime among all the animals.[f]

---

[e] ὁ δὲ παρακύψας εἰς ΝΟΜΟΝ ΤΕΛΕΙΟΝ ΤΟΝ ΤΗΣ ᾽ΕΛΕΥΘΕΡΙΑΣ, οὗτος ΠΟΙΗΤΗΣ – οὗτος μακάριος ἐν τῇ ΠΟΙΗΣΕΙ αὐτοῦ ἔσται. James 1:25. [Hamann slightly revises the verse, drawing attention to the dual meaning in Greek of poet/doer and poesis/deed: "Whoso looks into THE PERFECT LAW OF FREEDOM, this DOER – this man shall be blessed in the DEED."]

[f] τό τε γὰρ μιμεῖσθαι σύμφυτον τοῖς ἀνθρώποις ἐκ παίδων ἐστὶ καὶ τούτῳ διαφέρουσι τῶν ἄλλων ζῴων ὅτι μιμητικώτατόν ἐστι καὶ τὰς μαθήσεις ποιεῖται διὰ μιμήσεως τὰς πρώτας, καὶ τὸ χαίρειν τοῖς μιμήμασι πάντας. σημεῖον δὲ τούτου τὸ συμβαῖνον ἐπὶ τῶν ἔργων· ἃ γὰρ αὐτὰ λυπηρῶς ὁρῶμεν, τούτων τὰς εἰκόνας τὰς μάλιστα ἠκριβωμένας χαίρομεν θεωροῦντες, οἷον θηρίων τε μορφὰς τῶν ἀτιμοτάτων καὶ νεκρῶν. αἴτιον δὲ καὶ τούτου, ὅτι μανθάνειν οὐ μόνον τοῖς φιλοσόφοις ἥδιστον ἀλλὰ καὶ τοῖς ἄλλοις ὁμοίως, ἀλλ᾽ ἐπὶ βραχὺ κοινωνοῦσιν αὐτοῦ. διὰ γὰρ τοῦτο χαίρουσι τὰς εἰκόνας ὁρῶντες, ὅτι συμβαίνει θεωροῦντας μανθάνειν καὶ συλλογίζεσθαι τί ἕκαστον, οἷον ὅτι οὗτος ἐκεῖνος. Aristotle, *Poetics* 4 [1448b]. ["From childhood men have an instinct for representation, and in this respect man differs from the other animals in that he is far more imitative and learns his first lessons by representing things. And then there is the enjoyment people always get from representations. What happens in actual experience proves this, for we

[14] Refers in the theological sense to a prefiguration of an event in the New Testament by one in the Old Testament.

[15] Psalms 22:6.

[16] Cf. Herder, *Essay*: "It is the unique positive power of thought which, associated with a particular organization of the body, is called reason in man as in the animal it turns into an artifactive skill; which in man is called freedom and turns in the animal into instinct. The difference is not one of degree nor one of a supplementary endowment with powers; it lies in a totally distinct orientation and evolution of all powers" (tr. Gode, p. 110; cf. tr. Forster, p. 83).

[17] Invention, education, and imitation are key concepts of Herder's *Essay*, which is an answer to the question of how language was invented. He rejects the argument that it is learned as part of education or training, either divine or from our parents: "Parents never teach their children language without the latter, by themselves, inventing language along with them" (tr. Gode, p. 121; cf. tr. Forster, p. 92); "Had [the disposition to learn language] come to man through mere habit and training, why not to the bear?" (tr. Gode, p. 124; cf. tr. Forster, p. 94). Herder also defines "imitation" as a purely human activity: "The ape always apes, but it has never imitated" (tr. Forster, p. 95; cf. tr. Gode, p. 125).

Consciousness, attentiveness, abstraction, and even the moral conscience seem to a large degree to be energies of our freedom.[18]

Freedom involves not only undetermined powers but also the republican privilege of being able to contribute to their determination. These conditions were indispensable to human nature. The sphere of animals determines by instinct, it is said,[19] the orientation of all their powers and their drives in a particular and inclusive way; the perspective of men, in precise contrast, extends to the universal and almost becomes lost in the infinite.

Aristotle compares the soul with the hand, namely because the latter is the tool of all tools, while the former is the form of all intellectual and sensible forms.[g]

Presumably the senses stand in the same relation to understanding as the stomach does to the vessels which secrete the finer and higher fluids of the blood, without whose circulation and influence the stomach could not perform its office. Everything that is in our understanding has previously been in our senses, just as everything that is in our entire body has once passed through our own stomach or our parents'. The *stamina* and the *menstrua*[20] of our reason are thus in the truest understanding revelations and traditions which we accept as our property, transform into our fluids and powers, and by this means we become equal to our destiny, both to reveal the critical and archontic office of a political animal[21] and to transmit it.

---

enjoy looking at accurate likenesses of things which are themselves painful to see, obscene beasts, for instance, and corpses. The reason is this. Learning things gives great pleasure not only to philosophers but also in the same way to all other men, though they share this pleasure only to a small degree. The reason why we enjoy seeing likenesses is that, as we look, we learn and infer what each is, for instance, 'that is so and so'," tr. W. Hamilton Frye (Loeb Classical Library, 1927).]

[g] ὥστε ἡ ψυχὴ ὥσπερ ἡ χείρ ἐστιν· καὶ γὰρ ἡ χεὶρ ὄργανόν ἐστιν ὀργάνων, καὶ ὁ νοῦς εἶδος εἰδῶν καὶ ἡ αἴσθησις εἶδος αἰσθητῶν. Aristotle, *On the Soul* 3.8 [432a]. ["The soul then is like a hand; for the hand is a tool of tools, and the mind a form of forms, and sensibility a form of sensible objects."]

[18] Ibid.: "[Süssmilch] only explained laboriously that all the delicate and complex actions which we call attention, reflection, abstraction, etc., cannot very well be performed without signs to lend the soul support" (tr. Gode, p. 119; cf. tr. Forster, p. 90).

[19] See ibid., pp. 103–5 (tr. Gode) or pp. 77–9 (tr. Forster) on instinct and the sphere of animal activities; he refers to Reimarus' work on the topic.

[20] *Stamina*, a plural form, as the "rudiments or germs from which living beings or their organs are developed" and *menstrua* not only as discharge but also as the nutritive medium of the embryo.

[21] Another reference to Aristotle as quoted in footnote c. An archon was one of nine chief magistrates of Athens.

The analogy of animal housekeeping is the only ladder[22] for the ana-gogical[23] knowledge of spiritual economy,[h] which in all probability alone resolves and completes the phenomena and *qualitates occultae*[24] of that visible abridged half.

Suppose that man comes into the world like an empty skin. Then this very absence makes him all the more capable of enjoying nature through experiences and of sharing in the community of his race through traditions. Our reason at least has its source in the twofold instruction of sensible revelations and human testimonies, which are communicated through similar means, namely distinguishing marks,[25] and in accordance with similar laws.[i][26]

Philosophers have always given truth a bill of divorcement by putting asunder what nature has joined together[27] and vice versa. In this way there have arisen, among the other heretics of psychology, Arianists,

---

[h] Toutes les puissances du corps et de l'entendement ne sont-elles pas des facultés, et qui pis est des facultés très ignorées, de franche qualités occultes, à commencer par le mouvement, dont personne n'a découvert l'origine – – Je ne sais s'il n'y auroit pas dans cet abîme une preuve de l'existence de l'Être Suprême. Il y a un secret dans tous les premiers ressorts de tous les Êtres – Or comment ce secret sans que personne le sût? il faut bien qu'il y ait un être, qui soit au fait. Voltaire, *Questions sur l'Encyclopédie*. Part VI. Article "Faculté," pp. 13, 15. ["Are not all the powers of the body and of the understanding faculties and, what is worse, quite unknown faculties, pure occult qualities, to start with movement whose origin no one has discovered . . . I do not know whether there would be in that abysm a proof of the existence of the Supreme Being. There is a secret in all these first motives of all beings . . . How then this secret, with no one knowing it? There must be a being who is knowledgeable." The *Questions sur l'Encyclopédie* (1770–2), in nine volumes, is Voltaire's expansion of his more famous *Dictionnaire philosophique* (1764).]

[i] See *Recherches sur l'entendement humain d'après les principes du sens commun* by Thomas Reid; translated from English and published in Amsterdam in 1768. [Section 21 of Chapter 6, for example, of Thomas Reid's *An Inquiry Into the Human Mind on the Principles of Common Sense* (1764) is relevant to this discussion.]

[22] Herder, *Essay*: "The attempt has been made to think of man's reason as a new and totally detached power that was put into his soul and given to him before all animals as a special additional gift and which, like the fourth step of a ladder with three steps below, must be considered by itself" (tr. Gode, p. 110; cf. tr. Forster, p. 83).

[23] The mystical or spiritual sense of words or of their literal sense.

[24] Herder, *Essay*: "I do not suddenly ascribe to man – as an arbitrary *qualitas occulta* – a new power providing him with the ability to create language" (tr. Gode, p. 107; cf. tr. Forster, p. 81). A "qualitas occulta" is a hidden quality.

[25] In Herder's *Essay*, with the recognition of a distinguishing mark human language was invented (tr. Gode, p. 116; cf. tr. Forster, p. 88).

[26] The second part of Herder's *Essay* discusses four natural laws by which men developed and came to invent language.

[27] Matthew 19:6: "What therefore God hath joined together, let not man put asunder."

Mohammedans, and Socinians,[28] who claim to have explained everything on the basis of a unique positive power[29] or entelechy[j] of the soul.

The mystery of the marriage between natures so opposed as the outer and the inner man, or body and soul, is great; in order to arrive at a comprehensive concept of the fullness within the unity of our human essence, several distinguishing earthly marks must be recognized.[30]

Man therefore is not only a living field but also the son of the field, and not only field and seed (in the system of materialists and idealists) but also the king[k] of the field,[31] who is to grow good seed and hostile tares; for what is a field without seeds and a prince without land and income? These Three in us are therefore One, namely Θεοῦ γεώργιον,[l] just as the three profiles on the wall are the natural shadow of a single body illuminated by a double light behind it – – –

---

[j] ἔστι γὰρ ἐξ ἐντελεχείᾳ ὄντος πάντα τὰ γιγνόμενα. Aristotle, *On the Soul* 3.7 [431a]. ["For all things that have come into being are from the entelechy of being."]

[k] Qui igitur exisse ex potestate dicuntur, idcirco dicuntur, quia non sunt in potestate *mentis*, cui *regnum totius animi* a natura tributum est. Cicero, *Tusculan Disputations* 3.5.

Omnem enim naturam necesse est, quae non solitaria sit neque simplex, sed cum alio iuncta atque connexa habere aliquem in se principatum, ut in homine mentem in belua quiddam simile mentis – Principatum autem id dico, quod Graeci ἡγεμονικόν vocant: quo nihil in hoc genere nec potest, nec debet esse praestantius. Cicero, *On the Nature of the Gods* 2.11.

Marcus Aurelius Antoninus, *Meditations* 5.19.

Dux et Imperator vitae mortalium animus est. Sallust, *The Jugurthine War* 1.

["Those then who are described as beside themselves are so described because they are not under the control of mind to which the empire of the whole soul has been assigned by nature," Cicero, *Tusculan Disputations* 3.5, tr. J. E. King (Loeb Classical Library, 1971).

"For every natural object that is not a homogeneous and simple substance but a complex and composite one must contain within it some ruling principle, for example in man the intelligence, in the lower animals something resembling intelligence . . . I use the term 'ruling principle' as the equivalent for the Greek *hēgemonikon*, meaning that art of anything which must and ought to have supremacy in a thing of that sort," Cicero, *On the Nature of the Gods* 2.11.29, tr. H. Rackham (Loeb Classical Library, 1956).

"Things of themselves cannot take the least hold of the Soul, nor have any access to her, nor deflect or move her; but the Soul alone deflects and moves herself, and whatever judgments she deems it right to form, in conformity with them she fashions for herself the things that submit themselves to her from without," Marcus Aurelius Antoninus, *Meditations* 5.19, tr. C. R. Haines (Loeb Classical Library, 1916).

"The ruler and leader of the life of mortal men is the mind," Sallust, *The Jugurthine War* 1. Sallust's *animus* has been translated as "mind," but it might also have been translated "soul."]

[l] In 1 Corinthians 3:9, this is what Paul calls the Church; the scholastic term is as ambiguous as the names of the soul and of human nature are even to this day. ["The field of God"; cf. the King James Version: "ye are God's husbandry."]

[28] All three are unitarian, that is, they reject the doctrine of the Trinity.

[29] See n. 16.   [30] See n. 25.

[31] "Field" in the phrase "king of the field" translates *Feld*; all other occurences of "field" in this paragraph translate *Acker*.

After I have wangled myself upward as far as the empyrean holiness of human nature, or to put it a better way, after my peripatetic[32] soap bubbles have blown ahead of me for long enough, so at length they burst mid-way into the following dewdrops:[33]

"Man learns to use and to govern all his limbs and senses, and therefore also the ear and tongue, because he can learn, must learn, and equally wants to learn. Consequently the origin of language is as natural and human[34] as the origin of all our deeds, skills, and crafts. But notwithstanding the fact that every apprentice[35] contributes to his instruction to learn in keeping with his inclination, talent, and opportunities, learning in the true understanding is not invention any more than sheer recollection is."[36]

I did not go far out of the way with my ideas, for we come to our goal at once, to wit:[37] the most recent Platonic proof of the origin of language.

Nothing could be more ridiculous than to conduct a proof that is the contrary of a truth that has been not only firmly proven[38] but also crowned.[m] [39] Hence I find myself under the pleasant obligation of being able to burn the incense of doubt to the fashionable spirit of my age.

Out of the vast hovering dream of images which pass by my soul when, seven months ago, I read the *Academy's Prize-Essay*, I collect myself in a moment of wakefulness in order to dwell at will on a single doubt and to observe it clearly and more correctly.[40] This One Doubt consists solely in

m   – – contendere durum
                Cum victore – –
                    Horace, *Satires* 1.9.42–3
                ["... it is hard to fight with the victor ..."]

32   That is, Aristotelian, and in contrast to Herder's "Platonic" account of the origin of language.
33   Cf. Herder, *Essay*: "The contemporary French philosopher ... made dazzling ... no more than an air bubble which for a while he keeps blowing ahead of himself but which not even he can prevent from unexpectedly bursting as he proceeds along his way" (tr. Gode, pp. 114; cf. Forster, p. 86).
34   Ibid.: "Invention of language is therefore as natural to man as it is to him that he is man" (tr. Gode, p. 115; cf. tr. Forster, p. 87).
35   Ibid.: "an apprentice finds it easiest to develop them for himself in this fashion" (tr. Gode, p. 110; cf. tr. Forster, p. 83).
36   The Platonic theme of anamnesis, or recollection.
37   Cf. Herder, *Essay*: "And then, in straightening out these concepts, I did not actually go out of my way, for of a sudden we find ourselves at our goal! To wit:" (tr. Gode, p. 115; cf. tr. Forster, p. 87).
38   Ibid.: The argument that language is of human origin "has everything speaking for it and nothing at all against it" (tr. Forster, p. 163).
39   Crowned, that is, by the Berlin Academy, which awarded Herder's *Essay* its prize.
40   Herder, *Essay*: "He manifests reflection when, confronted with the vast hovering dream of images which pass by his senses, he can collect himself into a moment of wakefulness and dwell at will on one image, can observe it clearly and more calmly" (tr. Gode, pp. 115–16; cf. tr. Forster, p. 87).

this: "whether the Platonic apologist ever had a serious intention to prove his theme or only to touch upon it?"[n]

I was induced to make this doubt and no other my theme by a whole ocean of distinguishing marks,[41] from which I intend to single out only a few, and the least of them at that, to wit: that the entire Platonic proof is composed of a closed circle, a perpetual merry-go-round,[42] and non-sense neither hidden nor refined; that it is based on the hidden powers of arbitrary names and the slogans or favorite ideas of society; that finally it amounts to a divine Genesis, which is indeed more supernatural, sacred, and poetic than the oldest oriental creation stories of heaven and earth. If the learned author had written in all seriousness, do you think he would have exposed himself so wantonly and rashly to a pressed-down, shaken-together,[43] hyperbolic-pleonastic re-retaliatory measure of criticism, or misused polemical weapons as wounds to himself, as stripes to himself,[44] or would he always have done the opposite of what he promises his readers, vows to them, and believes he is impressing upon them? – –

Platonic proof of the human origin of language
The human species stands above the animals not by stages of more or of less but in kind (p. 108 or p. 81)[45] because it is assured that

n
> ... curriculo pulverem Olympicum
> Collegisse iuvat, metaque fervidis
> Evitata rotis.
>> Horace, *Odes* 1.1.3–5
>
> Quis circum pagos et circum pagita pugnax
> Magna coronari contemnat Olympia, cui spes,
> Cui sit conditio dulcis sine pulvere palmae?
>> Horace, *Epistles* 1.1.49–51

[There are some whom "it delights to gather the Olympic dust, and the turning-post grazed by the glowing wheels."
"What boxer in the villages and at the cross-roads would refuse to crown himself with an Olympic wreath if he had the hope or the offer of the sweet palm without dust?"]

[41] Ibid.: "the vast ocean of sensations" (tr. Gode, p. 115; cf. tr. Forster, p. 87).
[42] Ibid.: "I have called Süssmilch's way of arguing a perpetual merry-go-round" (tr. Gode, p. 121; cf. tr. Forster, p. 91).
[43] Luke 6:38: "Give, and it shall be given unto you; good measure, pressed down, and shaken together."
[44] Exodus 21:23–5: "thou shalt give life for life ... Burning for burning, wound for wound, stripe for stripe."
[45] Hamann's summary of Herder's argument stays close to Herder's own words. In it, Hamann gave the page numbers of the treatise when he quoted a passage; I have instead given the corresponding page numbers in the two English translations by Gode and Forster.

man is vastly inferior to the animals in the intensity and reliability of his instincts, and indeed that he does not have at all what in many animal species we regard as innate artifactive skills and drives (p. 103 or pp. 77–8), whereas unlike the animals language, like senses and conceptions and drives, is congenital and directly natural (p. 107 or p. 80). This lack of an instinct, which pulls all the powers darkly toward a single point (p. 111 or p. 84) and limits them to a single point (p. 111 or p. 84), is replaced in man by reflection, which consists of an orientation of all powers which as such is peculiar to his species (p. 112 or p. 85) and in the tempering of the powers in subservience to this major orientation (p. 113 or p. 85), by which man becomes a creature whose positive power expressed itself in a vaster realm, after a finer organization, with greater light (pp. 111–12 or p. 84) and pursues its work more freely (p. 112 or p. 85).

Man, placed in the state of reflection which is peculiar to him, and given with this reflection full freedom of action for the first time, did invent language. For what is reflection? What is language? (p. 115 or p. 87).

Language, from without, is the true differential character of our species, as reason is from within (p. 127 or p. 96). Language is the natural organ of reason, a sense of the human soul, as the power of vision (in the story of the sensitive soul of the Ancients) builds for itself the eye and the instinct of the bee builds its cell (p. 128 or p. 97).

Reflection is characteristically peculiar to man and essential to his species; and so is language and the invention of language. Invention of language is therefore as natural to man as it is to him that he is man (p. 115 or p. 87).

A vast ocean of sensations permeates through all the channels of the senses[46] – in order at the end to make the reader attend to the academic thumbfull of apperception. – In short, "This first distinguishing mark within his reflection is a work of the soul! With it human language is invented!" Εὕρηκα![47]

---

[46] Herder, *Essay*: "in the vast ocean of sensations which permeates it through all the channels of the senses" (tr. Gode, p. 115, more freely than usual; cf. tr. Forster, p. 87).

[47] Ibid.: "The first act of this acknowledgement results in a clear concept; it is the first judgment of the soul – and through what did this acknowledgement occur? Through a distinguishing mark which he had to single out and which, as a distinguishing mark for reflection, struck him clearly. Well, then! Let us acclaim him with shouts of eureka! This first distinguishing mark, as it appeared in his reflection, was a work of the soul! With it human language is invented!" (tr. Gode, p. 116; cf. tr. Forster, p. 88). Hamann uses a more technical philosophical term for acknowledgement, namely apperception.

An archpriest[48] well-known in his diocese recalled with the most inward grief that he had heard, at some church festival devoid of moral and reason, a village preacher who had divided his subject into two parts, each of which contained in it an antithesis and both of which appeared to cancel out the other, but which actually proved, intuitively, that which they were supposed to prove: namely, a very peculiar, incomprehensible, and supernatural arithmetic. Despite all my most inward grief at having lost five thalers, alas!, every arduous, hard-working month of my precious life because of an extremely political arithmetic,[49] I cannot refrain, confronted with the similarity of the Platonic proof and that subject of a village preacher who is presumably poor in spirit, from smiling.

The Platonic proof of the human origin of language consists of two parts, one negative and one positive. The first includes reasons why man is not an animal, and the second includes reasons why man is nonetheless an animal. Such an apocalyptic[50] creature as neo-Platonic man, who is not an animal yet is an animal, can and must be the inventor of language because an animal cannot invent language and a God must not invent it.[51]

If I had the least desire to immortalize myself through stadium lengths[52] and notes to a meager text that are as impertinent in their erudition as in their volume, or through a philosophical commentary on two Latin words, and to become a writer for great minds and even greater fools, then the purely negative part of the Platonic proof could provide me with the most fertile material for a historical critical masterpiece – After many an edition and translation in our enlightened quarter of the earth, perhaps it would occur to a Chinese emperor[53] of the next age to

---

[48] Johann Joachim Spalding (1717–1804); "archpriest" as a councillor of the Upper Consistory (*Oberkonsistorialrat*) in Berlin (a position he held since 1764). In a letter of October 7, 1772, Hamann refers to him as the "court preacher of the Solomon of the North" (*Briefe*, vol. III, p. 18). In 1772 Spalding published anonymously, *Über die Nutzbarkeit des Predigtamtes und deren Beförderung* ("On the utility of the ministry and its promotion"), in which he recalls the sermon on the "divine arithmetic" of the Trinity.

[49] Hamann's salary had recently been cut as part of an austerity drive of the government; he complains about it in a letter to Herder on October 6, 1772 (*Briefe*, vol. III, p. 18) and at the end of *To the Solomon of Prussia*.

[50] Revelation 17:8: "the beast that was, and is not, and yet is."

[51] Closely follows Herder, *Essay*, tr. Gode p. 127, tr. Forster p. 96.

[52] Perhaps another reference to Pindar.

[53] Frederick the Great, whose poem to his favorite cook was entitled "Epître au Sieur Noël par l'Empereur de la Chine."

have a hearty extract[54] of my masterpiece canonized as a family devotional reader, or to sell a raked-over coal of ideas and doubts in the High German mother tongue (which is as consummately barbaric and beggar-proud as that of the late Bayle of most blessed memory and of M. Henry Ophellot de la Pause)[0] to his subjects for the hare in the moon which so inspired the sacred Confucius.[55] However, because I am a sworn enemy to all the thieves' cant and Chinese charlatanry of authorship and because criticizing the negative part of the Platonic proof does not even call on my present interest, I therefore eagerly concede that "man is not an animal and has no instincts at all"; I do this all the more readily as the most recent apologist of the human origin of language seems to presuppose in every animal an instinct as essential as genius is in every man who is at least an author. By this means instinct, needless to say, becomes a *conditio sine qua non* of every animal, in order to raise and promote man out of the sphere of the animals with all the more intensity and reliability[56] into a higher order of creatures that is differentiated by kind and not by stages – – –

In the history of our present age, we have more than one shining example of how little is involved in being a standing, lying, sitting, or even hither and thither wandering creature who not in stages but in kind is above those animals that are commonly called subjects; a creature who because of its more freely working positive power[57] is called a tyrant or a god of the earth, in accordance with the diversity of heavenly zones, tongues,

---

[0] – – – cette langue herissée encore de termes barbares, qui se traîne peniblement avec tout son attirail minutieux d'articles et de verbes auxiliares et qui n'oppose que son orgueilleuse pauvreté à la magnificence de l'idiome de Cervantes, à la douceur du Tasse et à l'energie de celui des Bolingbrokes et des Shaftesburys. Preface to *Histoire des douze Césars de Suetone* etc., p. xii. [". . . this language still bristling with barbarisms that crawls along with difficulty with all its minute gear of articles and auxiliary verbs and does nothing but oppose its proud poverty to the magnificence of Cervantes' idiom, the sweetness of Tasso's, and the energy of the Bolingbrokes and the Shaftesburys." The quotation is by "Henri Ophellot de la Pause" (an anagram of "le philosophe de la nature" and the pseudonym of Delisle de Sales (1741–1816)), in the preface to his translation of Suetonius, published in 1770.]

54 In 1765 the *Extrait du Dictionnaire historique et critique de Bayle* was published in Berlin.
55 In Chinese legend, the hare in the moon can be seen mixing the elixir of life with mortar and pestle. It is likely that "Confucius" refers metaschematically to an enlightened philosopher under Frederick (the "Emperor of China").
56 Herder, *Essay*: "It seems assured that man is by far inferior to the animals in the intensity and reliability of his instincts" (tr. Gode, p. 103; cf. tr. Forster, p. 77).
57 Ibid.: "If man was not to be an instinctual animal, he had to be – by virtue of the more freely working positive power of his soul – a creature of reflection" (tr. Gode, p. 112; cf. tr. Forster, p. 85).

and times; a creature whose character in the overall determination of all higher powers within the total complex of the lower powers,[58] all of whose psychology, has been turned into a pitiful wasteland in recent times through the tiresome fault of some canting philosophers and their German brothers[59] – a shining example, I say, from the history of the living age before our eyes that nothing under the sun is easier than to be and to make such a creature, but that it may be miserably hard to support it and have it come of age, especially if it is newly minted and quite young.

Despite all the positive power, its orientation, the tempering of all powers in subservience to the major orientation, in spite of the vaster realm, the finer organization, etc., and all the heavy expenses squandered on the negative part of the Platonic proof, the majesty of man and his species unexpectedly bursts as we proceed along our way because of the positive part.[60] For does the whole positive part of the Platonic proof state anything more positively and explicitly than that man thinks and speaks out of instinct – – that the positive power to think and to speak is congenital and directly natural[61] – – that it like the instinct of the animal is pulled, drawn, and steered toward the single point of a distinguishing mark – that with the first word the whole language was invented, despite the law of eternal progression;[62] – that the invention of language is as essential to man as the web to the spider and the honeycomb to the bee[63] – and that nothing more is needed than to place man in the state of reflection which is peculiar to him in order to invent what is natural

---

[58] Ibid.: "the overall determination of his powers of thought within the total complex of his senses and of his drives" (tr. Gode, p. 111; tr. Forster, p. 84).

[59] Ibid.: "in modern times this entire area of psychology has been turned into a pitiful wasteland because French philosophers . . . have turned everything upside down, while German philosophers arrange most of these concepts more for the benefit of their systems" (tr. Gode, p. 115; cf. tr. Forster, p. 87).

[60] Ibid.: "which not even he can prevent from unexpectedly bursting as he proceeds along his way" (tr. Gode, p. 114; cf. tr. Forster, p. 86).

[61] Ibid., tr. Gode, p. 107; cf. tr. Forster, p. 80; in context the remark is applied only to the non-human language of animals.

[62] The first of the natural laws discussed in the second part of Herder's *Essay*; see p. 127 in Forster's translation.

[63] Three passages in Herder's *Essay* are combined here: "In that case language would become as essential to man as it is essential that he is man" (tr. Gode, p. 108; cf. tr. Forster. p. 81); "The bee in its hive builds with a wisdom that Egeria could not teach her Numa . . . the spider weaves with the skill of Minerva" (tr. Gode, p. 104; cf. tr. Forster, p. 78); and "the instinct of the bee builds its cell" (tr. Gode, p. 128; cf. tr. Forster, p. 97).

o him[64] – As a curse and a blemish of our enlightened age there lives an outlived mad spermologue,[65] on whose bald scalp, but for the impenetrable shield of the tolerance that obtains in Olympia,[66] fiery coals from heaven would long ago have rained[67] – – I do not mean the immortal citizen of Mount Krapac[68] but the childish ex-rector C. T. D.[69] * * * – – O abomination of desolation[70] (such a thing may well have been heard in heathen mythology but not in any church history of the old and new Israel!) – to resume that low trick of the Gallic[71] Jupiter on his father[72] – and indecently to assault the poetic privy parts of a sacred person, whom I could name with as little shame as even our cleverest and most modest orthodox doubt his testimonium[73] – in order not be abused for having taken the poetic intensity from the Platonic apology for the human origin of language, I will break into song with a fragment of the most recent Genesis in the oriental dialect[74] on the Pindaric lyre-for-hire as praise and incense for the Pythian[75] victor.

[64] Two passages from Herder's *Essay* are alluded to: "Man, placed in the state of reflection which is peculiar to him, with this reflection for the first time given full freedom of action, did invent language . . . Invention of language is therefore as natural to man as it is to him that he is man" (tr. Gode, p. 115; cf. tr. Forster, p. 87); "Language has been invented . . . as naturally and to man as necessarily as man was man" (tr. Gode, p. 118, tr. Forster, p. 89).

[65] A spermologue, σπερμολόγος, is "one who picks up and retails scraps of knowledge, an idle babbler, gossip," is translated as "babbler" in Acts 17:18. Here Hamann is referring to the rector of a gymnasium in Berlin, Christian Tobias Damm (1699–1778), who published the first volume of his *Vom historischen Glauben* ("On Historical Faith") in 1772, a skeptical treatment of the miracles of the Old Testament.

[66] A reference to Frederick's Berlin; called "sotadic tolerance" in *The Knight of the Rose-Cross*. In Damm's preface, he writes that the phrase "scriptum est" acts as an "impenetrable shield of superstition." (*Hamanns Hauptschriften erklärt*, vol. IV, p. 244; quoted on p. 247).

[67] Cf. Psalms 68:21: "But God shall wound the head of his enemies, and the hairy scalp of such an one as goeth on still in his trespasses"; Psalms 140:10: "Let burning coals fall upon them"; Romans 12:20: "Therefore if thine enemy hunger, feed him; if he thirst, give him drink: for in so doing thou shalt heap coals of fire on his head."

[68] Unknown; one suggestion is that the referent is Elijah, who did not die but was taken up to Heaven.

[69] In a judgment before the Oberkonsistorium, Damm was obliged not to instruct youth in theology. "Childish" may also be appropriate given his disdain for "childish" belief in miracles.

[70] Matthew 24:15 (echoing Daniel 9:27, 11:31, and 12:11).

[71] The Galli were the self-castrating priests of Cybele.

[72] Jupiter castrated his father Uranus.

[73] The Holy Spirit, whose creative power had been denied by enlightened theologians.

[74] The third section of the first part of Herder's *Essay* praises the "old unpolished languages" and especially the "Oriental languages," a theme that is developed in the second part.

[75] The Pythian games were sacred to Apollo, and "Apollo" refers metaschematically to the Enlighteners.

Courage, allons, prends ta harpe bénie[p]
Et moque-toi de son Académie – –

He created him a nonanimal and animal from a vast ocean of sensations, from the vast hovering dream of images which passed by his senses and which as an act of their acknowledgement, as a distinguishing mark for reflection[76] stuck out the rifle before him.[77] High above the animals, not by stages but by kind of instinct, stood the Platonic androgyne[78] as a nonanimal – without instinct.

Go have dominion over the fowl of prey and things of the sea;[79] but be mute and dumb! said the andriantoglyph[80] to the protoplast[81] of language – for in the moment that you distinguish the fruit of your inner and outer instinct, your mouth shall be opened[82] and you will be an animal full of the instinct of outer and inner, and your nonanimal character will wither like grass.[83]

As yet the Platonic androgyne stood, born mute, in the sleep of hidden powers – Behold! in a moment it happened that he fell deeper and deeper into his element – into a vast ocean of sensations – into a vast hovering dream of images, and that he was placed in a state of reflection and rapture which however was peculiar to him. And behold! in that very same moment it happened that the first sound of his outer instinct escaped him, as a characteristic mark and a word of communication of the inner

---

[p] St. George, in Voltaire, *La Pucelle d'Orléans*, canto 16, ll. 99–100. ["Be brave, come on, take up the blessed harp / And make sport of your Academy"; Hamann directs Voltaire's lines to Herder.]

[76] The phrases come from Herder's *Essay*, pp. 115–16, tr. Gode (pp. 87–8, tr. Forster).

[77] Alludes to Damm's preface (see n. 66): "However, as soon as [the phrase "scriptum est"] becomes an impenetrable shield of superstition, which is opposed, without any further investigation, to all reasonable designs and in front of which everyone points his rifle, then it becomes a loathsome thing."

[78] Plato, *Symposium* 189c–193c: human beings were originally two-bodied and four-limbed, before Zeus split them in half.

[79] Genesis 1:28: "God said unto them, Be fruitful, and multiply, and replenish the earth, and subdue it: and have dominion over the fish of the sea, and over the fowl of the air, and over every living thing that moveth upon the earth"; James 3:7: "For every kind of beasts, and of birds, and of serpents, and of things in the sea, is tamed, and hath been tamed of mankind."

[80] ἀνδριαντογλύφος, carver of statues.

[81] "Protoplast" means not only the first formed or created but also, as probably here, the first former or creator.

[82] Genesis 3:5: "For God doth know that in the day ye eat thereof, then your eyes shall be opened."

[83] Psalms 37:2: "For they shall soon be cut down like the grass, and wither [*verwelket*] as the green herb"; Isaiah 15:6: "For the waters of Nimrim shall be desolate: for the hay is withered away, the grass faileth [*verwelket*], there is no green thing." Isaiah 64:6: "we all do fade [*verwelket*] as a leaf."

instinct.[84] And the outer and the inner instinct were the first word,[85] and the nonanimal placed above the animals through the lack of instinct was a creature driven by the instinct of outer and inner, that is, a reflective and language-creating[86] animal; Hail to the inventor of language! Let us acclaim him[87] with a Solomonic מצאתי![q] With this divine organ of the understanding[88] the whole Koran of the seven arts and the whole Talmud of the four faculties[89] are discovered, and upon this rock stands the stronghold of our age's philosophical faith, before which all the gates of oriental poetry must bend.[90]

I called this supernatural proof of the human origin of language "Platonic" because it starts with the neologic coinage of reflection,[91] as an "individual point and shining spark of the perfect system"[92] and in the end returns to a Greek synonymy,[93] and because the Platonists chewed over and over the λόγος ἐνδιάθετος or ἐνθυμηματικός and λόγος προφορικός,[94] the inner and the outer word, like that Swedish coop-prophet,[95] *ab intra et extra* and *ad nauseam*.

[q] "Voici ce que j'ai *trouvé* c'est que Dieu a créé l'homme juste; mais ils ont cherché beaucoup de discours." Ecclesiastes 7:[29]. ["Lo, this only have I found, that God hath made man upright; but they have sought out many inventions." Hamann quotes from the Olivetan-Martin version of the Bible, perhaps preferring the French "beaucoup de discours" to Luther's "viel Künste." The Hebrew word for "I have found" is used instead of Greek εὕρηκα, "eureka" or "I have found."]

84 Herder, *Essay*: "The first characteristic mark which I conceive is a characteristic word for me and a word of communication for others!" (tr. Gode, p. 128; cf. tr. Forster, p. 97).
85 Genesis 1:5: "And the evening and the morning were the first day."
86 Contrast Herder, *Essay*: "I do not suddenly ascribe to man . . . a new power providing him with the ability to create language" (tr. Gode, p. 107; cf. tr. Forster, p. 81).
87 Ibid.: "Let us acclaim him with shouts of eureka!" (tr. Gode, p. 116; cf. tr. Forster, 88).
88 Ibid.: "Thus language appears as a natural organ of the understanding" (tr. Gode, p. 128, with "understanding" substituted for "reason" [Herder has *Verstand*]; cf. tr. Forster, p. 97).
89 The seven arts are the seven liberal arts of the Middle Ages, and the four faculties are those of the medieval university (arts, theology, law, medicine).
90 Matthew 16:18: "upon this rock I will build my church; and the gates of hell shall not prevail against it."
91 Herder, *Essay*: "This creature is man, and this entire disposition of his nature . . . we shall call reflection" (tr. Gode, p. 112; cf. tr. Forster, p. 84).
92 Ibid. (on bees): "They are individual points, shining sparks from the light of God's perfection" (tr. Forster, p. 130).
93 Ibid.: "In more than one language, word and reason, concept and word, language and cause have hence one designation, and this synonomy comprises their full genetic origin" (tr. Gode, p. 127; cf. tr. Forster, pp. 96). The Greek word "logos" bears all those meanings.
94 Distinctions among kinds of λόγος. Thought and word were distinguished among Stoics as λόγος ἐνδιάθετος and λόγος προφορικός, respectively; the λόγος ἐνθυμηματικός is, presumably, a λόγος in the logical form of the enthymeme.
95 Emanuel Swedenborg (1688–1772), Swedish scientist, philosopher, and theologian.

Philo counts the γόνιμος φώνη as the sixth sense[r] [96] and, what is more, seems to speak of the genesis of language almost like the *"nisus* of the embryo to speak at the moment when it reaches maturity";[s] [97] he sees it, however, as a great audacity to "point to bodies through shadows, things through words."[t]

I could, if it were worth the trouble, explain the whole proof woven through with arbitrarily assumed postulates and false axioms about the nature of language, from more than one side, and have the apologist appear in a certain light in which however he is not intended to appear here.[98] I therefore take only that part of his legislation of the origin of a continually progressing human language and a continuing progressing human soul which is thoroughly misjudged, misunderstood, and obscured.

[r] τὸ μὲν γὰρ ἄλογον ψυχῆς μέρος ἑξαχῇ διελὼν ὁ δημιουργὸς ἐξ μοίρας εἰργάζετο, ὅρασιν, ἀκοήν, γεῦσιν, ὄσφρησιν, ἀφήν, γόνιμον φώνην. Philo, "Qui rerum divinarum haeres," *Omnia quae extant opera*, Frankfurt 1691, pp. 512–13. [Philo, "Who is the heir of divine things," 232 [508]; cf. Loeb edn. of the works of Philo (1932), vol. IV, p. 398. "For the Maker divided the irrational part of the soul sixfold and produced six parts, sight, hearing, taste, smell, touch, and fertile voice." However, a more modern text has "seven" rather than "six" parts by separating γόνιμος from φώνη (it also inverts their order): "sight, hearing, taste, smell, touch, voice and reproductive faculty."]

[s] ὁ γὰρ διοιγνὺς μήτραν ἑκάστων, τοῦ μὲν νοῦ πρὸς τὰς νοητὰς καταλήψεις, τοῦ δὲ λόγου πρὸς τὰ διὰ φώνης ἐνεργείας, τῶν δὲ αἰσθήσεων πρὸς τὰς ἀπὸ τῶν ὑποκειμένων ἐγγινομένας φαντασίας, τοῦ δὲ σώματος πρὸς τὰς οἰκείους αὐτῷ σχέσεις τε καὶ κινήσεις ἀόρατος καὶ σπερματικὸς καὶ τεχνικὸς καὶ Θεῖός ἐστι λόγος. Ibid. p. 497. [Philo, "Who is the heir of divine things," 119 [489]; cf. Loeb ed. of the works of Philo (1932), vol. IV, pp. 340–2. Apart from a few minor errors in Greek, the text in the note may be translated: "For he that opens the womb of each of these, of mind, to mental apprehensions, of speech, to the activity of the voice, of the senses, to receive the pictures presented to it by objects, of the body, to the movements and postures proper to it, it is the invisible, seminal artificer, the divine word," tr. Colson and Whitaker, the Loeb edn. of the works of Philo (1932), vol. IV, p. 341).]

[t] τόλμημα οὐ μικρόν, διὰ σκιῶν μοι σώματα, διὰ ῥημάτων πράγματα, ἅπερ ἀμήχανον ἦν δεικνύναι. Ibid. p. 491. [Philo, "Who is the heir of divine things," 72 [483]; cf. the Loeb edn. of the works of Philo (1932), vol. IV, p. 318. "Great indeed was its audacity, that it should attempt the impossible task to use shadows to point me to substances, words to point me to facts" (tr. Colson and Whitaker, the Loeb edn. of the works of Philo (1932), vol. IV, p. 319).]

[96] In the bilingual (Greek–Latin) edition of Philo's works from which Hamann is quoting, the γόνιμος φώνη is translated as "vox pronunciativa," a pronouncing voice; however, the Greek word γόνιμος means "productive, fertile."

[97] Herder, *Essay*: "the genesis of language is as much an inner imperative as is the impulse of the embyro to be born at the moment it reaches maturity" (tr. Forster, p. 129). *Nisus*, in Latin, is a straining or thrusting forth.

[98] Ibid.: "I cannot possibly explain the whole section in its totality here, woven through with arbitrarily assumed postulates and false axioms about the nature of language as it is, because the author would always appear in a certain light in which he is not intended to appear here" (tr. Forster, p. 135, with "not intended to" for "should").

Nor do I touch on the poetic fragment for the archaeology of the history of language to any greater degree.[99] However, if with the first word human language was invented, then perhaps the archaeologist understands by word, in keeping with a turn of expression common to the Orient,[100] a quite different thing. For in accordance with the Wachterian *Concordia naturae*[101] and "as the early inventors wanted to say everything at once" (p. 162 or p. 123), the first word may well turn out to be neither a noun nor a verb,[102] but rather a whole period at the least[u] – in strength and intensity standing in inverse ratio to our contemporary Aphthonian chriae[103] of III pages – "And beyond this let us not play with words!"[104]

Man must therefore be a creature, as our dear Plato has proved in accordance with the wisdom that has been granted to him as the most sure word of prophecy which shines in a dark place,[105] a creature who

---

[u] Like the Chinese script of which Boulanger says in his "essays sur la population d'Amérique" (Amsterdam, 1767), vol. IV, p. 278: "Les *charactères chinois* n'étant pas des lettres, mais des mots, des termes, ou des *phrases.*"

Or like the oldest statues, ὧν τέχνη ἐδόκει ἡ συστολὴ καὶ ἰσχνότης. Demetrius of Phaleron, *De elocutione* 14.

In order to produce and transfer some concept about the *very most ancient language*, that a language is as *possible without any of our grammar* as it is with no *tongue* or *aperture* of the *mouth* according to the most recent belly-talkers or engastrimyths, etc., I simply refer to my countryman, Theophilus Siegfried Bayer, *Museum Sinicum* (St. Petersburg, 1730). [The quotation from Boulanger, "The Chinese characters, not being letters but rather words, expressions, sentences," has not been traced.

In context, the passage from Demetrius reads, "So there is something neat and trim in the older method of writing. It resembles ancient statues, the art of which was thought to consist in their succinctness and spareness" (tr. W. Rhys Roberts, Loeb Classical Library, 1927, p. 307).

The full title of Bayer's work may be translated as "The Chinese Museum, in which the principle of the Chinese language and literature is explained." An "engastrimyth" is the Greek form of "ventriloquist," both meaning "belly-speaker" (it is found in the title of ch. 58 of Rabelais' Fourth Book). Hamann mocks the concept of a grammar-less language by comparing it to the blemmyae of fable.]

[99] Ibid.: "which I consider here only as a poetic fragment for the archaeology of the history of peoples" (tr. Forster, p. 153).

[100] Ibid.: "Amongst the Orientals it has come to be a common turn of expression to call the recognition of a thing the naming of it" (tr. Gode, p. 127; cf. tr. Forster, pp. 96–7).

[101] Johann Georg Wachter, *Naturae et scripturae concordia* (1752).

[102] Herder, *Essay*: "From the verbs it was that the nouns grew and not from the nouns the verbs" (tr. Gode, p. 132; cf. tr. Forster, p. 100).

[103] Aphthonius was a fourth-century sophist and rhetorician whose *Progymnasmata* was an important pedagogical text for humanists in the Renaissance; according to the *Oxford English Dictionary* article which quotes the standard Greek–English Lexicon, a *chreia* or *chria* is "A pregnant sentence . . . borrowed from some other author, and worked out by certain rules."

[104] Herder, *Essay*, tr. Gode, p. 115; cf. tr. Forster, p. 87.

[105] 2 Peter 1:19: "We have also a more sure word of prophecy; whereunto ye do well that ye take heed, as unto a light that shineth in a dark place."

stands above the animals not by stages but by kind in order to become worthy of his true destiny, the critical and archontic office of a political animal, if that is still present with our readers.

In criticism and politics, therefore, consists the entire canon of human perfection, which my friend Herder –

Much-beloved reader! My name is the Magus of the North[v] – – and I make it my evening's festivity and my last duty of my life to recognize in the crowned Pythian victor my friend Herder, to embrace and bless him,[106] publicly and solemnly, against whom I have heretofore fenced with eyes blindfolded, – – He stooped down – who shall rouse him up? – – His eyes shall be red with wine, and his teeth white with milk – –[w]

Reader! fear not; I am not a specter, as walks in darkness or wastes at your noonday,[x] nor even the shade (now enlightened by his friend Herr Carl Renatus H–s–e) of the Royal Prussian Privy Councillor and Ordinary Professor of Philosophy and Eloquence at the University of Halle, etc., who once lived *in genio seculi* magnificently and heartily.[107] No; I am nothing but the Magus of the North and as him I will and must die – as innocently as I became him[108] – sun, moon, and stars are already dark to me behind clouds after rain,[109] and my teeth have as few festive hours

---

[v] – – "il n'y a point d'exorde plus beau que celui-cy: mes très chers frères, mon nom est Macaire." *Œuvres du comte Algarotti*. Dulces ante omnia Musae.

Traduit de l'Italien, à Berlin. 1772, vol. VII, p. 390. [Francesco Algarotti (1712–64) was an Italian writer and connoisseur of the arts. The quotation comes from a letter of 1752: "There is no more beautiful exordium than this: 'my very dear brothers, my name is Macarius.'" (Algarotti refers to the life of Macarius of Rome, as told for example in the *Vitae patrum*; see the *Patrologia Latina* 73, col. 422b.)

The motto "Dulces ante omnia Musae" ("sweet above all things the Muses"), which appears on the title pages of Algarotti's works in this edition, is taken from Virgil, *Georgics* 2.475.]

[w] Genesis 49:9, 12. [Genesis 49:9: "he stooped down . . . who shall rouse him up?"; Genesis 49:12: "His eyes shall be red with wine, and his teeth white with milk."]

[x] un démon du midi. ["A demon of midday"; cf. Psalm 91:5–6: "Thou shalt not be afraid . . . Nor for the pestilence that walketh in darkness; nor for the destruction that wasteth at noonday."]

[106] In a letter of August 1, 1772 (*Briefe*, vol. III, p. 15), Herder had asked Hamann for a blessing instead of a curse.

[107] The shade is Christian Adolph Klotz, an enemy of Herder, who published his *Genius seculi* ("Genius of the age") in 1760 and who had died in 1771. His "friend" is Carl Renatus Hausen, who took Klotz as his subject in *Leben und Charakter Herrn Christian Adolph Klotzens, Königlich-Preussischen Geheimden-Raths und ordentlichen Professors der Weltweisheit und Beredsamkeit auf der Universität Halle u.s.w.* ["Life and character of Herr Christian Adolph Klotzen, Royal Prussian Privy Councillor and Ordinary Professor of Philosophy and Eloquence at the University of Halle, etc."] in 1772.

[108] Since the name was applied to Hamann (by Karl von Moser), not chosen by him.

[109] Ecclesiastes 12:2: "While the sun, or the light, or the moon, or the stars, be not darkened, nor the clouds return after the rain."

as the mill-maid of Solomon the Preacher.[110] The sacred inquisition of political arithmetic – more melancholy-clever than an auto da fé – has condemned the last child[y] below the age of majority of those wise men from the east to an iron furnace,[z] where he is to starve and freeze because the timber of our costly thirsty canals[111] grows more expensive from year to year, so that all my fellow citizens (although no Magi) must freeze for the sake of making this iron furnace of an Egyptian master-hand warm,[112] never mind glowing and seven times more heated than the lime furnaces in the north are wont to be. Why should I not go with peace and joy[113] to the generation of my fathers[114] accompanied by the sound of the cornet, flute, harp, sackbut, psaltery, dulcimer, and all kinds of music,[115] of which the *beaux esprits* of this age are indeed *virtuosi*, and who by cultivating the "middle sense in its range of receptivity from without"[116] have made a greater name for themselves than the God of the Jews through the trumpets of his priests, which may well cause cities to collapse[117] but are not able to build any, like our contemporary Amphions[118] – – all through the sheer power of music and their musical taste that hears the grass grow: But why do I continue to talk this much? It was one day decided by the decree of the watchers[119] through political arithmetic that the Magus is no longer to burn but rather to freeze and starve, even

---

[y] Non sine Dîs animosus infans.
  Horace, Ode 3.4.20 ["The child courageous not without the protection of the gods."]
[z] Daniel 3:19. ["That they should heat the furnace one seven times more than it was wont to be heated."]

[110] Ecclesiastes 12:3: "the grinders cease because they are few." In Luther's version, the mill-grinders are explicitly female, hence Hamann's "mill-maids." Hamann is complaining that because of the pay-cut he suffered, the hours in which he can eat good food are few.
[111] In 1772, at the first partition of Poland, Frederick the Great obtained territory linking East Prussia with the rest of his domains and began to build canals linking them together.
[112] Deuteronomy 4:20: "But the Lord hath taken you, and brought you forth out of the iron furnace, even out of Egypt."
[113] The opening of Luther's hymn, "In peace and joy I now depart."
[114] Psalm 49:19: "He shall go to the generation of his fathers."
[115] Daniel 3:5: "That at what time ye hear the sound of the cornet, flute, harp, sackbut, psaltery, dulcimer, and all kinds of musick, ye fall down and worship the golden image that Nebuchadnezzar the king hath set up."
[116] A reference to the sense of hearing, from Herder, *Essay*, tr. Gode, p. 142; cf. tr. Forster, p. 108; in this section of the essay, the sense of hearing is discussed at length. Here applied ironically to Frederick's love of music.
[117] Joshua 6.
[118] Amphion, king of Thebes, fortified the city by playing his lyre; the stones assembled themselves into the wall by the power of his music.
[119] Daniel 4:17: "This matter is by the decree of the watchers."

assuming that 7,000 of his brothers were in the land,[120] but of course I cannot determine the number without the higher revelation of political arithmetic, which I cannot think of without the most inward grief of my entrails, just like a certain court preacher and the divine arithmetic.[aa]

Ought not[121] my friend Herder, in order to chase after the mark, the jewel of the announced prize, within the limits of the academy,[122] ought he not to have run as uncertainly, fought as one that beats the air?[123] Indeed he suffered as a fine soldier[124] and was legally crowned because he strove lawfully.[bb] As a clever steward of the mammon of unrighteousness[125] he could take nothing but the revelations and traditions of his age as the basis of his treatise and he could only build his proof on sand,[126] piecework, wood, hay, stubble[127] – – but of course: everything in accordance with the latest model of his age – Is it his fault that in our economic, blissfully-sensitive,[cc] mercilessly righteous age (contrary to some few usages and prejudices of the veiled and revealed Judaism whose influence as charitable as it is secret but which the blind world does not know because it does not see it) Arabic tournaments are still being tolerated, as Count Algarotti[dd] (may whose bones lie as gently as they do

---

[aa] Johann Joachim Spalding, *Über die Nutzbarkeit des Predigtamtes und deren Beförderung* (Berlin, 1772), p. 134. ["I still remember with the most inward grief a sermon . . . who had for its theme: divine arithmetic, according to which, first of all, One is Three and secondly, There is One"; see also n. 48.]

[bb] νομίμως, 2 Timothy 2:5. ["And if a man also strive for masteries, yet is he not crowned, except he strive lawfully"; the Greek word means "lawfully."]

[cc] *sentimental*. [Hamann parodies the fashionable term.]

[dd] C'est aux *Arabes*, qu'on doit l'usage des *Thèses publiques*, que l'on pourroit nommer les *Tournois* et *les joutes* de la Philosophie. *Œuvres du comte Algarotti*. Dulces ante omnia Musae. Traduit de l'Italien, à Berlin, 1772, vol. V, p. 464. [The quotation is taken from his "Pensées diverses": "It is to the Arabs that we derive the practice of public disputations, which we could call the tourneys or the jousts of philosophy." See also note v.]

[120] 1 Kings 19:18: "Yet I have left me seven thousand in Israel."
[121] Luke 24:26: "Ought not Christ to have suffered these things, and to enter into his glory?"
[122] Hamann draws closely on the language of Philippians 3:12 and 14 and 1 Corinthians 9:24, which because of differences between Luther's Bible and the King James Bible I have not been able to reproduce here.
[123] 1 Corinthians 9:26: "I therefore so run, not as uncertainly; so fight I, not as one that beateth the air."
[124] 2 Timothy 2:3: "Thou therefore endure hardness, as a good soldier of Jesus Christ."
[125] Luke 16:8–9.
[126] Matthew 7:26: "And every one that heareth these sayings of mine, and doeth them not, shall be likened unto a foolish man, which built his house upon the sand," and other passages.
[127] 1 Corinthians 3:12: "Now if any man build upon this foundation gold, silver, precious stones, wood, hay, stubble."

luxuriously!)[128] writes? Ought he not to have delivered a sonnet[ee] if he intended to satisfy a public doting about questions and strifes of words?[129] – Ought he not to have accommodated himself to the critical and archontic debility of an age whose politics is no mere solecism[ff] – nor gallionism[gg] but rather the mystery of the most holy contradiction which rules in the climate and is most active in children – in an age, in front of whose critical nose the Halle Johann Salomo Mathanasius[130] may pour out the full load of his undigested erudition, corrupted with acid and gall, indeed an age when great men in at least three faculties and worthy members of the education, defense, and welfare trades feed and strengthen their sound reason on the crap of historical faith;[hh] – in a moral age that listens with ears pricked up to the algebra[ii] of the realities to which the synagogue has given its imprimatur; – in a most Christian age when an angel of the congregation with a cloven foot[131] – (may lukewarm water, like his style, be in your mouth, posterity![132] his name!) can deny the spiritual priesthood and blaspheme the most sacred calling through twice unforgivable lies, in comparison with which all anacreontic clowning is genuine morality and all the pythanological paralogisms[133] about the origin of language are gold and precious stones – – In order to be gone up through

---

[ee] Les Académies fondées par les Princes recueillent pour ainsi dire les *Sonnets* des Sciences – et jamais un *livre*. Ibid., p. 369. ["The academies of royal foundation gather, so to speak, the sonnets of the sciences . . . and never a book" from pp. 396–7 of vol. v (the "Pensées diverses").]

[ff] Le Solecisme de vouloir la fin sans employer les moyens, qui y conduisent. Ibid., vol. vii, p. 385. ["The solecism of wanting the end but not using the means that lead to it"; from a letter of 1756.]

[gg] οὐδὲν τούτων τῷ Γαλλίωνι ἔμελεν. Acts 18:17. The city Shushan was perplexed; meanwhile the king and his project director, who was presumably at once a leaseholder of wit and bon ton, sat down to drink. Esther 3:15. [Acts 18:17: "Gallio cared for none of these things." Esther 3:15: "and the king and Haman sat down to drink; but the city Shushan was perplexed."]

[hh] Of C. T. D. *Vom historischen Glauben* (Berlin, 1772). The book was published at the author's expense. [Christian Tobias Damm, "Of historical faith"; see n. 65.]

[ii] Toutes les actions de la vie se réduissent à autant de problèmes de Maximis et Minimis, Algarotti already prophesied. Ibid., vol. v, p. 291. ["All the problems of life may be reduced to as many problems of maxima and minima"; from "Pensées diverses."]

[128] Frederick raised a monument to Algarotti in Pisa.

[129] 1 Timothy 6:4: "He is proud, knowing nothing, but doting about questions and strifes of words."

[130] Johann Salomo Semler, professor of theology in Halle, challenged the divine authority of the Bible. The name "Mathanasius" implies pedantic learning and was the pseudonym of Thémiseul de Saint-Hyacinthe in his popular satire on pedantry, *Le Chef-d'œuvre d'un inconnu* (1714).

[131] A pun in German on Spalding's name ("Spaltung" means cleft); see n. 48.

[132] In order, that is, for posterity to spew it out, as in Revelation 3:16: "So then because thou art lukewarm, and neither cold nor hot, I will spue thee out of my mouth."

[133] "Pythanological" may be Hamann's coinage, from πυνθάνομαι, to learn; a paralogism is a piece of false reasoning.

great victories,[134] my friend Herder could not write otherwise than as a satyr[135] for a wicked, adulterous generation[136] that is neither nonanimal nor inhuman, but a prodigy with iron arm, an ant's belly, and the countenance of Anubis[jj] – for a generation that denies God, and rushes to become rich, and through miscellaneous works in poetry and prose means to conquer heaven and earth! The angel of death and the heir of their full barns is calling them by name[kk] – – in a tragic comic age when even a Magus in Europe is not ashamed to run his head against the wall and to whimper[ll]

[jj] Je feray ce que dit le Florentin: Bras de fer, ventre de fourmi, ame de chien. C'est à dire: Pour devenir riche, j'endureray tant de travail que mon corps en pourra porter; je me passeray aux plus petis despens qu'il me sera possible; de conscience j'en auray autant qu'un chien. Lequel dernier point s'accorde assez bien avec cest autre proverbe: Pour devenir bien-tost riche, il faut tourner le dos à Dieu. Henri Estienne, *Apologie pour Hérodote* (November 1566), p. 47 [Part 1, chapter 6]. ["I will do what the Florentines say: 'Arm of iron, belly of the ant, soul of a dog.' That is: to become rich, I will bear as much work as my body will carry; I will proceed at the lowest possible expense; I will have no more conscience than a dog. This last point is in good agreement with another proverb: 'To become rich quickly, you have to turn your back on God'". Anubis as the dog-headed Egyptian divinity is recalled with the "soul of a dog."]

[kk] Luke 12:20. [The full parable is in Luke 12:16–20: "The ground of a certain rich man brought forth plentifully: And he thought within himself, saying, What shall I do, because I have no room where to bestow my fruits? And he said, This will I do: I will pull down my barns, and build greater; and there will I bestow all my fruits and my goods. And I will say to my soul, Soul, thou hast much goods laid up for many years; take thine ease, eat, drink, and be merry. But God said unto him, Thou fool, this night thy soul shall be required of thee: then whose shall those things be, which thou hast provided?"]

[ll]
Supplées, s'il vous plait.
– – ce mot des Français révéré
mot énergique au plaisir consacré
Mot – – – –

"qui est au jurement des Italiens ce que l'action est à l'instrument." Don Apuleius Riforius, Benedictine.

["Fill in the blank please.
– this word revered by the French
energetic word sacred to pleasure,
Word – – – –"

"which is to the curses of Italians what action is to an instrument."

The lines of verse are quoted from Voltaire, *La Pucelle d'Orléans*, canto 11, ll. 135–7; Joan of Arc had just repelled an attempted rape, and the frustrated Englishman uttered an obscenity. Hamann truncates the description of the profanity (the lines continue "Word which the vulgar profane often pronounce shamefully in their anger"), and substitutes part of Voltaire's note on the line, comparing the curses of different Europeans.

"Don Apuleius Risorius, Benedictine" is credited with the preface to the poem and was one of Voltaire's pseudonyms.]

[134] Genesis 49:9: "my son, thou art gone up." In Luther's Bible, "through great victories" follows immediately.

[135] In the sense both of "satyr" and "satirist."

[136] Matthew 12:39: "An evil and adulterous generation"; Matthew 12:45: "this wicked generation"; Mark 8:38: "this adulterous and sinful generation."

in the highest tone of elegy: – – *Arithmétique politique rends moi mes 5 écus!*[137]

Do not weep, readers whom I have touched!, over the Magus in the North, whom you see before you with a little half-year-old muse or grace[138] in his right arm and a little three-year-old Apollo[139] on his left hand – you see that there is not a third left for me to profane, like the canting giant of Monsieur Marmontel[140] – Assuming, therefore, that the Magus of the North is destined to starve, which however I doubt in the reign of a Frederick who, like God, is kind toward the unthankful[141] and dwells in an unapproachable light[142] and under the administration of a Maecenas[143] who is not ashamed to be a friend of the German Horaces and Virgils and an advocate for a publican – I doubt it just as much as I doubt the intensity and reliability of all my ideas, which perhaps mean nothing more, nothing less, than the apparition of the Northern Lights[mm] – Assuming therefore that the Magus dies today or tomorrow, then know, Readers!, that he dies as a Magus who loved God, his king, and his country – that he is angry over their similar fate – NON OMNIS[144] – because he leaves a boy and girl to his friend Herder to raise.

To him, the worthiest of all my friends, who are each not only great, true, and tender – but are also numberless – – (go, Judas Ἰσκαριώτης, hang yourself, and get out of the way!)[145] – in the North and in Germany – – (for what do the peoples of Burgundy, Champaigne, Gascony, and the French Swiss, have to do with me?) – to my Herder, the worthiest of all my friends in the North and in Germany I bequeath my

---

mm   pectus inaniter angit
                                 irritat, mulcet, falsis terroribus implet
                                 ut MAGUS – – –
                                Horace, Epistle 2.1.[211–13]

["who by illusions tortures my breast, provokes, soothes, and fills it with false terrors, like a MAGUS."]

[137] "Political arithmetic, give me back my five écus!" See n. 49.
[138] Elisabeth Regina, born on April 12, 1772.   [139] Johann Michael, born on September 27, 1769.
[140] Bélisaire, the hero of Jean-François Marmontel's popular novel of that title, published in 1767; the novel became famous because it contains a chapter pleading for religious tolerance.
[141] Luke 6:35: "for he is kind unto the unthankful."
[142] 1 Timothy 6:16: "dwelling in the light which no man can approach unto."
[143] Perhaps Baron von Zedlitz, the Minister of Culture, is meant.
[144] "Not entirely," from Horace's Ode 3.30.6: "I shall not entirely die," words which were inscribed on Algarotti's mausoleum in Pisa.
[145] Judas Iscariot hangs himself at Matthew 27:5.

joy and my crown, yes! so I die truly as Magus, father, and friend! the true blood of my heart! Let him give you bread and wine[nn] – but to me however no memorial of stone. EXEGI.[146]

[nn] Lamentations 2:12. ["They say to their mothers, Where is bread and wine?"]

[146] Horace, Odes 3:30.1: "I have made a memorial more lasting than bronze." Horace is referring to his poetry; Hamann to his writings, family, and friends, and is contrasting himself with Algarotti.

To the

Solomon of Prussia[1]

Exquisite dishes entice the Prussians,
Have changed them into Epicureans.

* *

Illusion, deception, and hunger
Might make us all anthropophages.[2]

---

[1] Frederick the Great, whom Voltaire had addressed as the "Solomon of the North" in his 1740 "Ode au roi de Prusse sur son avènement au trône" (l. 51; see the Voltaire Foundation's edition of the work, vol. XXA, 531–6). Hamann's essay was written in French, the language in which Frederick wrote.

[2] From the poem "Epître au Sieur Noël par l'Empereur de la Chine, à Pekin 1772," by Frederick the Great to his cook. It was printed in *Lobschrift auf Herrn Noel* (1772). Lines 57–8 and 18–19 of the French are quoted, respectively.

Save, Lord. Let the King
hear us when we call.

Psalms 20:9.[3]

In amicitia gerenda, sicut in certamine currendi, non ita convenit
exerceri, ut, quoad necesse sit, pervenire possis: sed ut productus
studio et viribus, ultra facile procurras . . . propterea quod in cursore
tantum velocitas esse oporteat, ut efferatur usque ad finem: in amico
tantum benevolentiae, ut ultra, quam [quod] amicus sentire possit,
procurrat amicitiae studio.

Rhetorica ad Herennium, Book 4, chapter 47.[4]

[3] Hamann quotes this verse in a standard translation of the French Protestants (the French of his
biblical allusions matches closely the language of Olivetan's version revised by David Martin).

[4] "In maintaining a friendship, as in running a race, it is a good idea to be trained not only so that
you can reach as far as the finish-line but also, drawn on by will and strength, that you can run
beyond it easily . . . for there should be enough speed in a runner to go beyond the finish and
enough goodwill in a friend in his zeal for friendship to go beyond what his friend is capable of
noticing."

SIRE,

I am a poor devil,[5] crazy about my bastards, whom I have just bestowed on a young man, lost for his country,[6] but worthy to be the President of the Academy of Sciences,[7] by which he has been crowned for a treatise that is as nasty as this century which lets the magi die of hunger rather than throwing them into a burning fiery furnace.[8]

Your Majesty is what the wise men of the century call a Supreme Being of the Earth,[9] and You, Sire, have made the superiority of Your Genius shine far beyond all other kings by so many wonders that the LORD of the Jews has made your name glorious beyond all the Idols of the Nations.[10]

The Magus of the North adores you, Sire!, with a devotion which rivals that which inspired the Wise Men of old from the East. Blessed be the LORD thy God[11] who has judged the ends of Prussia, who has given strength unto his King, exalted the horn to His Anointed,[12] and fulfilled the good promise[13] given to Your Fathers five hundred years ago. Because the Eternal God has loved his people, SOLOMON has been made KING over all the Prussians![14]

But where are the temples? the altars? priests consecrated to the religion of the Supreme Being of Prussia?

---

[5] "Le Pauvre Diable" is the title of a satire Voltaire wrote in 1758.

[6] Herder, a Prussian, was at the time of the essay in the service of Count Wilhelm von Schaumburg-Lippe in Bückeburg in Lower Saxony.

[7] The presidency of the Berlin Academy of Sciences had been unfilled since the death of Maupertuis in 1759. Euler had initially assumed the leadership of the Academy, though not the presidency, which Frederick offered to d'Alembert in 1763 (d'Alembert was not willing to move to Berlin and rejected the offer; nonetheless, for more than two decades he advised Frederick on matters related to it).

[8] The reference is to Herder and his *Treatise on the Origin of Language*, the prize-winning essay in a competition on that topic set by the Berlin Academy of Sciences. Hamann was known as the "Magus of the North" (as he refers to himself below). The "burning fiery furnace" refers to Daniel 3.

[9] "Supreme Being" is a deistic term for God.

[10] Psalms 86:9–10: "All nations whom thou hast made shall come and worship before thee, O Lord; and shall glorify thy name. For thou art great, and doest wondrous things." Psalms 96:5: "For all the gods of the nations are idols: but the LORD made the heavens."

[11] 1 Kings 10:9: "Blessed be the LORD thy God."

[12] 1 Samuel 2:10: "the LORD shall judge the ends of the earth; and he shall give strength unto his king, and exalt the horn of his anointed."

[13] 1 Kings 8:56: "there hath not failed one word of all his good promise, which he promised by the hand of Moses his servant."

[14] 2 Chronicles 2:11: "Then Huram the king of Tyre answered in writing, which he sent to Solomon, Because the LORD hath loved his people, he hath made thee king over them." Perhaps "five hundred years ago" refers to the period in which the Teutonic Knights colonized Prussia.

The sublime taste of Your Majesty, like the Spirit of Christianity, desires no worship but that in spirit and in truth,[15] nor any altars but the hearts of his subjects, nor any ministers but those who love and preach the truth, who love and practice virtue. But where is this chosen generation? this royal priesthood? this holy nation? this peculiar people who show forth the virtues of him who has called them from darkness to his marvelous light?[16] Where are the Magi who present their bodies a living sacrifice, holy and acceptable to Your Majesty who in all his states desires only a reasonable service?[17]

O God! the heathens are come into Thine inheritance; THY holy temple have they defiled![18] – O Lord! Remember the reproach wherewith THINE enemies have reproached the footsteps of his Anointed[19] – –

Your century, Sire!, is a day only of trouble and of rebuke and blasphemy.[20] All the sarcasms, countless and in good standing, against the Providence of the FATHER, who is in heaven, against the gospel of his Son and against the manifold works of the Holy Spirit, are just smiles and songs compared to the sacrilegious thoughts and words by which Your August Name[21] is blackened, and the Wisdom of Your Kingdom and the Oracles of Your Will and of Your Spirit.

The greatest Monster in society, as one[a] of these modern writers says, is a Free-thinking Slave. It is clear, then, just how far all your subjects will

---

[a] *Nouvelles Lettres persannes*, p. 297. [George Lyttelton published *Letters from a Persian in England* anonymously in 1735. Hamann quotes from the French translation of 1770, *Lettres d'un Persan en Angleterre, ou, Nouvelles lettres persannes*. The quotation in English is found at the end of Letter

[15] John 4:24: "God is a Spirit: and they that worship him must worship him in spirit and in truth." The keywords of this paragraph – goût, esprit, verité, vertu, raisonnable – are those of the Enlightenment, but Hamann restores them to a biblical context.

[16] 1 Peter 2:9: "But ye are a chosen generation, a royal priesthood, an holy nation, a peculiar people; that ye should shew forth the praises of him who hath called you out of darkness into his marvellous light."

[17] Romans 12:1: "I beseech you therefore, brethren, by the mercies of God, that ye present your bodies a living sacrifice, holy, acceptable unto God, which is your reasonable service."

[18] Psalm 79:1: "O god, the heathen are come into thine inheritance; thy holy temple have they defiled."

[19] Psalms 89:50–1: "Remember, Lord, the reproach of thy servants; how I do bear in my bosom the reproach of all the mighty people; Wherewith thine enemies have reproached, O Lord; wherewith they have reproached the footsteps of thine anointed." (Cf. Zephaniah 2:8: "I have heard the reproach of Moab, and the revilings of the children of Ammon, whereby they have reproached my people, and magnified themselves against their border" and Lamentations 5:1: "Remember, O Lord, what is come upon us: consider, and behold our reproach.")

[20] 2 Kings 19:3: "This day is a day of trouble, and of rebuke, and blasphemy."

[21] Voltaire had praised Frederick's name in his 1740 "Réponse à une lettre dont le roi de Prusse honora l'auteur": "Lui seul est vraiment roi, sa gloire est toujours pure;/Son nom parvient sans tache à la race future" ("He alone is truly king, his glory is always pure;/His name unblemished reaches the future race"; Voltaire Foundation edition, vol. XX A, p. 543).

debase themselves through the insolence and corruption of these *beaux-esprits* whose ingratitude surpasses that of the famous rebel Absalom.[22] The Jews did not imagine their God so ravenous for the flesh of bulls and the blood of goats[23] that we would have grown accustomed to the idea of a Genius voracious of the sweat and blood of the children of his Kingdom in order to fatten his little dogs,[24] on whom an idolatrous Century lavishes mausoleums[25] despite the divine principle of thrift.[26] But I would rather chew my stammering tongue in order to spit it in the face of Your Enemies, and I would rather, as St. Paul says,[27] give my body to be burned, than translate or abridge[28] all the abominations established in the Holy place of the Supreme Being of Prussia. May the Posterity that reads of them not pay attention!

But Sire! You thought it not robbery the form[29] of a Supreme being which is able to destroy souls and bodies all the way to the fires of Hell,[30] and You have made yourself of no reputation, even making yourself in the likeness of this King of the Jews,[31] who is the King of Kings[32] and who nonetheless was numbered among the transgressors, the bandits, the rogues.[33] You humbled Yourself and being found in fashion as an unhappy Prussian,[34] you will at last succeed in becoming our FATHER, who will

LXXVI: "The unthinking may be passive from Delusion, or at least from Inadvertency; but the greatest Monster and worst criminal in Society, is a Free-thinking-Slave."]

[22] 2 Samuel 13–19.
[23] Psalms 50:13: "Will I eat the flesh of bulls, or drink the blood of goats?"
[24] The allusion to Matthew 15:26–7 is clearer in French, in which appear "the little dogs," rather than the simple "dogs" of the King James Bible: "But he answered and said, It is not meet to take the children's bread, and to cast it to dogs. And she said, Truth, Lord: yet the dogs eat of the crumbs which fall from their masters' table."
[25] The graves of Frederick's dogs at Sans Souci; perhaps this is also a reference to the monument he raised to Algarotti in Pisa.
[26] Perhaps also a reference to the principle of least action, Maupertuis' most famous discovery. In his *Essai de cosmologie* (1750), he attempted to give the principle a cosmic and theological significance. Voltaire satirized Maupertuis devastatingly in a subsequent controversy over whether Maupertuis plagiarized the principle.
[27] 1 Corinthians 13:3: "And though I bestow all my goods to feed the poor, and though I give my body to be burned, and have not charity, it profiteth me nothing."
[28] Hamann translated letters of petition and complaint for the French officials in charge of the General Excise and Customs Administration.
[29] Philippians 2:6: "Who, being in the form of God, thought it not robbery to be equal with God."
[30] Matthew 10:28: "And fear not them which kill the body, but are not able to kill the soul: but rather fear him which is able to destroy both soul and body in hell."
[31] Philippians 2:7: "But made himself of no reputation, and took upon him the form of a servant, and was made in the likeness of men."
[32] "King of Kings": see Daniel 2:37, 1 Timothy 6:15, and Revelation 17:14 and 19:16.
[33] Cf. Mark 15:28 and Luke 22:37 (and Isaiah 53:12).
[34] Philippians 2:8: "And being found in fashion as a man, he humbled himself, and became obedient unto death, even the death of the cross."

know well how to give good things, like our Father who is in Heaven;[35] for

> – – he is the best of Fathers,
> not dulling us with laws that are too strict,
> he wants his children, as little Libertines,
> to amuse themselves with the work of his hands:
> He will postpone the prize to next year.[b]

Be ye therefore, Sire, perfect, even as YOUR Father which is in heaven is perfect,[36] and Your Name will be hallowed above every name.[37] The honor, brightness, and glory of Your Kingdom will be established and added unto;[38] for the Eternal has highly exalted You in giving you a Royal Majesty such as no King before YOU has had, and YOU will be seated on the Throne of the Eternal to be the King of Kings. All Prussia will obey you and your will will be done in earth as it is in Heaven.[39]

After having become the Paradigm of Kings, the Prince of Virtues, Arms, and Laws and indeed the Father of Your Prussian Peoples,[40] with neither the stilts of a good man like Sully nor those of a Controller-General of Finances,[41] You, Sire, will have in addition the good fortune of being the Creator of an original Historian of his nation and of Your Century.[42] Is not the gleaning of the grapes of a Genius better than the whole vintage of a servile and precarious imitation? –[c]

---

[b] "Les Systèmes," by Voltaire. [Voltaire's satirical poem was first published in 1772. God decides to award a prize to the best solution to the philosophical problems of existence. At the end of the poem, no one wins, and he defers the contest to next year. Hamann quotes lines 97–101.]

[c] Judges 8:2. ["Is not the gleaning of the grapes of Ephraim better than the vintage of Abi-ezer?"]

[35] Matthew 7:11: "If ye then, being evil, know how to give good gifts unto your children, how much more shall your Father which is in heaven give good things to them that ask him?"

[36] Matthew 5:48: "Be ye therefore perfect, even as your Father which is in heaven is perfect."

[37] Philippians 2:9: "Wherefore God also hath highly exalted him, and given him a name which is above every name."

[38] Cf. Daniel 4:36: "At the same time my reason returned unto me; and for the glory of my kingdom, mine honour and brightness returned unto me; and my counsellors and my lords sought unto me; and I was established in my kingdom, and excellent majesty was added unto me."

[39] Matthew 6:9–10, Luke 11:2.

[40] The full title of Sully's *Memoirs* praises "Henry Le Grand, l'exemplaire des roys, le prince des vertus, des armes et des lois, et le père en effet de ses peuples françois," which Hamann here translates and adapts.

[41] The Duc de Sully (1560–1644), a Huguenot, became the head of King Henri IV's financial system. The Controller-General of Finances in Prussia was La Haye de Launay, who headed the General Excise Administration (or "Regie"), a new ministry Frederick introduced, run by Frenchmen, and responsible for collecting certain taxes. In Frederick's *Memoirs*, Launay is called the Director-General of Finances (régisseur-général des finances).

[42] Presumably a reference to Herder.

The blood of the great Winckelmann will be avenged,[43] and your natural subjects will no longer exile themselves nor risk being massacred by these Bandits who love gold and silver antiquities as passionately as the *beaux esprits* of today love the antiquities of Truth and Virtue. Herder will be the Plato and the President of Your Academy of Sciences. Prussia will produce its Rabelaises and its Grécourts,[d] and they will be more brilliant than the apes and the peacocks of Ophir,[44] and you, Sire, will be like the good Lord,

  – – who did nothing but laugh.[45]

The Magus of the North will burn, and his seven thousand brothers[e] will no longer die of hunger, but will come forth from their tombs and be like these birds of the air which shall tell the matter.[f]

Blessed be the LORD thy God,[46] the Queen of Sheba will say; for God has established Solomon to make judgment and justice between Europe and Asia.[47]

---

[d] Scheffner of the Marienwerder War and Domains Board, author of very fine and pitiful poems, translator of Guarini, whom Augustus himself would recognize as a putissimum penem and a homunculum lepidissimum. [Johann George Scheffner (1736–1820), author in 1771 of *Gedichte im Geschmack des Grécourt* (*Poems in the Taste of Grécourt*), and translator in 1773 of Guarini. Jean-Baptiste Joseph Willart de Grécourt (1683–1743) frequented libertine circles and wrote much light verse. Battista Guarini (1538–1612), court poet at Ferrara.

A "putissimus penis" is a "most genuine penis" and a "homunculus lepidissimus" is a "most charming little man."

The provincial War and Domains boards had been established by Frederick William I and were also an important feature of Frederick the Great's administration. In 1772, the year this essay was written, Marienwerder (Kwidzyn) became Prussian through the first division of Poland, and Scheffner was moved from Königsberg to there.

Hamann's marginal annotation is in German, apart from the Latin phrases.]

[e] – – Nam multo plures sumus ac veluti Te
Judaei cogemus in hanc concedere turbam. Horace, *Satire* 1.4.

[Lines 142–3: "For we are much more numerous and like the Jews we will force You to give in to our mob." Horace's mob consists of the poets.]

[f] Ecclesiastes 10:20. ["for a bird of the air shall carry the voice, and that which hath wings shall tell the matter"]

43 The Prussian historian and critic of ancient art was murdered in Italy in 1768 by an acquaintance to whom he had shown his gold and silver medals. His *Thoughts on the Imitation of Greek Works in Painting and Sculpture* (1755) was influential.

44 See 1 Kings 10:11 and 22 and 2 Chronicles 9:10, 21.

45 From the last line (l. 118) of Voltaire's "Les Systèmes."   46 1 Kings 10:9.

47 A reference to the first partition of Poland among Frederick, Maria Theresa, and Catherine the Great.

The Solomon of Prussia will have at sea a navy,[48] but even the fleurs de lys[49] will no longer part the garments of Solomon, nor upon his vesture will they cast lots.[50]

All the inhabitants of the New Prussia[51] will seek to Solomon, to hear his wisdom, which God has put in his heart.[52] Each one will bring his present,[53] and all hearts, Sire, will burn with love for the immortality of your name, the glory of your kingdom, and the fulfillment of your will, with a love stronger than death and more envious than the grave is of a Treasure.[54]

Money will not be prized in Prussia more than the Systems and projects of a Punic faith,[55] and money will be nothing accounted of in the days of our Solomon,[56] for the trial of the Prussian Faith will be much more precious than gold tried by fire, that everyone might be found unto praise and honor and glory at the appearing[57] of The Solomon of Prussia.[g]

g   Iam FIDES et PAX et HONOS, PVDORque
                      PRISCVS et neglecta redire VIRTVS
                      Audet, adparetque BEATA pleno
                      COPIA cornu.
                                     Horace.

[Horace, *Carmen saeculare* 57–60: "Now FAITH and PEACE and HONOR and ANCIENT MODESTY and neglected VIRTUE dare to return, and BLESSED PLENTY shows itself with its brimming horn."]

[48] 1 Kings 10:22: "For the king had at sea a navy of Tharshish with the navy of Hiram: once in three years came the navy of Tharshish, bringing gold, and silver, ivory, and apes, and peacocks." The Prussian maritime trade society (a trade credit society) was founded in 1772.

[49] A reference to the French tax collectors, with perhaps an allusion to Matthew 6:28: "And why take ye thought for raiment? Consider the lilies of the field, how they grow; they toil not, neither do they spin."

[50] Matthew 27:35: "And they crucified him, and parted his garments, casting lots: that it might be fulfilled which was spoken by the prophet, They parted my garments among them, and upon my vesture did they cast lots."

[51] A reference to the recently conquered territories of Prussia.

[52] 1 Kings 10:24: "And all the earth sought to Solomon, to hear his wisdom, which God had put in his heart."

[53] 1 Samuel 10:27: "But the children of Belial said, How shall this man save us? And they despised him, and brought no presents."

[54] "Treasure" may also be translated as "treasury" or "public revenue." Song of Songs 8:6: "for love is strong as death; jealousy is cruel as the grave."

[55] Bad faith, faithlessness.

[56] 1 Kings 10:21: "And all king Solomon's drinking vessels were of gold, and all the vessels of the house of the forest of Lebanon were of pure gold; none were of silver: it was nothing accounted of in the days of Solomon." The allusion is closer in French, where *argent* means both "silver" and "money."

[57] 1 Peter 1:7: "That the trial of your faith, being much more precious than gold that perisheth, though it be tried with fire, might be found unto praise and honour and glory at the appearing of Jesus Christ."

The ruler of the feast will bear witness thereof to Peking, crying like a Chinese swine:[58] every sovereign does at the beginning serve good wine, but You! my Apollo[59] and my Lord! You have kept the good wine until now.[60]

But as for the toll – –

I burn[h] and I die calling unto the Lord like the Judge of Israel with the jawbone of an ass:[61] O Lord God, remember me, I pray thee, and strengthen me, I pray thee, O Supreme Being, that I may be at once avenged for my two eyes[62] – May I die with these political arithmeticians who take five écus a month[63] without rhyme and without reason, and I am too convinced that Your Majesty loves both the one and the other.[64]

VIXI.[65]

---

[h]
> – – o mare! o terra! ardeo.
> Quantum neque atro delibutus Hercules
> Nessi cruore, nec Sicana fervida
> Furens in Aetna flamma.
>> Horace, *Epode* 17.

[Lines 30–3: "O sea! o earth! I burn more than Hercules, smeared with the gore of Nessus, and more than the Sicanian flame raging in boiling Aetna."]

[58] Hamann alludes to Voltaire's "Relation du bannissement des Jésuites de la Chine" (1768): "And then they invited our Lord Jesus to a village wedding, and as the wedding stewards were drunk and out of wine, our Lord Jesus Christ changed the water into wine on the spot, after having been rude to his mother. Some time later, finding himself in Gadara, or Gesara, near the small lake of Gennesareth, he met some devils in the bodies of two who were possessed. He drove them away as fast as he could, and sent them into a herd of two thousand swine, who went grunting to throw themselves in the lake and drown there; and what proves still more the greatness and the Truth of this miracle is that there were not any swine in this country." (Voltaire adapts two gospel stories: the wedding feast at Cana, recounted in John 2, and the Gadarene swine, in Matthew 8, Mark 5, and Luke 8.) This passage quoted is found on p. 9 of vol. XXVII of the 1877–85 *Œuvres complètes*; it is projected to appear on vol. LXVII of the Voltaire Foundation edition.

[59] Elsewhere, Hamann connects the "Apollo of theism" with Frederick (See *Werke*, vol. III, p. 159). Voltaire had compared Frederick to Apollo.

[60] John 2:9–10: "When the ruler of the feast had tasted the water that was made wine, and knew not whence it was: (but the servants which drew the water knew;) the governor of the feast called the bridegroom, And saith unto him, Every man at the beginning doth set forth good wine; and when men have well drunk, then that which is worse: but thou hast kept the good wine until now."

[61] That is, like Samson. Judges 15:15–16: "And he found a new jawbone of an ass, and put forth his hand, and took it, and slew a thousand men therewith. And Samson said, With the jawbone of an ass, heaps upon heaps, with the jaw of an ass have I slain a thousand men."

[62] Judges 16:28: "And Samson called unto the lord, and said, O Lord God, remember me, I pray thee, and strengthen me, I pray thee, only this once, O God, that I may be at once avenged of the Philistines for my two eyes."

[63] Hamann's salary had recently been cut as part of an austerity drive of the government; he complains about it in a letter to Herder on October 6, 1772 (*Briefe*, vol. III, p. 18) and in *Philological Ideas and Doubts* (note 49).

[64] That is, as a poet and a philosopher.

[65] "I have lived." Hamann varies, "*dixi*," "I have spoken," formerly used at the end of speeches.

New

Apology

of the

Letter *h*

Or:
Extraordinary
Observations
on the
Orthography
of German
by
H. S.,[1]
Schoolmaster

– – et nobilis et decens,
Et pro solicitis non tacitus reis,
Et centum puer artium
Late signa feret militiae TVAE.[2]

Second, improved edition

Pisa, 1773[3]

---

[1] Hamann implies that the essay was written by a Königsberg teacher, Heinrich Schröder. See the letter to Herder, November 13, 1773 (*Briefe*, vol. III, p. 63).

[2] Horace, Ode 4.1.13–16: "both noble and graceful, not silent on behalf of anxious defendants, youth of a hundred skills, he will bear the standards of YOUR warfare widely" (Hamann's capitals).

[3] The place of publication and the claim that this was a second, improved edition are feigned; it was published in Frankfurt.

The occasion for the present observations on orthography is given to me by an extraordinary religious teacher with the initials "C. T. D.," who says of himself that "he was authorized by universal, sound, and practical human reason to tell our German heads how the unpronounced letter *h* has been inserted between syllables by inattentive and unthinking hack writers and so-called chancellery writers; and that this spelling of this letter *h* is a pointless, groundless custom that appears barbaric in the eyes of all foreigners and injurious to the nation and must be abolished."[4]

For all the mildness of his true religion, for all the thoroughness of his effort to refute the charge of promiscuous enthusiasm, he labels as slaves all the German heads who write a never-pronounced *h* in the middle and at the end of syllables! – Indeed, he closes his "Chance Thoughts Related to the Main Subject" with the oracular pronouncement: "Whoever is not faithful in the orthography of the little letter *h* is[5] easily unfaithful and unjust also in the great revelations and mysteries of universal, sound, and practical human reason."[6]

The author offers himself the laudable testimony "that he everywhere insists on the most distinct clarity of thoughts, explains every word with entire exactitude, has nothing to do with any statute whose basis is not in view, pretends to no knowledge of impossible and exaggerated

---

[4] C[hristian] T[obias] D[amm], *Betrachtungen über die Religion* (1773; "Observations on religion"). The quotation is adapted from a passage on p. 232 and another on pp. 233–4.
[5] Reading "ist" for "ich."
[6] Cf. Damm, *Betrachtungen*, p. 234 ("He who is not faithful in small matters . . . is easily unfaithful and unjust also in great matters"); the allusion is to Luke 16:10.

postulates, etc." All this self-praise, however, is all the more impertinent as he does not touch with one of his fingers the whole burden of his method[7] in the prevailing matter of the letter *h*. So palpable an unfaithfulness and so screeching an injustice with an orthographic and almost infantile pedantry will persuade the most reasonable persons in the entire nation what kind of poor sinner the extraordinary religious teacher is in the eyes of his own so-called universal, sound, and practiced human reason, and how little grace he himself may hope for before its merciful throne of judgment.

If an enthusiast in the German language is a man inspired,[8] then the author of the "Chance Thoughts Related to the Main Subject" seems, in regard to the letter *h*, "to produce from the impulse of his highly praised human reason the most unusual and unclear sayings, and in an all-too-powerful transport of an emotion or from an exaggerated idea" he seems to preach crucifixion against an innocent breath, which some hairsplitters of language have refused even to recognize as a letter.

Gentle reader! I am neither a retired nor a dismissed school teacher, though one already rather advanced in years. From some occasional pages, which I, as a teacher seeking what is truly best for youth, had printed, it is known quite generally how it has always been the single focus of my attention to lead my students (who currently number 120) to a proper spelling of our mother tongue. Supported by my dear wife and eldest daughter in a post which demands both blood and sweat, I eat my salt and bread with joy, and after having performed my labors, I drink my small pot of beer with good cheer. May our dear Father on high preserve me in my late days from the triple temptation "to secure myself food through an extraordinary making of books,[9] to fall into a fleshly and pharisaical trust in the orthodoxy of my orthography, and to license for use among the flock of both sexes entrusted to me such a mongering of letters as the extraordinary religious teacher plots to introduce among the nations of Germany."

I know the name of my adversary only by his three initials. For the benefit of the gentle reader, who may know him even less, I will communicate on the basis of the information before me a short extract of his life and

[7] Luke 11:46: "ye lade men with burdens grievous to be borne, and ye yourselves touch not the burdens with one of your fingers."
[8] *Begeisterter.*   [9] Ecclesiastes 12:12: "of making many books there is no end."

opinions, in order to justify myself in taking him to be a man with whom, hopefully, I may not be ashamed to exchange a couple of printed sheets or to be drawn into an orthographic duel.

"Some forty or fifty years ago, Herr C. T. D. studied rather meagerly, it appears, at a rather doubtful university. – In more enlarged circumstances he perused with mechanical thoughtfulness the writings of an immortal Wolff in the German and Latin language, over some years, at one of the best, and in addition invariably appointed, hours of the day, in order to arrive at a knowledge of the meaning of concepts, connection of thoughts, and thinking – Several hundred times in the past he preached publicly against his better knowledge and belief, as he now writes; apart from some Greek and Latin books, he translated and expounded more than once the New Testament and some sections of it" – Is it not a terrible shame that a life so laudably employed should be darkened by the worst treachery against an innocent letter!

Notwithstanding the fact that, by the author's own admission, his opinions are neither new nor unknown, they all appear to be suited to the dignity of an extraordinary religious teacher and the taste of his illuminated century. He takes his soul to be "a property of his body that has been arranged extremely artfully and wisely," but in the very next days the body will founder like a decrepit, uninhabited, old house. "A property deriving from that bodily property is its reason," great as Diana of the Ephesians,[10] miraculous as her image fallen from heaven,[11] and a sacred virgin just as immaculate. "His universal, sound, and practical religion, and the clear paternal will of GOD over all the vermin and weeds of the earth, is no more than a careful exercise of the dimmest instincts" – Among all the comprehensible, mutually contradictory, and sterile observations on his religion of humanity is the strange apparition of an orthographic canon, a true god *ex machina*, to which my present observations are dedicated.

Because letters are signs not only of articulated sounds, but often also of syllables and sometimes of words, and indeed can even represent the name of an extraordinary religious teacher of our time, it is therefore easy

[10] Acts 19:28: "Great is Diana of the Ephesians."
[11] The palladium, the image of Athena (Diana) which fell from heaven, protected the city of Troy for as long as it was preserved there.

to believe that his philosophical concept of a letter will be sufficiently general to suit also a mere breath or *spiritus*.

Now let us proceed to the main subject and see whether we succeed in viewing the sufficient reason for the proposition that the letter *h* must not be written either in the middle or at the end of syllables.

First, potential answer: because it is not pronounced

I do not claim this answer is anything but potential and do not actually burden my adversary with it, so that I am not obliged to start being ashamed of him too soon, in case he seriously intended to claim as a fundamental principle of our orthography and of universal human reason: "that no letter which is not pronounced may be written and thus that the pronunciation of letters must be the sole and highest arbiter of correct spelling for German heads."

If *h* is to be omitted from the middle and end of syllables because it is not pronounced, then it would be even more necessary to discontinue the doubling of consonants at the end of each syllable. Is it possible for a human tongue, however universal, sound, and practiced, to pronounce an *ll*, *ss*, *tt*, *mm*, *nn*? Despite this, the author makes use of an extraordinary doubling (a usage peculiar to himself) in the prefix *ann*, without my believing him capable of any miracle in the pronunciation of this double consonant other than by the modification of a vowel. But would not the sign of aspiration be more suitable for a given modification in pronouncing vowels than the redoubling of a certain articulated sound which is just as impossible for the tongue?

The canon of writing no letter which is not pronounced is the most impossible and exaggerated postulate in the exercise. Why is the author himself unfaithful to his own propositions, not only in regard to all the other letters, but even to *h*? Why does he not write *in* instead of *ihn*, and *inn* instead of *in*, or *ir* instead of *ihr*, and *tun* instead of *thun*, in order to comply at least with the appearance of an analogy? What reason can indeed be envisaged for his biased exception of all the remaining letters and his unjustified severity toward a breath, which is not even an articulated sound?

If the pronunciation of letters is to be elevated to a universal judgment throne over correct spelling such as the one so-called human reason arrogates to itself (under cover of liberty) over religion, then it is easy to foresee the destiny of our maternal language. What divisions! what Babylonian confusion! what mongering of letters! All the great diversity of dialects and speech and their shibboleths[12] would pour into the books of each province, and what dam[13] could withstand this orthographic deluge? The *h*, turned out from the raw midnight of Germany, would prolifherate itself in the writings of the greater and milder nations of the Holy Roman Empire with such opulence that would not be comparable to the wise generosity of a famous translator[14] of sacred parchment rolls in very isolated cases. – In short, the whole social bond of literature among the German nations would be destroyed in a few years, to the great disadvantage of the true, universal, practical religion, its dissemination, and the peace promised by it – –

With what sort of conscience, however, can a man who insists on the most distinct clarity of thoughts and a careful fidelity in minutiae clear out of the way the small orthographic aids to clarity and better distinctness of concepts? – A German head,[15] with whose calf Wolff ploughed his way to immortality judged all the roots of our maternal language to be monosyllabic, and the imperative form to be the roots of verbs. *Führ*, therefore, is the stem of the verb *führen*.[16] Why should the etymological property of letters, which the author seems not yet to have denied or forsaken, not be an excellent advantage of the letter *h*, in order to make the difference in the following two lines of an old hymn evident and obvious to the senses:

> Der du für mich gestorben
> Führ auch mein Herz und Sinn.
>
> [You, who died for me
> Guide also my heart and mind.]

But does the pronunciation of the letters alone determine the pronunciation of the word? How is the mere pronunciation of letters supposed to be able to determine the correct spelling? Can a child read, then, as soon as he is ready with the A B C? Can it really be unknown to an extraordinary religious teacher of our illuminated century that all children must spell

---

[12] "Shibboleth" was the Hebrew word used to distinguish two groups of people, only one of which could pronounce the *sh*; see Judges 12:4–6.

[13] In German, *Damm* is an exact pun on "dam" and "Damm."   [14] Luther.

[15] Leibniz, whose teachings Christian Wolff popularized.

[16] *Führ* is the imperative "lead" or "guide," and *führen* is the infinitive "to lead," "to guide."

the letters before they can learn to read, and that they are instructed in the proper pronunciation of syllables as well as letters? –

Gentle reader, despite my earnest intention to rid myself of all chance thoughts no matter how suited to the main subject and nobly to resist them as so many irksome temptations of the dim powers of imagination, I must on this one occasion offer in passing that I am willing to see that far more justice is done to my adversary than he may expect from certain political gatekeepers of German literature in their universal, frigid, and indifferent reviews; who pile on to their privileged infidelity and injustice in judgments the grossest ingratitude toward the extraordinary religious teacher of their illuminated public, while with the suet of their opinions they sprinkle their novels, dictionaries, provincial letters, and essays, in order to invite all the heathen and fools in Germany to the free board of their new heaven, and to make all the wise men after the flesh, all the mighty, all the noble,[17] as blessed in the spirit as, according to a well-known lyricist of your universal church, the once indefatigable Hercules enjoyed himself at the joyful table of his jovial father.[a]

It is admittedly the case that the little *h* is a great stone of stumbling[18] and that in general the arduous yoke of spelling may be unspeakably lightened by the canon of omitting all the letters that are not pronounced, especially the little insignificant *h*. A writer who, as our author, has never written a letter without thought and reflection, has felt this difficulty of defending spelling in the harsh light of human reason more clearly and vividly than is necessary or possible for the unthinking hack writer. That is why he had the good-hearted idea of clearing, as well as he could, this rock of offence from out of the way of his readers.

My intention is certainly not to offend in any way our German heads, although I simple-mindedly believe that neither writers nor even critics of our illumined century may succeed in clearly viewing the sufficient reason why *o–h* is written but *o* alone is pronounced, or why *s-i-e-h* is announced by a mere *si*.

---

[a]   – – Sic Jovis
Interest epulis impiger Hercules. ["As indefatigable Hercules shares in the banquets of Jove"; Hamann adapts Horace, Ode 4.8.29–30.]

[17] 1 Corinthians 1:26: "not many wise men after the flesh, not many mighty, not many noble, are called."

[18] 1 Peter 2:7–8: "the stone which the builders disallowed, the same is made the head of the corner, And a stone of stumbling, and a rock of offence."

Thus it would be a very worthy enterprise for a publisher patriotically disposed toward universal, sound, and practical human reason to prepare a new edition of *Observations on Religion by C. T. D.* in the most rigorous spirit of the new orthographic canon and with the complete omission of all letters not pronounced, without regard to the person of a vowel or consonant, to serve as a general school text. Through such an edition the former yoke of teachers and students and all the ceremonies of spelling would become superfluous.

According to an observation[b] already made by wise Aristotle, the first seed of pernicious faith without the understanding of sufficient reason is sown with spelling, when a child in good faith learns to pronounce a syllable of three letters i. m.[19] *i-e-h* as a single *i*. It is here, then, that the blind adoration of propositions which are incomprehensible, contradictory to all childish reason, and most unproductive as well starts to be taught and to be hammered into the heads of students.

With the luxury of letters the soul of the child further receives its very first impressions of harmful superfluity and of opulence in the fashions of artificial diligence and wit, at which universal, sound, and practical human reason, religion, and orthography, alas!, laugh up their sleeve.

Such a new edition of the *Observations*, in the most rigorous spirit of the orthographic canon of pronunciation, prepared with care regarding the correct spelling, would soon unite all the nations of Germany concerning the name and character of the extraordinary religious teacher. All previous divisions and schisms – "whether man is a faithful or faithless -ox, -anite, -ist or a mere *quod dicere nolo?*"[20] – would be abruptly resolved and cut off. All Germany would recognize with an unanimous voice the mark of universal, sound, practical reason in the very orthography of its prophet, would bless him aloud and immortalize his extraordinary merit through a charitable prytaneum for him and his intimate brothers in spirit, who are not tired of cutting, trimming, purifying, and edifying the system of universal human reason through novels, dictionaries, provincial letters, and short essays, in order to make wide and broad the strait gate and

---

[b] δεῖ γὰρ πιστεύειν τὸν μανθάνοντα. Ἀριστοτέλης, Περὶ σοφιστικῶν ἐλέγχων 1.2. ["the learner must take things on trust." Aristotle, *On Sophistical Refutations* 1.2 (165b).]

[19] I have taken Hamann's "Z. E." as an abbreviation for "zur Erinnerung" and translated with the abbreviation for "in memoriam."

[20] Perhaps "orthodox," "Wolffianite," and "Encyclopedist" are intended. The Latin phrase, "which I do not want to say," comes from Juvenal, *Satire* 8.275.

narrow way to life,[21] even to make, contrary to the whole destiny of his nature, a holy ministry to serve the public good for all the heathens and fools among the nations of Germany – –

Still I would ten times rather talk myself out of breath into the wind with a man born blind about the first and fourth days of the Mosaic history of creation,[22] or with a man born deaf about the harmony of a tiny nightingale and a foreign gelding, than fall out any longer with an adversary who is not even capable of seeing that a universal, sound, practical human language, and human reason, and human religion, without arbitrary fundamental principles, are his own furnace of ice.[23] Thus I hasten to the

Second, actual answer

"The unpronounced letter *h* has been inserted between syllables by inattentive scribes. It is the usage of the so-called chancellery writers and the custom of unthinking hack writers. Someone who writes thoughtfully should not be guided by such people. It is a groundless custom, appearing barbaric in the eyes of foreigners, and therefore injurious to our nation; its fetters are not suitable for the freedom of German minds, eyes, and fingers."

Gentle reader! I know a man – whether he is a villain or just a fop, the all-knowing searcher of hearts knows better than you and I – This man served in vain at two chancelleries, for one month and for six months – He was unable to succeed in obtaining the modest happiness of becoming a gatekeeper, before the superior concurrence of invalid shoeblacks and moonlighters. Presently he is one of the schoolteachers who seek what is truly best for youth, which is fundamentally more worthy of veneration than being a well-installed land-toiler, horse-broker, and Jourdain Mamamouchi[24] of three night-caps[25] with no head except for money – –

---

[21] Matthew 7:13–14: "Enter ye in at the strait gate: for wide is the gate, and broad is the way, that leadeth to destruction, and many there be which go in thereat: Because strait is the gate, and narrow is the way, which leadeth unto life, and few there be that find it."

[22] On the first day God created light and on the fourth day the stars in the heavens (Genesis 1:3 and 14).

[23] *Betrachtungen über die Religion*, p. 65: "Think of a furnace of ice; you do indeed think of what is individually possible . . . but you cannot think of the two together."

[24] In Molière's *Le Bourgeois Gentilhomme*, the main character, Monsieur Jourdain, is an ambitious merchant who permits his daughter to marry the man she has chosen only by an elaborate deceit: he believes that the prospective son-in-law is the son of the Grand Turk, and in one scene he himself is ennobled as a "Mamamouchi" in a fantastic ceremony.

[25] In a letter to Herder on December 20, 1774 (*Briefe*, vol. III, p. 130), Hamann writes that the three night-caps signify the three revenue offices at Königsberg, Gumbinnen, and Marienwerder. The

To praise our German heads, the chancellery writers of universal human reason and religion have stayed loyal even to this day to the stylistic usage in writing the little letter *h* and are more ashamed of orthographic liberty than all the remaining and extraordinary opinions of their lame Master Martin[c] – –

However, if, in keeping with his own confession of faith, language and its correct spelling were grounded "on the custom of the best informed persons in the entire nation," how in all the world could a few unthinking hack writers and so-called chancellery writers ever have succeeded in making such a barbaric and injurious profiteering of the letter *h* so universal? Was there then not a single conscientious councillor or director of the chancellery to curb this nonsense? Were the eyes of all readers as bewitched as the fingers of some unthinking hack writers? Did the entire state consist of philosophers *à la turque*?[26] A poetical narrative of this event, without date or place, would be uncommonly entertaining for the historical meditation of our century – –

But which foreigners does the extraordinary prophet have in mind? Why does he not speak clearly and distinctly? Does he mean the French? – – From youth on I have been fearful of their language because of the hateful, ambiguous name[27] – – Does he mean the English? – – As a schoolteacher, I have come to know the English disease, but not, thank God!, with any of the children of my flesh; but in my time their language was not yet in fashion.

Although I do not know whether these two nations are in fact so conscientious as to pronounce every written *h* with distinct clarity and *alta voce distincta*, like that merry Latinist, nonetheless in my poor fatherland I have heard a very large number of large and small Frenchmen speak German, who mishandled our German *h* just as irresponsibly as

---

[c] Cf. P. Gerundio. [In José Francisco de Isla's satirical romance *Historia del famoso predicador fray Gerundio de Campazas* (1758), the lame schoolmaster Martin maintains an allegiance to three contradictory opinions about orthography. Among other complaints, he grieves that España is spelled without the "H" which etymologically belongs to it. The work had a wide European fame, and Hamann read it in German translation.]

three night-caps contrast with the three horse-tails which a pasha of the highest class bore on his standard. Hamann is teasing Johann Jakob Kantner (1738–86), a publisher, book-merchant, and lottery director.

[26] Presumably another reference to Molière: M. Jourdain is dressed "à la turque" for his fake ennoblement.

[27] The French disease, *morbus gallicus*, is syphilis; the English disease is rickets.

the extraordinary religious teacher, and anyway I have so many prejudices against both nations that I cannot compare them at all with our German heads.

Is it then, say, the Dutch who label us barbarians on account of a small letter? – –

Gentle reader! as great a friend as I have been until the present day of tabagies,[28] I have nonetheless once and for all made a solemn vow not ever to be drawn in my lifetime into any Dutch quarrels whether concerning orthography or orthodoxy – It has cost me, alas!, more than one black eye. These barbarians understand neither wit nor Christianity; they are, in a word, Dutch! Their language is a polished knife. I come now with agitated pen to the:

final, merely probable response to the question
"How did the extraordinary religious teacher fall into the orthographic heresy of omitting the letter *h* in the middle and at the end of syllables (with the exception of all foreign words and some arbitrary details) because it is not pronounced and of ruining the correct spelling of his maternal language through the embezzlement and suppression of a little letter, which is as ungrounded as unauthorized, which appears in the eyes of all reasonable readers to be in bad taste, and which is injurious to the fingers themselves of the author?"

In keeping with my previous observations and the appendix of the effects of dimly imagined ideas, it can only be inferred that so extraordinary a spirit of persecution regarding an innocent letter must be an effect of the crassest ignorance and most ridiculous vanity.

There is a kind of ignorance in the will, and it can be cured neither by Christian-Wolffian merits in Latin and German nor by careful translations and explications of sacred scripture. This kind of ignorance "is pure in its own eyes, and yet is not washed from its filthiness."[29] "O how lofty are its eyes! and its eyelids are lifted up"[30] instead of being ashamed by their disgrace. This kind of ignorance puffs itself and speaks with swelling cheeks: "Our reason is universal, sound, and sufficiently practiced!" without knowing "that it is wretched, and miserable, and poor, and blind, and

---

[28] A tabagie is "a group of smokers who meet in club fashion" (*Oxford English Dictionary*).

[29] Proverbs 30:12: "There is a generation that are pure in their own eyes, and yet is not washed from their filthiness." "Generation" corresponds to *Art*, as in "kind [*Art*] of ignorance."

[30] Proverbs 30:13: "There is a generation, O how lofty are their eyes! and their eyelids are lifted up."

naked."[31] Is it, to speak humanly, even possible that such a one could arrive at the clear awareness of an idiotism implanted in his soul presumably at his earliest existence, indeed perhaps already in the womb of his artful body, notwithstanding the fact that he reveals himself as obviously in his whole life as in the opinions adopted by him; but to his own eyes he is hidden – –

The crassest ignorance and most presumptuous vanity! – – Powerful errors and a more than miraculous superstitious faith in lies and mysteries of darkness and wickedness! – – Obstinate stupidity *in pallio philosophico*[32] and ravening brutality in sheep's clothing[33] against the only true God and the express image of his invisible person in human nature![34] – – Dumb horror and death to the soul! – A cup of trembling[35] – – of drunken, belching reason, for which because of its corrupt stomach or heart the blood of the witnesses of JESUS, the strength of their proofs, rose to the zenith – – –

O you ignorant despiser of divine providence and universal human reason!, do not regard as a blind game of chance the fact that the orthography of the extraordinary religious teacher is as closely related to the main subject as to the spirit of his illuminated century, whose philosophical and political history is a true dithyramb for the historical faith of those old wives' creatures which tremble! and whose existence is denied, notwithstanding the palpable influence, their inspiration, by the preacher of their historical faith, merely because the hoary Wolffian in his time just wrote in ideas. – –

Gentle reader! My three classes are waiting for me, and I must take my leave of you without any hope of seeing your face again. My family name will be struck from the book of life[36] soon enough and perish along with the obsolete Lutheran translation of the Bible, where you can find him,

---

[31] Revelation 3:17: "thou . . . knowest not that thou art wretched, and miserable, and poor, and blind, and naked."

[32] "In philosophical clothing"; *pallium* is an outer garment particularly associated with the Greeks.

[33] Matthew 7:15: "Beware of false prophets, which come to you in sheep's clothing, but inwardly they are ravening wolves."

[34] Cf. Colossians 1:15: "Who is the image of the invisible God," and Hebrews 1:3: "Who being the brightness of his glory, and the express image of his person." "Person" corresponds to *Wesen* in Luther and Hamann.

[35] Isaiah 51:17: "Awake, awake, stand up, O Jerusalem, which hast drunk at the hand of the LORD the cup of his fury"; cf. Isaiah 51:22.

[36] Revelation 3:5: "I will not blot out his name out of the book of life."

if you care to, in the prophecies of Jeremiah against Moab, 48:12.[37] The little letter *h*, with which my good Christian name Heinrich begins, may speak for itself if there is breath in its nostrils. I will no longer concern myself either with its future fate or with the whole world, which is in a sorry state, and every evening I look forward to sleep and sleep's brother with my pipe and pot of beer. My father in heaven will care for my poor widow and my young children without it being necessary for them to bow before Baal and his ministers and priests or to become extraordinary mongers in letters, reason, or religion – Fare well! – yea, eternally well!

[37] "I will send unto him wanderers"; Luther has "Schröter" for "wanderers," an oblique reference to the putative author of the essay, Heinrich Schröder.

New
Apology
of the
Letter *h*
by
Itself

You little prophets of Böhmisch-Breda!^d Be not amazed that I speak unto you with a human voice like that dumb beast of burden,[38] to punish your transgression. Your life is what I am – a breath. Do not think therefore that I should crawl before you, whine and beg to be preserved, or lament if I am altogether banished or eliminated from your writings. I view it as an honor and a favor to be subject to the bondage of your vanity[39] less than my vocalizing and consonating brothers.

My existence and preservation is a matter for him who bears all things with his strong word and who has sworn, saying: "Till heaven and earth pass, one jot or one tittle shall in no wise pass"[40] –

You little prophets of Böhmisch-Breda! I perceive that in all things you are too superstitious.[41] The invisible GOD, who is therefore unknown to you,[42] is of course the father of reason and religion, which however are

---

^d *Le Prophète de Böhmisch Breda*. Grimm contra Rousseau. [Friedrich Melchior Grimm published a satire on French opera, *Le Petit Prophète de Boehmischbroda*, in 1753 (repr. in *La Querelle des bouffons*, ed. Launay, 1973, vol. I, pp. 135–92). The prophet is a destitute, naive musician, whose dream is to succeed at the Prague carnival; "Grimm's point is to argue that even this simple Bohemian lad possesses musicality superior to many French musicians" (Daniel Heartz, *From Garrick to Gluck*, 2004, p. 213). Grimm's satire anticipated Rousseau's *Lettre sur la musique française* (1753).]

[38] Balaam smote his ass three times when it refused to advance when the angel of the Lord blocked the way; the Lord gave the ass voice, and Balaam saw that he was a sinner; see Numbers 22.

[39] Romans 8:20: "For the creature was made subject to vanity, not willingly."

[40] The collocation "hath sworn, saying" occurs in Judges 21:1 and 21:18 and in Isaiah 14:24. Matthew 5:18: "For verily I say unto you, Till heaven and earth pass, one jot or one tittle shall in no wise pass from the law." Hamann and Luther write "the smallest letter" instead of "jot."

[41] Acts 17:22: "Ye men of Athens, I perceive that in all things ye are too superstitious."

[42] Paul preaches the "unknown God" to the Athenians in Acts 17:23. The Lord is the "invisible God" in Colossians 1:15 and 1 Timothy 1:17.

spirit and truth and thus as hidden from your senses as the invisible GOD, who is therefore unknown to you.

"Eye hath not seen, nor ear heard, neither have entered into the heart of man" – Herein is the only religion which is worthy of a supreme creature and befitting to him, and which GOD has prepared for them that love him.[43]

However, is human love possible without familiarity and sympathy? – You glory that you know GOD; how have you come to this glorious knowledge? – Through the observation of his works – How do you know that these works know him better than you yourselves, and are they not far less capable than you yourselves of this high revelation and of communicating it to you? To become acquainted with a mere man – and the most familiar of them all – would you depend on outward works? How dissimilar, how remote and strange, are such works, indeed how they contradict the depths of the inward man hidden in his heart!

Lie not against the truth[44] with your vainglorious knowledge of God; for lies belong to the wisdom which is earthly, human, and devilish. All the articles of your so-called universal, sound, and practiced reason are lies – more incomprehensible, contradictory, and sterile than all mysteries, wonders, and signs of the most holy faith which you persecute just as vainly as the extraordinary religious teacher of your century in his "Chance Thoughts Related to the Main Subject" persecutes me, I who am talking with you, like that dumb beast of burden, in order to avert the foolishness of the prophet whom it bore and who smote it in the heat of his incredulity or his yet more excessive credulity.

You little prophets of Böhmisch-Breda! In order actually to produce the knowledge of the supreme being on your little wandering star,[45] as you yourself call it, probably no more natural and reasonable means is left than for one of your brothers to travel to heaven and descend again into the abyss of the dead; for GOD is not a GOD of the dead but of the living.[46] You however are dead while you live,[47] and your true destiny is to press through to life only through death.

---

[43] 1 Corinthians 2:9: "But as it is written, Eye hath not seen, nor ear heard, neither have entered into the heart of man, the things which God hath prepared for them that love him."

[44] James 3:14: "glory not, and lie not against the truth."

[45] That is, planet; cf. also Jude 1:13: "wandering stars, to whom is reserved the blackness of darkness for ever."

[46] Matthew 22:32: "God is not the God of the dead, but of the living"; cf. Mark 12:27.

[47] 1 Timothy 5:6: "But she that liveth in pleasure is dead while she liveth."

Do not blaspheme with a lying tongue, which, inflamed by hell, turns black the whole artificial mechanism of your course. Your hate against GOD, like his wrath upon you, is infinite; the worm of your hate is undying, and the fire of his wrath is unquenchable.[48] For do not speak of the natural love toward GOD until all the bodies of your earth deny the force of their inertia and the fundamental laws of gravity through the cord of your miraculous voice.

The direction of all your tendencies, the striving and imagining of your heart from youth onwards, is aimed at the center of the earth. An unhindered expression of your natural capacity would remove you from the father of light into infinite darkness, were it not for his higher, gracious, unmediated force of attraction from above; for all that is in the world is not of the Father, but is of the world.[49] But you belong to the world, and he who is not of this world, his language you do not know and cannot hear his words.

You little prophets of Böhmisch-Breda! The object of your observations and devotion is not GOD but a mere verbal image which you have deified through a more than poetic license into a real person, and you make so many gods and persons of this sort through the transubstantiation of your verbal images that on judgment day the coarsest heathendom and the blindest popery, in comparison with your philosophical idolatry, will be justified and perhaps absolved.

Is the property, then, of these verbal images as unknown to you as the jealous God[50] whose name and honor you, like thieves and murderers,[51] violate – Is all your human reason anything other than tradition and inheritance, and is anything much involved in tracing the pedigree of your trite, bald, and twice dead opinions[52] to the roots of the family tree? Is not your human reason an indeterminate organ, a nose of wax,[53] a weather-cock, to which the letter of a holy canon, which was once written and has lasted till now, is to be preferred? Is the famous *principium coincidentiae*

---

[48] Mark 9:44, 46, 48: "Where their worm dieth not, and the fire is not quenched"; cf. Isaiah 66:24.
[49] 1 John 2:16: "For all that is in the world, the lust of the flesh, and the lust of the eyes, and the pride of life, is not of the Father, but is of the world."
[50] Exodus 34:14: "for the LORD, whose name is Jealous, is a jealous God," and elsewhere.
[51] John 10:8: "All that ever came before me are thieves and robbers." Hamann's allusion to the Luther Bible is more exact, as Luther has "thieves and murderers" (*Diebe und Mörder*).
[52] Jude 1:12: "trees whose fruit withereth, without fruit, twice dead, plucked up by the roots."
[53] "A thing easily turned or moulded; a person easily influenced, or of a weak character" (*Oxford English Dictionary*).

*oppositorum*ᵉ entirely unknown to you? It is the spirit that quickens;⁵⁴ the letter is flesh, and your dictionaries are straw!

You little prophets of Böhmisch-Breda! Who need ask of you a solemn pledge that you do not give a fig for posterity and truth and that the majority of voices and coins is your heart and your highest good. You say: "Our fathers taught the dull routine of their time, but the ears of our time are itching, and we must caress them." Hypocrites! Are you not witnesses yourselves that you are the children of your fathers,⁵⁵ and condemn both them and yourselves out of hand! – –

A standard-bearer of his age, like Saul – and a groundling similar to him may be fobbed off with the puppet-show of a dead prophet and an old woman;⁵⁶ however, to breathe into a letter as small as I am an apology as new as mine, is, truly, no matter for you, you great prophets of Böhmisch-Breda!

> Qualem ministrum fulminis alitem,
> cui REX DEORVM regnum in aves vagas
>   permisit, expertus *fidelem*
>   Iuppiter in Ganymede flavo,
>
> – – – mox in *ovilia*
> demisit hostem vividus impetus,
>   nunc in reluctantes *dracones*
>   egit amor *dapis* atque *pugnae*!⁵⁷

ᵉ Giordano Bruno. [According to the "principle of the coincidence of opposites" (or "reconciliation of contraries"), deriving from Nicholas of Cusa rather than Bruno, all opposites coincide in God.]

⁵⁴ John 6:63: "it is the spirit that quickeneth."

⁵⁵ Matthew 23:31: "Wherefore ye be witnesses unto yourselves, that ye are the children of them which killed the prophets."

⁵⁶ Saul consulted a woman with a familiar spirit; see Numbers 28.

⁵⁷ Horace, *Ode* 4.4.1–4, 9–12: "Like the winged bearer of the lightning, to whom the KING OF GODS gave dominion over the roving birds, having found him *faithful* in the case of fair-haired Ganymede . . . next with eager onset he swoops down as foe upon the *sheepfolds*; then love of *plunder* and the *fight* drives him against the struggling *snakes*" (tr. Bennett, Loeb Classical Library; Hamann's capitals and italics).

Golgotha and Sheblimini![1]

By a

Preacher in the Wilderness[2]

Moses.
Who says of father and mother:
"I have not seen him"
Nor acknowledges his brethren,
Knows nothing of his children, — —
They instruct Jacob in thy judgments
And Israel in thy law:
They only put incense before thee,
And whole burnt sacrifice upon thine altar.[3]

Jeremiah.
Behold! I will feed them with wormwood, and make them drink the water
of gall: for from the prophets of Jerusalem is profaneness gone forth into
all the land.[4]

1784.

[1] Golgotha: Calvary, where Christ was crucified. Sheblimini: Hebrew for "Sit thou at my right hand," from Psalms 110:1 ("Sit thou at my right hand, until I make thine enemies thy footstool"). At Hebrews 1:13, the command was addressed to Christ. By linking Golgotha, where Christ was humbled, with the command "Sheblimini!," by which he was exalted, Hamann emphasized the kenotic pattern of Christ's life (cf. especially Philippians 2:5–11). Christians traditionally connected Psalms 110:1 with Christ, and Luther did so with special emphasis; he also used *Sheblimini* as a name for his tutelary spirit. Hamann repeatedly invoked *sheblimini* in his letters and works, in a wide range of meanings.

[2] Like John the Baptist; cf. Matthew 3:1: "In those days came John the Baptist, preaching in the wilderness of Judaea."

[3] From Deuteronomy 33:9–10. "Moses" is triply appropriate. The verses come from Deuteronomy, that is, from the "Fifth Book of Moses" as it is known in German. Moreover, they are taken from the blessing spoken by Moses. Finally, Hamann gives the verses in the translation by Moses Mendelssohn (1783). By omitting the second half of verse 9 which gives the reason for ignoring parents, brethren, and children ("they observe thy word and keep thy covenant"), Hamann presents Mendelssohn as an apostate from his own faith.

[4] Jeremiah 23:15.

"I, too, cannot fail to mention the pleasurable[a] sentiments [*Gesinnungen*] which pay no heed to benevolence and are not amenable to any coercion,[5] toward Herr Moses Mendelssohn, which the perusal of his *Jerusalem* has produced in me. It combines (in the judgment of one authority) everything that can secure for a work a successful entrée into the hearts of its readers, everything by which all good writing has always had success: perfect clarity in the individual thoughts, a smooth and lucid coherence among the thoughts as they progress, evident and useful truth at many points, and expressions of noble and virtuous convictions [*Gesinnungen*] on the part of the author." But as far as the theory of rights, duties, and contracts[6] is concerned, the art of making rational decisions in cases of collision[7] satisfies me less than the commonplace opinion of old Cicero and his most recent, excellent translator and commentator.[8] Over this disputed point and a few similar ones I shall converse with my gentle [*andächtigen*] reader at length and breadth, height and depth, this way and that, to cut a long story short.

Since however a great gulf between our religious and philosophical principles has been firmly established, equity demands that the author be compared only with himself and to no standard other than the one which he himself professes. Herr Mendelssohn believes in a state of nature,[9] which he partly presupposes and partly opposes to society (as dogmatists do with a state of grace). I grant him and every dogmatist his belief, even if I am myself incapable of making either a proper concept or use of this

---

[a] Christian Garve, notes on the first book of Cicero's *Offices*, pp. 95–6. [Christian Garve, *Philosophische Anmerkungen und Abhandlungen zu Cicero's Büchern von den Pflichten* (1783; "Philosophical notes and essays on Cicero's books on duties"). Garve's volume of annotation accompanied his translation of Cicero's *De officiis*. Hamann translates from a footnote on pp. 95–6, in which Garve praises Mendelssohn's *Jerusalem*, adapting it so that Mendelssohn's characteristic vocabulary of "duties" and "convictions" appears.]

[5] Moses Mendelssohn, *Jerusalem*, tr. Allan Arkush (Hanover, NH, 1983), p. 61: "In general, men's convictions [*Gesinnungen*] pay no heed to benevolence, and are not amenable to any coercion."

[6] Ibid., p. 56: "this theory of rights, duties, and contracts."

[7] Ibid., p. 49: "the *art of making rational decisions in cases of collision*." Everyone in the state of nature has the right to determine for himself how to resolve conflicting duties of conscience.

[8] Hamann praises Garve as an excellent translator of Cicero's *De officiis* ("On duties"); Mendelssohn had praised Garve as an excellent translator of Adam Ferguson (*Jerusalem*, p. 55n). The "commonplace opinion" of Cicero may refer to his recourse to the concept of equity, the traditional humanistic method of matching general laws to particular circumstances. See, for example, *De officiis* 1.10, in which Cicero discusses how duties change because of changed circumstances (and see fn. a above).

[9] *Jerusalem*, pp. 35–7, 47–9, 52.

hypothesis so familiar to most of the men of letters[10] of our century. I do no better with the social contract! For both of us, the divine and eternal covenant with Abraham and his seed must be all the more important because the blessing is based on this attested solemn contract, pledged and promised to all the peoples of earth.

For the benefit of the speculative friends of natural law, and with their philosophical and juristic assistance,[11] the author has spent a great deal of effort to define the first principles of natural law,[12] in order in the end to be able to explain rationally some of the rabbis' assertions; thus the Gordian knot of annulling the ecclesiastical law[13] seems very likely to be a consequence of that idle and fruitless effort. Because it is applied to the difference between church and state, from which Herr Mendelssohn started and to which he again returns,[14] this theory is as it were the golden hip of its master, whose metal must above all be assayed.[15] For the privilege granted to speculative taste, that is the privilege of twelve pages which the dissident reader is permitted to skip,[16] is a double bribery, and what matters the most with first principles is whether they can be accepted or placed into doubt before we move on to applying them.

Without forging three moral entities or persons[17] out of state, religion, and liberty of conscience (whose immoral dissension and feuds are all the

---

[10] Ibid., p. 104: "In a word, we are *literati, men of letters*. Our whole being depends on letters; and we can scarcely comprehend how a mortal man can educate and perfect himself without a *book*."

[11] Perhaps puns on Mendelssohn's "very worthy friend," *Assistenzrath* Ernst Ferdinand Klein, the philosophical jurist (*Jerusalem*, p. 55).

[12] *Jerusalem*, p. 45: "I court the danger of becoming too speculative for some readers . . . To the friends of natural law it may not be disagreeable to see how I sought to define for myself its first principles."

[13] In *Searching for Light and Right*, the work that provoked *Jerusalem*, the anonymous author (August Friedrich Cranz) argues that since Mendelssohn rejects ecclesiastical law, he has in fact already broken with Judaism; see *Jerusalem*, pp. 84–5. On p. 130, Mendelssohn quotes the rabbis to support his view that with the destruction of the Temple, punishments to enforce ecclesiastical law were no longer legal.

[14] *Jerusalem*, p. 56: "Let us now apply this theory of rights, duties, and contracts to the difference between state and church, from which we started."

[15] Ibid., p. 81: "Must one never doubt principles? If so, men of the Pythagorean school could dispute forever how their teacher happened to come by his golden hip, and no one would dare to ask: Did Pythagoras actually have a golden hip?"

[16] Ibid., p. 45: "I court the danger of becoming too speculative for some readers. Yet everyone is free to skip what does not suit his taste." In the English translation, the subsection on "the origin of the rights of coercion and the validity of contracts of men" runs from page 45 to 55.

[17] Ibid., p. 33: "Some thought it proper to separate these different relations of societal man into moral entities"; p. 45: "civil society, viewed as a moral person"; p. 57: "The state, or whoever represents

more startling if morality has to do with laws which cannot contradict each other),[18] they are first and foremost three phrases which at first glance say everything, or rather nothing; therefore, they are related to other words as the indefiniteness of man is to the definiteness of the animals.[19]

"Very well! If the dispute allowed itself to be settled by a verbal definition"[20] – yet the three of them stand right in the antechamber of the theory.[21] With the moral capacity, it seems to me (*in parenthesi*) to be precisely the same story as with a moral entity. This capacity is called moral if it is consistent with the laws of wisdom and goodness;[22] so then wisdom combined with goodness ought to be called morality.[23] Instead, the combination is called justice; in that case the capacity that is consistent with the laws of wisdom and goodness ought by rights to be called just. Moreover, might and right are heterogeneous ideas even in state of nature;[24] so capacities, means, and goods appear to be far too closely connected to the idea of power for them not to amount before long to a monotonous sameness. – – Where, however, do the laws of wisdom and goodness come from? Suppose there are such laws; why is it still necessary to search for a light and law of nature?[25] Would these laws not already be in themselves the best law of nature? – Least of all do I grasp how from three initial definitions of right, morals, and goods, the conclusion follows that man

---

the state, is viewed as a moral person"; p. 73: "Hence the state is a moral person"; likewise divine religion "is a moral person" (p. 73).

[18] Ibid., p. 46: "The laws of wisdom and goodness cannot contradict each other."

[19] Ibid., p. 112. Defending the use of fables to convey moral truths, Mendelssohn writes: "Every animal has its definite, distinctive character, and presents itself in this light at first glance, since its features as a whole largely point to this peculiar mark of distinction . . . Indeed, even inanimate objects have something more defined in their exterior than man has for man. At first glance, man reveals nothing, or rather, everything . . . His distinctive character, therefore, does not strike the eye."

[20] Ibid., p. 38.

[21] State, religion, and liberty of conscience are introduced as three moral entities on the first page of *Jerusalem* (p. 33 in translation).

[22] *Jerusalem*, p. 45: "The *authority* [*Befugnis*] (the moral capacity) to make use of a thing as a means for promoting one's felicity is called a *right*. This capacity is called moral if it is consistent with the laws of wisdom and goodness."

[23] Ibid., p. 46: "Wisdom combined with goodness is called *justice*."

[24] Ibid., p. 37: "*Might* and *right* are, therefore, different things; and in the state of nature, too, they were heterogeneous ideas."

[25] Alludes to *Searching for Light and Right* (see n. 13). In German, *Recht* may mean either "law" or "right," depending on context.

therefore has a right to certain goods or means,[26] unless a right to felicity is being arbitrarily assigned; the universality of such a right, however, can be maintained as little as a universal right to divine law–giving and direct revelation.

The theorist needs two groups to define his rudiments: those who hold rights and those who bear duties. Swiftly he creates the former out of a moral capacity, and the second out of a moral necessity.[27] Once again a dilemma of philosophical indefiniteness! The holders of rights are taken simply with regard to the state of nature, while the bearers of duties are taken with regard also to the state of society, and through an expression turned askant, not doing and passively suffering could all the more rashly be confounded.[28]

However, to every right there corresponds a duty.[29] Thus to the moral capacity to make use of a thing as a means for promoting one's felicity there corresponds also a moral incapacity to do so; need rather than necessity. Thus in the state of nature there are nothing but duties of omission,[30] no doing but pure not-doing.

If I have a right to make use of a thing as a means for promoting my felicity, then everyone in the state of nature has an identical right; just as in wartime a soldier has the right to kill his enemy, and the enemy to kill him.[31] Or are the laws of wisdom and goodness as diverse as my self and every other self? or is the metaphysical law of royal self-love and *amour propre* part of the law of nature?[32]

---

[26] *Jerusalem*, pp. 45–6: "Man has, therefore, a right to certain goods or means toward felicity, insofar as this right does not contradict the laws of wisdom and goodness."

[27] Ibid., p. 45: "The *authority* (the moral capacity) to make use of a thing as a means for promoting one's felicity is called a *right*. This capacity is called moral if it is consistent with the laws of wisdom and goodness"; p. 46: "Whatever must be done in accordance with the laws of wisdom and goodness, or the opposite of which would be contrary to the laws of wisdom or goodness, is called *morally necessary*. The moral necessity (obligation) to do, or omit doing something is a *duty*."

[28] Ibid., p. 47: "Man cannot be happy without *beneficence* [*Wohltun*], not without *passive* [*leidendes*], but also not without *active*, beneficence."

[29] Ibid., p. 46: "To every right, therefore, there corresponds a duty; to the right to act, there corresponds the duty to suffer [the action]."

[30] Ibid., p. 48: "Only the duties and rights of omission are perfect [i.e., enforceable] in the state of nature."

[31] Ibid., p. 46n: "One may object that, in time of war, the soldier has the right to kill an enemy, without the latter being obligated to submit to being killed."

[32] Frederick the Great published "Essai sur l'amour-propre envisagé comme principe de morale" ("Essay on self-love conceived as a moral principle") in 1770.

Let it be conceded that the laws of wisdom and goodness cannot contradict each other; are not cases of collision between them just as easy to imagine as between one's own use and benevolence?[33] Is there no dissension, are there no campaigns, between moral qualities as there are between moral entities?[34] – and there, as here, does not freedom fall victim to moral necessity and the terrible imperative of the laws of wisdom and goodness,[35] in which after all a right of coercion[36] is already present?

Is it wisdom and goodness, however, to trim and maim further with laws the meager capacity of our possessions and our right (perfect or imperfect,[37] I do not know) to the means of our felicity? Or are these laws, too, of such a nature that, through them, all conditions under which the predicate "a means to happiness" may belong to a thing are invested in both groups?[38] Now these laws, on which our moral capacity and incapacity depend, are assumed to be known the world over and revealed to the entire human race; or, since they presumably have reference to inner convictions, does their perfection lie in the fact that they do not necessarily have to be expressed, and that therefore an explicit account of them may not be given even for a speculative reader?

All the same, for all the verbal bolts on which every definition of a theorist is fixed, the matter seems to me to amount to this: man in the state of nature holds a right, so long as his use of a thing as a means toward his felicity is consistent with the laws of wisdom and goodness; on the other hand, he bears a duty as soon as the use of a thing as a means towards his felicity contradicts these laws. The former therefore has an active natural law to enjoy, while the latter has a passive-suffering natural

---

[33] *Jerusalem*, p. 52: "exclusively to man in the state of nature belongs the right to settle cases of collision between his *own use* and *benevolence*."

[34] Ibid., p. 33: "Immeasurable evils have hitherto arisen, and still threaten to arise, from the dissension between these moral entities."

[35] Ibid., p. 46: "Whatever must be done in accordance with the laws of wisdom and goodness, or the opposite of which would be contrary to the laws of wisdom and goodness, is called *morally necessary*."

[36] Ibid., p. 45: "civil society, viewed as a moral person, can have the *right of coercion*."

[37] Imperfect and perfect rights are discussed in ibid., pp. 46–7; only the latter are compulsory and may be exacted by force.

[38] Ibid., p. 46: "The law of justice on which a right is founded is either of such a nature that all the conditions under which the predicate may belong to the subject are invested in the holder of the right, or they are not. In the first case, it is a *perfect*, in the second an *imperfect right*." The two groups are the right-holders and the duty-bearers.

law in which to be consoled. – – Despite all the pharisaical hypocrisies with which the men of letters of our illuminated century make mention of the principles of contradiction and of sufficient proof, they are the worst defilers of their own house!

Because of these cases of collision between positive and negative authority, between one's own use and one's wearisome dependence on the benevolence of someone in the state of natural independence whose own use is wiser, there appears from the brain of the theorist, like Pallas *ex machina*,[39] the law of justice![40] – What an extravagance of these mystical laws, in order to adduce a miserable law of nature that is scarcely worth saying and suits neither the state of society nor the matter of Judaism! "Even that which they build," an Ammonite would say, "Even that which they build, if a fox go up, he shall even break down their stone wall."[41] Let one try to explain rationally certain assertions of the rabbis of divine reason without such principles.[42]

As a duty-bearing reader, I freely content myself with the fact that I can scarcely deny to any right-holding penman the authority to make use of a superannuated, Leibnizian[43] verbal definition as a means to discuss the first letters of his law of nature; after all, the laws of wisdom and goodness that never contradict each other have fallen out, against the knowledge and will of the theorist who could do nothing to stop it and they must be bound anew through justice.

As a right-holding man of letters I would, however, wish to have gentle readers of better knowledge and belief [*Wissen und Gewissen*] to whom I might pose one question only: "How is justice, which gives to each its own, supposed to be able to stop being what it is, deny its own essence, rob wisdom and goodness of what is theirs, and exchange its own immutable oneness for two things that are as distinct from each other as they both are from justice itself?"

---

[39] *Maschinenpallas*: perhaps conflates the story of Pallas Athena born fully grown and armed from the head of Zeus with the *deus ex machina*. It may be a reference to the palladium, the image of Athena that protected Troy as long as it was preserved in the citadel there.

[40] See n. 38.   [41] Nehemiah 4:3.

[42] *Jerusalem*, p. 130: "Let one try to explain rationally, without my principles, this assertion of the rabbis!"

[43] Mendelssohn adopted his definition of justice ("wisdom combined with goodness") from Leibniz; see the commentary by Alexander Altmann which accompanies the English translation of *Jerusalem*, p. 174.

Is it wisdom and goodness to give and to leave to each its own? Of course it is in the sole case where there is no other law of property than the wisdom and goodness of the giver. However, this case is the only one of its kind. Now how is a generic term proper for an individual thing which refuses to be stacked with anything and which cannot be put under the same rubric with anything else?[44]

Leibniz was therefore correct for that sole case which can be discussed only in a theodicy. Our fine and good-natured wits, drunk on the strong drink of their universal wisdom and brotherly love and prattling out all the feeling of justice in edicts and homilies and Aphthonian chriae,[45] are also right, in keeping with the coherent and systematic conclusiveness of the Roman-metaphysical despotism[46] whose transcendental intellect itself prescribes its laws of nature.

The law of justice,[47] however, is of such a nature that what matters with it are conditions and a relation of predicate to subject. In fact, through conditions the categorical perfection of a law is diminished, and the relation of predicate to subject appears to be an attribute purloined from logical truth. In the meantime I have no intention of being very particular about this botched attempt at philosophical justice, since in this entire law I do not even quite know what subject and what predicate are actually in question. Suppose that all the conditions under which a right belongs to someone are invested in the holder of the right: then the bearer of the duty is perfectly robbed of his knowledge and scruple [*Wissen und Gewissen*] and all his moral capacity. With imperfect rights, however, a distinct share (namely the conditions that have not been invested) is dependent on the knowledge and scruple of the duty-bearer, for duties and scruple seem to be entirely expendable concepts for the right-holder, unknown quantities and *qualitates occultae*.[48] Who may denounce his scrupulousness? Who is

---

44 *Jerusalem*, p. 131: "But why do you seek a generic term for an individual thing, which has no genus, which refuses to be stacked with anything, which cannot be put under the same rubric with anything else?"

45 Aphthonius was a sophist and rhetorician of the fourth century AD whose *Progymnasmata* was an important pedagogical text for humanists in the Renaissance; according to the *Oxford English Dictionary* article which quotes the standard Greek–English Lexicon, a *chreia* or *chria* is "A pregnant sentence . . . borrowed from some other author, and worked out by certain rules."

46 *Jerusalem*, p. 34: "Yet he who considers tranquillity in doctrine and life to be felicity will find it nowhere better secured to him than under a Roman Catholic despot."

47 See n. 38.

48 Cf. Hume, *Dialogues Concerning Natural Religion*, part 4: "It was usual with the peripatetics, you know, Cleanthes, when the cause of any phenomenon was demanded, to have recourse to their

to force on him the scales for such a critical decision? The right is even in his hand![49] Such a law of justice is glossed with greater decency and seemliness by that amusing addition of the commentators: "Break the barrel, but don't let the wine run out!" Or, as the muses of the fish-market sing, "Wash my back, but don't get it wet!"

Through the serpent's deception of language, in all Jerusalem there circulates, in verbal forms as varied as manifold, the eternal *petitio* of one and the same hypocritical *principii* of outward perfection of rights and actions, of inner imperfection of duties and convictions – Yet everything does depend on the two questions which I must repeatedly touch on:

> I. According to the law of reason, are there rights to persons and things which are connected to doctrines and which can be acquired by assent to doctrines?

Like worms through children, laws pass through sickly men of letters; laws are the golden emerods[50] and the nymph Egeria[51] of many a philosophical government. If a connection between the physical and the moral cannot be denied,[52] and if the different modifications of writing and modes of designation must also have had different effects upon the progress and improvement of concepts, opinions, and knowledge,[53] then I do not know where the difficulties come from in imagining a connection between moral capacities and doctrines. According to the law of reason (i.e., the immutable coherence and essential connection of ideas which either presuppose or exclude one another),[54] doctrines are as closely

---

faculties or occult qualities; and to say, for instance, that bread nourished by its nutritive faculty, and senna purged by its purgative. But it has been discovered, that this subterfuge was nothing but the disguise of ignorance." See also pp. 93 and 117, above.

[49] Cf. Job 2:6: "And the Lord said unto Satan, Behold, he is in thine hand." See also n. 296 below.

[50] 1 Samuel 6:4.

[51] Egeria instructed King Numa, legendary second king of Rome, in sacred rites.

[52] At *Jerusalem*, p. 37, Mendelssohn criticizes Hobbes' confusion of moral and physical capacities. Perhaps Hamann has *Jerusalem*, p. 42 in view. To the question "Which form of government is best?," Mendelssohn responds that it is as vague as the question "which food is the most wholesome": "Every complexion, every climate, every sex, and mode of life, etc., requires a different answer."

[53] *Jerusalem*, p. 110: "All these different modifications of writing and modes of designation must also have had different effects on the progress and improvement of concepts, opinions, and knowledge."

[54] Ibid., p. 91: "reason, that is ... an immutable coherence and essential connection of ideas, according to which they either presuppose or exclude one another."

connected to moral capacity in general as they are to the special right of decision in cases of collision. Assent to doctrines has an effect on our convictions, as these convictions do on our moral judgment and the conduct[b] that is consistent with it.

> II. Can perfect rights be produced through contracts unless there are imperfect duties prior to the contract, and do compulsory duties derive from duties of conscience?[55]

With perfect rights, physical force takes the place of moral capacity; and with perfect duties, physical necessity that has the force to extort actions. With such a perfection, the whole speculative law of nature is ruptured and flows out into the height of injustice [*Unrecht*][56] – to the end of that which is abolished.[57] In brief, all the highly praised laws of wisdom and goodness, the law of justice and the law of reason are lost in the all-merciful will and *bon plaisir* of that Roman marionettist and virtuoso,[58] and in his swan song: *Heu quantus artifex pereo!*[59] – Thine end is come, and the measure of thy covetousness.[60]

However, suppose that there is a social contract: then there is also a natural one, older and more genuine, and the conditions of the natural contract must be the basis of the social one. Through it all natural property becomes conventional again,[61] and man in the state of nature becomes dependent on its laws, i.e., positively obliged to act in accordance with the very same laws which all of nature and especially the nature of man has to thank for the preservation of existence and the use of all means and goods contributing to it. Since man bears duties to nature, he accordingly has least of all an exclusive right to and hateful monopoly over his abilities,

---

[b] See Adelung. [On *gebaren* ("conduct"), Johann Christoph Adelung, *Grammatisch-kritisches Wörterbuch* (1796, "Grammatical-critical dictionary") comments that it is used "not only of gestures but of all the ethical actions of man" and that "in High German it is obsolete."]

55 *Jerusalem*, pp. 46–7: "There are *perfect* and *imperfect duties* as well as *rights*. The first are called compulsory rights and compulsory duties; the others, however, are called *claims* (*petitions*) and *duties of conscience*."

56 Recalls the Latin tag *summa lex summa injuria*, "the height of the law is the height of injury."

57 2 Corinthians 3:13: "And not as Moses, which put a vail over his face, that the children of Israel could not stedfastly look to the end of that which is abolished."

58 I.e., Nero (and by implication Frederick the Great).

59 Hamann adapts Nero's words, "Qualis artifex pereo," "What an artist dies in me," as recorded by Suetonius.

60 Jeremiah 51:13.   61 *Jerusalem*, p. 47: "*Not all property is merely conventional.*"

neither to the products thereof, nor to the sterile mule of his industry and the sadder bastards of his usurping acts of violence over the creature made subject, against its will, to his vanity.[62]

Not to him, not to him alone,[63] is the moral capacity to make use of things as a means subordinated, but rather to those laws of wisdom and goodness which light our way in the immense kingdom of nature. All the conditions under which the predicate "felicity" may belong to the subject "duty-bearer" are invested in him as such and not as one who holds a right through the law of nature and the law of natural justice and of his own reason. He therefore has neither a physical nor a moral capacity for any other felicity than the one intended for him and to which he is called. All the means which he makes use of to attain a felicity not given to him as a blessing are a heap of natural offenses and decided injustice. All lust to improve one's existence is the spark of a hellish turmoil.[64]

It would not befit any Solomon, to whom the God of the Jews gave very great wisdom and understanding exceeding much, and largeness of heart, even as the sand that is on the sea shore;[65] – nor any Nebuchadnezzar, to whom the God of the Jews has given the beasts, despite their definiteness, to serve him;[66] it would befit only a philosopher without cares[67] or shame, only a Nimrod,[68] to call out in the state of nature with the force of a horned brow,[69] "To Me, and to Me alone, appertains the right to decide whether, for whose benefit, when, and under what conditions I am obliged to exercise beneficence."[70] – However if that me, even in the state of nature,

---

[62] Romans 8:20: "For the creature was made subject to vanity, not willingly."

[63] *Jerusalem*, p. 48: "Hence, in the state of nature, to me, and to me alone, appertains the right to decide *whether, to what extent, when, for whose benefit*, and under what conditions I am obliged to exercise beneficence."

[64] Ibid., p. 47: "For the *improvement of one's existence* is inseparable from *benevolence*."

[65] 1 Kings 4:29: "And God gave Solomon wisdom and understanding exceeding much, and largeness of heart, even as the sand that is on the sea shore."

[66] Jeremiah 27:6: "and the beasts of the fields have I given him also to serve him."

[67] Frederick the Great named his palace at Potsdam "Sans Souci."

[68] Nimrod, "a mighty one in the earth" (Genesis 10:8), has been taken since Augustine as the figure of a tyrant opposing God.

[69] According to Exodus 34:29 in the Vulgate (but not in Luther's translation or the King James Bible), when Moses came down from Sinai, he was unaware "quod cornuta esset facies sua." ("that his face was horned").

[70] *Jerusalem*, p. 48; see n. 63.

is unjust and overweening to this degree, and if every man has an identical right to Me! and to Me alone! – then let us rejoice over the We of God's Grace, and be thankful for the crumbs which their hunting-dogs and lap-dogs, greyhounds and bear-baiters leave behind for orphaned minors. "Behold, he drinketh up a river, and hasteth not: he trusteth that he can draw up Jordan into his mouth.[71] – – Who might constrain him to toss the beggared hinds a pourboire? Who might stop him absorbing the Foy! Foy![72] of the poor sinners?"

Should everyone intend to set up his unphilosophical Me as the royal umpire in cases of collision, neither a state of nature nor a state of society is possible. On the contrary, in both states decisions about natural or positive laws must fall to One universal Lord and heir.[73] So it is hardly worthwhile to continue to rummage around in the speculative and theoretical rubble of the right to property for one's own use, of the right to make decisions about beneficence, and of the totality of conditions logically necessary for the perfection of compulsory rights; instead, all social contracts derive, according to the law of nature, from the moral capacity to say Yes! or No!, and from the moral necessity to make good the word that has been given. The moral capacity to say Yes! or No! is based on the natural use of human reason and speech; the moral necessity to fulfill the word that has been given is based on the fact that our inward declaration of will can be expressed, revealed, or known only in speech or writing or action, and that our words like our deeds must be regarded as the natural signs of our convictions. Reason and language are therefore the inner and outer band of all social life. If that which nature, through having been established, has joined together is divorced or divided, then faith and fidelity are annulled, and lies and deceit, shame and vice, are confirmed and stamped as means to felicity. Fundamentum est iustitiae FIDES – dictorum constantia et veritas. – Est enim primum, quod cernitur in

---

[71] Job 40:23, the behemoth.

[72] I have translated "Pfuy" inexactly as "Foy" (both derive from Dutch "fooi"). "Foy" is "a parting entertainment, present, cup of liquor, etc., given by or to one setting out on a journey" (*Oxford English Dictionary*); "pfuy" refers more specifically to the money which customs officials were in the habit of receiving from shippers. James C. O'Flaherty notes that in 1782 Hamann's income was "reduced from 460 to 300 thaler" because of the loss of this money; see the chronology in his *Johann Georg Hamann* (Boston, 1979).

[73] Hebrews 1:1–2: "God . . . Hath in these last days spoken unto us by his Son, whom he hath appointed heir of all things."

universi generis humani societate, eiusque autem vinculum est RATIO et
ORATIO, quae conciliat inter se homines coniungitque naturali quadam
societate. – – Res a natura copulatas errore divellere, fons est fraudium,
maleficiorum, scelerum omnium.ᶜ

Every sophist is therefore not only a liar but also a hypocrite, and makes
use of language as mere puppetry,⁷⁴ in order to pass off his idol, the vain
fabrication of human art, as the overflow of divine reason and the daughter
incarnate of its voice,ᵈ to deceive superstitious readers by the snare of a
golden hip or golden calf,⁷⁵ and to insinuate himself like a thief and a
killer into their confidence at the cost and risk of unrecognized living
truths.

"If a ruler harkens to lies, all his servants are wicked."⁷⁶ All his claims
to a royal monopoly on injustice, all his efforts and ideas to fence in and
ruin his subjects, with edicts of gallows and shame, to keep them from
imitating him and infringing on his monopoly, have no other effect than
to make the sophistry of his rule the more contemptible and ridiculous in
the eyes of posterity.

"For he spake, and it was done."⁷⁷ – "and whatever the man called
every creature, that was the name thereof."⁷⁸ According to this model

---

ᶜ Cicero, *De officiis*, Book 1, chap. 7; Book 1, chap. 16; Book 3, chap. 18. [The first citation adapts
Cicero, *De officiis* ("On duties") 1.7.23: "Fundamentum autem est iustitiae fides, [id est] dictorum
[conventorumque] constantia et veritas" ("Moreover, the foundation of justice is good faith, [that
is], truth and fidelity to promises [and agreements]").

The second adapts Cicero, *De officiis* 1.16.50: "est enim primum, quod cernitur in universi generis humani societate. Eius autem vinculum est ratio et oratio, [quae docendo, dis-
cendo, communicando, disceptando, iudicando] conciliat inter se homines coniungitque naturali quadam societate" ("the first principle is that which is found in the society of the whole
human race; the bond of society is reason and speech, which [by teaching, learning, communicating, discussing, and judging] associate men with themselves and join them in a sort of natural
society").

The third adapts Cicero, *De officiis* 3.18.75: "[Sic enim cogitans: 'Est istuc quidem honestum,
verum hoc expedit,'] res a natura copulatas audebit errore divellere, qui fons est fraudium, maleficiorum, scelerum omnium" ["(For if he reasons, 'That way is the right way to be sure, but this
way brings advantage,' he will venture to tear asunder what nature has joined, which is the origin
of fraud, wrong-doing, and all crimes").]

ᵈ בַּת־קוֹל. [Bat qol, literally "daughter of a voice," is the means by which God communicated to men
after the end of biblical prophecy.]

⁷⁴ *Jerusalem*, p. 44: "Religious actions without religious thoughts are mere puppetry, not service of
God."

⁷⁵ Mentioned by Mendelssohn in ibid., p. 120. Cf. Exodus 32.

⁷⁶ Proverbs 29:12.   ⁷⁷ Psalms 33:9.   ⁷⁸ Genesis 2:19.

and image of definiteness, every word of a man ought to be and to remain the thing itself. It is on this likeness of stamp and motto to the perfect type of our race[79] and to the guide of our youth[80] – it is on this law of nature to make use of the word as the primary, noblest, and most powerful means of revealing[e] and communicating our inward declaration of will – that the validity of all contracts is based, and this mighty fortress of truth in the inward parts is superior to all frenchified practices, machinations, pedantries, and mongering. The misuse of language and of its natural testimony is therefore the grossest perjury; it turns the transgressor of this first law of reason and its justice into the worst misanthrope, the traitor and opponent of German uprighteousness and honesty, on which our dignity and felicity are based. A Punic preacher,[82] not in the wilderness, has found that nature hath made men German, and that all *Œuvres diverses*[83] of a cynical-sodomitical dialect, stinking of b . . and f. .[84] as of pitch and brimstone, are nothing but the black arts of a f. . diable of darkness.

In a valley of vision[85] full of indefinite and wavering ideas it is not good, your glorying of greater enlightenment![86] – – better development! more correct distinctions! the sublimed linguistic usage of healthy human understanding! – in opposition to the times and the system of Hobbes.[87] I have already censured the relationship between what one man calls

---

e   Cf. Luther's Preface. [Perhaps refers to Luther's "Preface to the Psalter": "Compared to a speaking man, a silent one is simply to be regarded as a half-dead man; and there is no mightier or nobler work of man than speech. For it is by speech, more than by his shape or by any other work, that man is most distinguished from other animals." See Luther's Works (American Edition), vol. XXXV, p. 254.]

79   God; cf. Genesis 1:27: "So God created man in his own image."
80   Jeremiah 3:4.   81   Psalm 51:6 .
82   Interpretations vary. Possibly Luther, an Augustinian (Augustine as North African was "Punic"); possibly an allusion to King Solomon, the preacher of Ecclesiastes 7:29: "Lo, this only have I found, that God hath made man upright."
83   Presumably refers to the works of Frederick the Great, though the reference is disguised in order to pass through the censors.
84   The "b . . ." and "f . . ." could stand for a number of expressions, some quite vulgar, including *bumsen* ("screwing") and *ficken* ("fucking").
85   Isaiah 22:1.   86   1 Corinthians 5:6.
87   *Jerusalem*, p. 36: "There is, at bottom, a good deal of truth in all Hobbes' assertions. The absurd consequences to which they lead follow solely from the exaggeration with which he propounded them, whether out of a love of paradox or in compliance with the needs of his time. Moreover, in his day the concepts of natural law were, in part, still not sufficiently enlightened . . . The ideas of *right* and *duty*, of *power* and *obligation*, have been better developed; one has learned to distinguish

177

right and another power. Compulsory duties, whose perfection consists in the fact that they can be exacted by force,[88] seem to verge right on the obligation of fear.[89] Furthermore, if as much is won by the expression of beneficence as is lost by self-sacrifice, then the cases of collision between beneficence and one's own use, or between duties toward oneself and toward one's neighbor, are as much the fruits of a pitiful sophistry as the illusory conflict between the rights of the Deity and the rights of man, the conflict to which the theorist imputes all the evils that have been perpetrated from time immemorial under the philosophical and political cover of truth and justice.[90] The love of our fellow man is an innate weakness, and benevolence little more than a foppery into which and then immediately out of which one seeks to lure oneself,[91] which pesters and flatters the reader with scholastic jargon while it, incidentally, treats itself to the guzzled contents of ideas and, with the empty skins, has a good laugh about the biased public. In brief, Penelope's whole web[92] amounts to the nimbleness that lets each thing that is inseparable from the other[93] appear double but then swiftly lets them merge again in each other. The result is that through hocus-pocus of this kind, viewpoint and horizon are continually being shifted under both aspects, and the speculative letterer becomes dizzy on the slender dance-rope.[94] Meanwhile the ephah of theory in the land of Shinar is lifted up between heaven and earth, and

more correctly between physical and moral ability, between might and right. These distinctions have become so intimately fused with our language that, nowadays, the refutation of Hobbes' system seems to be a matter of common sense, and to be accomplished, as it were, by language itself."

[88] Ibid., p. 47: "Compulsory rights may be *exacted* by force."

[89] Ibid., p. 35. According to Hobbes' system, "all *right* is grounded in *power*, and all *obligation* in *fear*."

[90] Ibid., p. 58: "all the evils which from time immemorial have been perpetrated under the cloak of religion by its fiercest enemies, hypocrisy and misanthropy, are purely and simply the fruits of this pitiful sophistry, of an illusory conflict between God and man, the rights of the Deity and the rights of men."

[91] Ibid., p. 63: "Without God, providence, and a future life, love of our fellow man is but an innate weakness, and benevolence is little more than a foppery into which we seek to lure one another so that the simpleton will toil while the clever man enjoys himself and has a good laugh at the other's expense."

[92] Which she undid at night (see *Odyssey*, Book 2).

[93] *Jerusalem*, p. 40: "One is inseparable from the other" (i.e., the spiritual and the earthly, the present and the future).

[94] Ibid., pp. 39–40: "Delusions of this kind shift the viewpoint and the horizon of the weak-sighted man who has to walk along a narrow path; he is in danger of becoming dizzy and of stumbling on a level road."

Jerusalem shall no more be inhabited in her own place, even in Jerusalem, but shall come to be under the meridian of Babel.[f] –

In fact one confuses ideas, and it is, in the strictest sense, neither in keeping with the truth nor advantageous to the reader's welfare to oppose state and church, to sever inner felicity so neatly from external tranquility and safety, as the temporal from the eternal.[95] The child of the one mother was overlaid by her in its sleep, and the still living child is already squirming beneath the blow of the upraised sword of the Solomonic executioner, to be cut in two, half to the one, half to the other[96] –

Actions and convictions belong to the true fulfillment of our duties and to the perfection of man.[97] State and church have both as their object.[98] Consequently, actions without convictions and convictions without actions are a cleaving of complete and living duties into two dead halves. When grounds for action may no longer be grounds of truth, and grounds of truth are no longer suited to grounds of action; when the creature depends on necessary understanding, and reality on contingent will, then all the divine and human unity in convictions and actions comes to an end. The state becomes a body without spirit and life – carrion for eagles![99] The church becomes a ghost, without flesh and bone – a scarecrow for sparrows! Reason, with its immutable coherence of ideas which either presuppose or exclude one another,[100] stands still, like the sun and the moon upon Gibeon and in the valley of Ajalon.[101]

---

[f] Zechariah 10:10–11 and 12:6. [The first citation may be in error; Zechariah 5:9–11 seems to fit better: "Then lifted I up mine eyes, and looked, and, behold, there came out two women . . . and they lifted up the ephah between the earth and the heaven. Then said I to the angel that talked with me, Whither do these bear the ephah? And he said unto me, To build it an house in the land of Shinar: and it shall be established, and set there upon her own base."
"In that day will I make the governors of Judah like an hearth of fire among the wood, and like a torch of fire in a sheaf; and they shall devour all the people round about, on the right hand and on the left: and Jerusalem shall be inhabited again in her own place, even in Jerusalem."]

[95] Cf. ibid., three passages: p. 39: "it is, in the strictest sense, neither in keeping with the truth nor advantageous to man's welfare to sever the temporal so neatly from the eternal"; p. 39: "One confuses ideas if one opposes [man's] temporal welfare to his eternal felicity"; p. 35: Hobbes "regarded tranquility and safety, no matter how they were obtained, as the greatest felicity."

[96] 1 Kings 3.

[97] *Jerusalem*, p. 40: "Now, two things belong to the true fulfillment of our duties: *action* and *conviction* . . . Hence actions and convictions belong to the perfection of man."

[98] Ibid., p. 56: "Both state and church have as their object actions as well as convictions."

[99] Luke 17:37.

[100] *Jerusalem*, p. 91: "reason, that is . . . an immutable coherence and essential connection of ideas, according to which they either presuppose or exclude one another."

[101] Joshua 10:12.

Yet the theorist is of the opinion that the state may not be charged for the convictions of its subjects any more than the dear Lord may be for their actions. In this he not only contradicts his own scheme of Judaism, but also, in unison with Hobbes, he sets the highest felicity in external tranquility and safety no matter how it comes about[102] and no matter how perfectly dreadful it is, like that evening calm that prevails in a fortress that is to be taken during the night,[103] so that, as Jeremiah says, "they shall sleep a perpetual sleep, and not wake."[104] Through such verbal games of physiognomical and hypocritical indefiniteness, in our enlightened times of midnight every letter- and word-grocer gains a triumph over the most expert master, to whom at bottom he nevertheless owes this triumph;[105] but a confusion of ideas is not without practical consequences.[106]

Gentle reader, without fatiguing myself and you with the even more speculative application,[107] I would wish, for the sake of our mutual safety in the upper floor,[108] no such loose ground and sandy bottom for the new and tough theory of Judaism.

Since I, too, know of no eternal truths save as incessant temporality,[109] I therefore have no need to lose my way climbing up into the cabinet of divine intellect, nor into the sanctuary of divine will; nor to linger over the difference between direct revelation through word and script, which are intelligible only here and now, and between indirect revelation through

---

[102] *Jerusalem*, p. 35: Hobbes "regarded tranquility and safety, no matter how they were obtained, as the greatest felicity."

[103] Ibid., p. 34: "Your structure is completely built, and perfect calm reigns in all its parts. To be sure, only that dreadful calm which, as Montesquieu says, prevails during the evening in a fortress which is to be taken by storm during the night." (See *De l'esprit des lois*, 5.14.)

[104] Jeremiah 51:57.

[105] *Jerusalem*, p. 37: "In this fashion, in our day, every student of natural law can gain a triumph over Thomas Hobbes, to whom, at bottom, he nevertheless owes this triumph."

[106] Ibid., p. 39: "And this confusion of ideas is not without practical consequences."

[107] Perhaps refers to Mendelssohn's rebuttal, at the beginning of Part II of *Jerusalem*, of a reviewer's hypothetical test-case that had been intended to refute him. Mendelssohn quotes the words of the reviewer: "Let us . . . apply them (the denied principles) to a particular case," *Jerusalem*, pp. 81–2.

[108] Ibid., p. 87: "Now Christianity, as you know, is built upon Judaism, and if the latter falls, it must necessarily collapse with it into *one* heap of ruins. You say that my conclusions undermine the foundation of Judaism, and you offer me the safety of your upper floor."

[109] Ibid., p. 39: "At bottom, man will never partake of eternity; his eternality is merely an *incessant temporality*"; p. 89: "It is true that *I recognize no eternal truths other than those that are not merely comprehensible to human reason but can also be demonstrated and verified by human powers.*"

things (nature) and concepts, which by dint of their soul-script may be legible and comprehensible at all times and in all places.[110]

"Again and again to resist all theory and hypotheses, and want to speak of facts, to hear nothing but of facts, and yet should have the least regard for facts precisely where they matter most!"[111] – Yet I am neither hungry for the shewbread,[112] nor have leisure and strength for labyrinthine strolls and peripatetic labyrinths. Instead, I hasten to the point and concur entirely with Herr Mendelssohn that Judaism[113] knows of no revealed religion, in the very sense in which he himself understands it: that is, to them in actuality nothing has been made known and confided by God through word and script with the single exception of the sensory vehicle[114] of the mystery, the shadow of good things to come and not the very image of the things,[115] the real communication of which God reserved for a higher mediator, high-priest, prophet, and king than were Moses, Aaron, David, and Solomon. – Hence just as Moses was himself ignorant that his countenance shone, making the people afraid, so too all the legislation of this divine minister was a mere veil and curtain of the religion of the old covenant which unto this day remains untaken away,[116] swaddled, and sealed.

The characteristic difference between Judaism and Christianity[117] is not a matter therefore of either direct or indirect revelation in the sense

---

[110] Ibid., p. 126: "Judaism consisted, or, according to the intention of the founder, was to consist of: (1) Religious doctrines and propositions or *eternal truths* about God and his government and providence, without which man cannot be enlightened and happy. These are not forced upon the faith of the nation under the threat of eternal or temporal punishments, but, in accordance with the nature and evidence of eternal truths, recommended to rational acknowledgement. They did not have to be given by direct revelation, or made known through *word* and *script*, which are intelligible only *here* and *now*. The Supreme Being has revealed them to all rational creatures through *things* and *concepts* and inscribed them in the soul with a script that is legible and comprehensible at all times and in all places."

[111] Ibid., p. 96.

[112] Matthew 12:3–4: "Have ye not read what David did, when he was an hungred . . . How he entered into the house of God, and did eat the shewbread . . . ?"

[113] *Jerusalem*, pp. 89–90: "Judaism knows of no revealed religion in the sense in which Christians understand this term."

[114] Ibid., p. 115: "The spirit of truth . . . evaporated, and the empty vehicle that was left behind turned into a pernicious poison."

[115] Hebrews 10:1: "the law having a shadow of good things to come, and not the very image of the things." Hamann, like Luther, has "Wesen" ("essence") where the King James Bible has "very image."

[116] 2 Corinthians 3:14.

[117] *Jerusalem*, p. 89. The denial of direct revelation "constitutes a characteristic difference between it [the Jewish religion] and the Christian one."

in which Jews and naturalists[118] understand it – – nor of eternal truths and doctrines – – nor of ceremonial and moral law: no, it is solely a matter of temporal truths of history, which occurred once and never come again – of facts which have become true at one point in time and place through a coherence of causes and effects, and which, therefore, can only be conceived as true in respect to that point in time and space,[119] and must be confirmed by authority. Authority can indeed humble, but it cannot instruct; it can suppress reason but not put it in fetters.[120] Nonetheless without authority the truth of history vanishes along with the event itself.[121]

This characteristic difference between Judaism and Christianity is a matter of historical truths, not only those of past times but also of times to come, which are proclaimed in advance and prophesied through the spirit of a providence as universal as it is particular, and which can, according to their nature, not be accepted in any other manner than on faith. Jewish authority alone gives them the required authenticity; these memorabilia of the former and future ages were also confirmed through miracles, proven by the credibility of the witnesses and those who handed down the tradition, and supported by evidence of real fulfillments that are sufficient to place the faith beyond all talmudic and dialectical doubts and hesitancy.[122]

Hence the revealed religion of Christianity is called, rightfully and with reason, faith, trust, confidence, firm and childlike reliance on divine pledges and promises[123] and on the majestic progress of its life unfolding itself in representations from glory to glory[124] until the full uncovering and apocalypse of the mystery which was hidden and believed from the

---

[118] Ibid.: "I, therefore, for my part, have nothing to advance that has not already been stated and repeated countless times by Jews and naturalists."

[119] Ibid., p. 91: "Besides these eternal truths, there are also *temporal, historical truths*; things which occurred once and may never occur again; propositions which have become true at one point in time and space through a confluence of causes and effects, and which, therefore, can only be conceived as true in respect to that point in time and space."

[120] Ibid., p. 85: "Authority can humble but not instruct; it can suppress reason but not put it in fetters."

[121] Ibid., p. 93: "Without authority, the truth of history vanishes along with the event itself."

[122] Ibid., p. 127: "as historical truths they can, according to their nature, not be accepted in any other manner than on *faith*. Authority alone gives them the required evidence; these records were also confirmed to the nation by miracles, and supported by an authority which was sufficient to place the *faith* beyond all doubts and hesitancy."

[123] Ibid., p. 100: "In fact, the word in the original language that is usually translated as *faith* actually means, in most cases, *trust, confidence*, and firm reliance on pledge and promise."

[124] 2 Corinthians 3:18: "we all . . . are changed into the same image from glory to glory."

beginning[125] in the fullness of beholding face to face:[126] just as father Abraham believed in the Eternal,[127] rejoiced to see his day, saw it, and was glad; for he staggered not at the promise of God through unbelief, but was strong in faith, giving glory to God.[128] Therefore it was counted to him even for merit. But the lawgiver Moses was flatly refused entry into the promised land; and through a similar sin of unbelief against the spirit of grace and truth[129] (a spirit which was to have been preserved[130] in the hieroglyphic usages of symbolic ceremonies and actions of valid meaning[131] until the times of refreshing,[132] outpouring,[133] and anointing), this earthly vehicle of a temporal, figurative, dramatic, animal law-giving and sacrificial worship decayed into the pernicious and deadly insidious poison of a childish, servile, literalistic, idolatrous superstition. The books of Moses entire, together with all the prophets, are the rock of the Christian faith,[134] and the chief cornerstone, elect, precious, which the builders disallowed, even to them is made the cornerstone, but a stone of stumbling, the rock of scandal,[135] so that from unbelief they stumbled at the word on which their whole house rests.[136] Moses, the greatest prophet and the law-giver to the nation, is but the smallest, most fleeting shadow of his office,

[125] Cf. Romans 16:25: "according to the revelation of the mystery, which was kept secret since the world began."

[126] Psalms 17:15: "As for me, I will behold thy face in righteousness"; 1 Corinthians 13:12: "For now we see through a glass, darkly; but then face to face."

[127] Genesis 15:6: "And he believed in the Lord; and he counted it to him for righteousness." At *Jerusalem*, p. 100, Mendelssohn translates, "Abraham trusted in the Eternal and it was accounted to him for piety."

[128] Romans 4:20: "He staggered not at the promise of God through unbelief; but was strong in faith, giving glory to God."

[129] John 1:17: "For the law was given by Moses, but grace and truth came by Jesus Christ."

[130] *Jerusalem*, p. 115: "The images lost their value as signs. The spirit of truth, which was to have been preserved in them, evaporated, and the empty vehicle that remained behind turned into a pernicious poison."

[131] Ibid., p. 119: "Therefore, each of these prescribed actions, each practice, each ceremony, had its meaning, its valid significance."

[132] Acts 3:19.

[133] Acts 2:17: "And it shall come to pass in the last days, saith God, I will pour out of my Spirit upon all flesh."

[134] Cf. Ephesians 2:19–20: "ye . . . are built upon the foundation of the apostles and prophets, Jesus Christ himself being the chief corner stone."

[135] In Greek, *skandalon* means a stumbling-block, offense.

[136] 1 Peter 2:6–8: "Wherefore also it is contained in the scripture, Behold, I lay in Sion a chief corner stone, elect, precious: and he that believeth on him shall not be confounded. Unto you therefore which believe he is precious: but unto them which be disobedient, the stone which the builders disallowed, the same is made the head of the corner, And a stone of stumbling, and a rock of offence, even to them which stumble at the word." Romans 9:33: "As it is written, Behold, I lay in Sion a stumblingstone and a rock of offence."

which he himself acknowledged as the mere ensample of another prophet who he promised his brethren and their descendants would be raised up, expressly commanding and enjoining them to obey Him.[137] The golden calf of the Egyptian tradition[138] and of the rabbinical ordinances governing men, through the agency of Aaron and the heads of the synagogue[139] and under the likeness of divine reason – (for the sake of the Eternal!) – was the complete destruction of the law, according to their own prophecy. By this final abomination of desolation,[140] Moses became the pope of the polluted nation, the corpse of putrefied law-giving became the relic venerated by superstition, houses of prayer became dens of thieves,[141] Bethel became Bethaven,[142] and the city of the bloody husband,[143] in spite of heathen and anti-Christian Rome, became a Babylonian whore[144] and the school of the reigning prosecutor,[145] was a slanderer, liar, and murderer from the beginning.[146]

Christianity therefore does not believe in the doctrines of philosophy, which is nothing but an alphabetical script of human speculation,[147] subject to the variable changes of moon and vogue! It does not believe in images and worship of images! not in worshiping animals and heroes! not in symbolic elements and password signs or in some black lines traced by the invisible hand of chance there on the white wall![148] not in pythagorean-platonic numbers!!![149] – not in any transitory shadows of

---

[137] Deuteronomy 18:15–18.

[138] At *Jerusalem*, p. 120, Mendelssohn describes the Israelites' clamoring for the golden calf (Exodus 32) as a relapse into the sinful delusion of the Egyptians.

[139] Ibid., p. 102: "It was with much reluctance that the heads of the synagogue resolved in later periods to give the permission – which had become necessary – to write about the laws."

[140] Matthew 24:15, Mark 13:14; cf. Daniel 9:27.   [141] Matthew 21:13.

[142] Bethel, "house of God," is the name Jacob gave to Luz, where he had his vision of the ladder (Genesis 28:19). In Hosea 10:5, the people of Bethaven mourn over it because the glory thereof has departed from it. (In Amos 5:5, "Beth-el shall come to nought.")

[143] Exodus 4:25–6: "Surely a bloody husband art thou to me . . . A bloody husband thou art." In the present context, the bridegroom of blood is Christ, and his city is Jerusalem.

[144] The Babylonian captivity; recall also Revelation 17–18.

[145] *Jerusalem*, p. 74: "the answer of the most supreme Judge to the prosecutor," that is, God's answer to Satan (Job 2:6).

[146] John 8:44: "He was a murderer from the beginning."

[147] *Jerusalem*, p. 118: "Images and hieroglyphics lead to superstition and idolatry, and our alphabetical script makes man too speculative."

[148] Ibid., pp. 113–14: If a "second" Omai [James Cook had brought the first Omai to Europe from the South Seas] were suddenly transported to the Temple of Providence [established in Dessau to serve the cause of natural religion], he "would find everything empty of images and ornaments; only there, on the white wall, he would see some black lines [i.e., the words, 'God, all wise, all-powerful, all-good, rewarding the good'], traced, perhaps, by chance."

[149] Pythagoras, his school, and numbers are discussed at ibid., p. 117.

actions and ceremonies which do not last, do not endure, and to which mysterious power and inexplicable magic are ascribed![150] – not in any laws that must be followed even without faith in them, as the theorist puts it somewhere, in spite of his Epicurean-Stoic word-splitting over faith and knowledge![151] – – No, Christianity knows and recognizes no other shackles of faith[152] than the sure word of prophecy[153] within the most ancient documents of the human race[154] and within the holy scriptures of genuine Judaism, without Samaritan segregation[155] and apocryphal Mishnah. – That depository made the very Jews into a peculiar generation, instructed of God, anointed, and called and chosen before all the peoples of earth for the salvation of mankind.[156]

A horde that was stolen from the iron furnace[157] of Egyptian brickmaking and forced labor needed, it is true, shackled actions,[158] and a taskmaster for the impending creation of a peculiar state. As the leader of the host was enraged in spirit, to the point of sanctioning curses and death;[159] so their coarse vanity and childish impatience for a king distressed the spirit of the last judge[160] to the point of the longsuffering vengeance of all-wise love, which seeks to lead to moral improvement by means of physical misery.[161]

---

[150] Ibid., p. 119: "Man's actions are transitory; there is nothing lasting, nothing enduring about them that, like hieroglyphic script, could lead to idolatry through abuse or misunderstanding."

[151] Ibid., p. 101: "everything depends . . . on the distinction between *believing* and *knowing*."

[152] Ibid. Mendelssohn thanks God that the proposed thirteen articles of the Jewish catechism "have not yet been forged into shackles of faith."

[153] 2 Peter 1:19.

[154] The Old Testament. The phrasing alludes to Herder's work of similar title, published 1774–6; for Hamann's response, see *Werke*, vol. III, p. 123.

[155] The segregation between Jews and Samaritans is recorded in the New Testament; cf. John 4:9: "for the Jews have no dealings with the Samaritans." Perhaps Hamann's phrase also refers to Samaritans' exclusive dependence on the Pentateuch, "segregated" from the rest of the Hebrew Bible.

[156] 1 Peter 2:9: "But ye are a chosen generation, a royal priesthood, an holy nation, a peculiar people."

[157] Deuteronomy 4:20: "But the Lord hath taken you, and brought you forth out of the iron furnace, even out of Egypt."

[158] Contrast the "shackles of faith," *Jerusalem*, p. 101. Also, cf. pp. 118–19: the great maxim of ceremonial laws "seems to have been: *Men must be impelled to perform actions and only induced to engage in reflection.*"

[159] The taskmaster and leader of the host is Moses. His rage at the golden calf is recounted in Exodus 32.

[160] Samuel was the last of the Old Testament judges; the elders of Israel, however, demanded a king.

[161] *Jerusalem*, p. 124: "Whenever I transgress the laws of God, the moral evil thereby engendered makes me unhappy; and God's justice, that is, his all-wise love, seeks to guide me to moral improvement by means of physical misery."

The extraordinary taste for law-giving and the Royal luxuriance in it demonstrates just as large an incapacity to govern oneself as to govern one's equal; it is a mutual need for slaves and despots who resemble the slaves. One part of Mosaic wisdom was (like the people's possessions) loot from the Egyptians;[162] Midianite[163] shrewdness contributed also its mite; and in order to make the masterpiece of eternal perdurance even more tangled and colorful, at the end a Wolffian[164] divining rod revealed the vein of a Chinese ceremonial, which had been tied to transitory actions of valid meaning,[165] but fell victim to the inevitable misunderstandings and unsociable abuses of oral transmission,[166] just as the catechism of the universal religion of man, implemented and pursued in the days when the legislation was being prepared, fell to the lax babbling[167] of Aaron by which he intended to make it elegant[168] –

In comparison with the two questions of the best form of government and the most wholesome food,[169] the heavenly politics[170] had on the contrary to condescend to the earthly there and the temporal then, without thereby becoming shackled to here and now,[171] in order (like the sun) to complete its bright circle[172] from the faith of Abraham before the law, to the faith of his children and heirs of promise[173] after the law; for the

---

[162] Exodus 12:36. Hamann presumably refers to Mendelssohn's claim that the Hebrew script was originally hieroglyphic (*Jerusalem*, p. 110).
[163] The Midianites sold Joseph to Potiphar (Genesis 37). Jethro, a Midianite priest, was the father-in-law to Moses (Exodus 2). Later the Midianites were enemies of Israel.
[164] Mendelssohn's argument in *Jerusalem* is cast within the frame of natural law in the tradition of Pufendorf and Wolff (see *Jerusalem*, p. 27).
[165] *Jerusalem*, p. 119: "Therefore, each of these prescribed actions, each practice, each ceremony had its meaning, its valid significance." See also n. 150 above.
[166] At *Jerusalem*, p. 127, Mendelssohn argues that the written laws become incomprehensible over time, and that the instruction transmitted orally restores it to its precise meaning. He also praises oral instruction on pages 102–3.
[167] 1 Timothy 6:20, 2 Timothy 2:16 and, in Luther's translation, Exodus 32:25.
[168] The allusion to Exodus 32:25 cannot be captured in English, since Luther's translation differs from English ones. KJB: "And when Moses saw that the people were naked; (for Aaron had made them naked unto their shame among their enemies)." Luther: "When Moses saw that the people had become lax (for Aaron had made them lax through vain babbling, by which he intended to make them [*sic*] elegant)."
[169] *Jerusalem*, p. 42. The question *Which form of government is best* is "too vague a question, almost as vague as a similar one in medicine: *Which food is the most wholesome?*"
[170] Ibid., p. 131: "Just as, according to Plato, there is an earthly and also a heavenly Eros, there is also, one might say, an earthly and a heavenly politics."
[171] Ibid., p. 126. Eternal truths did not have to be "made known through *word* and *script*, which are intelligible only *here* and *now*."
[172] Ibid., p. 120: "It was not long before this brilliant circle, too, had been completed."
[173] Hebrews 6:17.

promise, not a law, was given as the token of the covenant in his flesh to righteous Abraham.[174] We see directly in this true politics, as a philosopher said, a deity, where ordinary mortals see the stone.[175] Therefore, the valid meaning of transitory actions[176] was probably aimed at the lost or distorted key of knowledge,[177] which was so inconvenient to the heads of the synagogue that they availed themselves of the unauthorized permission[178] to destroy utterly the whole lock of the law, thereby shutting up the kingdom of heaven against men, not themselves entering in, and them that were entering in they suffered not to go in;[179] instead, the rabbis of divine reason[180] turned into the *literati III literarum,*[181] the most perfect men of letters[182] and Masoretes[183] in the holiest and most fruitful sense.

By the nature and idea of the thing, the abrogation of the Mosaic constitution[184] (which depended on the possession of the land and institutions governing it, and which was related to temple, priesthood, and laws of purification)[185] was reported more intelligibly and publicly than

---

[174] Genesis 17:11: "And ye shall circumcise the flesh of your foreskin; and it shall be a token of covenant betwixt me and you"; Romans 4:13: "For the promise, that he should be the heir of the world, was not to Abraham, or to his seed, through the law, but through the righteousness of faith."

[175] *Jerusalem*, p. 132: "If we look at it directly, we shall see in true politics, as a philosopher said of the sun, a deity, where ordinary mortals see a stone." The reference presumably derives from Socrates in Plato, *Apology* 26d.

[176] See n. 165.   [177] Luke 11:52: "for ye have taken away the key of knowledge."

[178] *Jerusalem*, p. 102: "It was with much reluctance that the heads of the synagogue resolved in later periods to give the permission – which had become necessary – to write about the laws. They called this permission a destruction of the law."

[179] Matthew 23:13: "for ye shut up the kingdom of heaven against men: for ye neither go in yourselves, neither suffer ye them that are entering to go in."

[180] *Jerusalem*, p. 130: "What divine law commands, reason, which is no less divine, cannot abolish."

[181] "The literati of the three letters"; possibly refers to the three (different) letters of the tetragrammaton or the three letters FUR, Latin for thief (an allusion to Plautus, *Aulularia* 325–6); or perhaps a reference to the triliteral roots of Hebrew.

[182] *Jerusalem*, p. 104: "We do not need the man of experience; we only need his writings. In a word, we are *literati, men of letters.*"

[183] Masoretes are the Jewish scholars held to be responsible for the present Hebrew text of the bible. "Masorete" comes from Hebrew *masorah* ("tradition"), which was believed to derive from *masar* ("to deliver," "to hand down") but in fact comes from *masoret* ("bond").

[184] *Jerusalem*, p. 131: "This constitution existed only once; call it the *Mosaic constitution*, by its proper name. It has disappeared, and only the Omniscient knows among what people and in what century something similar will again by seen."

[185] Ibid., p. 134: "Laws that depend on the possession of the land and institutions governing it carry their exemption with them. Without Temple and priesthood, and outside Judea there is no scope for either sacrifices or laws of purification or contributions to the priests, insofar as these depend on the possession of the land."

that disposition of angels[186] was in a position to convey in an Arabian desert on the fire-burning, smoke-steaming mount that was touched by meteors of dark tempests, by means of the sound of the trumpet and the voice of words, which they that heard entreated that the word should not be spoken to them anymore (for they could not endure that which was commanded).[187] With a soul-script[188] so audible, indelible, and legible that he may run that reads it,[189] the heavenly kingdom of the anointed was introduced – and like a butterfly escaped the empty cocoon and the dead chrysalis of Judaism! Nonetheless, the ears of the sophist, uncircumcised[190] in heart and senses, are buzzing with so many doubts and ruminations, hypotheses and theories, that he neither hears nor can hear the voice of calm common sense[191] for all the roar of his artillery! – – Without fire and hearth, one is no citizen; without land and people, no prince; and the priestly nation of a mere bookbag-religion is, according to the expression of Scripture, a reproach to God and to divine reason.[192] Indeed, it would be a greater miracle than what happened with the shoes and clothes[193] if that legislation for the benefit of a horde of fugitive bondsmen wandering in the desert (who moreover were to form the first papal state)[194] could possibly be as adequate for a rabble without state or religion, scattered to the four winds, as its mummy has been down until the present day and back and forth over the entire globe. No, the whole mythology of the Hebraic household was nothing but a type[195] of a

---

[186] Acts 7:53: "Who have received the law by the disposition of angels, and have not kept it."

[187] Hebrews 12:18–20: "For ye are not come unto the mount that might be touched, and that burned with fire, nor unto blackness, and darkness, and tempest, And the sound of a trumpet, and the voice of words; which voice they that heard intreated that the word should not be spoken to them any more: (For they could not endure that which was commanded . . .)."

[188] *Jerusalem*, p. 126: "The Supreme Being has revealed [eternal truths] to all rational creatures through *things* and *concepts* and inscribed them in the soul with a script that is legible and comprehensible at all times and in all places."

[189] Habakkuk 2:2: "Write the vision, and make it plain upon tables, that he may run that readeth it."

[190] The sophist is Mendelssohn, whom Hamann accuses of being pagan rather than Jewish.

[191] *Jerusalem*, p. 97: "the sophist whose ears are buzzing with so many doubts and ruminations that he can no longer hear the voice of common sense."

[192] Ibid., p. 129: "*An executed man is*, according to the expression of Scripture, *a reproach to God.*" Cf. Deuteronomy 22:23: "for he that is hanged is accursed of God." Mendelssohn quotes from his translation of the Pentateuch.

[193] Deuteronomy 29:5: "And I have led you forty years in the wilderness: your clothes are not waxen old upon you, and thy shoe is not waxen old upon thy foot."

[194] *Jerusalem*, p. 131. Many believe that "Judaism was a hierocracy, an ecclesiastical government, a priestly state, a theocracy, if you will."

[195] In the theological sense: "a person, object, or event of Old Testament history, prefiguring some person or thing revealed in the new dispensation" (*Oxford English Dictionary*).

more transcendent history, the horoscope of a heavenly hero, by whose appearance everything is already concluded and will be yet that which is written in their law and their prophets: "They shall perish, but thou shalt endure: yea, all of them shall wax old like a garment; as a vesture shalt thou change them, and they shall be changed"[196] – –

Infinitely more than that silhouette of the Jewish papal state and their exclusive right of citizenship, a philosopher and citizen of the world ought to value the most ancient document[197] because it concerns the entire human race and also because Moses illuminates the human race's true relationships to his people without selfish prejudices. He deserves the immortality he made himself for the most recent posterity, as much through the individual fragments of the primordial age as through the full plan of providence which elected him to be the instrument of its public institutions. For what are all the *miracula speciosa*[198] of an *Odyssey* and *Iliad* and their heroes against the artless but richly significant phenomena of the patriarchs' venerable wandering? What is the gentle, loving soul[199] of the blind Maeonian[200] ballad-monger against the spirit of Moses, aglow *a priori* and *a posteriori* with its own deeds and high inspirations!

However favorable the most recent etymology of the word *Adel* ["nobility"] from an Arabic root may be to the European centaur-knighthood,[g] the Jew nevertheless is still the authentic first nobleman of the entire human race, and the prejudice of their family and ancestral pride is grounded more deeply than all the titles in the ludicrous chancery style of heraldry. Even the discrepancy of their small order dispersed throughout the whole world compared to the rabble of all other peoples fits within the concept of the matter; just as the caricature of the document speaks in favor of the authenticity and gray antiquity of its charter and shouts down the wittiest mockery. The duration of its legislation is fully the strongest proof of its author's power, of the superiority of its ten words[201] over the craved Twelve Tables,[202] hydropic monsters and

---

[g] See Köster's *Di[s]p[utatio]*. [Not traced; some commentators believe that "Köster" refers to the Orientalist Johann Bernhard Köhler, whom Hamann knew in Königsberg.]

[196] Psalms 102:26; echoed at Hebrews 1:11–12.   [197] The Old Testament; see n. 154.
[198] "Splendid wonders," Horace, *Ars poetica* 144.
[199] *Jerusalem*, p. 121: "In Homer himself, in that gentle and loving soul."
[200] Homer, born in some accounts at Smyrna in Maeonia.
[201] The Ten Commandments.   [202] Traditional basis of Roman Law.

gourds which come up in a night, and perish in a night,[203] that shadow and gladness are gone.[204] Moses is still the great Pan, against whom all pharaohs and their black artists[205] are utterly *servum pecus*.[206]

An Egyptian priest chided the Greeks for being children.[207] One of their games – they made a name for themselves in inventing and practicing it – is the *globe aspirant*[208] of philosophy. Although the ignorance of their epoch is neither suitable nor appropriate to our own century, the little foxes and masters of Greek wisdom still affect the sheer nakedness and amateurism of pagan ignorance with such naivete of taste that as the prophet says they "know neither their owner nor the crib of their master."[209] Systematic atheism thus is an atticism par excellence, the means by which the common sense of some of the spermologues[210] distanced itself from the universal and unavoidable superstition of popular idolatry, without however being able to supply the phenomena of indefinite objects with anything better than some transcendental whims, which more often than not have no other credentials [*Creditiv*] or sufficient reason than the *relationes curiosae*[211] of oriental legends and rumors, homegrown folktales, premonitions, dreams, puzzles, and more childishness of that sort.

But ever since the gods of the earth[212] appointed themselves the very highest philosophers, Jupiter (once the *summus philosophus!*) was obliged to crawl away and hide in the cuckoo-shape of a pedagogue; and although Herr Mendelssohn to some extent seems to be offended that his late friend[213] conceived the divine education of the human race under the influence of who-knows-which historian of mankind,[214] he himself

---

[203] Jonah 4:10: "Thou hast had pity on the gourd . . . which came up in a night, and perished in a night."

[204] Jonah 4:6: "And the Lord God prepared a gourd, and made it to come up over Jonah, that it might be a shadow over his head, to deliver him from his grief. So Jonah was exceeding glad of the gourd."

[205] Exodus 8:18–19.   [206] Horace, *Epistles* 1.19.19: "Oh imitators, a servile herd."

[207] See Plato, *Timaeus* 22b.

[208] Perhaps "suction ball," formed by analogy with "pompe aspirante" ("suction pump").

[209] Isaiah 1:3: "The ox knoweth his owner, and the ass his master's crib."

[210] In Greek, a σπερμολόγος is "one who picks up and retails scraps of knowledge, an idle babbler, a gossip." In Acts 17:18, the Greek philosophers ask of Paul, "What will this babbler say?"

[211] "Curious reports"; Hamann read the *relationes curiosae* of Eberhard Werner Happel (published in 1683–90).

[212] *Jerusalem*, p. 37: "Hobbes . . . is, in fact, less indulgent to the gods of the earth than his system would lead one to expect." By "gods of the earth," Mendelssohn was referring to temporal authorities; Hamann is pointing to Frederick the Great and his philosophical pretensions.

[213] Lessing died in 1781.

[214] *Jerusalem*, p. 95: "I, for my part, cannot conceive of the education of the human race as my late friend Lessing imagined it under the influence of I-don't-know-which historian of mankind."

nonetheless molded the concept of religion and church into that of an institution of public education. Moreover, in respect to pedantry, he parroted and spelled out so many trivial things about the leading reins of speech and script and their natural parallelism with the religious power possessed by scraps of masoretic letters and scholastic words[215] that a gentle reader can hardly refrain from yawning at least at some point in his speculative slumber. For Herr Mendelssohn, it is a completely ungrounded article of faith[216] to consider "our alphabetical script to consist merely of signs of sounds."[217] According to his rational grounds, *invita Minerva experientiae*,[218] the road that script takes across and through speech to things is nothing less than necessary.[219] Yet with a scarcely credible and almost unpardonable conviction he maintains that script is the "immediate designation of things."[220] It is such a shame that only philosophers who were born deaf may lay claim to this privilege! – With such a sidling away of the understanding, the immeasurable, without any flight of inventiveness, can easily be thought of as measurable,[221] and vice versa – – just as easily as all German literature, by the immediate designation of things, can be thought of as surveyed and even improved by an emperor in Peking[222] as by a Johann Ballhorn[223] who was born deaf! –

However, if all human knowledge can be reduced to a few, fundamental concepts,[224] and if the same sounds often occur in the spoken language as do the same images in different hieroglyphic tablets, though always in

---

[215] Mendelssohn gives his theory of the origin and development of language at ibid., pp. 107–12.

[216] Ibid., p. 100: "Hence, ancient Judaism has . . . *no articles of faith.*"

[217] Ibid., p. 108: "The opinion of some that our alphabetical script consists merely of signs of sounds . . . is, to be sure, completely without foundation."

[218] Hamann alters the expression "invita Minerva" (literally, "when Minerva is unwilling," and idiomatically, "against one's natural inclination," or "when one is not in the mood or is without inspiration") so that it means "against the natural inclination of [one's] experience."

[219] *Jerusalem*, p. 108: "For us, therefore, the road from script to things leads across and through speech; but there is no reason why it should be necessarily so."

[220] Ibid.: "To one born deaf, script is the immediate designation of things."

[221] Ibid., p. 109: "one sees at any rate how men may have been led, step by step, without any flight of inventiveness, to think of the immeasurable as measurable."

[222] By Peking, Hamann means Berlin. The emperor, Frederick, attempted to survey and improve German literature in a treatise he wrote in French, *De la littérature allemande* (1780).

[223] Johann Ballhorn was a Lübeck publisher of the sixteenth century. One of his "enlarged and improved" editions was so incompetent that an eponymous verb, "to ballhorn," was introduced into German, meaning to introduce corruptions into a text.

[224] *Jerusalem*, p. 101: "To be sure, all human knowledge can be reduced to a few, fundamental concepts."

different combinations, by means of which they multiply their meaning;[225] if this were true, then this observation would also apply to history, and the entire range of human events and the whole course of their vicissitudes would be encompassed and divided into subsections just as the starry firmament is divided into figures, without knowing the stars' number[226] – Hence the entire history of the Jewish people, by the allegory of their ceremonial law, appears to be a living, mind- and heart-rousing[227] primer of all historical literature in heaven, on and under the earth, – an adamantine hint[228] forward to the Jubilee year and a state-plan for divine rule over all creation from its beginning to its close. The prophetic riddle of a theocracy is reflected in the fragments of this smashed vessel, like the sun "in the showers upon the grass, that tarrieth not for man, nor waiteth for the sons of men";[229] for yesterday the dew from the Lord was upon Gideon's fleece only, and it was dry upon all the earth; today dew be on all the ground, and it was dry upon the fleece only[230] –

It is not just that the entire history of Judaism was prophecy, but rather that its spirit of prophecy was occupied, beyond all other nations (to whom perhaps the analogue of a similar dim premonition and intuition cannot be denied), with the ideal of a savior and knight, of a man of might and wonder,[231] of a goel[232] whose descent according to the flesh was to be of the stem of Judah[233] but whose departure from the heavens was from the bosom of the Father.[234] The Pentateuch, the Psalms, and the Prophets

[225] Ibid., pp. 108–9: "Since one very often had occasion to transform script into speech and speech into script, and thus to compare audible and visible signs, one must soon have noticed that the same sounds often recur in the spoken language, as do the same parts in different hieroglyphic images, though always in different combinations, by means of which they multiply their meaning."

[226] Ibid., p. 109: "one sees at any rate how men may have been led, without any flight of inventiveness, to think of the immeasurable as measurable, and to divide, so to speak, the starry firmament into figures, and thus to assign to every star its place, without knowing their number."

[227] Ibid., p. 102: "The ceremonial law itself is a kind of living script, rousing the mind and heart."

[228] Lessing, *The Education of the Human Race*, § 46–7: "By a 'hint' I mean that which already contains any germ, out of which the, as yet, held back truth allows itself to be developed. Of this character was the inference of Christ from the naming of God 'the God of Abraham, Isaac, and Jacob.' This hint appears to me to be unquestionably capable of being worked out into a strong proof. In such previous exercitations, allusions, hints, consists the positive perfection of a Primer" (tr. F. W. Robertson).

[229] Micah 5:7: "And the remnant of Jacob shall be in the midst of many people as a dew from the Lord, as the showers upon the grass, that tarrieth not for man, nor waiteth for the sons of men."

[230] Judges 6:36–40.

[231] Isaiah 9:6: "his name shall be called Wonderful, Counsellor, The mighty God."

[232] From the Hebrew verb *redeem*. The nearest male relation had certain obligations to his next of kin and was a goel; God is the goel of his people.

[233] Hebrews 7:14.   [234] John 1:18: "the only begotten Son, which is in the bosom of the Father."

are full of signs and glimpses toward this appearance of a meteor over the pillar of the cloud and the pillar of fire,[235] a Star out of Jacob,[236] a Sun of righteousness with healing in his wings![237] – toward the marks of the contradiction in the ambiguous form of his person;[238] his message of peace and joy; his travails and sorrow; his obedience unto death, even the death of the cross!;[239] his being raised from the mortal dust of a worm to the throne of immovable majesty – – toward the kingdom of heaven, which this David, Solomon, and Son of Man would plant and conclude as a city which has foundations, whose builder and maker is God,[240] as a Jerusalem above, which is free and the mother of us all,[241] as a new heaven and a new earth, without sea[242] and without temple therein.[243]

These historical truths, temporal and eternal, of the king of the Jews, the messenger of their covenant,[244] the firstborn and head of his church,[245] are the A and Ω,[246] the foundation and the summit of our wings of faith. However, the end and the grave of the Mosaic papal state became the occasion and the workshop of meta–Mosaic shackled actions,[247] of a more than Egyptian bondage and a more than Babylonian captivity.[248]

Unbelief in the most essential, historical sense of the word is thus the only sin against the spirit of the true religion,[249] whose heart is in heaven and whose heaven is in the heart. The mystery of Christian godliness consists not in services, sacrifices, and vows which God demands from men,[250] but rather in promises, fulfillments, and sacrifices which God

---

[235] Exodus 13:21–2.   [236] Numbers 24:17.   [237] Malachi 4:2.

[238] Christ as fully divine and fully human; or specifically the kenotic paradox whereby Christ is highest and lowest, Golgotha and Sheblimini.

[239] Philippians 2:8.

[240] Hebrews 11:10: "For he looked at a city which hath foundations, whose builder and maker is God."

[241] Galatians 4:26: "But Jerusalem which is above is free, which is the mother of us."

[242] Revelation 21:1: "And I saw a new heaven and a new earth . . . and there was no more sea."

[243] Revelation 21:22: "And I saw no temple therein."

[244] Malachi 3:1: "and the Lord, whom ye seek, shall suddenly come to his temple, even the messenger of the covenant."

[245] Colossians 1:18: "And he is the head of the body, the church: who is the beginning, the firstborn from the dead."

[246] Revelation 1:8: "I am Alpha and Omega, the beginning and the ending, saith the Lord."

[247] See n. 152 and n. 158.

[248] In Hamann's view, Mendelssohn, a meta-Moses, offers something more restrictive than Mosaic law and more confined than the Jewish ghetto.

[249] Mendelssohn had argued that "not unbelief, not false doctrine and error" were punished under Mosaic law but "misdeeds against the fundamental laws of the state" (*Jerusalem*, p. 130).

[250] Ibid., p. 58: "The parallel has been drawn too far. Toward God – toward man – one thought. Just as from a sense of duty toward our neighbor we sacrifice and relinquish something of our own,

made and did for the welfare of men. It consists not in the noblest and greatest commandment which he laid down,[251] but in the highest good which he freely gave; not in legislation and moral teachings[252] which are relevant merely to human convictions and human affairs, but in the carrying out of the divine will through divine counsels, works, and institutions for the salvation of the whole world. Dogmatic faith[253] [*Dogmatik*] and ecclesiastical law belong only to the public institutions[254] of education and administration and as such are subject to the arbitrary will[255] of the authorities, an external discipline that is sometimes coarse and sometimes refined, depending on the elements and the degrees of the prevailing aesthetic. These visible, public, and common institutions are neither religion nor wisdom that descends from above, but are earthly, sensual, devilish[256] in accordance with the influence of foreign cardinals or foreign ciceroni, poetic father-confessors or prosaic paunchy priests and in accordance with the variable system of statistical weights and balances, or armed tolerance and neutrality – churches and schools have often, like the monsters and creatures of the state and of reason, contemptibly sold themselves to the state and to reason, and betrayed them just as contemptibly. Philosophy and politics have needed the sword of superstition and the shield of unbelief for all their joint deceits and violent actions, and as much through their love as through their hate they have mistreated dogmatic faith more grievously than Amnon did the sister of his brother Absalom[257] –

so we should do likewise from a sense of duty toward God. Men require *service*; so does God. . . . Nobody will expressly agree with these absurd propositions if they are put before him in plain language."

[251] Matthew 22:36–7: "Master, which is the great commandment in the law? Jesus said unto him, Thou shalt love the Lord thy God with all thy heart, and with all thy soul, and with all thy mind." Christ gives the second commandment, the "golden rule," at verse 39: "Thou shalt love thy neighbor as thyself." Mendelssohn, quoting Hillel, gives the golden rule as the "quintessence" of "God's commandments and prohibitions" (*Jerusalem*, p. 102).

[252] *Jerusalem*, p. 58: "the moral teachings of reason will be sacred, just as religion is."

[253] Ibid., p. 63: "Nor need it [the state] trouble itself with all the principles which a dominant or merely tolerated faith [*Dogmatik*] may adopt or reject."

[254] Ibid., p. 41: "Public institutions for the formation of man that concern his relations with God I call *church*."

[255] A marginal note has been deleted.

[256] James 3:15: "This wisdom descendeth not from above, but is earthly, sensual, devilish."

[257] 2 Samuel 13:4, 14–15. Amnon said "I love Tamar, my brother Absalom's sister" and "being stronger than she, forced her, and lay with her" and "then hated her exceedingly; so that the hatred wherewith he hated her was greater than the love wherewith he had loved her."

In the infinite disrelation of man to God, the "public institutions for the formation of man that concern his relations with God"[258] are just absurd propositions in dry language; they infect the blood the more a speculative creature imbibes them.[259] To get hold of the infinite disrelation in the first place and clear it out of the way, man must – before there can be any discussion of relations which are to serve public institutions as the *fundamentum relationis*[260] – participate in a divine nature or else the godhead must assume flesh and blood. The Jews, through their divine legislation, and the naturalists,[261] through their divine reason, have each seized a palladium to make the equation. As a result, there is no mediating concept left to Christians and Nicodemuses[262] except to believe with all their heart, with all their soul, with all their mind:[263] For God so loved the world[264] – – This faith is the victory that overcomes the world.[265]

A similar disrelation of man to man seems to adhere just as naturally to all the public institutions of the state; hence the disrelation of double the regular fee[266] is neither striking nor surprising in a system *de convenance* which ennobles all the citizens of the kingdom and country into bondsmen *deterioris conditionis* through a Jewish and Turkish circumcision of their salt-bread and bread of cares, which is changed into fleshpots and roasted birds of passage for the benefit of foreign Galileans, triflers, and adventurers of philosophical industry.[267] Yet according to another faith

---

[258] *Jerusalem*, p. 41.

[259] Ibid., p. 58: "Nobody will expressly agree with these absurd propositions if they are put before him in plain language, yet everyone has more or less imbibed them, as it were, and infected his blood with them."

[260] *Beziehungsgrund*, in German. In scholastic logic, the *fundamentum relationis* refers to "Those elements of the objective world that constitute the terms of a relation" (*Oxford English Dictionary*).

[261] See n. 118; "naturalists" practice natural religion.

[262] Nicodemus acknowledged Christ in secret (John 7). Nicodemism attempted to combine inward faith with outward conformity to authority.

[263] Matthew 22:37 (for example); see n. 251.   [264] John 3:16.

[265] 1 John 5:4: "this is the victory that overcometh the world, even our faith."

[266] *Jerusalem*, p. 62n: "Some time ago, in an otherwise rather tolerant state, a board composed of learned and distinguished men made certain dissidents pay double the regular fee for approbation. When they were called to account for this action by the authorities, they excused themselves by saying that, surely, dissidents were everywhere *deterioris conditionis* in civil life." "*Deterioris conditionis*" can be translated as "of inferior legal status."

[267] A critique of Frederick's Prussia, in which Hamann believes ordinary citizens are taxed (their bread is "circumcised") in order to support an arbitrary government (system *de convenance*), its foreign administrators ("Galileans" are foreign and here stand for the French), and its philosophers. The Gospels, in contrast, present a different faith.

[*Dogmatik*], to take little and give twice are not beliefs or actions *deterioris conditionis*[268] –

Exclusive self-love[269] and envy are the legacy and trade of a Jewish naturalism,[270] contrary to the Royal Law to love one's neighbor as one-self.[271] A being who needs our benevolence, requires our assistance, or immorally claims any of our physical capacities for his own use,[272] who extorts with force, and who, the mightier he would appear, the more he requires the labor of his helots – Such a being is nothing but a dead god of the earth,[273] like him who owed the toleration of his wise maxims and heroic experiments in skin for skin[274] to the answer of the supreme judge: He is in thy hand.[275] The one true God in Heaven and father of men sends his rain and sunshine[276] without respect of persons.[277] But the Jews were against his good deeds and especially against those institutions which through their offices were to contribute to the palingenesis[278] of creation; they were minded like our *illustres ingrats*[279] and wicked sophists who turn even all the regalities of nature, fortune, and providence into the idols of their vanity, into the snare of their covetousness. Like the dumb beast who bore the sacred objects in the fable,[280] they zealously usurp and appropriate the worship of their kindred mob for their Midas-profits and the merit of their ears[281] under the yoke of animal definiteness,[282] and they think it not robbery.[283] Through contemptuous and angry feelings, full

---

[268] "Of an inferior condition"; see n. 266.   [269] See n. 32.   [270] See n. 118 and n. 261.

[271] James 2:8: "If ye fulfill the royal law according to the scripture, Thou shalt love thy neighbour as thyself, ye do well." See also *Jerusalem*, p. 102 and n. 251 above.

[272] *Jerusalem*, p. 57: "God is not a being who needs our benevolence, requires our assistance, or claims any of our rights for his own use."

[273] Temporal authority. See ibid., p. 37 and n. 212 above.

[274] Job 2:4: "Skin for skin, yea, all that a man hath will he give for his life."

[275] Job 2:6: "And the Lord said unto Satan, Behold, he is in thine hand." Cf. *Jerusalem*, p. 74.

[276] Matthew 5:45.   [277] 1 Peter 1:17.

[278] Regeneration, rebirth. Also an allusion to Charles Bonnet's *Palingénésie philosophique* (1769). In 1770, Johann Caspar Lavater, the German translator of this work, added a dedication to it calling on Mendelssohn either to refute Christianity or to convert to it.

[279] Though the phrase occurs in Corneille's *Cinna*, the reference here is to Voltaire's *Henriade*: "Amitié, plaisir des grandes âmes, / Amitié, que les rois, ces illustres ingrats, / Sont assez malhereux pour ne connaître pas," which Frederick is said to have quoted during his trip incognito to Holland in 1755 (the anecdote is told in Thomas Carlyle's biography of Frederick).

[280] An allusion to Aesop's fable in which an ass who was carrying a sacred image believed that the crowd which had prostrated themselves before the image were honoring him.

[281] Midas turned everything he touched to gold. In another myth, his ears were turned into those of an ass for preferring Pan's music to Apollo's; "to have asses' ears" denotes an incapacity to appreciate something.

[282] *Jerusalem*, p. 112; see n. 19 above.   [283] Philippians 2:6.

of lies and wrath, the entire mechanism of religious and political legality is driven with a demonic zeal that consumes itself and its own work, so that at the end nothing remains but a *caput mortuum*[284] of the divine and human form. – A kingdom that is not of this world[285] can therefore claim for the church no other right than to be barely tolerated and endured, because all public institutions of merely human authority cannot possibly exist next to a divine law-giving but instead like Dagon run the risk of losing head and hands,[286] so that, on its own threshold, only the stump, *turpiter atrum desinens in piscem*,[287] of the beautiful philistine nature would be left to it –

State and church are Moses and Aaron; philosophy, their sister Miriam, the leprous prophetess.[288] The younger brother is a god to the first-born, who in turn is his mouth,[289] but Moses was slow of speech, and of a slow tongue,[290] his hands were heavy,[291] and his rod was heavier still, before which even he was once afraid,[292] and with which he sinned unto death in the desert;[293] but the light and right, the Urim and Thumim,[294] of the state rested on Aaron's wave-breast, and hung on both his heave-shoulders[295] – –

Herr Mendelssohn had quoted an addendum from the commentators that mocked the answer of the supreme judge in the most ancient legal case as ridiculous nonsense.[296] He himself treats almost as rabbinically the answer given by the founder of our religion. To give everyone his due, to Caesar his tribute, and to God the glory due his name:[297] this in his eyes

---

[284] "Worthless residue"; an old term from alchemy and chemistry.

[285] John 18:36.   [286] 1 Samuel 5:4; Dagon was the god of the Philistines.

[287] Adapted from Horace, *Ars poetica* 3–4: "becoming an ugly black fish below." The word "Dagon" has commonly been connected to the Semitic root for "fish."

[288] Numbers 12:10: "And the cloud departed from off the tabernacle; and, behold, Miriam became leprous."

[289] Exodus 4:16: "And he [Aaron, the younger brother of Moses] shall be thy spokesman unto the people: and he shall be, even he shall be to thee instead of a mouth, and thou shalt be to him instead of God."

[290] Exodus 4:10: "And Moses said unto the Lord . . . I am slow of speech, and of a slow tongue."

[291] Exodus 17:12: "But Moses' hands were heavy."

[292] See Exodus 4:2–3.   [293] See Numbers 20.

[294] "Light and right" is how Luther rendered "Urim and Thummim" (Exodus 28:30; Leviticus 8:8; Deuteronomy 33:8).

[295] The two offerings (wave-breast and heave-shoulder) occur together at Leviticus 10:14–15.

[296] *Jerusalem*, p. 74: "to grant the church disciplinary power without injuring civil felicity, is like the answer of the most supreme Judge to the prosecutor: *Let him be in your hands; but spare his life!* Break the barrel, as the commentators add, but don't let the wine run out!" See Job 2:6.

[297] Psalms 29:2: "Give unto the Lord the glory due unto his name."

is "a manifest opposition, a collision of duties."[298] But was it a jesuitical precaution to call hypocrites and tempters by their correct names?[299] The blind guides[300] abused the lectern of Moses,[301] and laid heavy burdens, grievous to be borne, on others' shoulders, but they themselves did not move them with one of their fingers.[302] They paid tithe of mint and anise and cummin with mathematical scrupulousness, but they left the weightier matters of the law, righteousness, mercifulness, and fidelity, in the lurch,[303] filtered gnats and swallowed camels.[304] That just answer, full of wisdom and goodness, to render unto Caesar his tribute and unto God his glory, was thus no pharisaical advice to serve two masters[h] and to run with the hare and with the hounds, in order for a free naturalist-people without religion and state to be able to cherish and enjoy the pride of beggars and the happiness of rogues at the expense of the human race.

Gentle reader! Let me, old Marius,[305] rest a little on the rubble of the philosophical-political Jerusalem, before I bless you in parting. – – In the

---

[h] To halt between two opinions, Luther on Psalms 35:15. [In Psalms 35:15, where the King James Bible has *abjects* ("the abjects gathered themselves together against me"), the Luther Bible has *halting ones*. In his commentary on that verse, Luther glosses "the halting ones" as "they who run with the hare and with the hounds, who serve God yet serve the devil."
See *Jerusalem*, pp. 132–3: "serve two masters with patience and devotion"; and recall Matthew 6:24: "No man can serve two masters." "To halt between two opinions" recalls 1 Kings 18:21.]

[298] *Jerusalem*, pp. 132–3: "*Render unto Caesar that which is Caesar's and unto God what is God's. Manifest opposition, a collision of duties!* . . . Here is demand against demand, claim against claim. 'To whom shall we give? Whom shall we obey?' Bear both burdens – went the advice – as well as you can; serve two masters with patience and devotion. Give to Caesar, and give to God too!" See Matthew 22:21, etc.

[299] *Jerusalem*, p. 72: "I can conceive of a state of mind in which it is pardonable before the tribunal of the all-righteous Judge if one continues to mix into his otherwise salutary exposition of truths beneficial to the public some untruth that, perhaps, on account of an erroneous conscience, has been sanctioned by the state. I would, at any rate, be careful not to accuse, on this account, an otherwise honest teacher of hypocrisy or Jesuitry, unless I were thoroughly acquainted with his circumstances and state of mind – so thoroughly as perhaps no man ever can be with his neighbor's state of mind."

[300] For "blind guides," see Matthew 23:16, 24, where they are the "scribes and pharisees, hypocrites." Hamann writes "Wegweiser" where Luther has "Leiter."

[301] Matthew 23:2: "The scribes and the Pharisees sit in Moses' seat." Hamann writes "Katheder" where Luther has "Stuhl." The Greek is καθέδρα, the Latin *cathedra*.

[302] Matthew 23:4: "For they bind heavy burdens and grievous to be borne, and lay them on men's shoulders; but they themselves will not move them with one of their fingers."

[303] Matthew 23:23: "for ye pay tithe of mint and anise and cummin, and have omitted the weightier matters of the law, judgment, mercy, and faith."

[304] Matthew 23:24: "Ye blind guides, which strain at a gnat, and swallow a camel."

[305] Gaius Marius, Roman general (157–86 BC); in European painting and literature, typically depicted meditating among the ruins of Carthage (see Plutarch's *Life*).

wilderness there is the reed that is shaken by the wind,[306] but no patriotic Catos[307] – "What doest thou here Elijah?"[308] Religion and pay![309] – For heaven's sake! Oaths and the Sermon on the Mount![310] – Has the theorist not proved to our face that we (if we may say so without boasting) reverend clergymen have become his brothers-in-business according to the flesh,[311] just as he himself, alas!, has become, through vain deceit after the tradition of Greeks and after the rudiments of the world,[312] a circumcised brother-in-faith in the spirit and essence of heathen, naturalistic, atheistic fanaticism; – for whosoever denies the Son, the same has not the Father,[313] and he that honors not the Son honors not the Father which has sent him.[314] But he that has seen the Son has seen the Father.[315] HE and the son is One Being,[316] whose oneness is such as not to admit the least division or plurality in either the political or metaphysical sense.[317] No man has seen God; the only begotten son, which is in the bosom of the father,[318] has given the only exegesis of the fullness of his grace and truth. –

But then it is sorrowful not to know what one is, oneself,[319] and almost risible to be the exact opposite of what one wants and intends. The Jew, that is, has been without any god besides the one over whom the archangel contended three thousand years ago;[320] the Greek has been waiting for

---

[306] Matthew 11:7.
[307] The "patriotic" Cato most likely refers to Cato the Younger (or Cato Uticensis) who committed suicide after Caesar's victory. He was the great-grandson of Cato the Elder (or Cato the Censor), whose name became a byword for stern morality.
[308] 1 Kings 19:9.
[309] *Jerusalem*, p. 60: "But if the church has no property, who is to pay the teachers of religion? Who is to remunerate the preachers of the fear of God? Religion and pay – teaching virtue and salary – preaching the fear of God and remuneration. These notions seem to shun one another."
[310] At ibid., pp. 64–5, Mendelssohn discusses the purpose of oaths (they help steel the will of weak, irresolute, and vacillating men and rouse their conscience). Christ forbade all oaths in his Sermon on the Mount (Matthew 5:34–7).
[311] Mendelssohn argued that religious oaths were inadmissible as conditions on which clergymen take office (*Jerusalem*, pp. 63–72).
[312] Colossians 2:8: "Beware lest any man spoil you through philosophy and vain deceit, after the tradition of men, after the rudiments of the world, and not after Christ."
[313] 1 John 2:23.   [314] John 5:23.   [315] John 14:9: "he that hath seen me hath seen the Father."
[316] John 10:30: "I and my Father are one."
[317] *Jerusalem*, p. 128: "God, the Creator and Preserver of the world, was at the same time the King and Regent of this nation; and his oneness is such as not to admit the least division or plurality in either the political or the metaphysical sense."
[318] John 1:18: "No man hath seen God at any time; the only begotten Son, which is in the bosom of the Father, he hath declared him."
[319] Hamann questions whether Mendelssohn is Jew or Greek.
[320] That is, the body of Moses. See Jude 1:9.

two thousand years for a science and a queen[321] who is still to come and of whom it may one day be said: This is Jezebel![322] The Jew: with no anointed one but him whom his own people lifted up, with the assistance of the Roman governor[323] in collusion with his friend Herod,[324] as Moses lifted up a serpent of brass[325] – with schools[326] instead of temples, schools like the birthplace of the one who was lifted up! – with no other sacrifice than his eloquent blood – cursed like Canaan, instead of Joseph's dreams of a universal monarchy,[327] a servant of servants unto his brethren.[328] The philosopher *à la grecque*, a king of peace and righteousness![329] His circumcision knife extends to everything that carries a purse, his priests and Levites do not bathe in the blood of calves and goats,[330] nor skin their pelt, but rather are *Maîtres des hautes œuvres & des basses œuvres*[331] to their own natural kind – The Capitolium[332] is a Bedlam, and Coheleth[333] a Calvary!

It even happens that a David Hume judaizes and prophesies, like Saul the son of Kish.[334] To the hypocrite Cleanthes, Philo the Pharisee finally confesses his fit of astonishment and of melancholy over the greatness and obscurity of the unknown object, and his contempt of human reason which can give no solution more satisfactory with regard to so extraordinary and magnificent a question of the unknown object's existence.[335] Therefore,

---

[321] Metaphysics; cf. the preface to the first edition of the *Critique of Pure Reason* (1781), where Kant recalls the time when metaphysics was acknowledged to be the queen of the sciences.

[322] 2 Kings 9:37: "And the carcase of Jezebel shall be as dung upon the face of the field in the portion of Jezreel; so that they shall not say, This is Jezebel."

[323] Pontius Pilate.

[324] Luke 23:12: "And the same day Pilate and Herod were made friends together: for before they were at enmity between themselves."

[325] Numbers 21:9; John 3:14.

[326] I.e., synagogues; in the Luther Bible, synagogues are always called schools. At Matthew 13:54, Christ taught in the synagogue of his own country.

[327] Genesis 37:8–9.

[328] Genesis 9:25: "And he said, Cursed be Canaan; a servant of servants shall he be unto his brethren."

[329] Frederick II; cf. Hebrews 7:2.

[330] Hebrews 9:12: "Neither by the blood of goats and calves, but by his own blood he entered in once into the holy place."

[331] The "master of high works" was the hangman.   [332] I.e. Berlin, the capital.

[333] Coheleth is the Latin version of the Hebrew name for Ecclesiastes. Hamann may intend it as an ironic reference to the wisdom of the Academy of Sciences in Berlin.

[334] 1 Samuel 10:11: "What is this that is come unto the son of Kish? Is Saul also among the prophets?"

[335] Refers to the penultimate paragraph of Hume's *Dialogues Concerning Natural Religion*, where Philo says to Cleanthes, in regard to natural theology: "Some astonishment, indeed, will naturally arise from the greatness of the object; some melancholy from its obscurity; some contempt of human reason, that it can give no solution more satisfactory with regard to so extraordinary and magnificent a question."

the whole piety of natural religion is lost in the Jewish anachronism[336] of a longing desire and expectation that Heaven would be pleased to dissipate the shame of such a profound ignorance, or at least to alleviate it[337] through another gospel than that of the cross, through a paraclete that is still to come ("adventitious Instructor").[338]

This adulterous psilosophy,[339] which speaks half in the speech of Ashdod and not in the pure language of the Jews[340] – does it not deserve to be contended with and its hair plucked off (Nehemiah's deed[341]), that it seeks to spoil for us not only all the labor of the vineyard – ("thou, O Solomon, must have a thousand, and the keepers two hundred"[342]) – but also every one of life's vows since no one can swear in good conscience to the permanence of his convictions,[343] as for example to swear to the permanence of his feelings after, like before, enjoying love and its proceeds. Vows, needless to say, seem to be a very superfluous evil in a country where judgments and opinions and convictions, without corresponding actions, are privileged small change that may be legally tendered.

Yes, for all that it is indeed written in the law of Moses: thou shalt not muzzle the mouth of the ox.[344] However, in the opinion of the philosopher,

---

[336] That is, the natural theologians (like the Jews) are hoping for a Messiah to come, an anachronism for Christians, who believe the Messiah has already come.

[337] From the penultimate paragraph of Hume's *Dialogues Concerning Natural Religion*: "But believe me, Cleanthes, the most natural sentiment, which a well-disposed mind will feel on this occasion, is a longing desire and expectation, that Heaven would be pleased to dissipate, at least alleviate, this profound ignorance, by affording some particular revelation to mankind, and making discoveries of the nature, attributes, and operations of the divine object of our faith."

[338] From ibid., penultimate paragraph: "A person, seasoned with a just sense of the imperfections of natural reason, will fly to revealed truth with the greatest avidity: While the haughty dogmatist, persuaded that he can erect a complete system of theology by the mere help of philosophy, disdains any farther aid, and rejects this adventitious instructor."

[339] Psilosophy is opposed to genuine philosophy, love of wisdom. "Psilos" means "bare" or "mere"; in particular contexts it might also be translated "depilated" or "unsupported by evidence" or "defenseless." For Hamann, "pure" reason is helpless, mere reason.

[340] Nehemiah 13:24: "And their children spake half in the speech of Ashdod, and could not speak in the Jews' language, but according to the language of each people." In 1 Samuel 5, Ashdod is the seat of the Dagon and his priests.

[341] Nehemiah 13:25: "And I contended with them, and cursed them, and smote certain of them, and plucked off their hair."

[342] Song of Songs 8:11–12: "Solomon had a vineyard at Baal-hamon; he let out the vineyard unto keepers; every one for the fruit thereof was to bring a thousand pieces of silver. My vineyard, which is mine, is before me: thou, O Solomon, must have a thousand, and those that keep the fruit thereof two hundred."

[343] Mendelssohn opposes oaths in *Jerusalem*, pp. 63–72. Cf. ibid., p. 66: "I may feel sure of something right now, but a moment later, some slight doubt of its certainty may sneak or steal its way into a corner of my soul."

[344] Deuteronomy 25:4: "Thou shalt not muzzle the ox when he treadeth out the corn."

this would have been said out of a divine predilection for the Israelite bulls and oxen, and not altogether for our sakes,[345] for our sakes alone. Teaching and consoling and preaching, then, are not actions which tire the body?[346] Or is a pure, light tongue of the learned that knows how to speak a word in season to him that is weary[i] not worth as many pieces of silver[347] as the pen of that most accomplished and hale writer who does nothing but sign his name and often scribbles it so idiotically that it is not possible, without the special grace and inspiration and aid of a sheblimini, to understand either how to digest the content or to read the signature? Was not even Melchizedek paid alms for his blessing with a tenth part of everything?[348]

I too shall conclude with the broken echo of the above-mentioned solemn protestation against whatever pathetic sophistry and spiteful, small-minded consistency may have been compelled or coaxed out of me by a good many contagious objects – and even with the result – – *reparabilis adsonat Echo!*[j]

Belief and doubt act upon men's cognitive faculty, as fear and hope do upon their appetitive urge.[349] Truth and untruth are instruments for the intellect: (true or untrue) notions of good and evil are instruments for the will.[350] For we know only in part,[351] and all men's rational arguments

---

[i] Isaiah 32:4. ["The heart also of the rash shall understand knowledge, and the tongue of the stammerers shall be ready to speak plainly." Cf. Isaiah 50:4: "The Lord God hath given me the tongue of the learned, that I should know how to speak a word in season to him that is weary."]

[j] Persius, *Satires* 1.102. ["The restoring echo sounds." The phrase ends a bombastic passage quoted in that satire which an ancient commentator attributed to Nero.]

[345] 1 Corinthians 9:9–10: "For it is written in the law of Moses, Thou shalt not muzzle the mouth of the ox that treadeth out the corn. Doth God take care for oxen? Or saith he it altogether for our sakes?"

[346] *Jerusalem*, p. 45: "The only aid religion can render to the state consists in *teaching and consoling.*"

[347] Hamann opposes Mendelssohn's argument that the "church does not remunerate; religion buys nothing, pays nothing, and allots no wages" (*Jerusalem*, p. 61).

[348] Hebrews 7:1–2: "For this Melchisedec, king of Salem, priest of the most high God, who met Abraham returning from the slaughter of the kings, and blessed him; to whom also Abraham gave a tenth part of all."

[349] *Jerusalem*, p. 62: "Fear and hope act upon men's *appetitive urge*, rational argument on their *cognitive faculty.*" Cf. ibid., p. 100: "Belief and doubt . . . are not determined by our faculty of desire, by our wishes and longings, or by fear and hope, but by our knowledge of truth and untruth."

[350] Ibid., p. 62: "Notions of good and evil are instruments for the *will*, those of truth and untruth for the *intellect.*"

[351] 1 Corinthians 13:9: "For we know in part, and we prophesy in part."

consist either of belief in truth and doubt about untruth or of belief in untruth and doubt about truth. "This (partly negative, partly positive) belief is prior to all systems. It produced them first in order to justify itself."[k] So says the admirable friend of Herr Mendelssohn.[352] However, if the intellect believes in lies and acquires a taste for them, doubts truths and despises simple fare, then the light in us is darkness[353] and the salt in us is no longer a seasoning[354] – religion is pure church-procession – philosophy is empty verbal pomp, outmoded and meaningless opinions, obsolete and impotent rights! Skepticism about truth and credulous self-deception are thus symptoms as closely bound together as chills and hot fits in a fever. The man who thinks that he is farthest removed from this disease of the soul and who most ardently wishes to be able to cure all his fellow men of it himself admits that he performed this cure on himself and tried it on others so often that he has become aware of how difficult it is, and what little hope one has of success[355] – Woe to the unfortunate who finds something to criticize in these modest, purified words![356]

What is truth?[357] A wind that blows where it lists, whereof one hears the sound but cannot tell: whence? whither?[358] – A spirit that the world cannot receive, for it sees him not and knows him not.

Gentle reader, what does the peace which the world gives have to do with you and me? We know perfectly that the day of the Lord so comes as a thief in the night. When they shall say, Peace and safety, then sudden

---

[k] "We have invented them." Garve on Ferguson, pp. 296–7. [Christian Garve published his translation, with commentary, of Adam Ferguson's *Institutes of Moral Philosophy* in 1772. On pp. 296–7, Garve writes, "We all believe in the existence of virtue. This belief is prior to all systems. It produced them first; in order to justify it, we have invented them."]

[352] I.e., Garve.

[353] Matthew 6:23: "If therefore the light that is in thee is darkness, how great is that darkness!"

[354] Cf. Matthew 5:13: "Ye are the salt of the earth: but if the salt have lost his savour, wherewith shall it be salted?"

[355] *Jerusalem*, p. 67: "I am perhaps one of those who are the farthest removed from that disease of the soul [i.e., skepticism], and who most ardently wish to be able to cure all their fellow men of it. But precisely because I have so often performed this cure on myself, and tried it on others, I have become aware of how difficult it is, and what little hope one has of success."

[356] Ibid., p. 138: "woe to the unfortunate, who comes a day later, and who finds something to criticize even in these *modest, purified* words!"

[357] John 18:38.

[358] Cf. John 3:8: "The wind bloweth where it listeth, and thou hearest the sound thereof, but canst not tell whence it cometh, and whither it goeth."

destruction comes upon them[359] – And HE, the God of peace, who is higher than all reason, sanctify us wholly, that our spirit and soul and body be preserved blameless until the coming[360]–

"He that testifieth these things saith: Surely I come quickly! Amen!"[361]

---

[359] 1 Thessalonians 5:2–3: "For yourselves know perfectly that the day of the Lord so cometh as a thief in the night. For when they shall say, Peace and safety; then sudden destruction cometh upon them."

[360] 1 Thessalonians 5:23: "And the very God of peace sanctify you wholly; and I pray God your whole spirit and soul and body be preserved blameless unto the coming of our Lord Jesus Christ."

[361] Revelation 22:20.

Metacritique on the Purism of Reason

Sunt lacrimae rerum – o quantum est in rebus inane![1]

A great philosopher has asserted that "all general ideas are nothing but particular ones, annexed to a certain term, which gives them a more extensive signification, and makes them recall upon occasion other individuals."[2] Hume[a] declares this assertion of the Eleatic, mystic and

---

[a] See *A Treatise of Human Nature: Being An Attempt to Introduce the Experimental Method of Reasoning into Moral Subjects*, vol. I: Of the Understanding (London, 1739), p. 38. To my knowledge, this first masterpiece of the famous David Hume is said to be translated into French but not yet, like his last, into German. Also, the translation of the astute Berkeley's philosophical works has unfortunately not progressed. The first part appeared in Leipzig in 1781 and contained only the *Dialogues between Hylas and Philonous*, which had already appeared in Eschenbach's *Collection of Idealists* (Rostock, 1756). [Berkeley's *Dialogues* appeared in Johann Christoph Eschenbach, *Samlung der vornehmsten Schriftsteller die die Wirklichkeit ihres eignen Körpers und der ganzen Körperwelt läugnen* ("Collection of the most excellent writers who deny the reality of their body and of the entire physical world") in Rostock in 1756.]

[1] "There are tears for things – o what emptiness in things!" From Virgil, *Aeneid* 1.462, and Persius, *Satire* 1.1.

[2] David Hume, *A Treatise of Human Nature*, book 1, part 1, sect. 7: "A great philosopher [Berkeley] has disputed the received opinion in this particular, and has asserted, that all general ideas are nothing but particular ones, annexed to a certain term, which gives them a more extensive signification, and makes them recall upon occasion other individuals, which are similar to them. As I look upon this to be one of the greatest and most valuable discoveries that has been made of late years in the republic of letters . . ." Hamann translates freely.

The relevant passages from Berkeley appear in his introduction (sect. 11–18) to *A Treatise Concerning the Principles of Human Knowledge* (he was writing in reaction to Locke's account of the signification of general words in *An Essay on Human Understanding*, book 3, chap. 6, sect. 39; see also book 3, chap. 3, sect. 6).

Berkeley was the Church of Ireland bishop of Cloyne. Hamann calls him "Eleatic" because like the Eleatic pre-Socratic philosophers he casts doubt on the validity of sense experience. Cf. Kant, *Prolegomena to Any Future Metaphysics* AA 4.374: "The dictum of all genuine idealists, from the

enthusiast Bishop of Cloyne to be one of the greatest and most valuable discoveries that has been made of late in the republic of letters.

First of all, the recent skepticism seems to me to owe infinitely more to the older idealism than this single and fortuitous occasion would have us superficially understand, and that without Berkeley, Hume would hardly have become the great philosopher that the *Critique*, with a similar indebtedness, declares him to be.[3] But as for the important discovery itself: it lies open and uncovered, without any special profundity, in the very use of language of the most common perception and observation of the *sensus communis*.

Among the hidden mysteries[4] the problem of which (let alone the solution)[5] has apparently not yet entered into a philosopher's heart[6] is the possibility of the human knowledge of objects of experience without and before any experience[7] and after this the possibility of a sensible intuition before any sensation of an object.[8] The matter and form of a Transcendental Doctrine of Elements and Method[9] is grounded on this double im-possibility and on the mighty distinction of analytic and synthetic judgments.[10] For besides the characteristic distinction of reason as object or source of knowledge or even as kind of knowledge,[11] there is

Eleatic school to Bishop Berkeley, is contained in this formula: 'All knowledge through the senses and experience is nothing but illusion'" (translations from the *Prolegomena* are given in the version by Carus revised by Ellington, sometimes further revised).

[3] Kant's indebtedness to Hume is famously expressed in the preface to *Prolegomena* AA 4.260.

[4] See Kant, *Critique of Pure Reason* A 10: "A certain mystery lies here hidden" (all translations are taken from Norman Kemp Smith, sometimes revised). Kant adds that "if it had occurred to any of the ancients even to raise this question," the course of philosophy would have been spared many vain attempts.

For the sake of convenience, references to both editions of the *Critique of Pure Reason* (the "A" text of 1781 and the "B" text of 1787) will be given, except when (as here) a passage appears only in the first edition.

[5] Kant, in contrast, claims that in his work "there is not a single metaphysical problem which has not been solved" (A xiii).

[6] 1 Corinthians 2:9: "neither have entered into the heart of man, the things which God hath prepared for them that love him."

[7] See in the Preface and Introduction to the *Critique of Pure Reason*, Kant's initial discussion of knowledge that is *a priori*, independent of experience (A xii, A 2).

[8] See, for example, A 20 (B 34): "the pure form of sensible intuitions in general . . . must be found in the mind *a priori*"; and, in general, the transcendental aesthetic.

[9] Kant's *Critique of Pure Reason* is divided into the Transcendental Doctrine of Elements and the Transcendental Doctrine of Method. They are "matter and form" because the Doctrine of Elements provides the materials for the edifice of pure reason and the Doctrine of Method provides the plan (A 707 = B 735).

[10] The distinction is elaborated in A 6–10 (B 10–14).

[11] Kant's *Prolegomena* (AA 4.265): "If we wish to present knowledge as a science, we must first determine exactly its differentia, which no other science has in common with it and which therefore

a still more general, sharper, and purer distinction which enables reason to ground all objects, sources, and kinds of knowledge. Itself none of the three, and consequently in need neither of an empirical or aesthetic nor of a logical or discursive concept, it consists solely in the subjective conditions whereby Everything, Something, and Nothing[12] can be thought as object, source, or kind of knowledge. Like an infinite maximum or minimum,[13] it can be given (and if necessary taken) for immediate intuition.[14]

The first purification of reason consisted in the partly misunderstood, partly failed attempt to make reason independent of all tradition and custom and belief in them. The second is even more transcendent[15] and comes to nothing less than independence from experience and its everyday induction. After a search of two thousand years[16] for who knows what beyond experience, reason not only suddenly despairs of the progressive course of its predecessors but also defiantly promises impatient contemporaries delivery, and this in a short time,[17] of that general and infallible philosopher's stone,[18] indispensable for Catholicism and despotism. Religion will submit its sanctity to it right away, and law-giving its majesty, especially at the final close of a critical century[19] when empiricism on

is characteristic of it . . . What is characteristic of it may consist in a simple distinction of object, or of the sources of knowledge, or of the mode of knowledge."

[12] *Prolegomena* AA 4.263: "In the sphere of this faculty [i.e., reason] you can determine either everything or nothing."

[13] The infinitely great and the infinitesimal coincide by the "coincidentia oppositorum," as in Nicholas of Cusa, *De docta ignorantia* ("On learned ignorance") 1.4. They are also the limits invoked by calculus.

[14] A 19 (B 33): "In whatever manner and by whatever means a mode of knowledge may relate to objects, intuition is that through which it is in immediate relation to them . . . But intuition takes place only in so far as the object is given to us."

[15] Kant distinguishes between "transcendent" and "transcendental." A 296 (B 352–3): "The principles of pure understanding . . . allow only of empirical and not of transcendental employment, that is, employment extending beyond the limits of experience. A principle, on the other hand, which takes away these limits, or even commands us actually to transgress them, is called transcendent." See also *Prolegomena* AA 4.374 (the footnote).

[16] See David Hume, *A Treatise of Human Nature*, chap. 36, §7: "Two thousand years with such long interruptions, and under such mighty discouragements are a small space of time to give any tolerable perfection to the sciences; and perhaps we are still in too early an age of the world to discover any principles, which will bear the examination of the latest posterity."

[17] A xx: "Metaphysics . . . is the only one of all the sciences which dare promise that through a small but concentrated effort it will attain, and this in a short time, such completion as will leave no task to our successors."

[18] Contrast *Prolegomena* AA 4.366: "Critique stands in the same relation to the common metaphysics of the schools as chemistry does to alchemy."

[19] A xi (footnote): "Our age is, in especial degree, the age of criticism, and to criticism everything must submit. Religion through its sanctity, and law-giving through its majesty, may seek to exempt themselves from it. But they then awaken just suspicion, and cannot claim the sincere respect

both sides, struck blind, makes its own nakedness daily more suspect and ridiculous.

The third, highest, and, as it were, empirical purism is therefore concerned with language, the only, first, and last organon and criterion of reason,[20] with no credentials[21] but tradition and usage. But it is almost the same with this idol as it was with the ideal of reason[22] for that ancient.[23] The longer one deliberates, the more deeply and inwardly one is struck dumb and loses all desire to speak. "Woe to the tyrants when God troubles himself about them! Why then do they seek after Him? Mene, mene, tekel to the sophists! Their small change will be found wanting and their banks broken!"[24]

Receptivity of language and spontaneity of concepts![25] – From this double source of ambiguity[26] pure reason draws all the elements of its doctrinairism, doubt, and connoisseurship.[27] Through an analysis just as arbitrary as the synthesis of the thrice old leaven,[28] it brings forth new

---

which reason accords only to that which has been able to sustain these tests of free and open examination."

[20] Hamann alludes to Edward Young's *Night Thoughts*, Night 2, l. 469: "Speech, Thought's Canal! Speech, Thought's Criterion too!"

[21] In the *Prolegomena* (AA 4.278), Kant writes that the credentials of pure reason consist only in its answer to the question "How is synthetic knowledge *a priori* possible?"

[22] That is, God. In "The Ideal of Pure Reason" (chap. 3 of book 2 of the "Transcendental Dialectic"), Kant treats metaphysical arguments about the existence of God, concluding "A Supreme Being is, therefore, for the speculative reason, a mere ideal" (A 641 = B 669).

[23] That is, Simonides. Cicero records the anecdote that when Hiero asked Simonides about the being and nature of God, Simonides repeatedly delayed giving an answer because, he said, "the longer I deliberate, the more obscure the question seems to me," *De natura deorum*, 1.60. The story is also told by Philo in Hume's *Dialogues Concerning Natural Religion*, part 2.

[24] "Mene, mene, tekel" is the writing on the wall which Daniel interprets for Belshazzar, in Daniel 5. "Tekel" means "Thou art weighted in the balances, and art found wanting" (Daniel 5:27). Jesus overthrows the tables of the money-changers in the temple at Mark 11:15.

[25] Cf. Kant's "receptivity for impressions" and "spontaneity of concepts." A 50 (B 74): "Our knowledge springs from two fundamental sources of the mind; the first is the capacity of receiving representations (receptivity for impressions), the second is the power of knowing an object through these representations (spontaneity of concepts). Through the first an object is given to us, through the second the object is thought in relation to that representation." A 68 (B 93): "Concepts are based on the spontaneity of thought, sensible intuitions on the receptivity of impressions."

[26] In the *Prolegomena* (AA 4.269), Kant writes that the "ambiguity of the expression" has led to philosophical errors.

[27] These correspond to Kant's three steps of dogmatism, skepticism, and criticism, A 761 (B 789).

[28] Matthew 13:33: "Another parable spake he [Jesus] unto them; The kingdom of heaven is like unto leaven, which a woman took, and hid in three measures of meal, till the whole was leavened" (also Luke 13:20–1). 1 Corinthians 5:7–8: "Purge out therefore the old leaven, that ye may be a new lump, as ye are unleavened . . . Therefore let us keep the feast, not with old leaven, neither with the leaven of malice and wickedness; but with the unleavened bread of sincerity and truth."

phenomena and meteors[29] on the inconstant horizon, creates signs and wonders[30] with the All-creator and destroying[31] mercurial[32] caduceus of its mouth or with the forked goose quill[33] between the three syllogistic writing fingers of its Herculean fist – –

The hereditary defect and leprosy of ambiguity adheres to the very name "metaphysics." It cannot be set aside, still less transfigured, by going back to its birth-place[34] in the accidental synthesis of a Greek prefix.[35] But even if we grant that in the transcendental topic[36] the empirical distinction between *behind* and *beyond* would matter even less than a hysteron-proteron[37] in the case of an *a priori* and *a posteriori*; nonetheless, the birthmark of its name spreads from its brow to the bowels of the whole science, and its terminology has the same relation to every other language of art, pastures, mountains, and schools as quicksilver to other metals.

A good many analytic judgments indeed imply a gnostic hatred of matter or else a mystic love of form. Yet the synthesis of predicate with subject (the proper object of pure reason) has for its middle term[38] nothing more

---

[29] In Hamann's time, the word "meteor" had a broader signification than it does today; it included a range of atmospheric lights, including the *ignis fatuus*.

[30] "Signs and wonders" is a common collocation in the Bible, in both testaments.

[31] Mendelssohn's reference to the "all-crushing Kant" was made in *Morgenstunden* (1785), that is, after Hamann had written the *Metacritique*.

[32] Besides "quicksilvery," perhaps a reference to the Enlightenment journal *Der teutsche Merkur*.

[33] In German the adjective "split" (*gespalten*) may refer specifically to confusing or equivocal language.

[34] Kant, *Prolegomena* AA 4.379: "it is thereby established that metaphysics has a hereditary failing, not to be explained, much less set aside, until we ascend to its birthplace, pure reason itself." On Kant's *erklärt* ("explained") Hamann offers a pun, *verklärt* ("transfigured").

[35] The *Oxford English Dictionary* describes the ambiguity that adheres to the word "metaphysics," a name subsequently applied to Aristotle's treatise on the topic but which Aristotle himself never used: "This title doubtless originally referred (as some of the early commentaries state) to the position which the books so designated occupied in the received arrangement of Aristotle's writings . . . It was, however, from an early period used as a name for the branch of study treated in these books, and hence came to be misinterpreted as meaning 'the science of things transcending what is physical or natural.' This misinterpretation is found, though rarely, in Greek writers, notwithstanding the fact that meta does not admit of any such sense as 'beyond' or 'transcending.' In scholastic Latin writers the error was general (being helped, perhaps, by the known equivalence of the prefixes μετα- and trans- in various compounds)."

[36] A 268 (B 324): "Let me call the place which we assign to a concept, either in sensibility or in pure understanding, its transcendental location. Thus the decision as to the place which belongs to every concept according to difference in the use to which it is put, and the directions for determining this place for all concepts according to rules, is a transcendental topic."

[37] In Aristotle, the logical fallacy of establishing "the antecedent [*proteron*] by means of its consequents [*hysteron*]; for demonstration proceeds from what is more certain and is prior" (*Prior Analytics* 2.16 [64b30–2]).

[38] *Mittelbegriff*, the "middle term" of a syllogism (linking the major and minor terms).

than an old, cold prejudice for mathematics[39] before and behind it. The apodeictic certainty[40] of mathematics depends mainly on a curiological,[41] so to speak, portrayal of the simplest, most sensible intuition and then on the ease of proving and representing its synthesis and the possibility of its synthesis in obvious constructions or symbolic formulas and equations, by whose sensibility all misunderstanding is excluded of itself. However, while geometry determines and fixes even the ideality of its concepts of points without parts,[42] of lines and surfaces even in ideally divided dimensions, by means of empirical signs and figures, metaphysics abuses the word-signs and figures of speech of our empirical knowledge by treating them as nothing but hieroglyphs and types of ideal relations. Through this learned troublemaking it works the honest decency of language into such a meaningless, rutting,[43] unstable, indefinite something $= x$[44] that nothing is left but a windy sough, a magic shadow play, at most, as the wise Helvétius says,[45] the talisman and rosary of a transcendental superstitious belief in *entia rationis*,[46] their empty sacks and slogans.[47] Finally it is on the verge of being understood that if mathematics is able to lay claim to

---

[39] See for example A 4 (B 8): "Mathematics gives us a shining example of how far, independently of experience, we can progress in *a priori* knowledge"; A 712 (B 740): "Mathematics presents the most splendid example of the successful extension of pure reason, without the help of experience"; etc.

[40] A 46–7 (B 64): "the propositions of geometry are synthetic *a priori*, and are known with apodeictic certainty" (similarly, A 25 = B 39, etc.). See also A xv.

[41] "Curiological" refers to "that form of hieroglyphic writing in which objects are represented by pictures, and not by symbolic characters" (*Oxford English Dictionary*). The word was first applied in this sense by St. Clement of Alexandria; it regularly appeared in eighteenth-century discussions of the origin of script. Elsewhere Hamann alludes to Johann Georg Wachter's account (in *Naturae et scripturae concordia*, 1752) of the three stages in the development of script: curiological, symbolic or hieroglyphic, and characteristic.

[42] Euclid's *Elements* begins, "A point is that which has no part."

[43] Or "agile," "speedy."

[44] A 250: "All our representations are, it is true, referred by the understanding to some object; and since appearances are nothing but representations, the understanding refers them to a something, as the object of sensible intuition. But this something, thus conceived, is only the transcendental object; and by that is meant a something $= x$, of which we know, and with the present constitution of our understanding can know, nothing whatsoever." See also A 105 and A 109.

[45] Claude-Adrien Helvétius (1715–71), philosopher of the French Enlightenment. *De l'homme* (1773), p. 200 (vol. I, sect. 2, chap. 19): "When one attaches precise ideas to each expression, the scholastic who has so often confounded the world will be nothing but an impotent magician. The talisman which was the source of his power will be broken. Then all those fools who, under the name of metaphysician, have wandered such a long time in the land of chimeras and who in the windy beyond cross in every direction the depths of the infinite will no longer say that they see what they do not see and that they know what they do not know."

[46] "An entity of reason, a being that has no existence outside the mind" (*Oxford English Dictionary*). Kant defines *ens rationis* as an "empty concept without object" (A 292 = B 348).

[47] *Losung* means both "slogan" and "droppings."

the privilege of nobility because of its universal and necessary reliability, then even human reason itself would not be the match of the infallible and unerring instinct of insects.

If then a chief question indeed still remains – how is the faculty of thought possible?[48] the faculty to think right and left, before and without, with and beyond experience? – then no deduction is needed to demonstrate the genealogical priority of language, and its heraldry, over the seven holy functions of logical propositions and inferences.[49] Not only is the entire faculty of thought founded on language, according to the unrecognized prophecies and slandered miracles of the very commendable Samuel Heinicke,[50] but language is also the centerpoint of reason's misunderstanding with itself,[51] partly because of the frequent coincidence of the greatest and the smallest concept, its vacuity and its plenitude in ideal propositions, partly because of the infinite [advantage] of rhetorical over inferential figures, and much more of the same.

Sounds and letters are therefore pure forms *a priori*,[52] in which nothing belonging to the sensation[53] or concept of an object is found; they are the true, aesthetic elements of all human knowledge and reason. The oldest language was music, and along with the palpable rhythm of the pulse and of the breath in the nostrils, it was the original bodily image of all temporal measures and intervals. The oldest writing was painting and drawing, and therefore was occupied as early as then with the economy

---

[48] A xvii: "For the chief question is always simply this: – what and how much can the understanding and reason know apart from experience? not: – how is the faculty of thought itself possible?"

[49] Kant identifies twelve logical functions of the understanding in judgment (A 70 = B 95), arranged under four heads, each in three moments (perhaps Hamann added the four heads and three moments to yield seven, a numerological indication of perfection). Cf. the "Table of Categories," A 80 (B 106).

[50] Samuel Heinicke (1727–90) founded the first school for the deaf and dumb in Germany, in 1778. He wrote *Beobachtungen über Stumme und die menschliche Sprache* (1778; "Observations on the mute and human language") and *Über die Denkart der Taubstummen* (1780; "On the thought of deaf-mutes"), which Hamann read closely. Heinicke insisted on the priority of the spoken language for both deaf and hearing people; he argued that abstract thinking follows only after one has learned to use speech to deal with concrete objects perceived through the senses. His views on deaf education were contested by the Abbé de l'Epée, who promoted sign language. Both the Academy of Zurich (in 1783) and the University of Leipzig (in 1784) decided the question in favor of l'Epée, and his institute for deaf instruction went into decline. (See further Robert Harmon, "Samuel Heinicke," *Gallaudet Encyclopedia of Deaf People and Deafness* (1987), vol. II, pp. 35–8.)

[51] For Kant, not language but errors in the non-empirical employment of reason set "reason at variance with itself"; he claims to have solved the problem by "locating the point at which, through misunderstanding, reason comes into conflict with itself" (A xii).

[52] For Kant, space and time are the pure forms; see A 22 (B 36): "there are two pure forms of sensible intuition, serving as principles of *a priori* knowledge, namely, space and time."

[53] A 20 (B 34): "I term all representations pure . . . in which there is nothing that belongs to sensation."

of space, its limitation and determination[54] by figures. Thence, under the exuberant persistent influence of the two noblest senses sight and hearing, the concepts of space and time have made themselves so universal and necessary in the whole sphere of the understanding (just as light and air are for the eye, ear, and voice) that as a result space and time, if not *ideae innatae*, seem to be at least *matrices* of all intuitive knowledge.[55]

The sensibility and the understanding arise as two stems of human knowledge from One common root, in such a way that through the former objects are given and through the latter thought:[56] to what end is such a violent, unjustified, willful divorce of that which nature has joined together![57] Will not both stems wither and be dried up through a dichotomy and rupture of their common root? Would not a single stem with two roots be an apter image of our knowledge, one root above in the air and one below in the earth?[58] The first is exposed to our sensibility whereas the latter is invisible and must be thought by the understanding, which is in greater agreement with the priority of the thought and the posteriority of the given or taken, as well as with the favorite inversion of pure reason in its theories.

Perhaps there is even now a chemical tree of Diana[59] not only for the knowledge of sensibility and understanding but also for the explication and ampliation[60] of the two domains and their limits.[61] These have been made so dark, confused, and desolate by a pure reason, christened *per*

---

[54] A 32 (B 48): "every determinate magnitude of time is possible only through limitations of one single time that underlies it."

[55] The theory of innate ideas was opposed to the theory of the "tabula rasa," the blank slate. "Matrices" are wombs.

[56] A 15 (B 29): "there are two stems of human knowledge, namely, sensibility and understanding, which perhaps spring from a common, but to us unknown, root. Through the former, objects are given to us; through the latter, they are thought." See also A 51 (B 75): "The understanding can intuit nothing, the senses can think nothing. Only through their union can knowledge arise."

[57] Matthew 19:6: "What therefore God has joined together, let no man put asunder."

[58] A 835 (B 863): "the common root of our faculty of knowledge divides and throws out two stems, one of which is reason. By reason I here understand the whole higher faculty of knowledge."

[59] The Tree of Diana, or Arbor Dianae, is "the dendritic amalgam precipitated by mercury from a solution of nitrate of silver" (*Oxford English Dictionary*). The close resemblance of its structure to living vegetation was of great interest to investigators in the eighteenth century who were seeking a naturalistic explanation for the origin of life. See Maupertuis' *Vénus physique* (1756), chap. 17, p. 100 and Elizabeth B. Gasking, *Investigations into Generation 1651–1828* (1967), p. 73.

[60] See A 7 (B 11), where Kant calls analytic judgments "explicative" and synthetic judgments "ampliative."

[61] A 238 (B 297): "the understanding ... oversteps the limits of its own domain."

antiphrasin,[62] and its metaphysics which serve the prevailing indifferentism (that ancient mother of chaos and night in all sciences of morals, religion, and law-giving!),[63] that the dew of a pure natural language can be born only from the dawn[64] of the promised imminent regeneration and enlightenment.[65]

Without, however, my waiting for the visit of a new Lucifer rising from on high[66] nor violating the fig tree[67] of the great goddess Diana![68] the evil snake in the bosom[69] of the common, popular language gives us the finest parable of the hypostatic union[70] of the sensible and intelligible natures, the joint communication[71] of the idiom of their powers, the synthetic mysteries of the forms *a priori* and *a posteriori* corresponding and contradicting themselves, together with the transubstantiation[72] of subjective conditions and the subsumptions[73] into objective predicates and

---

[62] "By antiphrasis"; antiphrasis is "a figure of speech by which words are used in a sense opposite to their proper meaning" (*Oxford English Dictionary*). See Kant, *Prolegomena* AA 4.260: "sound common sense, often so called *per antiphrasin*."

[63] A x: "And now, after all methods, so it is believed, have been tried and found wanting, the prevailing mood is that of weariness and complete indifferentism – the mother of chaos and night in all sciences, but happily in this case the source, or at least the prelude, of their approaching reform and restoration. For it at least puts an end to that ill-applied industry which has rendered them thus dark, confused and unserviceable."

[64] Alludes to Psalms 110:3 in Luther's translation ("your children will be born unto you as the dew of the dawn").

[65] A x: "their approaching reform and restoration."

[66] Hamann's words (*aus der Höhe aufgehenden*, "rising from on high") recalls Luther's translation of Luke 1:78 (*der Aufgang aus der Höhe*, "the dayspring from on high," KJB).

[67] Luke 13:6–9: "He spake also this parable; A certain man had a fig tree planted in his vineyard; and he came and sought fruit thereon, and found none. Then said he unto the dresser of his vineyard, Behold, these three years I come seeking fruit on this fig tree, and find none: cut it down; why cumbereth it the ground? And he answering said unto him, Lord, let it alone this year also, till I shall dig about it, and dung it: And if it bear fruit, well: and if not, then after that thou shalt cut it down."

[68] Acts 19:35: "Ye men of Ephesus, what man is there that knoweth not how that the city of the Ephesians is a worshipper of the great goddess Diana, and of the image which fell down from Jupiter?" (also Acts 19:27).

[69] In one of Aesop's fables (Hausrath and Hunger, *Corpus fabularum Aesopicarum*, vol. I, p. 85), a farmer's son warms a frozen snake on his breast. The snake recovers, then bites and kills him.

[70] With reference to the Incarnation, the hypostatic union refers to the union of the divine and human natures in Christ.

[71] Alludes to the *communicatio idiomatum*, "the interchange of the properties," the theological doctrine that "while the human and Divine natures in Christ were separate, the attributes of the one may be predicated of the other in view of their union in the one Person of the Saviour" (*Concise Oxford Dictionary of the Christian Church*). See Luther's "The Word Made Flesh," *Luther's Works* (American Edition) vol. XXXVIII, p. 254.

[72] The Roman Catholic doctrine by which the elements of the Eucharist are converted into the body and blood of Christ; the Lutheran doctrine is sometimes called consubstantiation.

[73] A 137 (B 176): "subsumptions of an object under a concept"; see also A 132 (B 171).

attributes[74] through the copula[75] of an authoritative or expletive word[76] for cutting short dull whiles and filling out empty space in a periodic galimatias[77] *per thesin et arsin.*[78] –

O for the action of a Demosthenes and his triune energy of eloquence[79] or the mimic art, said to be coming, without the panegyric tinkling of an angel's tongue![80] Then I would open the eyes of the reader that he might perhaps see – hosts of intuitions ascend to the firmament of pure understanding and hosts of concepts descend to the depths of the most perceptible sensibility, on a ladder which no sleeper dreams[81] – and the dance of these Mahanaim or two hosts[82] of reason – the secret and vexing chronicle of their courtship and ravishing – and the whole theogony

---

[74] A 89 (B 122): "how subjective conditions of thought can have objective validity."

[75] For Kant's use of the copula, see A 74 (B 100), A 266 (B 322), and A 598–9 (B 626–7). In the last citation, Kant argues that since being "is merely the copula of a judgment," the statement "There is a God" adds nothing to the concept of God, which expresses merely what is possible.

[76] In a treatise written to combat the view of the Eucharist as merely symbolic or representational, Luther argues that Christ spoke an "authoritative word," a *Machtwort*, and not merely a *Nachwort* (an imitative word) when he instituted that sacrament: "his word is indeed not merely an imitative word but an authoritative word, which accomplishes what it expresses" (*Confession Concerning Christ's Supper*, p. 181 of vol. XXXVII of *Luther's Works*, American Edition). Also contrast Luther's discussion of the copula "is" (p. 308 and elsewhere) with Kant's dismissal of it.

[77] A galimatias is "confused language, meaningless talk, nonsense" *(Oxford English Dictionary)*, a word Hamann found in Rabelais.

[78] "By thesis and arsis," that is, by the downbeat and upbeat (Hamann inverts the normal order, "arsis and thesis"). A fugue "per arsin et thesin" is a fugue by inversion.

[79] Demosthenes was one of the greatest orators of ancient Greece. Both "action" and "energy" have technical meanings in rhetoric: "action" refers to the delivery or enunciation of a speech, and "energy" to the force or vigor of expression. "Triune" recalls the anecdote in which Demosthenes was asked which quality was of the greatest importance in oratory; he replied "action" and went on to give the same answer when he was asked what was of the second and third importance (see Cicero, *Brutus* 142 and *De oratore* 3.213 and also from Plutarch's *Moralia*, "Lives of the ten orators" 845a–b).

[80] Johann Jakob Engel (1741–1802), whose forthcoming *Ideen zu einer Mimik* ("Ideas on gestures and facial expressions") had been announced; it appeared in 1785–6. "Panegyric" because Engel had written a panegyric to Frederick II in 1781. "Engel" in German means "angel"; hence the allusion to 1 Corinthians 13:1: "Though I speak with the tongues of men and of angels, and have not charity, I am become as sounding brass, or a tinkling cymbal."

[81] Unlike Jacob's ladder, in Genesis 28:12: "And he dreamed, and behold a ladder set up on the earth, and the top of it reached to heaven: and behold the angels of God ascending and descending on it."

[82] Mahanaim is taken to mean "two camps" or "two hosts." Genesis 32:1–2: "And Jacob went on his way, and the angels of God met him. And when Jacob saw them, he said, This is God's host: and he called the name of that place Mahanaim." See also Song of Songs 6:13: "Return, return, O Shulamite; return, return, that we may look upon thee. What will ye see in the Shulamite? As it were the company of two armies" (for "company of two armies" Luther has "the dance to Mahanaim").

of all the giant and heroic forms of the Shulamite and muse,[83] in the mythology of light and darkness – to the play in forms[84] of an old Baubo with herself – *inaudita specie solaminis*, as Saint Arnobius says[85] – and of a new immaculate virgin, who may not however be a Mother of God for which Saint Anselm[86] took her –

Words, therefore, have an aesthetic and logical[87] faculty. As visible and audible objects they belong with their elements to the sensibility and intuition; however, by the spirit of their institution[88] and meaning, they belong to the understanding and concepts. Consequently, words are pure and empirical intuitions as much as pure and empirical concepts.[89] Empirical, because the sensation of vision or hearing is effected through them; pure, inasmuch as their meaning is determined by nothing that belongs to those sensations.[90] Words as the undetermined objects of empirical intuitions are entitled, in the original text of pure reason, aesthetic appearances;[91] therefore, according to the endlessly repeated

---

[83] The Shulamite is the beloved of the Song of Songs. At the beginning of the *Theogony*, Hesiod invokes the Muses, describes their birth, and accounts for their importance to kings and singers.

[84] *Prolegomena* AA 4.327: "the occupation of reason with itself alone"; A 680 (B 708): "Pure reason is in fact occupied with nothing but itself."

[85] Arnobius, in *Adversus nationes* 5.25, recounts the story of Ceres, who after the abduction of her daughter wanders disconsolately until she reaches Eleusis, where Baubo does what she can to comfort the goddess. Unsuccessful, Baubo changes tactics and tells coarse jokes. She then exposes her genitals, causing Ceres to laugh and providing an "unheard-of kind of solace" for the goddess. (Arnobius has "inauditi specie solaminis.")

[86] The essay "De conceptione sanctae Mariae" ("On the conception of St. Mary"), in support of immaculate conception, was formerly attributed to Anselm (who in fact had argued against it).

[87] A 52 (B 76): "We therefore distinguish the science of the rules of sensibility in general, that is, aesthetic, from the science of the rules of the understanding in general, that is, logic."

[88] Hamann's vocabulary is theological. "Institution" refers to the establishment or ordination of the sacrament of the Eucharist with the words spoken by Christ. "Elements" are the bread and wine that become the body and blood of Christ during the sacrament of the Eucharist. For Luther, a sacrament (baptism as well as the Eucharist) was made by the unity of the institution and elements. In the *Large Catechism*, Luther quotes Augustine for both sacraments: "It is said, *Accedat verbum ad elementum et fit sacramentum*, that is, 'When the Word is joined to the external element, and it becomes a sacrament' . . . The Word must make the element a sacrament, otherwise it remains a mere element" (see p. 448 of the *Large Catechism* in *The Book of Concord*, tr. Tappert, 1959). "Element" forms a complex pun, invoking the letters of the alphabet and the materials of a sacrament, in contrast to the elements of mathematics and of Kant's *Critique*.

[89] Contrast A 50 (B 74): intuitions and concepts "may be either pure or empirical."

[90] A 20 (B 34): "I term all representations pure . . . in which there is nothing that belongs to sensation."

[91] A 20 (B 34): "The undetermined object of an empirical intuition is entitled appearance."

antithetical parallelism, words as undetermined objects of empirical concepts are entitled critical appearances, specters, non-words or unwords, and become determinate objects for the understanding only through their institution and meaning in usage. This meaning and its determination arises, as everyone knows, from the combination of a word-sign, which is *a priori* arbitrary and indifferent and *a posteriori* necessary and indispensable, with the intuition of the word itself; through this reiterated bond the concept is communicated to, imprinted on, and incorporated in the understanding, by means of the word-sign as by the intuition itself.

Now is it possible, idealism asks from one side, to discover the concept of a word from the intuition alone of a word? Is it possible from the matter of the word "reason" [*Vernunft*], from its 7 letters[92] or 2 syllables in German – is it possible from its form which determines the order of these letters and syllables – to elicit something of the concept of the word "reason"? Here the *Critique* answers with both scales equally balanced. In some languages there are indeed logogriphs,[93] charades,[94] and witty rebuses which can be constructed through an analysis and synthesis[95] of letters or syllables in new forms. However, these are then new intuitions and appearances of words which correspond to the given word as little as do the different intuitions themselves.

Is it furthermore possible, idealism asks from the other side, to find the empirical intuition of a word from the understanding? Is it possible to find from the concept of reason the matter of its name, that is, the 7 letters or 2 syllables in German or any other language? Here one scale of the *Critique* indicates a decisive No! But should it not be possible to derive from the concept of reason the form of its empirical intuition in the word, the form by virtue of which one of the two syllables stands *a priori* and the other *a posteriori* and the seven letters are intuited in a

---

[92] Hamann refers to the seven different letters of the word *Vernunft*.
[93] "A kind of enigma in which a certain word, and other words that can be formed out of all or any of its letters, are to be guessed from synonyms introduced into a set of verses. Occasionally used for: Any anagram or puzzle involving anagrams" (*Oxford English Dictionary*).
[94] Formerly charades involved not a dramatic representation but an oblique description of each syllable of the word that is to be guessed.
[95] Nadler reads "syllable" (Hamann's text is abbreviated to "Sy").

definite ordered relation? Here the Homer of pure reason snores[96] as loud a Yes! as Jack and Jill at the altar,[97] presumably because he has dreamed that the universal character of a philosophical language,[98] hitherto sought, is already found.

Now this last possibility of obtaining, from the pure and empty quality of our outward and inward sense,[99] the form of the empirical intuition with neither an object nor sign of an empirical intuition is the very Δός μοι ποῦ στῶ[100] and πρῶτον ψεῦδος,[101] the whole cornerstone of critical idealism[102] and its tower and lodge[103] of pure reason. The given or taken materials belong to the categorical and idealist woods, the peripatetic and academic supply-house.[104] Analysis is nothing more than the latest fashionable cut, and synthesis nothing more than the artful seam of a professional leather- or cloth-cutter. And what the transcendental philosophy metagrabolizes[105] I have, for the sake of weak readers, transferred in a figure to the sacrament of language,[106] the letter of its elements, the

---

[96] Horace, *Ars poetica* 359–60: "I resent whenever Homer dozes off; however, it is allowable that sleep creeps up on a long work."

[97] The names "Jack" and "Jill" correspond to the "Hans" and "Greta" of Luther's marriage service ("Hans, dost thou desire Greta to thy wedded wife," etc). See "The Order of Marriage for Common Pastors," pp. 110–15 in Luther's *Works* (American Edition) vol. LIII.

[98] The "universal character" (*character universalis* or *characteristica universalis*) refers to attempts to devise a writing system whose characters would be immediately intelligible to everyone without interpretation. Leibniz, prominently, wished to create an ideal philosophical language by means of the *characteristica universalis*.

[99] Kant writes (A 22 = B 37) that by the outer sense we represent objects as outside us in space and that by the inner sense the mind intuits itself in time.

[100] "Give me a place to stand"; from Archimedes' boast that with a place to stand outside of the world, he would move the world. He is quoted in Pappus, *Greek Mathematical Works*, tr. I. Thomas (Loeb Classical Library, 1941) vol. II, p. 34.

[101] The "first falsehood," that is, the initial false premise invalidating the later deductions; the term derives from Aristotle's *Prior Analytics* 2.18 (66a).

[102] See *Prolegomena* AA 4.375: "My so-called (properly critical) idealism."

[103] Perhaps a reference to the Tower of Babel and the Freemasons' lodge. See also A 707 (B 735): "we have made an estimate for the materials, and have determined for what sort of edifice and for what height and strength of building they suffice. We have found, indeed, that although we had contemplated building a tower which should reach to the heavens, the supply of materials suffices only for a dwelling-house."

[104] "Categorical" and "peripatetic" refer to Aristotle; "idealist" and "Academic" to Plato. Words for "wood" in Greek and Latin also refer to raw material of any kind, matter.

[105] "Metagrabolize," a word favored by Rabelais, means to puzzle, mystify, confound.

[106] 1 Corinthians 4:6: "And these things, brethren, I have in a figure transferred to myself and to Apollos for your sakes." For "transfer in a figure" ("metaschematize") Luther and Hamann have "deuten," to indicate or interpret.

spirit of its institution, and I leave it to each one to unclench the closed fist into an open palm.[107] – – [108]

[107] Cicero's *Orator* 32.113: "Zeno, the founder of the Stoic school, used to give an object lesson of the difference between the two arts; clenching his fist he said logic was like that; relaxing and extending his hand, he said eloquence was like an open palm" (tr. Hubbell, Loeb Classical Library). Also in Sextus Empiricus, *Adversus mathematicos* 2.7.

[108] The text printed by Nadler includes the following paragraph, which appears in the version of the *Metacritique* which Hamann sent to Herder in a letter on September 15, 1784 (*Briefe*, vol. v, p. 216):

> But perhaps a similar idealism is the whole partition between Judaism and heathendom. The Jew has the word and the signs; the heathen, reason and its wisdom – (What followed was a μετάβασις εἰς ἄλλο γένος, the finest of which has been transplanted in the little *Golgotha*.)

The "partition" between Jew and heathen (or Gentile; Luther's word *Heide* corresponds to both "heathen" and "Gentile") is an allusion to Johann August Starck, *Freymüthige Betrachtungen über das Christentum* (1780; "Frank observations on Christendom"), p. 59: "As there is only one God, who is the Creator, Father, and Ruler of the entire world; as we are all equally children, who all descend from the One, have equally valid claims to God, and are destined for a single end; so the partition between Jews and heathens, all divisions, and all particularism had to be lifted as soon as the true God was proclaimed."

Α μετάβασις εἰς ἄλλο γένος is a change into another genre (or race).

Disrobing and Transfiguration[1]

A
Flying Letter[2]
to
Nobody, the Well Known[3]

HORATIUS

Non fumum ex fulgore, sed ex fumo dare LUCEM
cogitat — — —[4]
— — conviva satur — —
IAM SATIS EST![5] — — : רב עתה

1 Kings 19:4[6]

1786

---

[1] The transfiguration is related in Matthew 17:1–13 (and in the other synoptic gospels). The disrobing of Christ occurs just before his crucifixion; see for example Matthew 27:28–35.
"Disrobing" (*Entkleidung*) also responds to the reviewer of *Golgotha and Sheblimini!* who wrote that Hamann's language is more disguise (*Verkleidung*) than dress (*Bekleidung*); see *Allgemeine deutsche Bibliothek*, vol. 63 (1785), p. 33.
[2] In German there is an allusion to Zechariah 5:1–3: "Then I turned, and lifted up mine eyes, and looked, and behold a flying roll. And he said unto me, What seest thou? And I answered, I see a flying roll . . . Then said he unto me, This is the curse that goeth forth over the face of the whole earth: for every one that stealeth shall be cut off as on this side according to it; and every one that sweareth shall be cut off as on that side according to it." Luther has "flying letter" rather than "flying roll."
[3] Hamann's first book, *Socratic Memorabilia*, was dedicated to "Nobody, the Well Known."
[4] Horace, *Ars poetica* 143–4: "He intends to give not smoke from lightning but light from smoke."
[5] Horace, *Satire* 1.1.119–20: ". . . a satisfied guest . . . IT IS ENOUGH" (Hamann's capitals). The long "s" in *satur* ("satisfied") makes the word resemble *fatur*, "says."
[6] Elijah "requested for himself that he might die; and said, It is enough; now, O LORD, take away my life; for I am not better than my fathers." The Hebrew words mean "It is enough."

[The conclusion of the first version of *Disrobing and Transfiguration* follows.]

I intend to do my work of faith in a different way, my labor of love in a different way,[a] from the Berlin friends of Job,[b] [7] over whose foolishness and vanity the shuddering *manes* of the "departed Mendelssohn with a mouth as sweet as sugar"[8] are perhaps howling and gnashing! I want to address and placate them, not with bronze and incense but rather

       Farre pio et saliente mica: Horace[9]

---

[a] Isaiah 28:21. ["For the LORD shall rise up . . . that he may do his work, his strange work; and bring to pass his act, his strange act." Hamann's words echo more closely the phrasing in Luther's Bible. See also Hebrews 6:10: "For God is not unrighteous to forget your work and labour of love."]

[b] Job 42:8. ["Therefore take unto you now seven bullocks and seven rams, and go to my servant Job, and offer up for yourselves a burnt offering; and my servant Job shall pray for you: for him will I accept: lest I deal with you after your folly, in that ye have not spoken of me the thing which is right, like my servant Job."]

[7] Mendelssohn died on January 4, 1786, in the midst of a polemical dispute with Friedrich Heinrich Jacobi (1743–1819) over Lessing and pantheism. The controversy became heated when Karl Philipp Moritz wrote a few weeks after Mendelssohn's death that "Lavater's importunity dealt his life the first blow . . . Jacobi completed the work" (see Alexander Altmann, *Moses Mendelssohn: A Biographical Study* [1973], 744–6; Frederick C. Beiser, *The Fate of Reason* [1987], 92–108; and Gérard Vallée, *The Spinoza Conversations Between Lessing and Jacobi* [1988], 36–45). Jacobi and Johann Kaspar Lavatar (1741–1801), Swiss physiognomist and devout Protestant writer, were friends of Hamann.

[8] The quotation, perhaps in an obituary notice by one of the "Berlin friends" of Mendelssohn, has not been traced.

[9] Horace, *Ode* 3.23.20: "By pious grain and crackling salt," an offering made by those who could not afford more elaborate gifts.

however much as I am able, to contribute to clothing over[c] and transfiguring the convulsive gesturing on the façade of his book.[10] I also intend
some day to be so vain and foolish as to doubt whether the biographer or
asclepian editor[11] of the *Opera postuma* (which is still to come), with its
kabbala and algebra, will be in a much better position than I to solve the
mystery of the sacred desecrated city and the mystical ratios of the unity
of its name, both for the promised heavenly kingdom of religious power
and for the eternally wandering earthly and lunar kingdom of Judaism?
That is why my sickle should not intrude on their harvest. To the progeny
of blood and courage is due the vintage of his contributions to the reigning natural religion and the intensity of its strength. The single cluster of
the typical name and its two symbols on the battlements of the title are
enough for me.[12]

The spirit of observation and the spirit of prophecy are the wings of
human genius. All that is present belongs to the domain of the former; all
that is absent, the past and the future, belongs to the domain of the latter.
Philosophical genius expresses its power through striving, by means of
abstraction, to make what is present absent; it disrobes actual objects into
naked concepts and merely conceivable attributes, into pure appearances
and phenomena. Poetic genius expresses its power through transfiguring,
by means of fiction, visions of the absent past and future into present representations. Criticism and politics resist the usurpations of both powers
and ensure that they are balanced, through these positive forces and means
of observation and prophecy.

What is present is an indivisible, simple point in which the spirit of
observation is concentrated, and out of which it has its effect on the whole
sphere of the common faculty of knowledge. What is absent has a twofold dimension and is divisible into past and future, as is appropriate for
the likewise ambiguous spirit of prophecy, to which the divided instinct

---

[c] 2 Corinthians 5:2 and 4. ["For in this we groan, earnestly desiring to be clothed upon with our
house which is from heaven . . . For we that are in this tabernacle do groan, being burdened:
not for that we would be unclothed, but clothed upon, that mortality might be swallowed up of
life."]

[10] A reference to the title of Mendelssohn's work, *Jerusalem: On Religious Power and Judaism*
(1783).

[11] Socrates' last words were "Crito, we owe a cock to Asclepius; pay it, don't be remiss" (*Phaedo*,
118a). The editor of Mendelssohn's posthumous works is therefore in the position of Crito.

[12] Jerusalem is a "typical" name because typologically it is both an earthly city (for Hamann, Berlin)
and a heavenly city. The two symbols are presumably "Religious Power" and "Judaism."

(it was divided recently in the grey twilight of the seventh *Morgenstunde*, pp. 120–32)[13] of our faculty of approbation – – –

> laudator temporis acti
> se puero – – – – –

and faculty of desire – – – *avidusque futuri* (Horace, *ad Pisones*, 170–1) also seems to refer.[14]

Since the sum of the present is infinitely small as against the manifold aggregate of the absent, and since the spirit of prophecy is infinitely superior to the simple spirit of observation, it therefore follows that our faculty of knowledge depends on the many-headed modifications of the inmost, darkest, and deepest instincts of approbation and desire, to which it must be subject.

The past of the sacred desecrated city is now a dead certainty, and its renewed rejuvenated future no longer seemed to the Jewish philosopher to be a philosophical question which would still be in need of a critical and political discussion. Its name is accordingly an undeniable object for the spirit of prophecy; consequently the historical and prophetic material for the true knowledge[15] of this absent city can be sought, found, and derived nowhere else but in and from the oldest documents and genuine relics of Judaism, where the entire past of its history and most glorious future of its palingenesis[16] through the spirit of prophecy "in living color and shape is comprehended in one little picture,"[d] which can be known, interpreted, and understood only through that spirit. In these fixed prophetic

---

[d] Luther, in the preface to the Psalter. [See *Luther's Works* (American Edition), vol. XXXV, p. 256.]

[13] In chap. 7 of *Morgenstunden* (1785; "Morning hours"), Mendelssohn argued that the common division of the faculty of the soul into a faculty of knowledge and a faculty of desire was insufficient and posited an additional faculty of approbation. The modern critical edition of *Morgenstunden* is found in Mendelssohn's *Gesammelte Schriften* (Jubiläumsausgabe), vol. III, part 2; pp. 61–6 correspond to the pages Hamann cites from the first edition.

[14] Horace, *Ars poetica* (also known as the epistle "ad Pisones") 172–4: "praiser of times past when he was young" and "greedy of the future."

[15] Mendelssohn discusses the "material of knowledge" in chap. 7 of *Morgenstunden*; see *Gesammelte Schriften* (Jubiläumsausgabe), vol. III, part 2, pp. 62–3.

[16] Palingenesis, one of the speculative theories of Charles Bonnet (1720–93), held that periodic catastrophes forced all life to evolve up the Great Chain of Being. Lavater had translated Bonnet's *La Palingénésie philosophique* in 1769 and in the dedicatory epistle challenged Mendelssohn to refute the work or convert to Christianity.

and apocalyptic words of Hebrew literature, one has a "fine, bright, pure mirror"[17] whose ricocheting reflection effusively transfigures and makes present the darkness of the twofold absence for the spirit of observation, whose foolish senses are strengthened and armed with the weapons of prophecy for the manifold views into the destroyed and promised Jerusalem.

Through such a telescope of historic and prophetic foreknowledge,[18] an exemplary ideal from a thick cedar grove would have laughed at the spirit of observation, as material for a work, before which the name of the holy city would have shone as *cornuta Moysi facies*[e] or the crown of gold upon the tiara of Aaron, an ornament of honor, a costly work, the desires of the eyes, goodly and beautiful;[f] – it would have moved like the creative spirit of the Godhead over the pregnant element of the sea,[19] which from the double forces of the past *Was!* and the future *Become!* was predestined, prepared, and warmed into an incorruptible, higher, new being!; – or it would have enticed and gathered, like a heavenly cluck,[20] the chicks of their religious and ritual power under the shadow of its shimmering wings of a dove.[g] Before such a work the name Jerusalem would have stood between the two mock suns,[21] as the only right source of light, and like the sun it would have poured forth with calm rays the most beneficent and diverse effects over this planet and its satellite.

The Jewish philosopher, however, was concerned only with a formula of knowledge, by which he sought to disclose and communicate, on the one hand, the reluctance and disapprobation of his soul toward the present jealous image[h] of religious power and, on the other, the strength, the feast

---

[e] Exodus 34. ["The horned face of Moses," the Vulgate translation of Exodus 34:30.]
[f] Ecclesiasticus 45. [Verse 12: "He set a crown of gold upon the mitre, wherein was engraved Holiness, an ornament of honour, a costly work, the desires of the eyes, goodly and beautiful."]
[g] Psalm 68:13. ["Yet shall ye be as the wings of a dove covered with silver, and her feathers with yellow gold"; the allusion is more exact in German.]
[h] Ezekiel 8:5. ["Behold northward at the gate of the altar this image of jealousy."]

[17] See *Luther's Works* (American Edition), vol. xxxv, p. 257.
[18] The first part of Mendelssohn's *Morgenstunden* constitutes the "Vorerkenntniss," literally "fore-knowledge," that is, what must be known or presupposed in advance.
[19] Genesis 1:2: "And the earth was without form, and void; and darkness was upon the face of the deep. And the Spirit of God moved upon the face of the waters."
[20] Matthew 23:37: "how often would I have gathered thy children together, even as a hen gathereth her chickens under her wings."
[21] The mock sun (or parhelion) frequently occurs in pairs on either side of the sun.

for the eyes, and the heart's pity[i] toward what is more nearly present to him, the horn of salvation[22] of his people of Israel. His faculty of knowledge thus took an opposite way of reaching the prefigured goal of his faculty of approbation and of desire. He imitated the giddy frenzy of his fathers, to whom a molten present calf[23] was extremely pleasing as an absent lawgiver and captain. He went out from the double present of religious power and Judaism, which lay before the open door of his senses, and wove, out of a distaff of ideas that was more acquired than inherited and out of manipulation, and thanks to an arbitrary fiction, a spanking new Jerusalem, without ever concerning himself with the past and future archetype, or making any inquiries about it. This vain organ of poetic modeling tempted his heart into denying and destroying divine credibility and positive truth formally with the cooperation of philosophical abstractions.

The self-creator and master builder of a present city of God (a city that is privative and nearest to him) once again lapsed into the two sins[j] of his fathers, despised the spirit of prophecy in the living waters of historical and prophetic truth, and hewed him out cisterns, broken cisterns, that had more holes than water. The form of his tree of knowledge[24] indeed had a Hebrew name for its root, but it was broken down into pure philosophical fibers, of which he hung the most impressive as the shield of his edifice; the remaining *disiecti membra poetae*[25] lie behind upon the face of the field in the portion of Jezreel.[k]

---

[i] Ezekiel 24:21. ["Behold, I will profane my sanctuary, the excellency of your strength, the desire of your eyes, and that which your soul pitieth."]

[j] Jeremiah 2:13. ["For my people have committed two evils; they have forsaken me the fountain of living waters, and hewed them out cisterns, broken cisterns, that can hold no water."]

[k] 2 Kings 9:37. ["And the carcase of Jezebel shall be as dung upon the face of the field in the portion of Jezreel."]

[22] The "horn of salvation" occurs in 2 Samuel 22:3, Psalm 18:2, and Luke 1:69. The "horn of his people" occurs in Psalm 148:14. The *Oxford English Dictionary* indicates that in such biblical uses "horn" is "an emblem of power and might; a means of defence or resistance; hence *horn of salvation* is used of God or Christ."

[23] Exodus 32:1–8.

[24] Mendelssohn, *Morgenstunden*, chap. 7: "We can . . . regard the knowledge of the soul under diverse considerations, either insofar as it is true or false, and this I call the material of knowledge; or insofar as it excites desire or reluctance, approbation or disapprobation in the soul, and this can be called the form of knowledge." See *Gesammelte Schriften* (Jubiläumsausgabe), vol. III, part 2, p. 62.

[25] Cf. Horace, Satire 1.4.62: "limbs of the dismembered poet."

The shrewd, attentive spirit of observation[1] of the Jewish philosopher must have been struck by the present collapse of Christendom and religious power; he must have been struck just as clearly by the physical influence of Judaism, which is growing and gaining the upper hand, not only in all the temporal and earthly hustle and bustle, temptations, and state projects for the *perpetuum mobile*[26] of the mint-lottery-factory-commerce-monopoly-stamp-uni- and re-form-asset- and stream-lining devastation, but also in the opinions, convictions, prejudices, and the philosophical-poetical, metaphysical-aesthetic *esprit* of these last days which are contrary to all the centuries since the Incarnation of the LORD but which most grossly contradict even themselves and are at variance with themselves, to the shame and disgrace, to the scorn and derision, of the *bon sens* of the only recently planted political toleration and the *bon ton* of hypocritical humanitarianism and freedom of thought, which has hitherto been announced and preached with the enormous loquacity of foreign evangelists and *chambellans du jour*.[27] They have no scruple about becoming even greater transgressors by tearing down their own articles *de convenance*[28] and systems of predetermined harmony than they were by erecting them. They would have nearly desecrated the religious partition of the old and new covenant and testament[m] and moved out of the way the holy boundary stone[29] of our historical and prophetic foreknowledge of faith. With just as much zealotry one would have happily humbled, for a wooden, burden-carrying beast of unbelief made for love, gulfs, and gaps, by a more than Ethiopian misunderstanding,[30] the SALOMON DU NORD[31]

---

[1]
> *Mire sagacem* falleret hospitem
> Discrimen obscurum, solutis
> Crinibus, ambiguoque vultu.
> Horace, Ode 2.5.22–4

["An exceedingly shrewd stranger, to his amazement, would fail to notice the difference that was obscured by his flowing hair and ambiguous face."]

[m] "*Ultima voluntas*, the jurists call it." Luther on the last words of David. [See "Treatise on the Last Words of David" in *Luther's Works* (American Edition), vol. xv, p. 270. The word translated as "testament" is *Seelrecht*, which "describes the provision one made for the salvation of his soul." Luther also calls it *ultima voluntas*, the last will.]

[26] "Perpetual motion."   [27] "Chamberlains of the day."
[28] "Of expediency" (or propriety, suitability).
[29] Deuteronomy 19:14: "Thou shalt not remove thy neighbour's landmark."
[30] In Acts 8:27–39, the Ethiopian eunuch does not at first understand the scripture which Philip read.
[31] "Solomon of the North," that is, Frederick the Great.

into a king of the Jews. They are now assiduous to set up walls against the contraband of superstition, to block the eyes of needles, at the cost of their lungs and rags, to shout down and oppress the easy testimonies of truth and peace through dazzling pretence and full-throated error.

Was it the magnetism of a "polluted friend"[32] and painted apologist of heathendom and Judaism or the *speciosa dehinc miracula*[33] of her critical chicaneries and political intrigues by which the Berlin Moses became so disorganized and disoriented that he thought of another name, and wrote another name, confounded an absent Jerusalem of the promised land with a foreign present Babylon, or like that great host of Syrians with horses and chariots imagined that he was in the city of Dothan besieged by them, and behold, they were in the midst of Samaria.[n]

The spirit of prophecy, which the circumcised philosopher seems formally to have renounced, does indeed permit itself, in its presumptuous apocalyptic language, some *quid pro quo* of dithyrambic license and barbaric *striblingines*,[o] [34] for the sake of which a smoothly unfolding, rather bland, and spinster-neat

> – – Cynthius aurem
> vellit et admonuit – –
> Virgil.[35]

In its spiritual dialect, the great city where our LORD was crucified is called Sodom and Egypt. The difference of language, however, is in the

---

[n] 2 Kings 6:13, 14, and 20. [In 2 Kings 6:13–20, the king of Syria sent "horses, and chariots, and a great host" (2 Kings 6:13) to capture Elisha in Dothan. The king's men surrounded the city; Elisha prayed, and God smote the men with blindness; Elisha then led them to Samaria.]

[o] *Stribligo, imparilitas* – "a versura scilicet et pravitate tortuosae orationis." Aulus Gellius, *Attic Nights*, Book 5, chap. 20. [Aulus Gellius, *Attic Nights* 5.20, "A solecism, which by Sinnius Capito and other men of his time was called in Latin *inparilitas*, or 'inequality,' the earlier Latin writers termed *stribligo*, evidently meaning the improper use of an inverted form of expression," tr. Rolfe (Loeb Classical Library). Hamann quotes the Latin for "improper use of an inverted form of expression."]

[32] In the preface to *Morgenstunden*, Mendelssohn wrote of his muse of philosophy, "Alas! she was in better years my truest companion, my only comfort in all the unpleasant circumstances of life; and now I had to flee from her on all paths, like a deadly enemy: or what is still harder, to shun her like a polluted friend who herself warns me to avoid all contact with her." See *Gesammelte Schriften* (Jubiläumsausgabe), vol. III, part 2, p. 3.

[33] Horace, *Ars poetica* 144: "the splendid marvels afterward." The lines follow just after the epigraph (see n. 4 above).

[34] The plural of *stribligo*, the Latin word for solecism (see fn. o above).

[35] Virgil, *Eclogue* 6.3–4: "the Cynthian god plucked my ear and gave a warning."

nature of things. Objects of a sensory clear present are related to objects of dark distance as the greater light which rules the day to the lesser light which rules the night;[36] as the eyesight of the eagle to the brightness of the sun,[37] so is the pale moonlight to the eye of the owl. And yet the coincidence and divergence of our judgments come into contact at a point which can be avoided by nothing other than the most exact parallelism of our concepts with their objects.

In my humble opinion the relative concept of religious power and the theory of this ἅπαξ λεγόμενον[38] or neologism[39] contains more δυσνόητά τινα[40] than St. Paul's speech on the veil of the woman because of the angels;[P] notwithstanding, the image of religious power seems to have been just as clear and present to the Jewish philosopher as a Jerusalem must have been present before his senses. Now if he had intended to mark and indicate the city which was actually present to him with the merely figurative name of a "still far-off" absent city, say by virtue of a rural euphemism, then the whole title of his book would stand like a Delphic tripod,[41] and all three limbs and *termini*[42] (Jerusalem: religious power: Judaism:) would be analogous and uniform objects of the present.

However, if Jerusalem is to retain the true signification of an absent city, then from out of the title a *centaurus biformis*[43] will grow, whose upper part belongs to the human faculty of knowledge; the four-footed lower part, however, belongs to the instincts of approbation and desire, by which at the same time we love and hate, are devoted to whom we love,

---

[P] 1 Corinthians 11:3–15. [In this passage Paul argues that women must cover their heads while praying or prophesying; an enigmatic reason is given at 1 Corinthians 11:10: "For this cause ought the woman to have power on her head because of the angels."]

[36] Genesis 1:16: "the greater light to rule the day, and the lesser light to rule the night."

[37] According to a traditional story, eagles were reared to look straight into the sun without blinking (see for example Pliny, *Natural History* 10.3.10). Owls are associated with Athena and thus with philosophers.

[38] Or "hapax legomenon," a word or phrase of which only one instance is recorded.

[39] "Neologism" refers not only to a newly coined word or phrase but may also allude to neology, the rationalist theology current in the midcentury Germany.

[40] 2 Peter 3:16: "some things hard to be understood."

[41] The Pythia, the priestess of Apollo at Delphi, was seated at the Delphic tripod when the oracle was to be consulted.

[42] The *termini* are the terms of the syllogism; the three terms of logic here correspond to the three legs of the prophetic tripod.

[43] "Biform centaur."

and despise whom we hate. Consequently, the double twofold or fourfold faculty of approbation and misapprobation, desire and loathing, would have to depend simply on the prophetic truth and knowledge of the past and future Jerusalem, as much in regard to the present religious power as to the present Judaism.

Is the author, however, to the detriment of his "easy gait, full of light, his systematic clarity and precision," supposed to have put forward with the diligence of the present city the mask of an absent city, without drawing the attention of the reader "anywhere and anytime"[44] to the reason and purpose for such an anomaly and exception from his circumcised lips and their purism? Is the departed Mendelssohn supposed to have been an Israelite indeed without guile,[45] rather than "an elegant writer, petty-minded, focused on secondary matters, and irritatingly obtuse,"[46] in keeping with the Jewish purse of holiness, the taste *du siècle*,[47] the horizon and meridian plane of his words and home? Is he supposed to have brought forward, before the brow of his Jerusalem, a masterpiece of deception[q] as a test of the later masterwork? Is it a finer or more gross self-deception, to confuse the absent with the present, or the subjective with the objective?

"If without a concept no object actually exists,"[48] why was the concept that was indispensable in every respect, the recognizable feature of a present or absent, destroyed or glorified, past or future Jerusalem withheld

---

[q] *Allgemeine Litteratur-Zeitung*, No. 7, p. 56. [Christian Gottfried Schütz reviewed Mendelssohn's *Morgenstunden* in the *Allgemeine Litteratur-Zeitung* ("General literary newspaper"), No. 7, January 1786. At the end of his discussion, Schütz included without attribution Kant's initial reaction to the work, which had been communicated to him in a letter in November 1785 (see Kant, *Correspondence*, tr. and ed. Arnulf Zweig [1999], 237–9). Hamann quotes from the beginning of Kant's opinion: "the worthy M[endelssohn]'s book must be regarded in the main as a masterpiece of the deception of our reason."]

[44] Mendelssohn, *Morgenstunden*, chap. 7; *Gesammelte Schriften* (Jubiläumsausgabe), vol. III, part 2, p. 63.

[45] John 1:47: "Jesus saw Nathanael coming to him, and saith of him, Behold an Israelite indeed, in whom is no guile!"

[46] Adapts a sentence from a letter to Jacobi from Lavater; see *Aus F. H. Jacobi's Nachlass*, ed. Rudolf Zoeppritz (1869), vol. I, p. 79. Jacobi quoted Lavater's sentence in a letter to Hamann of May 12, 1786; see *Briefe*, vol. VI, p. 385.

[47] A taste "[characteristic] of the century."

[48] Mendelssohn, *Morgenstunden*, chap. 16, "Something is knowable only if it is known, a feature exists only if it is noticed, without a concept no object actually exists." Quoted in Kant's letter (*Correspondence*, tr. and ed. Arnulf Zweig [1999], 238). See *Gesammelte Schriften* (Jubiläumsausgabe), vol. III, part 2, p. 145.

from the reader? In this absence of a clear and distinct concept (an absence which, alas, is now irreparable by the author himself) which he may have owed because perhaps he did not have a concept of the true object itself, lies the πρῶτον ψεῦδος[49] or the main mask[50] of the entire drama which he staged of the deception of our reason. If one were able to fish out the deceptive light of a decayed, glowing wood from a swamp and transfer it into a dry light, it would be an "easy thing" to explain the totality of the illusion in its natural condition according to the scholastic rabbi's own propositions, to solve the misunderstanding of his suffering lover, rival, and successor, to liberate the awakened senses of the universal German readers from the snares laid for their understanding by the ambiguous letter, and to represent the "conquered" or deviously acquired approval of a lunatic somnambulist[51] in his ridiculous-sad build and nakedness. For the sake of brevity I refer to his sixth morning hour, where he derives this spiritual sickness from the confusion of a subjective sequence of ideas with an objective sequence, with all the more credibility and plausibility because he seems to have experienced a similar condition in connection with the muse of his elegant scribbling.

In the first slumber (p. 6), he gave to an explanation, which as he himself must admit was not incorrect, a bill of divorcement merely because it did not seem to him to be fruitful.[52] His faculty of approbation, elicited by *aqua fortis*,[53] he himself explains (p. 125) as a *double emploi*[54] of political arithmetic and recognizes the artificially created two as natural expressions of one and the same positive power.

[49] The "first falsehood," that is, the initial false premise invalidating the later deductions; the term derives from Aristotle's *Prior Analytics* 2.18 (66a).
[50] Perhaps referring to the chief actor or protagonist of a Greek drama.
[51] In chap. 6 of *Morgenstunden*, Mendelssohn discusses the sickness of sleepwalking; see *Gesammelte Schriften* (Jubiläumsausgabe), vol. III, part 2, p. 52.
[52] In chap. 1 of *Morgenstunden*, Mendelssohn writes, "Even if this explanation is not incorrect, nevertheless it does not seem to be fruitful." See *Gesammelte Schriften* (Jubiläumsausgabe), vol. III, part 2, p. 10.
[53] *Aqua fortis* in German is *Scheidewasser*, "divorce water," so-called because alchemists used it to separate one component of an alloy from another.
[54] Either "useless repetition" (applied to a word) or "duplication of an entry" (applied to bookkeeping). Hamann is referring to Mendelssohn's admission in chap. 7 of the *Morgenstunden* that "Both of them, the faculty of knowledge as well as the faculty of approbation are . . . expressions of one and the same power of the soul." See *Gesammelte Schriften* (Jubiläumsausgabe), vol. III, part 2, p. 63.

I do not need to draw up a bill of divorcement for Jewish hard-heartedness[r] toward my aforegiven explanation of presence and absence, still less to prefer the pregnant to the legitimate. But here I must simply imitate the pseudo-models of my evening hours of long boredom and my partly flying, partly diving letter-posting: despite the division on my own authority of the intellectual universe into presence and absence, I do not pretend that these predicates are anything more than subjective conditions by which no actual duplication of the objects themselves is substantiated, but rather merely a relationship of the diverse views and sides of one and the same thing to the measure of the inward man which corresponds to them, to his negative, variable, finite power which is incapable of any omnipresence because this is the exclusive property of a positive immeasurability.

Likewise the spirits of observation and of prophecy are expressions of a single positive power which cannot be divorced by their nature but only in thoughts and for the use of thoughts; they in fact mutually presuppose themselves, refer to each other, and have effects in common. Hence when I compared the present with an indivisible point, the duplication of its power and its close connection with the past, as effect, and with the future, as cause, are not at all cancelled. Presence and absence can be subjective predicates of one and the same object as well as . . .[55]

Like God, great and unknown to us,[s] is the name of this king; strange,[t] like those of his messengers,[56] is the name of his city. Its history and visage unite all the merely conceivable ideas of our faculty of knowledge, all the ruling ideas that belong to it, for a sensory image of a godly state; all possible impressions and representations which seem worthy or unworthy of our applause and which cannot be indifferent either to the faculty of approbation or of disapprobation; all present and absent objects of greedy desire or loathing aversion; everything wherein heaven, earth, and hell, life and death, blessing and curse, deficiency and redundancy, bliss and

---

[r] Mark 10:[4]–5. ["And they said, Moses suffered to write a bill of divorcement, and to put her away. And Jesus answered and said unto them, For the hardness of your heart he wrote you this precept."]

[s] Job 36:26. ["Behold, God is great, and we know him not."]

[t] Judges 13:18. ["And the angel of the LORD said unto him, Why askest thou thus after my name, seeing it is secret?" Luther has "strange" for "secret."]

[55] The manuscript is discontinuous here.   [56] "Angel" is Greek for messenger.

misery, letter and spirit, being and seeming are set against each other, attract each other, and repel. In short, Jerusalem is an originary riddle of contradiction, whose seven inward and outward seals[57] no finite power, without the courage of a lion and the patience of a lamb, is in a position to open.

Prophecy is in the lips of the king;[u] prophecy lies in the name of his city, which was, will be, exists everywhere and yet nowhere.[58] That which from the beginning of the world no Michelangelo, no Raphael has beheld with spiritual eyes; no virtuoso David nor his choir-leader has heard; no Plato, nor Leviathan,[59] no Attic Cyropedist,[60] foreign quietist nor Machiavellist has had the heart, through abstraction and fiction, to make into a princely and stately model of light and darkness, certainly not in actuality, but possibly, conceivably, perceptibly, knowably and representably; all this and wildly more is already prepared and adorned to come down,[v] and the earnest expecting creature, who groans to become free from the bondage of corruption and waits for the redemption of its body, to manifest the glory of adult adoption.[w]

Such an ambiguous name for a concept that has not yet been determined and for an object that is doubly absent was both sufficiently far-reaching and a comfortable, nimble, fruitful instrument and mediating link for the Jewish philosopher, to profiteer from the treasury of his faculty of knowledge and spirit of observation then and there on the present situation of Christianity and Judaism without betraying either, and to release in a single word and communicate in a breath the divided faculties of approbation and desire which belong to his ruling taste and good will.

---

[u] Proverbs 16:10. ["A divine sentence is in the lips of the king."]
[v] Revelation 21:2. ["And I John saw the holy city, new Jerusalem, coming down from God out of heaven, prepared as a bride adorned for her husband."]
[w] Romans 8:19–23. ["For the earnest expectation of the creature waiteth for the manifestation of the sons of God. For the creature was made subject to vanity, not willingly, but by reason of him who hath subjected the same in hope, Because the creature itself also shall be delivered from the bondage of corruption into the glorious liberty of the children of God. For we know that the whole creation groaneth and travaileth in pain together until now. And not only they, but ourselves also, which have the firstfruits of the Spirit, even we ourselves groan within ourselves, waiting for the adoption, to wit, the redemption of our body."]

[57] Revelation 5–8.
[58] Cf. the lesser doxology: "as it was in the beginning, is now, and ever shall be, world without end."
[59] Thomas Hobbes, perhaps.
[60] Xenophon, author of *Cyropedia* ("The education of Cyrus").

"Pharaoh shall lift up thine head."[x] With this ambiguous oracle the patriarch Joseph prophesied to his two dreaming fellow state prisoners unlike fates: to one of them, reinstatement into his former office, which he lost; to the other, the most shameful death sentence. Likewise, with a similar spirit of prophecy, *Jerusalem, or on Christianity and Judaism!* was able to announce to the former a horror of waste and ruin and to the latter a rising up of David's promises and their fulfillment in his seed and name, according to the letter of the flesh and in the spirit of philosophical circumcision.

Such a mask for the title would be even finer and more artful than the facial expressions of the angel Gabriel, who appeared to the prophet at Shushan in the palace, by the river of Ulai;[61] the angel "would have been happy to say clearly" the highest and greatest bit of religious power, "but he acted as if he misspoke the word deliberately, for from great unwillingness he might not name it correctly as 'mass' but rather spoke 'mauzim.'"[y]

Jerusalem was inhabited again in her own place, even in Jerusalem;[z] became a cup of trembling, a burdensome stone, a fiery oven among the wood, a torch of fire in a sheaf,[62] a Babel of religious power; meanwhile Judaism put off the garment of its mourning and affliction, cast about

---

[x] Genesis 40:13 and 19. ["Yet within three days shall Pharaoh lift up thine head, and restore thee unto thy place" and "Yet within three days shall Pharaoh lift up thy head from off thee, and shall hang thee on a tree." The two statements are taken from Joseph's interpretation of the dreams of the Pharaoh's chief butler and chief baker, respectively, who were imprisoned with Joseph.]

[y] Luther's preface to the prophet Daniel and his interpretation of chapter 11, verse 38. [Daniel 11:38: "But in his estate shall he honour the God of forces." In his German version, Luther does not translate "of forces" but rather transliterates the Hebrew word (*mäusim* in the German transliteration). Luther does this in order to make a pun. "And marvellously with the word *Mäusim* the angel touches the great and highest bit, the worst abomination of the papacy, the mass; he would happily say *His God of the mass*, and he acts as though he deliberately misspeaks the word, *mass*, for from great unwillingness he may not name it correctly, *mass*, but rather speaks *Mäusim*." See Luther's *Werke* (Weimar Ausgabe), vol. XI, part 2, pp. 72–5. (The passage is not translated in the American Edition of Luther's works.)]

[z] Zechariah 12:2, 3, and 6. ["Behold, I will make Jerusalem a cup of trembling unto all the people round about,when they shall be in the siege both against Judah and against Jerusalem. And in that day will I make Jerusalem a burdensome stone for all people: all that burden themselves with it shall be cut in pieces, though all the people of the earth be gathered together against it . . . Jerusalem shall be inhabited again in her own place, even in Jerusalem."]

[61] Daniel 8:2: "And I saw in a vision; and it came to pass, when I saw, that I was at Shushan in the palace, which is in the province of Elam; and I saw in a vision, and I was by the river of Ulai."

[62] Zechariah 12:2: "Behold, I will make Jerusalem a cup of trembling"; Zechariah 12:3: "And in that day will I make Jerusalem a burdensome stone"; Zechariah 12:6: "I make the governors of Judah like an hearth of fire among the wood, and like a torch of fire in a sheaf."

it a double garment of the righteousness that comes from God, and set a glorious diadem of the Everlasting on its head; and its name shall be called the peace of righteousness, the glory of God's worship.[aa]

Perhaps that is why the name of a destroyed city became a type of the despotic system, broken into pieces, with whose steadfast testimony "the last Berlin Wolffian"[bb] concluded the course of his praiseworthy authorship, and by means of which a memorial was erected in advance, to the offense and annoyance of some "sensible fellow citizens and foreigners"[63] to whom as to the Tirshatha[64] it went out in its nightly circuit by the gate of the valley and to the dung port and on to the gate of the fountain and to the king's pool, where "there was no place for the beast that was under him to pass."[cc] Such rubble of systematic ruins and a haggard grey beard would be grounded in the typical meaning of the title.

These are sheer proofs of the indissoluble bond between the spirit of observation and the spirit of prophecy. Our knowledge is indeed in part, and our prophesying in part;[dd] united, however, it is a triple cord that is not quickly broken. If one falls, the other will lift up his fellow; if the two lie together, then they have heat.[ee] What would all knowledge of the present be without a divine remembrance of the past, and without an

---

[aa] Baruch 5:1–4. ["Put off, O Jerusalem, the garment of thy mourning and affliction, and put on the comeliness of the glory that cometh from God for ever. Cast about thee a double garment of the righteousness which cometh from God; and set a diadem on thine head of the glory of the Everlasting. For God will shew thy brightness unto every country under heaven. For thy name shall be called of God for ever, The peace of righteousness, and The glory of God's worship."]

[bb] Strabo's *Wöchentliche Nachrichten*, vol. XIV, part 12, p. 94. [Anton Friedrich Büsching (1724– 93) edited the *Wöchentliche Nachrichten von neuen Landcharten, geographischen, statistischen und historischen Büchern und Schriften* ("Weekly notices of new maps, geographical, statistical, and historical books and writings"). The specified issue discusses Mendelssohn and reports on a proposed memorial; the author remarks, "I would however prefer to call it a memorial for the last Berlin Wolffians." Wolffians are followers of the German philosopher Christian Wolff (1679– 1754). Hamann calls Büsching "Strabo" after the ancient geographer in an allusion to the title of Büsching's periodical.]

[cc] Nehemiah 2:13–14. ["And I went out by night by the gate of the valley, even before the dragon well, and to the dung port, and viewed the walls of Jerusalem, which were broken down, and the gates thereof were consumed with fire. Then I went on to the gate of the fountain, and to the king's pool: but there was no place for the beast that was under me to pass."]

[dd] 1 Corinthians 13:9. ["For we know in part, and we prophesy in part."]

[ee] Ecclesiastes 4:[9]–12. ["Two are better than one . . . if they fall, the one will lift up his fellow: but woe to him that is alone when he falleth; for he hath not another to help him up. Again, if two lie together, then they have heat: but how can one be warm alone? And if one prevail against him, two shall withstand him; and a threefold cord is not quickly broken."]

[63] On p. 94 of the *Wöchentliche Nachrichten*: "However, that non-Jews praise him [Mendelssohn] in an exaggerated way is repugnant to sensible Berliners and foreigners."

[64] Nehemiah 8:9: "And Nehemiah, which is the Tirshatha"; modern translations give "governor" for "Tirshatha."

even more fortunate intimation of the future, as Socrates owed to his daemon?[65] What would the spirit of observation be without the spirit of prophecy and its guiding threads of the past and future? It rains its gifts on the rebellious also,[ff] that the Lord might nonetheless be and dwell among them *in cognito* without their knowledge and will. However much, therefore, that the Jewish philosopher intended to renounce the spirit of prophecy, nonetheless the small troop staked out on the title, the little light of the faith of his fathers hung at the frontispiece of his book (a symbol and mark that the spirit of prophecy has not abandoned him, but rather accompanied him in a pillar of an invisible cloud and a pillar of fire),[66] seemed useful to him in case of emergency, in order to orient the weather-cock of philosophical speculation and to point in the direction of the wind.

Even the golden cup of Babylon that made all the earth drunken is in the LORD's hand.[gg] From his face that eager lying spirit went out in the mouth of all Ahab's prophets[hh] and of the woman Jezebel which calls herself a prophetess.[ii] The last pious king, for whom all Judah and Jerusalem mourned, fell and died because he did not hearken unto the words of Necho from the mouth of God.[jj] A spirit of prophecy still fills with wisdom the Bezaleels and Aholiabs,[kk] Nicolaitanes and Balaamites,[67]

[ff] Ψ 68:18. ["Thou hast received gifts for men; yea, for the rebellious also, that the LORD God might dwell among them." "Ψ" abbreviates Ψαλμοί, Psalms.]

[gg] Jeremiah 51:7. ["Babylon hath been a golden cup in the LORD's hand, that made all the earth drunken."]

[hh] 2 Chronicles 18:21. ["And he said, I will go out, and be a lying spirit in the mouth of all his [Ahab's] prophets."]

[ii] Revelation 2:20. ["Thou sufferest that woman Jezebel, which calleth herself a prophetess, to teach and to seduce my servants to commit fornication, and to eat things sacrificed unto idols."]

[jj] 2 Chronicles 35:22 and 24. [2 Chronicles 35:22–4: "Nevertheless Josiah would not turn his face from him, but disguised himself, that he might fight with him, and hearkened not unto the words of Necho from the mouth of God, and came to fight in the valley of Megiddo. And the archers shot at king Josiah; and the king said to his servants, Have me away; for I am sore wounded. His servants therefore took him out of that chariot, and put him in the second chariot that he had; and they brought him to Jerusalem, and he died, and was buried in one of the sepulchres of his fathers. And all Judah and Jerusalem mourned for Josiah."]

[kk] Exodus 35 and 36. [See, for instance, Exodus 35:35: Bezaleel and Aholiab "hath he filled with wisdom of heart, to work all manner of work, of the engraver, and of the cunning workman, and of the embroiderer, in blue, and in purple, in scarlet, and in fine linen, and of the weaver, even of them that do any work, and of those that devise cunning work."]

[65] Socrates' daemon was a voice which forbade him from undertaking certain future courses of action, for example becoming a politician (see Plato, *Apology* 32c–d).

[66] Numbers 14:14: "thou goest before them, by day time in a pillar of a cloud, and in a pillar of fire by night."

[67] Two sects, mentioned in Revelation 2:6 and 14–15. The former is also a reference to Friedrich Nicolai (1733–1811), writer and bookseller of the Berlin Enlightenment.

letter-men and writing-men of all times, to work all manner of work, of the engraver, and of the cunning workman, and of the embroiderer. The universal Germany has them to thank for the *prototype inspirateur, le mannequin précieux*[ll] [68] of the most recent criticism and politics.

Hence with the hecatombs of our fashionable writers that which the preacher[mm] prophesied of the sacrifice of fools is fulfilled: that they consider not that they do evil. They understand neither what they say nor whereof they affirm[nn] and so have the least faith in it themselves. They know some things better than can be told them, without belief, and they believe, though without fear and trembling,[oo] infinitely more than they themselves know. They flattered him with their mouth and lied unto him with their tongue.[pp] In their dogmatism is idle cursing and contradiction.[qq] They speak vanity with a double heart, and say, With our tongue will we prevail; our lips are our own: who is lord over us?[rr] Public taste depends on the illusions of our thirst for power, and the people are served thereby.[ss] – How can they who do not understand not[69] believe what they themselves write, how can they be capable of distinguishing, testing, and even of orienting the writings of their better brethren? Hence they are, even in the universal German bedlam and lazaret, so many invalids, afflicted with a variety of scourges and torments, possessed men, lunatic, struck by fits – and a good part are sleeping,

---

[ll] *Le Tableau de Paris*, vol. II, p. 213. [Louis-Sébastien Mercier (1740–1814) wrote *Le Tableau de Paris* (1781–9), sketches of Parisian life. In chap. 173, devoted to fashion, he writes: "The celebrated dummy, the fastidious mannequin, got up in the newest fashions, in a word the *inspirational prototype* crosses from Paris to London every month, and from there goes spreading its graces in all of Europe." See Mercier, *Le Tableau de Paris*, ed. Bonnet (1994), vol. I, pp. 409–10.]

[mm] Ecclesiastes 5:1. ["Be more ready to hear, than to give the sacrifice of fools: for they consider not that they do evil." The preacher is the name for Solomon as the speaker of Ecclesiastes.]

[nn] 1 Timothy 1:7. ["Understanding neither what they say, nor whereof they affirm."]

[oo] James 2:19, Philippians 2:12. [James 2:19: "the devils also believe, and tremble"; Philippians 2:12: "work out your own salvation with fear and trembling."]

[pp] Ψ 78:36. ["They did flatter him with their mouth, and they lied unto him with their tongues."]

[qq] Ψ 59:12. ["For the sin of their mouth and the words of their lips let them even be taken in their pride: and for cursing and lying which they speak."]

[rr] Ψ 12:2 and 4. [Psalm 12:2–4: "They speak vanity every one with his neighbour: with flattering lips and with a double heart do they speak. The LORD shall cut off all flattering lips, and the tongue that speaketh proud things: Who have said, With our tongue will we prevail; our lips are our own: who is lord over us?"]

[ss] Jeremiah 5:31. ["The prophets prophesy falsely, and the priests bear rule by their means; and my people love to have it so: and what will ye do in the end thereof?"]

[68] "The inspirational prototype, the fastidious mannequin."

[69] Reading *nicht* ("not") with Nadler, rather than *noch* ("yet, still").

like the blind heads of Homer,[70] with open eyes, as living memorials and harbingers which appear through their very existence to announce to us

Saeculum Pyrrhae nova monstra questae
Horace, Ode 1.2.6[71]

the epoch of a new eon which stands before the door and knocks[72] –

O you physiognomic seer with the angelically pure mouth![73] Even your cherub's eye has a craving to see miracles which everyone whose face is not covered with wings[74] sees before and around him always. Gird your loins, like a man, and declare unto me.[75] Is nature not the prime miracle by which alone the experience of metaphysical meteors[76] is made possible? Is reason not the prime miracle on which rests all belief in the miracles of extraordinary phenomena and rare exceptions of still stranger rules? Are not prophecy and chop-logic the universal magnetism of all our intellectual inertia and motive force within the entrails and brain of our small world? Are there no longer Sauls among the prophets?[tt] prophesying Caiaphases among the high priests?[uu] no *Pontii Pilati*[77] who despite their skepticism[vv] become the closest witnesses of truth? Are your blasphemers which say they are Jews, and are not, but rather liars from the synagogue of Satan,[78] no miracle-workers like

---

[tt] 1 Samuel 10:11 and 12; 1 Samuel 19:24. [The sentence "Is Saul also among the prophets?" occurs in the passages Hamann cites.]

[uu] John 11:51. ["Being high priest that year, he [Caiaphas] prophesied that Jesus should die for that nation."]

[vv] John 18:38. ["Pilate saith unto him, What is truth?"; chap. 1 of Mendelssohn's *Morgenstunden* is entitled "What is truth?"]

[70] Given Hamann's reference to a "universal" German bedlam, the blind heads of Homer may refer to the cover of the Enlightenment journal *Allgemeine deutsche Bibliothek* ("Universal German library").

[71] Horace, Ode 1.2.6: "The age of Pyrrha, who bewailed strange marvels."

[72] Revelation 3:20: "Behold, I stand at the door, and knock."

[73] Lavater founded a new pseudo-science of physiognomy.

[74] Cf. Isaiah 6:2: "Above it stood the seraphims: each one had six wings; with twain he covered his face."

[75] Job 40:7: "Gird up thy loins now like a man: I will demand of thee, and declare thou unto me."

[76] In Hamann's time, the word "meteor" had a broader signification than it does today; it included a range of atmospheric lights, including the *ignis fatuus*.

[77] Latin plural of "Pontius Pilatus."

[78] Revelation 3:9: "I will make them of the synagogue of Satan, which say they are Jews, and are not, but do lie"; cf. Revelation 2:9.

Simon,[ww] the Samaritan, and Elymas,[xx] the Paphian, no religious legates who are themselves transfigured into the heroes of their Ethiopian fables, who with the moonlight of their critical *principes de convenance*[79] and political love of truth set themselves up as saviors of the human race, and who fool the universal German writers and readers with their own philosophical enlightenment? Did these rivals of the Egyptian adepts and energumens[80] not apuleize[81] their guest into a Plutarch *loup-garou*,[82] whose *os rotundum*, with the worst dupe [*Duppe*] and the most naive *ingenium Graium*[83] of a perpetual child with might and main,[84] driveled out again the porridge spoon-fed and stuffed into him by his Boeotian[85] wet-nurse and attendant, like that painted[86] Homer?[87]

O you physiognomic seer with covered face! Companion in tribulation, and in the kingdom and patience of JESUS CHRIST![88] HE knows thy countless works, and the last to be more than the first.[89] HE

---

ww Acts 8:9. ["But there was a certain man, called Simon, which beforetime in the same city used sorcery, and bewitched the people of Samaria."]

xx Acts 13. [Verses 6–8: "And when they had gone through the isle unto Paphos, they found a certain sorcerer, a false prophet, a Jew, whose name was Bar-jesus: Which was with the deputy of the country, Sergius Paulus, a prudent man; who called for Barnabas and Saul, and desired to hear the word of God. But Elymas the sorcerer (for so is his name by interpretation) withstood them, seeking to turn away the deputy from the faith."]

79 "Principles of expediency" (or propriety, suitability).

80 An "adept" refers to someone who has mastered a secret art; an "energumen" is one who is possessed by a devil, or a fanatical adherent. With the epithet "Egyptian," Hamann generally has in mind contemporary heterodox theologians, like Johann August Starck (1741–1816), who denied Christ's divinity. For Hamann, such writers were adherents of gnosticism and as such worshippers of the Egyptian goddess Isis.

81 "Apuleize" may mean "metamorphosize"; the name is derived from Apuleius, the author of the *Metamorphoses* (more commonly known as the Golden Ass), in which the hero Lucius is transformed into an ass and finally restored by the Egyptian goddess Isis.

82 In the French translation of Plutarch's life of Alcibiades by Jacques Amyot (1559), Timon is "surnamed the Misanthrope, which is to say the Loup-Garou."

83 *Os rotundum* means "round mouth" (or "well-rounded utterance"), and *ingenium Graium* means "Greek genius"; both echo Horace, *Ars poetica* 323.

84 An Egyptian priest told Solon that "you Greeks are always children" (Plato, *Timaeus* 22b).

85 Boeotian is proverbial for dull or dimwitted; also, Plutarch, author of "On Isis and Osiris," was Boeotian.

86 In Hellenistic times, "the painter Galaton depicted Homer being sick, with the other poets drawing upon his vomit" (Aelian, *Historical Miscellany* 13.22, tr. Wilson, Loeb Classical Library).

87 The sentence is difficult. A conjectural interpretation runs: "You modern theologians transformed Christ into a misanthrope spewing dull Greek platitudes."

88 Revelation 1:9: "I John, who also am your brother, and companion in tribulation, and in the kingdom and patience of Jesus Christ."

89 Revelation 2:19: "I know thy works, and charity, and service, and faith, and thy patience, and thy works; and the last to be more than the first."

knows still the more excellent way[90] of your love, the hyperboles of your arduous Martha's labor[91] and all the *pia desideria*[92] of your Thomas faith[93] – –

Rather hear attentively the noise of his voice, and that unutterable sound that goes out of his mouth.[94] HE scolds the angels of Momus,[95] who buffet his elect. HE will take away the unclean garments from them, and clothe them with festive garments, and set a fair mitre upon their head.[yy] Lamps despised[zz] in the thought of them that rejoice in pride[aaa] are the little ones; among their angels who do always stand before the face of the Father which is in heaven[96] he will give you places to walk among.[97] His day will be like refiner's fire and fullers' soap[98] –

Have pity upon me, have pity upon me, O ye my friends; for the hand of God hath touched me.[99] Without your good deed and its favor my life would be like that of Job and Lazarus. The hope of the reunion in the true country of all strangers and pilgrims[100] and palmers[101] may be our farewell and our mutual comfort. Death needs neither shield nor reward.[102] You household gods, do not humble me through foolishness and vanity, and exalt no dead man into an idol. Take no thought to add a cubit

---

[yy] Zechariah 3:[3–]5 and 7. ["Now Joshua was clothed with filthy garments, and stood before the angel. And he answered and spake unto those that stood before him, saying, Take away the filthy garments from him . . . And I said, Let them set a fair mitre upon his head. So they set a fair mitre upon his head, and clothed him with garments."]

[zz] Job 12:5. ["A lamp despised in the thought of him that is at ease."]

[aaa] Zephaniah 3:11. ["I will take away out of the midst of thee them that rejoice in thy pride."]

[90] 1 Corinthians 12:31: "yet shew I unto you a more excellent way."

[91] Luke 10:38–42. Martha became a symbol of the active Christian life (and Mary of the contemplative life).

[92] "Pious desires," the title of a major work of German pietism (by Philipp Jakob Spener, 1675).

[93] The story of doubting Thomas is related in John 20:24–9.

[94] Job 37:2: "Hear attentively the noise of his voice, and the sound that goeth out of his mouth."

[95] The Greek god of censure and ridicule.

[96] Matthew 18:10: "Take heed that ye despise not one of these little ones; for I say unto you, That in heaven their angels do always behold the face of my Father which is in heaven."

[97] Zechariah 3:7: "I will give thee places to walk among these that stand by."

[98] Malachi 3:2: "But who may abide the day of his coming? and who shall stand when he appeareth? for he is like a refiner's fire, and like fullers' soap."

[99] Job 19:21: "Have pity upon me, have pity upon me, O ye my friends; for the hand of God hath touched me."

[100] Hebrews 11:13–14: "they were strangers and pilgrims on the earth . . . they seek a country."

[101] "An itinerant monk travelling from shrine to shrine under a perpetual vow of poverty" (*Oxford English Dictionary*).

[102] Genesis 15:1: "the word of the LORD came unto Abram in a vision, saying, Fear not, Abram: I am thy shield, and thy exceeding great reward."

either to me or to my stature. The measure of my "greatness"[103] is not a giant's nor an angel's, a hand no broader than a common human cubit. So that the world is not pillaged to dress up and transfigure a corrupt sinner with the nimbus of a "holy man," it would be better if you did not make moustaches in my life,[104] as long as I can still laugh along. However, I will myself disrobe, and spread forth my hands as he that swims spreads forth his hands to swim,[bbb] in order to swim across the soft-moving waters of oblivion or go under.

Do not worry my muse on her silver wedding anniversary and do not say: Why was this garbage made?[ccc] Even this last dalliance is torture.[ddd] I have stinted nothing in robing the exposed nakedness and in transfiguring the sacred desecrated title. If I forget you again Jerusalem, let all that my right hand has written be forgotten. Let my pen cleave to this thumb if I prefer not Jerusalem above my chief joy. I too sit and weep by the rivers of Babylon and hang this flying letter upon the willows,[105] *uvida vestimenta*,[106] the last breath of different trysts with their *stridenti stipula*[107]

> Carmina tum melius, cum venerit IPSE, canemus.
> Virgil, *Eclogues* 3.27 and 9.67[108]

[bbb] Isaiah 25:11. ["And he shall spread forth his hands in the midst of them, as he that swimmeth spreadeth forth his hands to swim: and he shall bring down their pride together with the spoils of their hands."]

[ccc] Mark 14:4. ["Why was this waste of the ointment made?"]

[ddd] Horace, *Epistle* 2.2.124. ["He will give the appearance of play, but he will be torturing himself."]

[103] In *Wider Mendelssohn's Beschuldigungen in dessen Schreiben an die Freunde Lessings* (1786; "Against Mendelssohn's accusations in his writing *To the Friends of Lessing*"), Jacobi had written that he considered Hamann to be a "great and holy man." See Heinrich Scholz, ed., *Die Hauptschriften zum Pantheismusstreit zwischen Jacobi und Mendelssohn* (1916), 355–6.

[104] As children draw moustaches on official images (Nadler suggests).

[105] Psalm 137:1–2, 5–6: "By the rivers of Babylon, there we sat down, yea, we wept, when we remembered Zion. We hanged our harps upon the willows in the midst thereof . . . If I forget thee, O Jerusalem, let my right hand forget her cunning. If I do not remember thee, let my tongue cleave to the roof of my mouth; if I prefer not Jerusalem above my chief joy."

[106] "Drenched clothes." Horace, *Ode* 1.5.14–16: "The sacred wall shows by the votive table that I have dedicated my drenched clothes to the god who rules the sea"; in context applied to the end of a love affair.

[107] "Creaking straw"; Virgil, *Eclogue* 3.27.

[108] Virgil, *Eclogue* 9.67: "We will sing better songs when HE has come."

Index of biblical passages

Index of names

CAMBRIDGE TEXTS IN THE HISTORY OF PHILOSOPHY

Titles published in the series thus far

Kant *Groundwork of the Metaphysics of Morals* (edited by Mary Gregor with an introduction by Christine M. Korsgaard)

Kant *Metaphysical Foundations of Natural Science* (edited by Michael Friedman)

Kant *The Metaphysics of Morals* (edited by Mary Gregor with an introduction by Roger Sullivan)

Kant *Prolegomena to any Future Metaphysics* (edited by Gary Hatfield)

Kant *Religion within the Boundaries of Mere Reason and Other Writings* (edited by Allen Wood and George di Giovanni with an introduction by Robert Merrihew Adams)

Kierkegaard *Fear and Trembling* (edited by C. Stephen Evans and Sylvia Walsh)

La Mettrie *Machine Man and Other Writings* (edited by Ann Thomson)

Leibniz *New Essays on Human Understanding* (edited by Peter Remnant and Jonathan Bennett)

Lessing *Philosophical and Theological Writings* (edited by H. B. Nisbet)

Malebranche *Dialogues on Metaphysics and on Religion* (edited by Nicholas Jolley and David Scott)

Malebranche *The Search after Truth* (edited by Thomas M. Lennon and Paul J. Olscamp)

Medieval Islamic Philosophical Writings (edited by Muhammad Ali Khalidi)

Melanchthon *Orations on Philosophy and Education* (edited by Sachiko Kusukawa, translated by Christine Salazar)

Mendelssohn *Philosophical Writings* (edited by Daniel O. Dahlstrom)

Newton *Philosophical Writings* (edited by Andrew Janiak)

Nietzsche *The Antichrist, Ecce Homo, Twilight of the Idols and Other Writings* (edited by Aaron Ridley and Judith Norman)

Nietzsche *Beyond Good and Evil* (edited by Rolf-Peter Horstmann and Judith Norman)

Nietzsche *The Birth of Tragedy and Other Writings* (edited by Raymond Geuss and Ronald Speirs)

Nietzsche *Daybreak* (edited by Maudemarie Clark and Brian Leiter, translated by R. J. Hollingdale)

Nietzsche *The Gay Science* (edited by Bernard Williams, translated by Josefine Nauckhoff)

Nietzsche *Human, All Too Human* (translated by R. J. Hollingdale with an introduction by Richard Schacht)

Nietzsche *Thus Spoke Zarathustra* (edited by Adrian Del Caro and Robert B. Pippin)

Nietzsche *Untimely Meditations* (edited by Daniel Breazeale, translated by R. J. Hollingdale)

Nietzsche *Writings from the Late Notebooks* (edited by Rüdiger Bittner, translated by Kate Sturge)

Novalis *Fichte Studies* (edited by Jane Kneller)

Reinhold *Letters on the Kantian Philosophy* (edited by Karl Ameriks, translated by James Hebbeler)

Schleiermacher *Hermeneutics and Criticism* (edited by Andrew Bowie)

Schleiermacher *Lectures on Philosophical Ethics* (edited by Robert Louden, translated by Louise Adey Huish)

Schleiermacher *On Religion: Speeches to its Cultured Despisers* (edited by Richard Crouter)

Schopenhauer *Prize Essay on the Freedom of the Will* (edited by Günter Zöller)

Sextus Empiricus *Against the Logicians* (edited by Richard Bett)

Sextus Empiricus *Outlines of Scepticism* (edited by Julia Annas and Jonathan Barnes)

Shaftesbury *Characteristics of Men, Manners, Opinions, Times* (edited by Lawrence Klein)

Adam Smith *The Theory of Moral Sentiments* (edited by Knud Haakonssen)

Spinoza *Theological-Political Treatise* (edited by Jonathan Israel, translated by Michael Silverthorne and Jonathan Israel)

Voltaire *Treatise on Tolerance and Other Writings* (edited by Simon Harvey)